RAY

Ray Martin

STORIES OF MY LIFE

The Autobiography

RAY

Ray Martin

WILLIAM HEINEMANN: AUSTRALIA

A William Heinemann book
Published by Random House Australia Pty Ltd
Level 3, 100 Pacific Highway, North Sydney NSW 2060
www.randomhouse.com.au

First published by William Heinemann in 2009

Addresses for companies within the Random House Group can be found at www.randomhouse.com.au/offices.

National Library of Australia
Cataloguing-in-Publication Entry

Martin, Ray, 1944–.
Ray: stories of my life.

ISBN 978 1 74166 782 0 (hbk).

Martin, Ray, 1944–.
Entertainers – Australia – Biography.

791.45028092

Cover photograph by Colin MacDougall
Cover design by Greendot Design
Typeset in 12/17 Minion by Post Pre-press Group, Brisbane, Queensland
Printed and bound by Griffin Press, South Australia

Random House Australia uses papers that are natural, renewable and recyclable products and made from wood grown in sustainable forests. The logging and manufacturing processes are expected to conform to the environmental regulations of the country of origin.

10 9 8 7 6 5 4 3 2 1

Contents

Prologue   Growing Up a Train Brat   1
Chapter 1   A Bush Boy   7
Chapter 2   Sydney or Bust   28
Chapter 3   An Island Idyll   46
Chapter 4   A Simple Twist of Fate   58
Chapter 5   Radio Daze   66
Chapter 6   Absence Makes the Heart Grow Fonder   79
Chapter 7   A New York State of Mind   93
Chapter 8   Waiting for . . . Fidel   102
Chapter 9   Imagine John Lennon   113
Chapter 10   Hail to the Chief   123
Chapter 11   The Name's Bond . . . Alan Bond   138
Chapter 12   Spies and Other Colourful Characters   145
Chapter 13   Tick. Tick. Tick . . .   159
Chapter 14   That Was a Bit Close   179
Chapter 15   Death Row and Other Fun Places   196
Chapter 16   Food for Thought   208
Chapter 17   Two-and-a-half Men   214
Chapter 18   And Baby Makes Three   222
Chapter 19   High Noon   231
Chapter 20   Maestro, Music please . . .   247
Chapter 21   Flying High   259
Chapter 22   A Dad for All Seasons   269
Chapter 23   Gold Rush!   279
Chapter 24   Housewife Superstar, and Other
               Truly Beautiful Women   285
Chapter 25   Three Women and a Funeral   298
Chapter 26   The Best of Times, the Worst of Times   314
Chapter 27   The Saddest Man I Ever Met   325

Chapter 28   Sir Don's Last Innings   337
Chapter 29   The King   352
Chapter 30   *Frontline* and Other Funny Business   359
Chapter 31   Revolts and Royals   376
Chapter 32   'Gentlemen, Include Me Out!'   393
Chapter 33   'This is Payback Time, Raymond'   407
Chapter 34   Back to the Future   415
Chapter 35   The Last Hurrah   424
Chapter 36   The Years of Living Dangerously   436
Epilogue   The Full Circle   453

Acknowledgements   458
Index   461

For Dianne, whose love I cherish, and my children, Luke and Jenna, who remain my greatest blessing. Without them I would have few stories to tell.

Prologue
Growing Up a Train Brat

Ah! A man must feel revengeful for a boyhood such as mine.
God! I hate the very houses near the workshop by the line;
And the smell of railway stations and the roar of running gear
And the scornful-seeming signboards saying
'Second Class wait here.'

– 'Second Class Wait Here', Henry Lawson

My earliest memory is of a slow-moving train. Eternally slow. Ghosting across the Australian bush. It seemed to be taking forever to reach nowhere. And that's where we were going: to nowhere.

'All change at Bogan Gate for Tottenham,' the conductor barked as he walked along the corridor, knowing that somebody on the Broken Hill Express was due to get off at this godforsaken spot. We were smack bang in the middle of New South Wales. Even Cobb & Co had hitched their coaches and abandoned this empty place a long time ago. Where we were going, ABC regional radio was hard to pick up except at night. And the farm telephone was a party line that half a dozen distant nosy neighbours could listen in on.

In the late 1940s our ticket to ride was one of those rusty-red dogbox carriages with the tiny varnished timber compartments,

1

mock-leather bench seats and steam heating gushing out from behind your feet. Outside, big gold lettering announced to all the Central West slopes and plains that we were in Second Class.

Inside, the walls were decorated with black-and-white photos of tourist favourites like the Three Sisters, at the Blue Mountains. They were stunning shots, which I would later learn were by award-winning photographers like Cazneaux and Moore. Still, as a kid I always wondered if they had coloured pictures in first class. I bet they did.

As I peered through windows licked with soot and steam, we rattled past railway sidings with strange-sounding names. Cookamidgera, Mugincoble and Nelungaloo, west of Orange.

With parents named George James and Mary Jane – and four kids called Lorraine, Kay, Joyce and Raymond George – my itinerant mob seemed strangely out of place. Out of country, too, as we stepped down from our carriage onto the deserted gravel platform. There was nothing there except a dilapidated parched-pink ticket office and a sorry sign that should have verified we were at Bogan Gate – but somebody had removed the 't' with a 12-gauge shotgun.

Close enough was good enough way out the back of New South Wales, where gagging on bush flies was as certain as 40-degree days in summer and where anybody who fretted about a 't' on a railway-station sign probably should jump the next train out. Round here, the hot afternoon wind can bleach the lanolin off a sheep. A bucket of zinc cream is still not enough.

The conductor helped Mum and Dad put our bags under the shade of a corrugated awning, promising that the branch-line train from Trundle – a town that proudly boasted having 'the widest main street in the West' – shouldn't be too long. He didn't sound convincing. He clambered back aboard, bound for Ivanhoe, leaving us in a cloud of coal smoke.

The single-carriage train from Trundle eventually turned up at Bogan Gate, two hours late. We were the sole passengers, edging our way imperceptibly towards our destination, the hamlet of Tottenham.

The town hasn't really changed much in sixty years. From memory there are still two large flowering kurrajong trees standing like sentinels, one at each end of the road. In the middle squats a stolid art-deco pub with the year 1931 inscribed high on its façade. There used to be a brick watering trough for stock horses making the run out across the Snakes Plains, heading for that place with the wishful-sounding name of Nevertire. That's gone, like the passenger line, which long ago melted into the shimmering plains.

I was only about four years old but my lifetime peregrinations had already begun. Before I even got to high school, I would live in thirteen different places, in three Australian states, mostly in the bush.

My wife and children would have none of this red dust in their veins or fiery heat haze in their souls. They are coastal, city people. Nor would they have a journeyer's history like me.

I would go far away from here but never really leave. Give a boy his first formative years in the Aussie bush and the bush has him forever.

For me as a kid, the idea of sitting in a TV studio wearing make-up and talking to royalty or to a screen legend like Audrey Hepburn was white-fella dreamtime stuff. Not even in the glossy pages of her *Australian Women's Weekly* bible could my mother have imagined such an alluring future for her only son. As it turned out, for me New York and Paris were just twenty years down the track from Tottenham. Not a long time, really. Yet they lay in another galaxy, a rocket-ship ride away from this sunburnt country with its 'pitiless blue sky'.

The images of my early childhood are all rich and indelible. I feel privileged to have had, as Albert Facey put it, 'such a fortunate life'.

I have to say my son Luke's eyes glaze over on family trips when I stop at every long-abandoned railway station or shearing shed to take photos. He travels with his music at full bore and misses the stark beauty of this forgotten past. I have a theory that iPods can send you blind.

I have revisited most of my childhood homes in recent years and lingered awhile. I must say there was no great epiphany. Some places have been drowned, like an abandoned church we lived in at Glenbawn Dam, up near Scone. Others, like the whole Sydney suburb of Hargrave Park, have been wiped off the map. My first house, near Richmond Hospital, where I was born, is about to be bulldozed for an expressway.

I was only young through my family's rambling years, so it didn't really bother me. But as we flitted from town to town, my poor sisters had to somehow cope with high-school exams, losing friends and the usual teenage turmoil. They're remarkable women to have survived and succeeded as they have. I don't know how they did it, to be honest.

My old man never actually worked on the railways, although he probably should have. We always seemed to be waiting at a station or sitting on a train. Always moving on. We'd pack the heavy leather suitcases, pull out of school and catch yet another train to yet another place.

I remember as a toddler sleeping tucked up in the luggage rack, clickitty-clacking over the Great Dividing Range through the long, empty night. When I was older, I got to stretch out on a king-sized spread made by stacking all our suitcases in between the train's bench seats. That's as long as nobody else tried to share our compartment. By night, windows and blinds were jammed shut to keep the cascading grit and cold out. My traveller's lullaby was wheels screeching to a stop, the train shunting and coupling on the hooks and buffers, and steam engines hissing as they were filled from track-side water tanks while fettlers shouted and laughed above the cacophony.

I knew there was a nocturnal world of feverish activity outside, but the only thing we ever saw was our imagination. Mum somehow always managed to say 'Close that blind' just as we thought of cracking it open for a peek. How do mothers do that?

At every rail junction we regularly passed through – like Werris Creek, Junee and Cootamundra – it was the same familiar routine. We'd stagger out into the platform chill and race to the Railway Refreshment Room, 'the Triple R' as it was called, for white-bread toast with Vegemite and a hand-warming china mug of railway coffee. It was about the only time we ever had coffee; ours was a working-class world of tea drinkers.

In those simpler times railway coffee was a mystery brew, usually chicory or low-grade beans shipped in from Brazil, with condensed milk. As a kid, it tasted like sweet velvet, forget the caffeine fix. And if the lady in the starched-white railways apron took pity, then, unlike Oliver Twist, you'd score an extra dollop.

Mark Twain once changed trains at Albury and condemned our 1890s railway coffee as an undrinkable slop of 'sump-oil and sheep dip'. He obviously didn't try it with a succulent squirt of condensed milk!

Occasionally, we'd stay overnight in one of the endless string of railway pubs with names like The Royal, The Imperial, The

National or The Railway. The pubs always had wide wooden verandahs and freezing toilets, which inevitably were at the end of a long linoleum hallway. There'd be glasses of sarsaparilla on the pub steps for us kids as the old man downed his schooner in the front bar, desperate to beat the notorious closing-hour event known as the six o'clock swill. Mum would sit alone with a shandy in the ladies' lounge. They were bizarre drinking rituals.

My memories of these sojourns, these strange little arcane details, have been topped up and coloured-in by the vivid reminiscences of my sisters. They're unique family photographs, which come not so much courtesy of Kodak but from the albums of our minds.

My father was a hard-working breadwinner type – until the booze took over and the kitchen arguments turned violent. We were, at times, dirt poor. Destitute. As J. K. Rowling said, 'poverty is romanticised only by fools'. I certainly wouldn't recommend it as a lifestyle.

Yet it's certainly not hunger, fear or a feeling of deprivation that stand out for me. The great Mr Lawson might have had good reason to feel 'revengeful for a boyhood' such as his. I certainly don't. I know of course that time sandpapers the jagged edges. I doubt my mother remembered our crazy gypsy life quite as fondly as my sisters and I do. Still, my overwhelming memories of my childhood are of fun, adventure and warmth.

That's probably because Mum was such a loving and resilient woman. Like scrub timber, she was hardy and tenacious. And she was a tiger when it came to looking after her kids. She had a mother's uncompromising bias, which left us in no doubt we could *do anything* if we wanted to badly enough. And in her eyes, we could do no wrong. I think everyone needs a person in their lives who offers such total love.

Let the life story begin.

Chapter 1
A Bush Boy

Bingara is a tiny town in the cypress-covered ranges of New England. That's where my mother, Mary Jane Lamey, was born into an itinerant shearer's family in 1912.

My grandfather, Frederick Lamey, was a gun shearer renowned across the New South Wales north-west for his skills with the blade. That's according to family folklore, anyway. There's certainly no disputing that he played a lively fiddle at bush dances and a sweet violin in the family parlour. Maybe that's why my mother loved to dance. She started as a skinny kid, kicking up her heels to her father's rhythmic reels. Fred Lamey came from uncompromising Irish convict stock who arrived in Australia from Kilkenny in the early 1830s. He died before I could remember him. A long, angular bloke with a droopy moustache, from his photo he looked like Henry Lawson on a dry day.

Mum came out somewhere in the middle of twelve Catholic kids born to a tiny hobbit of a woman, Mary Bettridge, my feisty and formidable grandmother. She was also of Irish ancestry.

A family tale passed down the generations tells of my grandmother decking one of her offspring with a rock because he gave her cheek then tried to run away. So whenever I was around Grandma, I was always wary – even though I was taller than her by the time I was about eight.

Grandma's brother, Bill Bettridge, was a militant member of the Australian Workers' Union and for years was banned from the giant woolsheds along the Darling River after he organised some seriously disruptive strikes. I wish I'd met Great Uncle Bill because he sounds like a good larrikin.

Grandma kept a photo of her husband, Fred, and his two brothers in her lounge room. As kids, my sisters and I used to squint at the aged trio hanging on the wall, convinced that one of the Lamey boys looked dark enough to be an Aboriginal. Mind you, we never suggested that aloud. You just didn't.

On our travels we inevitably regrouped at Grandma's place in Gunnedah, where the blackfella camp was a no-go zone on the other side of the Namoi River. Parts of the town were still segregated when I was growing up; the Aboriginal women and kids had to sit down the front at the picture show. Black kids were expected to shower before they were allowed into the town's swimming pool. They were shocking, racist times.

Many years later, while researching the family tree, my sister Kay came across an intriguing discovery: Fred Lamey's grandmother was a Kamilaroi woman named Bertha. My great, great grandmother Bertha married William Lamey out at Keepit Station, a vast sheep spread on the rich soil of the Liverpool Plains. The remarkable thing about their union was that weddings between white fellas and blackfellas were not only unusual but considered a bit unnecessary, too.

From the scant family records, it seems that the Lameys spent fifty years mustering and shearing on Keepit Station. They bred out there like rabbits for a couple of generations. I always figured there was a bit of irony in the fact that a century after Bertha and William's marriage my father actually helped build Keepit Dam, which put much of Bertha's sacred Kamilaroi country under water forever.

When William and Bertha's daughter, my great-aunt Jane, held her wedding up the railway line in Moree in the 1870s, it was described in the local paper as 'a grand affair, the first of its kind in the district'. Again it was a blackfella and white-fella religious union. Jane became a highly reputable midwife in Moree, delivering the babies of some of the wealthiest white families in the district, along with giving birth to ten children of her own.

My mother was the most tolerant of women, without a racist bone in her body. I find it strange that she never mentioned our family's Aboriginal connection. Maybe she felt there were enough working-class hurdles in her life without adding to the family's load. Maybe our Aboriginal heritage was considered a family secret to be kept locked in the closet. Maybe it didn't matter to her. Either way, I'm proud of that connection, as I am of my Irish ancestry.

My mum left school before her thirteenth birthday, joining two of her older sisters as housemaids at an Inverell hotel. It was considered a waste of time in those days to keep girls in school when they could be providing for the family. She always said she was happy to be out of the classroom and earning a quid. Maybe it was because of this early industriousness that Mum never stopped working, either in a factory or around the house. She was no good at wasting time.

The young Mary Lamey was a tall, slim brunette and 'by far the prettiest girl in Gunnedah', my uncles always used to tell us.

Later on, when circumstances and her marriage turned bad, she grew skinny and anaemic for a while. And a bit brittle. But that didn't last long because she was country tough.

There are family photos of Mary in her late teens looking a bit like Faye Dunaway in the movie *Bonnie and Clyde*. Mum's wearing a typical flapper's shift dress, with a bob haircut and one foot on the running board of a Ford Model T, holding on to a rifle. She always claimed to be a crack shot. But the only sport I ever saw Mum indulge in was dancing; she glided across the boards like Ginger Rogers. When I was a kid, the simple 3/4 beat of a waltz on the radio would set Mum off, twirling me round the house like a dervish. (In her late seventies she broke her leg when she slipped on the kitchen floor, still high-stepping, only this time with a granddaughter.)

Despite her meagre purse, my mother always dressed nicely and was always ironed and starched. She never swore, apart from the occasional 'Bugger it', and was a stickler for good manners. When it came to 'please' and 'thank you', she was like a sergeant major, drilling it into us kids.

Mum's handwriting was much better than mine, and she always consumed the afternoon papers and women's magazines. But I can't recall ever seeing my mother read a book. There were virtually no books in my childhood home, except the ones we borrowed from the school library and a pristine set of George Newnes Encyclopedias a door-to-door salesman once sold my mother, convincing her they'd be invaluable for Joyce and me.

Mum was determined that I should go to university. The only time I can ever remember her getting really cranky with me was when I suggested leaving high school and getting a job. 'I haven't worked my fingers to the bone so you can be ordinary,' she snapped. I would be the first in our extended

Irish-Catholic family of maybe two hundred kids to make it to university.

My father, George James Grace, was born in inner-city Glebe, in Sydney, in early 1911.

His grandfather, a colonial policeman who was also from Kilkenny, had landed in Hobart Town in the early 1850s and later headed north to Parramatta. (We kept the fact he was a walloper a deep, dark family secret.) It was very early in George's life that his luck ran out. His mother died of TB when she was barely twenty-six. His father, who married again, was killed shortly after in a car crash.

So at the age of about nine, George was left in charge of his two younger brothers. All three were sent to a Catholic orphanage up the Hawkesbury River, until an elderly aunt took pity. She rescued them and gave them something resembling a childhood, out at Maroubra in South Sydney.

Though he left school at twelve, just as my mother had, my father was intelligent and articulate. He was a somewhat handsome rooster, a bit of a ladies' man, with a shock of thick, wavy hair and a velvet speaking voice. He'd somehow read copious volumes of Australian history and would freely quote verses of the bush poets, from go to whoa. Not just Lawson and Paterson, but O'Brien, Ogilvie, Kendall and Adam Lindsay Gordon as well. As a kid, I was suckled on their naïve sentiments and rhyming jingoism. In fact, the first two books I ever owned were anthologies of Henry and Banjo, which I'd asked for as Christmas presents. I still have them.

My father knew all the answers to the questions on the radio quiz shows, which were hugely popular in the early 1950s. In fact, he seemed to know all the answers to everything. George was what used to colloquially be called a bush lawyer. He had the gift of the gab, loved an argument and rarely lost one, especially if it had anything to do with politics. The only person I ever saw take him on and beat him was my eldest sister, Lorraine. She challenged and defied the old man often, although sometimes at the cost of a slap across the face for her impudence. That only strengthened her resolve.

George was also a staunch unionist. At barely twenty, in 1931, he joined the Communist Party, in the middle of Jack Lang's brawls with the British banks. I can remember that in the early 1950s he used to sell the Party paper, *The Tribune*, and give soap-box speeches on Sundays. Oblivious to his political exhortations, my sisters and I would tear around the sumptuous lawns of the Domain and climb the old fig trees as if we were on a family picnic. At various times in his life, he was an altar boy, a committed Catholic and a grand pooh-bah at the masonic lodge. Go figure.

Whether it was because of his political bent or his eye for women, Mum's parents disapproved of her marrying George Grace, who'd only recently arrived in Gunnedah. They were so upset they actually refused to attend the wedding, at St Joseph's Catholic Church, even though it was just around the corner from the family's rented house. Mum used to laugh and tell the story of how the priest had to drag a couple of passing strangers in off the street to act as witnesses.

In later years Mum owned up to having broken off an engagement to another bloke, a 'nice Scottish fellow', she used to say, when Dad asked her to marry him. She would just shake her head and smile at the simple twist of fate.

At the time of their marriage, George was a qualified fitter and turner. He was offered a job in a Brisbane motorbike repair shop, so they headed north to Queensland. That's where Lorraine was born. Soon after, they went back to Gunnedah, and

Kay came along. It would become a sort of migratory pattern, either in crisis or out of habit. Every couple of years the family would retreat to Gunnedah, like the mission swallows returning to Capistrano. Joyce was born next, making it a trio of girls. Either side of Joy, Mum had a couple of miscarriages.

After a brief stint in the Navy as the Second World War began, George switched to the Air Force, becoming a mechanic and later joining a bomber flight crew. When he was interviewed for his flying job, Dad was found to be 'a good, stirring, determined type' and 'well-mannered, intelligent and alert', according to his confidential service records.

When the RAAF tried to transfer him away from his wife and daughters in Melbourne to Tocumwal, in country New South Wales, Mum wrote an impassioned letter to John Curtin, the prime minister. It was clearly drafted by Dad. In the letter, Mum accuses the RAAF brass of victimising George because of his 'political affiliations'. There's no record of a reply from Mr Curtin, but the transfer was rescinded. Mind you, there would be no further Air Force promotions for Corporal George Grace, either.

*　　　　*　　　　*

It was an auspicious date, 20 December. In 1915, the Allies successfully evacuated the beaches at Gallipoli. On the same day in 1944 Adolf Hitler's last major offensive – the Battle of the Bulge – got under way and General Douglas MacArthur was seen wading ashore in the Philippines. My old man used to tell me that was the day the war in both Europe and the Pacific turned in our favour. It was also the day I was born, 20 December 1944.

I am pleased to share my birthday with some friends, some true-blue legends like champion spinner Bill O'Reilly, champion sailor John Bertrand and just about my favourite photographer, Ken Duncan. (Sir Robert Menzies and Uri Geller are a bit of a worry.)

Anyway, I entered the world in the maternity ward of Richmond District Hospital, on the outskirts of Sydney. We lived in a rented fibro house alongside the runway, and stayed there until my father was discharged from the RAAF and went to work down the road at the Riverstone Meat Works. Like all the others, that job didn't last long. Dad tried to re-enlist in the Air Force in 1947 but was knocked back on so-called medical grounds. He was as fit as the proverbial bush pig, so it's a fair guess that it was his membership of the Party that did the trick. Within two years Menzies would ride into government on the back of a 'Reds under the bed' scaremongering campaign.

I think it was probably coincidental, but that's when we headed out to Tottenham, *via Bogan Gate*, such a great Aussie placename. Dad took his first job as a merino property manager on a 1700-hectare station called Waitara, just north of town. It had been settled in the 1920s by the Chase family, who today run a highly successful beef cattle property.

My strongest memories of Waitara are vast mobs of emus, my first kelpie pup and my father squirting warm milk straight from the family cow into my open mouth. And, of course, that incredible Aussie phenomenon of the forties and fifties, the rabbit plague. On Sundays, after church, there would sometimes be a massive rabbit hunt. We all formed a dragnet, beating the bushes while the dogs chased hundreds of the furry li'l pests into a huge warren at one end of the property. The blokes would then block up most of the exits with soil and pump smoke down some burrows and strategically place sticks of dynamite into others.

14

What happened next must have been like the Western Front under heavy shelling. I was only about four at the time, so it seemed as if the whole world was blowing up before my eyes. There'd be an explosion of dirt, rabbit parts and skin flying through the haze. Then, anybody who could wield a stick would begin thumping every dazed or delirious rabbit that poked its head up. And dozens of them did. It was an absolute killing field. The next month, the mongrels would be back, outnumbering the merinos five to one.

Nobody in the family quite knows why, but we packed up and left Waitara after less than a year. We were back on the train to Gunnedah – via Bogan Gate, of course – for my first of many happy Christmases at Grandma's.

The train chugged into Gunnedah's quaint little station at about five in the morning, when it was barely light and still misty. We heard the roosters wake up as we dragged ourselves and all our worldly possessions up the road to Grandma's, in Little Barber Street, just behind the picture show. She was already up with porridge cooking and water on the boil for tea.

There was an army of aunts, uncles and cousins all camped inside Grandma's broiling timber cottage, like a family bivouac. Even with the doors and windows wide open, Gunnedah was still a furnace. What made it all worthwhile was a performance that took place on the afternoon before Christmas. To me as a small boy it became a mega-event, the most eagerly anticipated event of the year.

It's hard to believe today but in Australia in the 1940s we never ate chicken. Not through the year, anyway. There was plenty of red meat but never chicken. We had chooks for their eggs, not for their breasts or legs. As for roast duck or baked turkey, I never even saw one – except in Hollywood movies. But Christmas at Grandma's meant chooks. Mum's older brother, Jim, who worked at the abattoir, arrived after he'd knocked off . . . with a few live, squawking chooks in a hessian bag. Uncle Jim was my boyhood hero. He only ever wore workboots, shorts and a blue singlet, with his hair brilliantined like Humphrey Bogart's. His arms were the size of an elephant's leg.

Down the back of Grandma's yard, past the chrysanthemums, past the old water tank, under the peppercorn tree, was the wood pile. On the way you had to duck your head to avoid the rickety clothes line, which always had a pair of men's trousers hanging from it. Grandma figured they'd scare off potential burglars, who'd think there was 'a man in the house'. I doubt that it fooled anyone – although, come to think of it, the old girl was never robbed, even though she always left her doors unlocked.

Anyway, down by the wood pile is where we waited excitedly for Uncle Jim. With exquisite timing more suited to the West End stage, he put the hessian bag down and sharpened the axe, milking the tension. A struggling chook appeared, as magically as a magician's dove. Except the chook ended up on the block and off came the head.

The drama of the guillotine on the streets of revolutionary Paris had nothing on Uncle Jim's Christmas chop in Gunnedah. It wasn't the decapitation that fascinated us kids. It was watching the headless chook take a few nerve-twitched steps across the lawn. Usually it would drop quickly, but every now and then a chook would seem to make a run for it.

The anticlimax – the boring bit – was helping Mum and the others pluck the feathers after the chooks had been thrown into a tub of boiling water. Eating them the next day was pretty good, though.

* * *

16

Our lives took another crazy twist after that first memorable chook spectacular. George decided the family's destiny lay just outside the Hunter Valley town of Scone, where work was beginning on the mighty Glenbawn Dam. Going ahead as a one-man advance party to find us suitable accommodation, he hit the jackpot. While most other workers' families had to pitch tents out in the open paddocks, my old man somehow scored us four walls and a tin roof. It was actually an abandoned wooden Methodist church, complete with pulpit, pews and a vast web of spiders that appeared to have been undisturbed since the Triassic period. Sixty years later you only have to say the name 'Scone' to my sisters and it sparks an arachno-phobic rush. They still scream with the kind of manic laughter that only genuine fear evokes. They'll tell you how the creepy-crawlies prowled over sleeping faces, into our beds and their school clothes. Or else they dropped from the blanket of cobwebs that covered the high church ceiling, dangling and taunting us.

This erstwhile house of the Lord had no electricity, no run-ning water and no toilet. No cooking facilities, either, until Dad improvised with a few bricks propping up a hot plate over an open fire. Years later, Mum would recall fondly that each time it rained the fire went out, usually when she was trying to cook dinner for a family of six. And in a Scone winter it rained every other day. My strongest memory of the town is a world of claggy mud thick enough to stop a charging rhino. It regularly bogged my sisters' school bus.

Dad would come home from the Scone pub at night with a skinful, having been turfed out after last drinks. Then, by candlelight, he'd make all of us, including Mum, dutifully sit in the pews while he stood in the pulpit and delivered a fire 'n' brimstone sermon. It was never about religion, more about life and how privileged we all were. Yeah, onya, Dad.

Over the next couple of years, like a family of Bedouins, we moved from one watering hole to the next. In Wellington, in Central New South Wales, Mum and Dad ran a milk bar for about six months. Then it was off to Canberra, where Dad toiled in a garage and on Saturdays sold hot dogs outside the original Civic Hotel, never missing out on a drink himself. Not yet six, I stood with him in the icy Canberra winds, passing the bottled tomato sauce to blokes who spilled out at closing time needing a quick feed before heading home to the missus for tea.

Life had become unbelievably chaotic for us kids. I hadn't yet started school, but my sisters were all at the local convent school. Mum was upset by our nomadic lifestyle and embarrassed that Lorraine and Kay were wearing uniforms from two high schools ago because we'd shifted so many times. So, reluctantly, she arranged to send the two older girls back to Gunnedah, where they might have a bit of stability under the watchful gaze of Grandma and Auntie Annie, Mum's closest sister. They stayed there for the best part of a year.

Meanwhile, Mum, Dad, Joyce and I lived in Queanbeyan, then Griffith, before heading via Tumut to a beautiful spot called Yarrangobilly, high up in the New South Wales Alps. Dad got a job in each of these towns for a few weeks, and then we'd pull up stumps and move on.

Yarrangobilly was without doubt my favourite childhood place, and I have a string of them to choose from. As a kid, if I could have lived anywhere forever, it would have been up there at Yarrangobilly.

It was one of those abandoned gold towns that litter the Aussie bush, with just a post office-cum-general store, a CWA hall and a few families scattered through the valley. The weekly mail truck would bring the groceries and our school lessons on a run across the mountains from Tumut to Cooma.

My father seemed to have an eye for abandoned churches and cottages. This time we lived in the village policeman's place, an old one-bedroom wood-slab hut, which had long been deserted. Again there was neither electricity nor running water; and the outhouse was across the rough paddock. There was no way that the old man was going to spoil Mum with any newfangled conveniences.

Dad went to work on the Snowy Mountains Scheme, so he was away in Kiandra sometimes for a month at a time. Though I missed him, family life was quiet and peaceful without his unpredictable drinking binges.

Yarrangobilly was where I started my formal school life, by correspondence course. Joyce was nine and I had just turned six. We'd listen to the teacher on the radio for about an hour each morning, and then Mum would take over the lessons for the next bit. She was a harsh schoolmistress, but we still got to run free most of the day.

Our Yarrangobilly world was open, fresh and lush green. Depending on the season, drovers would bring sheep and cattle through, and camp overnight on the meadow below our house.

I was Joyce's shadow and idolised her. We collected wild goose-berries, rode the drovers' horses, then sat around their crackling camp fire at night. We fished for slipperies, a local snow-stream trout, in the whitewater river. Sometimes we'd wander way into the bush, up dirt tracks, to visit other local families. We'd play all day with their rough-nut urchin kids, get fed scones and jam, and then run home before dark. For a couple of kids, things couldn't get any better than this. It was idyllic.

But without Lorraine and Kay, there was a hole in Mum's heart.

So the minute their high-school year finished in Gunnedah they joined us in Yarrangobilly and life returned to normal.

For our family, Sunday night was always bath night. It was too grand a performance to happen more often than that. Mum would stoke up the fire, boil the copper and pour the water into a big tin bath strategically placed in front of the open fire. We were supposed to take it in turns for the honour of bathing first, but because I was the youngest – and the only boy – I'd inevitably end up with the slops. To add to the theatre of bath night, the oil lanterns would be turned off. The highlight was always when Kay, all of fifteen years old, would warble like some sultry chanteuse and perform her family-favourite 'bubble dance', with just the flickering light of the open flames dancing across the lounge-room walls. You could see nothing except her sparkling eyes above the bubbles, with the occasional tease of a bare foot and calf. It was about as risqué as a good Catholic schoolgirl could get away with, but she brought the house down every time. She'd laugh so much she was always in danger of drowning in bubbles. The old man used to cackle, too, and predict that Kay would end up amongst the high-kicking showgirls at the Tivoli Theatre in Sydney. But she and Lorraine used to paint a much more extravagant picture, of Kay jumping the convent fence, jack-booted nuns pulling at her long, flowing hair as she fled further afield, to the Folies Bergère. Kay was so pretty, so coquettish and full of fun, she'd undoubtedly have been a sensation in the 9th Arrondissement. It was pretty basic family fun, but we loved it.

Lorraine played the piano at Saturday night dances in the CWA hall, and fifty people would come out of the hills with plates of food and sly grog. It was party time circa 1950. Wives and daughters would gather, chattering down one end of the hall in their nicest frocks. They would all fix their hair the best they could at home with hot curling irons and a stiff brush. There were no beauty salons for a hundred miles. As for the blokes, in between a stuttering barn dance or Pride of Erin they'd all drift outside to linger over a smoke and a swig of the local moonshine. If it happened to be someone's birthday, a high-priced bottle of rum or whisky might suddenly appear. And just as quickly disappear, as the empty bottle was hoiked into the trees below, out of sight of watchful wives.

On one memorable occasion at Yarrangobilly, Dad brought home fifty tiny ducklings. He reasoned that once they'd grown they would supply highly prized duck eggs and maybe even the occasional duck dinner, neither of which we had ever tasted. Of course, he went back to work on the Snowy, which meant Mum was left to nurture the fluff-balls until they were big enough for an outdoor pen. Which Dad hadn't yet built. Winter wasn't quite over, so Mum had to keep them inside the house in a big wooden box. We kids somehow cajoled her into letting them out in front of the big open fire at night. Naturally enough, this meant the whole place reeked of duck poo.

Now, this turned out to be a major family trauma, because my mother wasn't just a tidy person, she was clinically clean. Certifiably. Our house always smelt like a Pine o Cleen factory and was always spotless. (Pine o Cleen, Dettol and Laxettes were the holy trinity of our lives, keeping us antiseptically clean, healthy and regular!) My mother was one of those women who ironed socks, underwear and handkerchiefs, and always starched the bedsheets – which, of course, she then ironed, with razor-sharp edges on the side. So, not surprisingly, the noisy, shitty ducks drove Mum close to despair.

Somehow, they managed to survive – and thrive – until Dad returned a month or two later. Mum tongue-lashed him into building a duck pen out the back. Immediately. George wasn't just a good fitter and a mechanic, he was also your original 'can do' handyman. He was forever embarking on major backyard constructions: a mammoth fish pond, a cantilevered birdcage or . . . a duck pen. Conscious that there were foxes in the nearby hills, Dad dug a trench around the fortified pen and buried the chicken wire deep into the ground. It was much too high for the foxes to scale. So, in a triumphant ceremony, the ducks were shifted to their new home before it got dark. Mum had her first peaceful night in at least a month.

The next morning we awoke to disaster. The foxes had scratched their way to China – under the heavy chicken wire – and the place was awash in the blood and feathers of what used to be fifty prized ducks.

I went back to Yarrangobilly twenty years later, only to find my verdant childhood Shangri-la as dry and dusty as the worst drought in a century could deliver. The Snowy scheme had long ago sucked all the water – and the slipperies – from the river at the bottom of our yard. Our wooden cottage had collapsed. The abundant old apple tree was a barren scarecrow. All that remained of the Sunday night baths and the doomed ducklings were ripe memories and the brick foundations, which stood as stark as gravestones in the paddock. The flat, lush meadow where the drovers used to camp was just a rubble-strewn wasteland, taken over by the Main Roads mob.

As they say, you should never go back.

*   *   *

In 1951, after only about a year, our magical life in the mountains came to an end. It was out with the suitcases again. (I'm convinced the reason that in my adult life I collect books and paintings and copious junk is that it makes it too damn hard to move!) Now I stay in the same house for at least ten years.

Having Lorraine and Kay with us permanently meant that we couldn't stay at Yarrangobilly, because there was no high school. There was no choice but to head down the perilous, winding Talbingo Mountain road to Tumut, with a truck packed chock-a-block. I remember Lorraine and Joyce were always carsick, and when we stopped Mum would point out the mountain scenery in a futile attempt to distract me from watching.

Dad quit the Snowy and took a job as a salesman in the Austin car and truck dealership in Tumut, while Mum returned to her original work as a housekeeper, in one of the town's many pubs. Lorraine, after her absurdly broken, itinerant education, somehow topped her third year High School Certificate exam. She was an exceptional student. In later life, as a mature-age student, she would go back and complete her Leaving Certificate, breeze through her Master's Degree and end up teaching Chinese history at Macquarie University. With his vagabond habits, my father gave none of his daughters a real chance at education. Yet they would all succeed in spite of his feckless ways.

In a sense these were still innocent times in Australia and life had its rigid family routines, no matter where we lived. Especially when it came to food. For example, there was never meat for this Catholic family on Fridays, which always meant fish. At least, that was until I got a recalcitrant bone stuck in my throat. After that near-death experience we became devotees of the first widely available fast food: the fish finger. Dad always expected offal for Sunday breakfast, usually blood pudding, and Sunday lunch was always a roast and three vegetables. Because bakers knocked off at noon on Saturdays – like everybody else in post-war Australia – it meant there was no fresh bread on Mondays for school sandwiches. So I'd get two shillings to buy a salad roll and juice. In Tumut I quickly discovered that two bob could instead buy a ridiculous amount of lollies.

It was probably my second week at school when, walking out through the flyscreen door of the milk bar with my treasure, I ran straight into my father. His showroom was just around the corner, one of the mortal dangers for a small boy with contraband in a country town. The old man snatched the lollies out of my hand, gave me a clip across the ear and sent me back to the playground. I went lunch-less that day. Indeed, for the next month it was strictly stale bread 'n' cheese sandwiches from home every Monday.

We moved onto a farm at Gocup, about 11 kilometres outside Tumut, because that was the only house available. There was no school bus out there. So when Dad went early to work in his clapped-out khaki-coloured Land Rover we'd have to walk. Lorraine and Kay would race away in front, as teenagers do. Joyce would suffer, having to wait behind to keep an eye on me, but she never whinged. Avoiding the bulls, we'd cross every paddock we could to shorten the journey.

Sometimes Joy and I would get a lift with an old bloke who owned a horse stud out along the road heading to Gundagai. He was a kindly, gentle man who'd survived the horrors of the Burma Railway as a prisoner of the Japanese forces. We loved being picked up by him, and not just because he was a nice bloke. He drove a fancy British-racing-green two-door Riley sports saloon with an exhaust that sang like a contralto – until he changed gear. Then it became an English tenor. I remember he always wore soft suede driving gloves, which impressed me because I'd never seen a man in gloves before.

Suddenly we stopped coming across him. Word filtered out that in a period of black-dog depression, which intermittently plagued him, he'd taken a shotgun and killed himself. It was all too much for a seven-year-old to comprehend.

I'd grown up around guns, although until then I had only thought of them as tools for the day-to-day running of a farm. Every property had a range of shotguns and rifles, mostly for shooting kangaroos, rabbits and the occasional sheepdog that turned feral. Roo shooting brought farmers a bit of extra cash and often became an excuse for a get-together. Across the main road from us, a few kilometres deep into another valley, lived the Smythe family. My parents were close friends with Mr and Mrs Smythe, and we'd often visit them for a game of tennis, a barbecue or roo shooting. We'd jump on the open tray of Mr Smythe's Bedford truck and he'd do his best to shake us off with madcap sudden stopping-and-starting manoeuvres across the stony, dry creek beds. It was just the scariest, hairiest ride. He'd get locked up for doing it today. We loved it!

But easily my favourite pastime at their farm was to go across and help Mrs Smythe milk the cows. They were Friesians, big and irksome and mostly stupid. What I loved was Mrs Smythe's raucous performance in the milking shed. She'd wade around in her oversized gumboots, through all the mud and cow shit imaginable, swearing like a wharfie at every wayward beast and aiming an occasional loud spray at the cattle dogs if they dared get in the way. And they always did.

I had never heard a woman swear until I encountered the foul-mouthed Mrs Smythe. Shakespeare would have been impressed by her impiety. I used to think that you didn't have to repeat what Mrs Smythe said – just listening to her would automatically earn you ten Hail Marys from the parish priest. Maybe more.

The two Smythe boys, who had taken a shine to Lorraine and Kay, often came over to our place in their hotted-up truck, giant spotlights ablaze, under the pretext of taking the girls roo shooting. My strict parents had twigged, so they'd only let the girls go if Joyce and I went along, too, as under-aged chaperones. It was a boisterous, paddock-bouncing escapade laced with bullets and bravado. They'd bring home at least half a dozen roos, which would be sold to the tannery in Tumut, along with a hundred rabbit skins. Occasionally, Dad would grab his gun and come along for the roo shoot as well.

The old man's drinking bouts had started turning sour, so a loaded shotgun suddenly added a new element to our domestic saga. Friday and Saturday nights Dad would regularly drive home plastered, and our job was to get him into bed without him starting a verbal brawl with Mum, who'd developed a bad habit of not backing down. It wasn't easy.

One Saturday night he came home late, well after we'd all eaten and were getting ready for bed. Mum chipped him about being so late, and that sparked a noisy argument. All four kids tried to intervene but were brushed aside. We all ended up running around the table screaming. Plates and cups crashed to the floor when someone yanked the tablecloth. In the midst of the bedlam, Dad cornered my mother, hitting her in the face and cutting her lip. When Mum snatched a bread knife from the bench, the old man peeled off, saying he was going to get his shotgun. That's when we headed for the hills.

Out the back door we flew, climbing through the fence in the pitch dark and fleeing across the empty paddock. My sisters and

I can laugh about the whole absurd fracas now. But it didn't feel quite so funny at the time, when our adrenaline was pumping. Especially when we heard the old man slam the back door, shout a few expletives in our direction and then fire the shotgun. We eventually made it to a neighbour's house about 3 kilometres up the road, where we all bedded down for the night.

After an awkward Sunday breakfast the farmer drove us back home. There we found an embarrassed, remorseful father with a sizeable hangover. The old man apologised long and loud to everybody – even the dogs – insisting that he'd only fired into the night sky and nowhere near us. Yeah well, at the time we all accepted that but we'll never know for sure. The Tumut police sergeant paid us a cursory visit that afternoon, obviously tipped off by the farmer who'd put us up for the night. He must have had his doubts about the old man.

After this somewhat sobering episode my father's drinking spree eased for a while. The guns were also locked away in the shed, on strict advice from the cops.

But Mum had clearly had enough. She announced that we were leaving the bush as soon as Lorraine finished her exams. We were heading for the safety of Sydney.

Chapter 2
Sydney or Bust

For a raw country kid like me, Sydney's Central Station was like another planet compared to Tumut's tidy railway station, sitting at the end of a spur line. This elaborate sandstone and stained-glass terminal was easily the largest building I'd ever seen. With its gargantuan clock tower and its cold and cavernous main hall where a hundred placenames rattled incessantly on the departures-and-arrivals board – along with the mad, anarchic rush of people – Central Station symbolised the big smoke. It was all a bit intimidating.

Right outside Central, where bustling Broadway began, was the biggest neon sign I could ever have imagined. It depicted a long-necked blue bottle pouring white liquid into a red fluted glass. It must have been five storeys high. I remember staring boggle-eyed because where I'd come from there weren't even streetlights. I can't remember what kind of alcohol it was advertising, but I knew it was nothing like any drink I'd ever seen.

It was the end of 1951. The good news was that South Sydney

had won their second footy comp in a row, beginning a glorious golden era for rugby league. And for me. For a Souths tragic, listening to scratchy ABC bush-radio commentary was a poor substitute for actually seeing the boys run out onto Redfern Oval. My dad had been a fan since his boyhood in Maroubra, the heartland of the Mighty Rabbitohs, and he'd passed the obsession on to me. The old man and I would see the Bunnies win three more premierships over the next four years.

The bad news was that in Sydney we had nowhere to live. Neither did a lot of people. Servicemen had come home from the war en masse and were starting families, but the postwar building boom hadn't yet kicked in. New South Wales was in a housing crisis, in desperate need of three hundred thousand new homes. In those days, if you didn't have your own place to live and you couldn't find a boarding house, you always camped with relatives. So every time we passed through Sydney en route to my old man's latest job in the bush, we'd catch a tram and bunk down at Uncle Jack and Auntie May's. Jack was Mum's eldest brother, and he and Auntie May lived in a tiny terrace in Underwood Street, Paddington.

Before home telephones, on occasion we would turn up unannounced on their doorstep, all six of us, surrounded by suitcases. There'd be kisses and cuddles, and in we'd go, sleeping on lounges and down hallways. Dad and Uncle Jack would traipse up to the pub, while Mum and Auntie May would set up the beds and cook dinner.

At night voices echoed down the side lane, the sound of footsteps ricocheted off the old brick houses all squeezed together, and in the narrow street trucks passed by so close it seemed like they were coming through the front windows. These were the strange, exciting sounds of the city to my eager ears.

I forget what work Uncle Jack did – it was some kind of

manual labour – but I do remember he had incredibly strong hands. He'd sit near the front doorway in his favourite lounge chair and pretend to be reading the afternoon race guide. As I tried to silently slip past him, he'd strike like a death adder and latch on to my leg, just above the kneecap. His hand was a steel trap. I'd writhe and squeal and bash his arm, but he would take no notice. Then – when my leg had gone numb – he'd just as randomly let go, look up mock quizzically from his paper and ask, 'What?' My sisters, who bruised easily, would wear the insignia of his fingers for weeks. Years later we'd laughingly suggest we gave blood clots in lieu of rent.

After a fortnight, when Mum thought we'd probably outstayed our welcome at Paddo, the old man managed to snaffle us some accommodation. You could always depend on Dad's breathtaking ingenuity. This time he managed to rent a small rundown 'houseboat' moored in a grimy industrial stretch of the Parramatta River, at a place called Meadowbank. It was really more of a claustrophobic barge, but we couldn't whinge because there were plenty of other wretched families crammed into caravans or inner-city dosshouses. Besides, we at least had a water view.

The old man actually went to the expense of buying a couple of hand lines, with the inspired plan of catching the occasional fish dinner. All we ever managed to haul in were a couple of bearded toadfish – it was probably the same one, trying to commit suicide – and a couple of other weird-looking toxic river inhabitants that Mum refused to even think about chucking into the pan. Mum loathed trying to cook, wash and carry out the rest of her domestic duties in the middle of the Parramatta River.

Living on the houseboat was a bit of a Boy's Own adventure for me. To get ashore we'd have to row, which meant a hilarious daily dice with death. My sisters would deliberately rock the boat, and then when Mum read the riot act they'd break into fits of uncontrollable giggles, as only girls can.

My sisters were very pretty girls – country fresh, rosy cheeked and full of fun. As a couple of teenage beauties the older pair attracted some local louts who undertook yahooing circuits around our stationary houseboat, in a spluttering outboard dinghy. At least they did until Dad came home one night and threatened to sink the boys. Or worse. Mum was almost as bad, riding shotgun like some boarding-school mistress. Lorraine and Kay were young country women trying to bust the convent shackles in the big city, without much luck.

Dad took a job as a mechanic and then as a salesman flogging Citroën Light 15 sedans, the sort Inspector Maigret zipped around Paris in, in the movies. As a perk of the job, he occasionally got to bring one home. Like the old Ford Model T, you could have any colour Citroën you liked, as long as it was black. It sat low to the ground, had running boards down the side and was the sleekest-looking motor vehicle I'd ever seen. Dad once drove it down the so-called Mad Mile section of the Princes Highway, outside of Sutherland – with me breathlessly aboard – and cranked the speedo up to almost 80 miles an hour. I figured that was the next best thing to supersonic.

As a seven-year-old, I was also pretty stoked by my first ride in an electric train. My magic carpet had always been a smoke-belching steam train or a big diesel. When we were going into the city one day, I asked the old man what pulled the train, seeing as it obviously didn't have an engine. Dad was clearly glad I'd asked. With a captive audience in our packed peak-hour carriage, he explained there was an incredibly strong bloke who was actually *pushing* it. To catch his breath, the bloke would hitch a ride on the back on the flat and downhill runs.

When we arrived at Central, Dad took me down to the back of the train to introduce me to 'the incredibly strong bloke'. He even pointed out the little metal balcony where the bloke would stand. But as luck would have it, 'unfortunately, he must have ducked away', according to my dad. 'He was probably out of breath and went for a quick drink of water, to recover from his amazing ordeal.' Country gullible, whenever I caught the train after that I used to risk spinal damage twisting my neck to try to spy 'the incredibly strong bloke', as other electric trains whizzed past. It was months before my sisters put me straight. It was worse than discovering Santa didn't exist.

The fact my father had a job didn't help much when it came to finding permanent digs. There were simply no places to rent. Yet Mum was certainly persistent. Every day she would drag the four of us kids into the Housing Commission's main office, and we'd sit there for hours, along with other desperate families. But when the commission clerk discovered we were living on a houseboat, he shook his head and declared that made us ineligible for emergency housing, because strictly speaking we weren't homeless!

So, in a change of tactics, Mum booked us into the Salvation Army's People's Palace, in lower Pitt Street, down near Chinatown. The Palace was one of a chain of Salvo temperance hotels around Australia in which no alcohol, gambling or other evils were permitted. The motto of the People's Palace was 'A safe place for morals'. It was an ironic refuge for my intemperate, immoral old man.

Lorraine and Kay were sent back out to Paddington to stay with the rellos again, while Joyce, Mum, Dad and I shared a compact double bed at the Salvos' – the parents up one end, Joyce and me down the other. We slept that way for a few weeks. Every morning it was back to the Housing Commission office, where we'd rendezvous with Lorraine and Kay. We became pretty familiar with the layout of the place – where the toilets were, when the tea trolley was due and even the names of some of the staff. Mum would make sure we dressed properly, sat up straight and always spoke softly. My indefatigable mother was convinced the Housing Commission people were starting to feel sorry for us. (I certainly was.)

But there was a masterstroke yet to be played.

After receiving some illicit hushed-voiced advice from one of the clerks, Mum took Joyce and me back to Central Station, with our suitcases, blankets and coats. We weren't catching a train this time, though. My father arrived after work, and the four of us, who'd been reasonably comfortable in the Salvos' Palace, slept the night on the station's wooden benches, as the entire world passed by. And then we slept there again the next night. A couple of cops came across us early the second morning and spoke sympathetically to my father. Cops have a way of sticking in your memory – even the friendly ones. Anyway, it did the trick. They drove us down to the Housing Commission office, and that same day we were bumped up the queue.

We suddenly found ourselves on the electric train again, heading to our new suburb, Hargrave Park, on the western outskirts of Sydney, almost at the end of the line. Located right behind Warwick Farm racetrack, it had been a giant tent city for American forces during the Second World War. Then it became the Royal Navy's main shore base, where they built huts to house eight thousand British sailors. After the war, the Poms went home and the New South Wales government grabbed it for emergency housing; they brought in architects to quickly transform the Navy base into a small town, with almost a thousand rough housing units.

Ours was at one end of a huge corrugated-iron hut that had been turned into six units. There were rows and rows of similar huts and a shopping strip, a couple of churches, a primary school and the Navy's old makeshift movie theatre.

We had a combined kitchen and lounge room with a fuel stove, three tiny bedrooms and a bathroom with a tin bath and a chip heater, which always sounded like it was about to take off when you filled it up. What was truly amazing was that we also had our first-ever flushing toilet! 'What more could civilisation possibly need?' I wondered.

In summer you boiled, and in winter the cold winds whistled through holes in the corrugated walls – until the old man found a ladder and covered them with pieces of fibro. Sydney had regular blackouts in those days, and we'd have to drag out the primus lamps, just like in the bush. It was all pretty basic, but it was home.

We also had a handkerchief-sized piece of dirt out the front of our unit, with a crude picket fence. Mum quickly turned it into a brilliant flower garden, until light-fingered neighbours pinched the flowers.

It was a community of battlers living so close together you couldn't mind your own business even if you wanted to. Down the road from our unit was a communal laundry and clothes lines. They were used on a strict roster basis, and there were regular squabbles when somebody tried to grab a spot when it wasn't their turn. Tempers were likely to run high given that along with your washing you had to cart your own wood to fire up the coppers. Even more than the school or the shops, the laundry was where the not-so-secret women's business took place: it was gossip central.

The ice-cream man drove a motorbike, with the sidecar full of Paddle Pops. Chirpy vendors sold wood, vegetables, milk and contraband off the backs of trucks. As kids, we followed the iceman's van and picked up chipped-off pieces that fell to the ground as he cut the frozen blocks down to size to fit in his customers' ice chests. Few families in Hargrave Park had a fridge, or an electric stove.

But easily the biggest taste treat was when the bread man came in school holidays, carrying his basket of steaming hot loaves. Your only choice was white bread or white bread. But a hot slice slathered with butter and Vegemite was infinitely better than caviar has ever tasted to me. My mouth waters just thinking about it.

In summer we kids floated anything we could climb aboard down nearby Brickmaker's Creek – even though we didn't yet know how to swim. Over at the railway station, where the gypsies used to panhandle, I'd slide down the grassy embankments on the edge of the railway viaduct to wait for my father's train. In the open paddocks we'd kick footballs and fly kites, and on cracker night we'd let off shoeboxes full of double bungers, catherine-wheels and skyrockets. Before plastic took over our lives, shoeboxes were used to store the family's most treasured bits and pieces.

Our family didn't have much, but I certainly never felt poor, maybe because at Hargrave Park everybody was in the same boat, with a few much worse off. I used to occasionally have tea at a schoolmate's place and his family didn't even have a table or chairs. They'd throw a tablecloth over a tea chest, and there were wooden boxes to sit on. Nobody seemed embarrassed. Nobody had to apologise.

Every Saturday night we'd go to the picture show. We'd always sit downstairs, in the stalls. My old man told me that upstairs, in the dress circle, you could see the black-and-white movies in colour . . . and *again* I believed him. We mostly saw westerns or smash-hit musicals such as *Brigadoon* and *Seven Brides for Seven Brothers*. I remember a chorus of sniffling and nose-blowing when Mario Lanza finally carked it in his starring role as *The Great Caruso*. They could be a soft-hearted, emotional mob out there at The Park, as we called our suburb.

Sport became the staple of my life at Hargrave Park, starting out with junior boxing. I remember when I was building a balsawood model jet fighter and the razor blade slipped and sliced off the top of my middle finger. Well, it almost did. I felt sure it warranted weeks in hospital, maybe 'in an induced coma'. That was what I'd heard the woman next door mention to my mother when they were talking about a car-crash victim they both knew. Mum simply whacked on some Dettol and gently wrapped a strip of sticking plaster around it. We both agreed my father should not be told. Otherwise, he would stop the fight: I was a major entry that night on the fight card at the Hargrave Park Scouts hall.

After two action-packed rounds, the referee declared it a draw. But I knew I had whupped the other kid, as Muhammad Ali would say. It seemed that seven-year-olds only ever fought a draw. Otherwise the loser would end up bawling in his mum's lap, and that wouldn't look good on the family CV.

The only serious injury inflicted on me that big fight night came from my old man the instant he took off my glove, which happened to be filled with blood from my gaping war wound. He gave me a clip over the ear for not telling him.

What made the Scouts hall bout historic was that it was my first organised sporting appearance. That's if you forget the cricket match the previous month against Warwick Farm Primary, in the schoolyard dirt with a tennis ball. I was wicketkeeping when one of their opening batsmen swung viciously, and much too late, cracking open the top of my head. It seemed there was more blood pouring out of me than you'd see on a bad day on the floor of the Riverstone Meat Works, where my father had once toiled. Wrapped in towels like a turbaned Sikh, I was carted off to the local GP, who inserted four stitches and put me on the bus home. That time, too, I had suggested to Mum that a lesser man would have ended up in hospital, 'in an induced coma'. She acknowledged the heroism on my part, gave me a sausage with boiled cabbage – Mum boiled every vegetable beyond recognition – and then tucked me into bed, mindful of concussion.

It was from these humble beginnings that my lifelong obsession with sport began. The weird thing is that participating in sport simply wasn't in my family's DNA, which made me seriously wonder if I had been swapped at birth. The only workout my sisters undertook was getting hot and sweaty on a towel at Cronulla Beach as they chased a suntan.

I competed in the state swimming championships a couple of times and made it onto the state Under 16 basketball squad and a representative soccer team, but when I got back from a big sports carnival, Mum invariably forgot to ask me how I'd gone. I can't remember my father ever throwing or kicking a ball to me. But I do remember him teaching me to spar. It would always be in the lounge room, usually after he'd had a few schooners. He'd get me to adopt a crouched southpaw stance like 'the great Vic Patrick'. I'd throw a few loose straight lefts; he'd counter and come inside my defence with an open-palmed slap to the face. He never hurt me. It was always meant as a reminder, he said, 'of how lightning fast the great Vic had been'.

The old man and I must have gone to the Sydney Stadium at least a dozen times when I was a kid, catching an overcrowded tram from Central to Rushcutters Bay. The iconic Tin Shed, as it was known, was a fifty-year-old corrugated-iron wreck of a joint. There were two pairs of boxers in neon lights above the arched entrance. Each side of them were giant billboards for the 'Stamina suit'. They declared: 'Stamina . . . the self-supporting trousers!!!' The only long-legged trousers I owned were made by Stamina, a grey serge pair I wore in winter. I had no idea what 'self-supporting' meant. Whatever it was, it sounded flash.

The stadium was a mammoth barn with a capacity of about twelve thousand. Raked wooden chairs circled the ring and stretched up to the cheap seats. It was pandemonium, without any insulation against the roar of the crowd or the cold winds; with the rich smell of liniment and sweat, smoke and beer, pies and hot dogs; with loudmouth blokes spitting advice at the pugs and laughing. They demolished the Tin Shed in the early 1970s, with all its memories of fights, wrestling and rock concerts, to make way for the Eastern Suburbs railway. What a shame.

The American essayist Joyce Carol Oates once wrote: 'Boxing is for men, about men and is men. It's a celebration of the lost art of masculinity, all the more trenchant for being lost.' Certainly through my young boy's eyes, boxing was a world strictly for blokes. There were almost no women, except a couple of sultry young things hanging off the arms of blokes wearing too many gold rings to be trusted. I never saw such well-dressed men in sharp suits and ties as I saw at the stadium fights, always sitting ringside, always smoking cigarettes and cigars, always swigging brandy from silver hipflasks they passed along the row. They seemed a world away from my father and his new best mates, who'd only ever drink beer out the back of the bleachers, handing round a dented packet of Craven A cigarettes.

We once saw a skinny bantamweight named Jimmy Carruthers, who was Australia's first World Champ, defend his crown.

He went in against a ripple-muscled white American bloke with the weird name of Henry 'Pappy' Gault. I remember, probably because it was such a strange name, that he was from a place called 'Spartanburg, South Carolina'. Jimmy easily won the fight, although I didn't notice much in the latter rounds because I was too busy watching the skirmishes and full-blooded stoushes that erupted amongst the crowd like scrub fires fuelled by testosterone and booze.

A few days later Sydney doctors revealed the reason Jimmy had fought a bit sluggishly. It turned out the champ had been carrying a 30-foot tapeworm in his gut. Thirty foot! That's over 9 metres long. The story disgusted my sisters so much they couldn't stop talking about it, until Mum actually banned the subject from the tea table. For years afterwards, if someone in the family ate a lot or seemed unusually hungry it would spark the comment 'Must have a tapeworm, eh?' We'd all nod knowingly, like a panel of GPs.

*　　　　*　　　　*

Hargrave Park no longer exists. It was officially erased from Sydney's maps in the 1960s, when a new housing estate was built on the site. The bureaucrats feared that nobody would live there if it was still called Hargrave Park. In the space of just a decade, The Park had built up a shocking reputation. It was 'a tragic place' and 'a den of iniquity', in the words of one priggish magistrate. The *Daily Telegraph* called it 'filthy and vermin-infested' and 'worse than the inner city slums of Redfern and Surry Hills'. That was all crap. We didn't exactly fall in love with the place, but it was a rung above the Salvos' and the houseboat, let me tell you.

What all of us in The Park knew was that it was just a halfway house to something much better. That happened for my family about two years after we arrived. We were offered a brand-new three-bedroom house out at Jannali, nestled in the leafy Sutherland Shire, not far from Cronulla Beach. We had lots of Arcadian bush to run through and even a fresh waterhole to swim in. The name of our street, Second Avenue – which was followed by Third, Fourth, Fifth, et cetera – was about as original as the design of the houses. Our road was a thin, corrugated strip of sandy dirt with fibro boxes each side, facing one another. They looked exactly the same, as if a giant mirror had been laid down the middle of the road. No self-respecting architect would ever lay claim to them. Not that we whinged for a second; we thought it was a miracle to have our own house at last.

Mum took a shovel and transformed the clay and leftover builder's rubble in the yard into easily the best garden in the street. The old man was busy, too. Out the back – beyond the shiny new Hills Hoist – he built a substantial chook pen, a double-storey aviary for finches and wrens, and a trellised summerhouse entwined with passionfruit vines that filtered the sun. Out the front, smack bang in the middle of Mum's thriving couch lawn, he lovingly crafted a fish pond like an oversized plate on a pedestal. It was the sort of creation Italian masons built in ancient Rome, except Dad's was made out of rocks and Illawarra sandstone pieces that Mum had dug from her garden.

Jannali may have been a brand-new government housing estate, but the sewerage pipes would take another fifteen years to arrive. We had the old thunderbox out the back, and the dunny man came first thing every Monday morning, rain or shine. Not that we actually *saw* him often, because it was usually still dark

40

when he'd come trotting down the side path, past my bedroom, in his blue shorts and his spotless white Dunlop Volley tennis shoes, without socks. He always whistled, just in case someone might be caught short in the dunny and have a heart attack as he removed the can through the trapdoor.

He'd race down there, carrying only the empty replacement can, and stagger back up the path on his way out to the truck. Last thing every Sunday night, Mum would ask if my bike was safely under the house. It usually lay like a booby trap somewhere down the side. She had nightmares about the dunny man loaded up and coming a cropper. At Christmas we'd have to leave beer out for the milko, the garbos and the postie – and especially the dunny man!

*   *   *

I attended Jannali Primary, just a few years behind Clive James. I vividly remember at the age of nine a school bus taking us to see the new queen on her first visit to Australia. I was too excited to sleep the night before. In our school uniforms we waited expectantly on the edge of the Princes Highway for at least three hours. Kids didn't wear hats in 1954. So we all just stood there baking on a hot February afternoon.

Suddenly there was an enormous roar from down the road. She was coming. This was it. I reached into my school bag to grab my little Aussie flag-on-a-stick so I could wave it 'with loyalty and devotion', just as the prime minister had asked.

But I missed her. Damn. I was too busy looking for my flag.

When I started to get some good marks in 6th class, the teachers all talked about me going to a selective school, probably Fort Street or Sydney Boys' High. Dad started muttering that I would go on to law at uni, just like the Labor Party barrister Clive Evatt QC – though God only knows where he got that idea from. The old man was now working as a travelling salesman, selling farm machinery around the bush, which meant he'd changed jobs at least half a dozen times since coming to Sydney. Mum was doing piecework in a plastics factory, the older girls caught the train together to jobs at the GPO, in Martin Place, and Joyce was excelling at high school. For the first time in my life, we seemed settled as a family. But it wouldn't last.

During school holidays I'd often go bush with my father in the big Buick V-8 company car. Most country roads were rough gravel in those days, making them slippery and treacherous in the wet. Quite frequently Dad would be half-drunk yet have another 50 or 60 miles to travel to the next town on his sales circuit. In a careless mood, he'd sit me on his lap to steer while he worked the accelerator and brakes, and off we'd go. No seatbelts or airbags in those days, either. I'd have to keep talking to him and jabbing him to make sure he stayed awake.

When he was in Sydney, Dad would now get full on Friday nights as well as having the usual Saturday-afternoon session. His drinking had become a lot worse. Occasionally he'd even roll in drunk on weeknights as well. You could hear a collective sigh of relief from everyone if he walked in the gate early and sober. When he was drunk, the violence was mostly verbal – he'd be belligerent and argumentative – although every so often he'd lash out at Mum and she'd cop a fat lip or a black eye. Because Mum would stand up to him, the older girls would often step in and calm Dad down, sending him off to bed. My mother would camp on the lounge.

As so often happens in family bust-ups, when it started to collapse everything unravelled quickly. The morning after one particularly abusive incident – he had kicked me for not feeding the dog and left a huge bruise on my leg – Mum finally went to the Sutherland police station and asked them to charge him. She had never done that before. A couple of cops arrived at the front door late that same afternoon, when the old man had come home early and was trying to make amends for the previous night's bastardry. I remember the chamber magistrate asking me whether I would sooner stay with my mother or father. I was only eleven; that was an impossible question to answer. I told him I wanted to stay with both of them. But I knew in my heart that wasn't going to be possible.

The embarrassing court episode chastened my father for a few months, but it wasn't long before the same destructive behaviour erupted. There were more futile attempts at reconciliation, yet things had clearly gone beyond that.

I think in today's Australia, Mum and Dad would have decided they'd both had enough of the bickering and fighting and gone their separate ways. But, back then, divorce, or even separation, had a real social stigma about it. Certainly it did for Catholics.

My eldest sister, Lorraine, who was in many ways the family's chief mediator and voice of reason, had had enough. As soon as she legally could, when she turned eighteen, she joined the Air Force and was posted to Melbourne. Kay also made it clear she was moving out the minute she could. That's when Mum finally made the decision to leave my father.

It was a brave move, reflecting both her strength and utter despair. After all, these were mean and hungry times for a single mother. There was no real community or church support network. Neighbours and even close family didn't really know what went on behind closed doors, because people didn't reveal personal failings such as relationship breakdowns. There were no refuges for abused women, no counselling services and certainly no welfare payments. That's why too often women stayed and copped the abuse.

As kids who'd seen and lived through the emotional torment and violence too many times, Joyce and I knew Mum had no choice but to leave and take us both with her. As much as we would have preferred their marriage to have the happily-ever-after storybook ending where the grey nomads drive off into the sunset together, that particular fairytale had turned sour long ago.

My father had threatened to kill Mum if she ever left him, and the shotgun incident and other violence made us all take him seriously. So my mother and sisters quietly hatched the great escape. Mum took me aside and calmly told me that we were going and swore me to secrecy. It was all a bit surreal, especially as Dad came home sober and pleasant for the last few days before we were due to leave. But even at my tender age I knew we'd reached a crisis point, and I was relieved to be getting out. I had no way of knowing what the future would be, but I was as anxious as my sisters and mother to be free of the violence and drunkenness.

Mum was understandably terrified, fearing Dad's reaction if he twigged to what was going on. We waited until he headed off to the bush for a week's work, then we packed our bags and fled the house in Jannali.

Suddenly I found myself back at our old stomping ground, Central Station. But this time we were going on the longest train trip we'd ever undertaken, as far away from the old man as we could run without crossing the Nullarbor. We were heading for Adelaide, via Parkes, Ivanhoe, Broken Hill and, of course, that old favourite, Bogan Gate. But we had no intention of getting off the Express this time.

At the Central Station ticket counter a strange thing happened when Mum was asked to fill out a form with our names on it. Petrified that Dad would somehow be able to trace where we'd gone, Mum wrote the name Martin, which Kay and Joyce both say was on a nearby advertising sign. It was a random choice, as random as the names chosen by customs officers for immigrants who couldn't write their names in English. It wasn't meant to be our permanent name, just a temporary one to get us through this crisis. But as the months turned into years it became part of our new persona, part of who we had become. So, some time later Mum formally changed our name by deed poll from Grace to Martin. It's given me a few laughs, the new name, especially during my *Midday* years, when people named Martin wrote me letters claiming to be long-lost relatives.

I was still only eleven when we shot through, and I would never see my father again. Through the rest of primary school and on into high school I simply told people that he had died. Still, for the next few years we were afraid that he might just resurrect himself and suddenly turn up.

Chapter 3
An Island Idyll

We didn't know anybody in Adelaide. For Mum this anonymity was part of the security, part of the appeal, along with Adelaide's isolation. She rented a small flat, just a few rooms, for the three of us – Mum, Joyce and me – in what in grander times had been a colonial mansion. It was on East Terrace, across from the Victoria Park racecourse.

There was a carriage house with stables out the back, and a champion equestrian jumper regularly put his horses over the fences in what used to be the mansion's grand garden. In those days horses were a magnet for me, so I loved it when the equestrian champ gave me a couple of shillings to walk his prized ponies after a workout.

Given the sorry circumstances surrounding our sudden arrival in Adelaide, my new primary school's Latin motto, *Vincit qui se Vincit* – 'He conquers who conquers himself' – seemed apt. Like every kid, that particular conquest was still somewhere in the distant future for me.

I can't really remember much about my final months of primary school, but I vividly recall the Melbourne Olympics, which happened around that time, in November 1956. Television was late arriving in Adelaide, so the only place you could see the Aussie triumphs was at the picture show, on the Movietone newsreels. And thank God for ABC radio. I couldn't get enough of all the Olympic glory, with Dawn Fraser, Betty Cuthbert, Murray Rose and all the other national heroes up on the dais collecting gold. Years later I would come to know some of them. They had no idea how much I had worshipped them as a boy.

Another abiding memory, again through the newsreels of the time, was seeing the atomic-bomb shelters that Americans were building under their houses. There was constant talk about a looming Cold War showdown, whatever the hell that was, in places such as Korea and Cuba, wherever the dickens they were. I wasn't even twelve and the world was about to end! The Third World War seemed a long way from Adelaide – until we saw footage of the Olympic water-polo match, in which the Russians and the Hungarians fought in the pool and there was blood in the water. Not even from the rugby-league gladiators had I seen such unbridled brutality.

I don't know whether it was the Olympic heroics that inspired me, but I finally got my chance to ride one of the equestrian champion's horses. He was as big as Phar Lap, and I was riding him bareback, just to cool him after a hose-down. As we turned at the top of the paddock, he spied the water jump and suddenly took off. So, in a pitiful display of cowardice, I pressed the eject button and slid off his wet rump, right into the muddy water. I finished up with mild concussion and both my coccyx bone and pride badly bruised. Mum ended my magnificent equestrian career right then and there, although she still let me go on earning a few shillings for walking the showjumpers. I also mucked out stables across at the racetrack on Saturdays. Then once a week I was a delivery boy for a local jeweller. I got to ride around Adelaide on my bike and get paid for it.

But – there's always a 'but' in life's stories, isn't there? – there was suddenly a domestic scare. We'd been holed up in Adelaide for barely four months when Mum got word that my father had somehow found out where we were. So it was panic stations, back on the road again – the railroad, actually. This time we fled by train to Lorraine's place in Melbourne. From there we flew by noisy DC-3 to Launceston, in Tasmania. It was my first plane trip and I sat holding the sick bag in my lap, just in case. While the trip on the DC-3 was the most thrilling ride I'd so far taken in my life, what lay in front of us in Tassie filled me with trepidation. We seemed to be living on the run.

Many years later, when I was working in television current affairs, I'd regularly get letters from viewers offering me a bit of free character analysis. Presuming to know my life story, they would ask 'How could you understand, with your silver-spoon upbringing?' or 'How would you have any idea what it's like to come from a broken home?' or 'How would you possibly know about a violent, abusive upbringing?'. All I ever used to say in reply was, 'Trust me. I do have some idea what you're going through.'

As it happened, Mum had an old family friend who'd grown up in Tassie, so the Apple Isle came highly recommended. Besides, going offshore meant there was now a big strip of water, namely Bass Strait, between us and my father. In a sense we now had a bloody big moat to protect us!

Our move to Tasmania would begin the most stable time of my young life. I have only warm, rich memories of my five years there. After all the turmoil Launceston became our tranquillity base, giving Mum, Joyce and me the chance to get on with our lives. Mum and Joyce quickly got jobs as machinists at the Patons & Baldwins knitting mill, the biggest employer of women in the state. I played sport every waking hour, discovered girls and began high school – in about that order of priority.

My maths teacher in the first year was a new uni graduate, an absolute maths wizard but a dunce when it came to teaching. We nicknamed him Blowfly. This was because, with his receding hair and his Coke-bottle glasses, that's exactly what he looked like. His classes were total mayhem, with punch-ups, rubbers and paper missiles hurtling around, and kids spending half the lesson AWOL. I went to a selective school, so these students were the cream of the crop, yet it was sheer pandemonium. Blowfly should have been in a lab researching chaos theory, rather than fostering chaos in his maths class.

My report card said it all. After finishing top of my year in primary school, I suddenly got 13 per cent in maths during my first term of high school. The class average was only 23 per cent, which had been skewed upwards by several girls who got marks in the 80s.

In the second term the headmaster, Mr Amos, took over, in a move somewhat akin to the Nazis annexing the Sudetenland. Lou Amos was about five foot tall, built like a panzer tank, with a flat-top crew cut. In another life he'd clearly been a bad-arse marine drill sergeant. Louie the Lip took no prisoners. I salvaged a mark of 50 per cent in the second term and 93 per cent to round out the year. Mum started to breathe a bit easier. Lou had pulled off the impossible, but he'd worn out a few canes doing it. This was the age of corporal punishment, and Lou Amos was a five-star general in that particular theatre of war.

I fondly remember an English teacher, an old battleaxe of a spinster, who became the female equivalent of Mr Chips for me. When I fell in love with Joseph Conrad's prose, she enthused and encouraged me. She also led me through the labyrinth of Shakespeare's 'simple' truths. My football coach was an impatient bully, but when he taught history he showed a different kind of passion – for the past. Both teachers left indelible marks on my boyhood psyche. They inspired me to want to teach high-school English and history.

It's funny what sticks in the memory from the schooldays' dreamtime. I recall a brittle boy named Jimmy. He suffered from what today we'd probably call acute Asperger's Syndrome, an awkward autism that made him an easy target for schoolyard taunts. A bit like the Dustin Hoffman character in *Rain Man*, Jimmy was a social misfit but a genius with numbers and scientific formulas. One morning he was tormented so badly by classmates that he cracked, ripping a wooden locker door right off its hinges with one hand and hurling it like a discus. It almost decapitated the row of kids who were lined up in front of the mirror carving their wet hair and trying to look like Elvis Presley. As his house captain I rescued Jimmy, who repaid me with unstinting loyalty. For the next year or so every time I turned around he'd be standing silently behind me. He was a nice kid, who I think went on to become a science boffin at university.

I cherish the memory of school holidays, catching wild brown trout at a mate's place out near Avoca in Tasmania; lazy afternoons in dappled light that I'd now love to photograph through a polarised lens; bucolic green valleys with wallabies and other wildlife aplenty; floating down slow-moving rivers on truck-tyre inner tubes; racing billycarts around rutted sheep tracks edged with sharp gorse bush; and launching off high riverbanks into streams that mirrored the sky. Just twist the kaleidoscope and the images change.

Like all the boys at Launceston High I had to join the cadet corps. I chose the Air Cadets because they had a much sharper light-blue uniform than the Army Cadets' khaki and navy bell-bottoms. Besides, they went flying instead of just slogging around the playground being bellowed at. At least that's what I thought the Air Cadets had going for it. About a month after I joined, we went on a camp outside Hobart. On day one, when everyone else went to the rifle range to shoot real bullets, a small group, including me, was handed kitchen duty: peeling the spuds for tea. When I voiced some mild adolescent objection, the RAAF sergeant promptly informed me I'd be peeling spuds the next day, too.

At that precise moment I decided that Her Majesty's Air Force and I had nothing, nought, nix in common and we would soon be parting ways. After a bit of sleuthing I discovered that one certain way to get out of high-school cadets – short of declaring that you were a homosexual – was to join the art class. (To some in Tassie at the time, I suspect it amounted to the same thing.) The school insisted that to drop out of cadets you had to be serious about sketches, oil paints and watercolours. In fact you had to be so serious that you intended to do art as a final-year matriculation subject. That was not a problem. They could stuff cadets, and kitchen duty, too. I was now a serious painter of pictures.

And how sweet it turned out to be. When an ex-cadet mate and I stepped up to our easels, we discovered we were the only boys amongst fifteen teenage girls. We loved those odds.

For one witless moment I even thought about teaching art. That was a silly idea, because I wasn't good enough. Art had rescued me safely from cadets and delivered me into the presence – if not the arms – of a bevy of schoolgirl beauties. I should quit while I was in front.

My best mate at Launceston High was John Honey. Together we ran the school radio station and edited the school newspaper and magazine. I guess you can picture us: a couple of budding mini media moguls making our move. 'Today the Tamar River, tomorrow the world.'

Au contraire. When I say we 'ran the school radio station', what we actually did was control the decibel level of the microphone and play a classical-music track during school assemblies. But it meant John and I could sit in a nearby office in leather-lounge-chair comfort and read a magazine while our classmates shuffled and tried to avoid the REM stage of sleep in the draughty assembly hall. (I doubt Reg Grundy began his brilliant career this way.)

Editing the school paper was slightly more proactive, but not exactly Walkley-award-winning stuff, either. I got to report on all the school sport, which usually involved John, me and our closest mates. John wrote what were loosely called 'news stories' for the paper. And together we helped edit the school magazine, *The Northern Churinga*, once a year. Looking back at some of the daggy photographs in the magazine, we should have enforced our rights as picture editors, too.

After uni, John Honey went on to read the ABC nightly news in Hobart and later directed the iconic feature film *Manganinnie*. He became the first boss of the Tasmanian Film Corporation, then moved on to Washington, DC, where he was an award-winning independent documentary maker. In recent times he's written scripts for TV shows such as *Macleod's Daughters* plus three novels, published by a company that he set up outside Hobart. Clearly, it was our high-school enterprise that kick-started his glorious multimedia career. (The simple fact that John is incredibly bright and talented probably helped, too.)

*　　　*　　　*

My introduction to television, which would come to dominate my working life, was quite basic, almost primitive. Like most families in Launceston in 1956, we couldn't afford a TV set, but even if we could have, it would have been a total waste of money. The signal had to come across Bass Strait from Melbourne's GTV, and even on a clear day it was more like radio with a few ghostly grey figures flitting across the screen. Still, that minor detail never quenched the latent thrill of TV. Mum, Joyce and I would join everybody else on the footpath in front of whatever electrical store was selling the latest TV models. It was quite a communal muster, especially Friday nights in later years when *Bonanza* was on. There was always an enthusiastic mob with collapsible chairs, Thermos flasks, sandwiches and cakes. Some even brought their dinner on a plate.

It was about this time in my life that I stopped spending pocket money on Bing Crosby records for my mother and started buying Elvis and Buddy Holly to take to parties at my friends' houses. (For a brief moment I even had a girlfriend whose name was Peggy Sue, which made her, by definition, irresistible.) This was also the time when I sang a Little Richard medley to my high-school music class in an attempt to break away from the regimen of medieval viola performances. (I sang it really badly, by the way. I still can't sing in tune. Even in the shower it's clear I'm singing off-key.) One lunchtime I was practising with some mates for the school athletics carnival when we heard the news that Buddy Holly, Ritchie Valens and the Big Bopper had all perished in a plane crash in Iowa. As Don McLean would later lament, that was 'the day the music died'. For us it was, anyway. We spent weeks in mourning. Thank God we at least had all their records. What else could you dance to? (My kids say I can't dance, either. What would they know? They didn't see me up hoofing it at the school dance.)

*   *   *

A regional centre of about seventy thousand people, Launceston was small enough to make your mark yet big enough to quietly slip away. It was the perfect place for an adolescent to have a go, make mistakes and probably survive them.

Ironically, my obsession with sport – cricket, in particular – was the only thing that ever got me into serious trouble at high school there. It was also responsible for my biggest newspaper headline at that stage of my life, and threatened to bankrupt my mother.

One Saturday, when for the third week in a row our match was abandoned due to rain, we ducked through a hole in the fence and into the adjoining cricket nets. They belonged to the Northern Tasmanian Cricket Association, the NTCA, where stars like Ricky Ponting and David Boon would later practise on their road to cricketing glory. We had a cricket ball but no bat, so we grabbed a stump to use instead. It had been good enough for the young Don Bradman, so why not us?

The trouble was, without meaning to, we made a mess of the practice pitches with the stump. What made our innocent misdeed so sensational was that Richie Benaud and the Aus-tralian Test team, en route to England for the Ashes tour, were due to practise in the nets the next Thursday. The *Launceston Examiner* emblazoned the story across its front page that Monday morning: HIGH SCHOOL STUDENTS VANDALISE TEST TEAM PITCH – MATCH IN DOUBT.

Lou Amos frogmarched us into his office and read the riot act: we were a disgrace to the school, it would cost our parents thousands of quid and what did we have to say for ourselves? All I could say was that my mother couldn't afford twenty quid, let alone a thousand. As the criminals' appointed spokesman I explained that all we wanted to do on the morning of the said felony was hit a cricket ball! We miraculously escaped the lash.

Instead, Lou dispatched us to apologise to the boss of the NTCA, who turned out to be a reasonable bloke. He said that under the same circumstances he probably would have done it too. We liked his style! After promising never to do it again, we were pardoned. Even better, he quietly slipped us each a free ticket to the big game with Richie Benaud and the boys. What a champ.

Not many of us high-school kids had a licence, let alone a car. The legal drinking age was twenty-one, so it wasn't worth even trying to buck the system when you were in your teens, because nobody was going to serve you or believe you. There were no other drugs, except for cigarettes. Condoms were scarce and the pill hadn't been invented, so girls were still scared. That was unfortunate.

In 1987 one of my old schoolmates organised a twenty-fifth reunion, and about 130 former students rolled up for a dinner in the same draughty assembly hall that John Honey and I used to assiduously avoid. I can report that the best-looking girls still looked pretty good. The girls who'd been notorious flirts were still up to their old fluttering-eyelash tricks. The boys who had been a pain in the arse hadn't changed much, either.

But what the students had done with their lives says a lot about Tasmania. There were no judges, no professors, no surgeons and no multimillionaire business types, as there would have been at a similar selective school in Melbourne or Sydney. Instead, the dux of our year had become a veterinarian. There was one law-yer. The vast bulk of these high achievers had become school principals and teachers. The government, I suspect, would look fondly on such a recidivist school system that turns its best and brightest brains back into education.

*　　*　　*

I have to say my mother and I got on famously through my teen-age years. Despite all the pop psychology about the turmoil of adolescence, I can't remember a cross word between us. Maybe we'd already had our fill of emotional chaos. I used to meet her at night outside the knitting-factory gates after she'd done an overtime shift, and we'd wander home, chatting away like a cou-ple of old tarts. Along with my wife, Dianne, Mum has easily been the strongest influence on my life. Whatever early success I've chalked up I owe primarily to Mary Jane.

Even before I had finished high school, my sisters had all mar-ried – within eighteen months of each other – and had moved on to different domestic worlds. With my old man out of the pic-ture, my brothers-in-law became good male role models for me. In fact, a decade later, my sister Lorraine's husband, Des, would be best man at my wedding.

By contrast with women today they all married very young. Maybe it was just a sign of the times. Maybe it was something deeper. In later life they'd sometimes ponder whether they had freely chosen the direction their lives had taken or whether they were motivated – even driven – into early marriage because of a desperate need to get away. It's not rocket science. How turbulent your life is as a child is a determining factor in how you end up. And who you are. It's an awesome responsibility being a parent.

But in the end all three of my sisters jumped those obstacles – the broken schooling, the crazy peripatetic lifestyle and domestic violence – and went on to be successful and productive. They also found contentment, and they laugh a lot.

*　　　*　　　*

In writing these stories and thinking about my early life, what I still find intriguing is that through all my school years my father never tried to make contact with me. Though Mum had hidden our whereabouts, if my father had wanted to send a message he could have done so through my relatives. He would occasionally turn up in Gunnedah out of the blue and have a cup of tea with my grandmother, yet I never heard a thing from him, not even a letter or a birthday card. There was certainly no offer from the old man to help out financially, during what were tough and expensive times for Mum, as every parent of a teenager knows too well. In a strange way it was almost as if he was the one who had disappeared, not us, as if he was the one who didn't want to be found. It wasn't until I joined *60 Minutes*, in a blaze of publicity more than two decades later, that George Grace tried to contact me. He showed up at the Channel 9 security gates and left a phone number. I didn't bother to call. The caravan had moved on. Besides, it seemed like a betrayal of my mother's selfless devotion and hard work.

Chapter 4
A Simple Twist of Fate

Nobody I knew of in my family had ever been to university. Nobody.

Indeed, for most Australians in the 1960s, technical colleges were the way to go if you wanted a tertiary education, because they were excellent institutions and were the usual entry into most professions and trades.

I wanted to go to university. But to do that you needed either family finances or a scholarship. I was lucky enough to pick up a Commonwealth scholarship and qualified for Sydney Uni. I felt privileged beyond belief; my mother felt that all the hours of overtime at the knitting factory in Launceston had paid off. And they had.

Obviously under the influence of some potent hallucinogen I decided to use my scholarship to enrol in *engineering*. I guess because I could. I lasted about three days before coming to the blinding realisation that changing a flat tyre was about the extent of my engineering prowess. Or care factor.

In sheer panic I fled across campus to the safety of the arts faculty, managing a last-minute switch to an education-department scholarship, with the intention of becoming a high-school English and history teacher. That was far more my natural style, even though the blokes in engineering looked more macho in tweed jackets with suede elbow pads and seemed to pull the best-looking female students.

My scholarship paid my fees and bought the basic books, leaving enough for train fares and a few beers. What more could I wish for? I lived at my sister Joyce's house on the southern fringe of the city, with her husband, their two small children and my mother, who now felt safe returning to Sydney. I spent three tedious hours a day commuting to and from uni on buses and trains.

There was still a sneering antipathy towards uni students, especially the long-haired, protesting variety. I wasn't actually long-haired or protesting when I asked the Town Hall stationmaster about a timetable change he'd just written on the blackboard. Looking at my bag full of books and then at me, the SM quipped sarcastically, 'You're the bloody genius, son. Work it out.' He then marched into his box and slammed the door. One of my brothers-in-law, who ran a fruit shop at Bankstown, was far more amiable, but he still jokingly called me 'Professor'. It was a different era.

When I wasn't slogging away at the books in the Fisher Library, I was playing basketball or squash. Opening the bowling for Australia against the Poms was still on the agenda.

As you've probably gathered by now, sport had given me my greatest pleasure in life. But sport was about to be gazumped by a girl. Not just any girl, either. She happened to be a girl who loved sport almost as much as I did. And if I was being honest, she was probably better at it than me. (But let's not be too honest.)

Dianne Mary Stephen was her name. I was barely nineteen and she was barely seventeen when I first gazed upon her playing at a squash club we were both members of at Gymea, in Sydney's Sutherland Shire. I couldn't take my eyes off her.

Dianne, a blue-green-eyed natural blonde, was undeniably beautiful. Tall and slim, with the best legs I ever saw on a squash court, she struck me as classy although somewhat aloof. It would have been love at first sight if I'd thought I seriously had a chance. For many months the best I could do was perv on her from an adjoining court and occasionally smile in her direction.

Then, my prospects suddenly picked up, thanks to another simple twist of fate.

Dianne played New South Wales Women's Grade, which at that time was probably the most elite squash competition in the world. Certainly she played against Heather McKay, the best player the game has ever seen, a woman known as 'the Don Bradman of squash'. Now, while Dianne could never beat Heather – no woman in the world ever did – Dianne won a number of trophies at our club. Which is where fate comes in.

In the midst of my end-of-year uni exams, I'd decided not to go to the annual squash club cabaret – but on the spur of the moment I changed my mind and put on a suit, fantasising that I might somehow get to dance with Dianne. Even better, I somehow ended up sitting at her table. Over a lifetime Dianne has always suggested that I manoeuvred it, although I've always insisted that she just got lucky. (That suggestion, by the way, is guaranteed to make her stick her finger down her throat.)

Either way, after I had scored a few dances, when Dianne was called up to collect the first of her many trophies she whispered, 'Hey, listen, will you please come with me? It's a long empty walk across that dance floor.'

What choice did a gentleman have?

Forty-something years later I clearly recall that was the same night Dianne leant forward and kissed me, in the dark, behind the cypress tree outside her parents' front door. Forty-something years later she reckons I'm dreaming.

In truth there was nothing about Dianne I didn't instantly like. Along with her natural beauty she was easygoing and fun to be with. From the outset I was comfortable talking with her, or just saying nothing. I loved her company and missed her when she wasn't around.

Dianne's upbringing had been very different from mine. Her mum and dad were happily married and would remain so for fifty-five years, until Bruce passed away of heart troubles, much too early. A divisional manager with a big transport company, he was absolutely – almost obsessively – devoted to his family. Her mother, Nancy, was a highly skilled dressmaker. They had lived in the same fibro house on the corner of a quiet suburban street in Lilli Pilli for over three decades. They were a tightly knit family, with four kids who were all equally sports crazy, including two brothers who played Grade cricket in Sydney. Just like their parents, Dianne's sister, Susan, and her two brothers have all enjoyed long and fruitful marriages. Without pretending to be a marriage-guidance counsellor, I've come to firmly believe there's a certain pattern to relationships: that stability breeds stability.

When I first met her, Dianne had just started working at the Sutherland Shire Council, with her elder brother, Brian. Like my sisters and most women of her generation, she was almost expected to leave school, get some secretarial skills and catch up with education later in life. What a stupid waste of talent. I'm thankful that times and opportunities have improved for our daughters.

Dianne and I spent our leisure time in the usual young lovers' whirl of sport, discos, parties, movies and more sport. Apart from the fact she barracked for the wrong football team, Dianne was perfect. I knew I'd probably have to marry her when she sat through five days of an Ashes test at the SCG with me!

*   *   *

While my personal world was terrific, I was starting to have uneasy, queasy feelings about teaching. It wasn't what I really wanted to do with the rest of my life. I loved studying and I adored history. Still do. I just didn't feel like *teaching* history. I wanted to get out there and see history being made. But without realising it, I compounded the dilemma by taking up an offer of an extra year at uni, an honours year in modern history.

Meanwhile, to make ends meet I laboured for an Eastern Suburbs pest-control firm in the university holidays. I crawled under floorboards chasing termites, hung off rooftops to extract nests filled with bird lice, trapped feral possums in ceilings, fumigated ships' holds for weevil infestation in bulk grain and squirted cyanide gas into plastic-sheet-covered golf greens.

Since it involved so many highly potent and toxic chemicals, it was damn dangerous. Not surprisingly, in those days people in the pest-control business had an alarmingly high casualty rate from cancer and lung disease. Blokes were dying, literally falling off the ladder, after only about a decade in the game. Safety rules were certainly lax. Lethal cocktails were freely sprayed around houses and yards; operators only sparingly used gas masks or protective clothing.

Then there was the rampant petty thievery. Maybe I was just unlucky to be working with a rare couple of freelance felons, but to me it seemed that the practice of pinching things from clients was almost ingrained in the trade. Inside houses we were fumigating, my co-workers would rifle through belongings and pocket spare cash and the occasional watch or trinket or carpenter's tool. Whisky and gin bottles would be given a hefty belt, no matter the time of day. One veteran exterminator I worked with was such a hopeless alcoholic he'd fossick through the kitchen cupboards and swipe the vanilla essence because, he explained, it was 85 per cent alcohol. He'd swig the tiny bottle en route to our next job and kick-start his whole day.

Things always seemed to be falling *onto* the back of our truck, not *off* it, as in The Great Chaff-bag Scam, a right royal rip-off that seemed to have been going on for years at the Kellogg's factory. Early Friday mornings while we fumigated piles of barley out the back, some insider would stuff about three dozen new empty chaff bags under the tarp of our truck. Then my workmates would go to a rag-and-bone merchant down the road, where they'd flog the stolen bounty for crisp cash. They picked up about forty bucks a time, a weekend bonus.

When we were fumigating an Italian cargo ship in Darling Harbour one Christmas Eve, the wharfies 'accidentally' dropped a huge wooden case filled with the latest fashion in knitted shirts from Milan. I watched in stunned disbelief as the dock workers flew into action – as frenzied as locusts in a wheatfield – layering on as many shirts as they could fit under their overalls. When they'd collected their booty, they invited us to hook in, too, and grab our own free Chrissie presents. I made some limp excuse and went off to collect the spray gear.

While still studying at university, I began desperately scanning the employment pages, looking for an exit strategy back into the real world. In quick succession I missed out on a cadetship at *The Sydney Morning Herald*, was accepted for an executive traineeship at Boral and sat an aptitude test at Honeywell computers. I heard the dull drone of a monster computer, circa 1964, that stretched the length of a cricket pitch. That's when I decided there were probably more laughs sitting under the dentist's drill. So I did a runner. I doubt the IT industry has suffered in my absence.

Trouble was, I now faced my own personal financial meltdown. My eldest sister, Lorraine, had signed on as guarantor for my education-department scholarship. But my rash decision to do Honours had doubled the penalty for dropping out of my teaching career. So I had to quickly come up with four hundred pounds to pay off my bond, which was the equivalent of about five thousand dollars today. Might as well have been five million.

There was no way I was going back to the pest-control game. That life of liquor and larceny was too fast for a boy from the bush. Besides, I couldn't face the prospect of a flying visit from the fraud squad. I figured that what I needed was regular factory work, no experience necessary, and endless overtime. I found an honest job on an assembly line at Namco Industries, out the back of Caringbah, screwing legs on kitchen tables.

It was perfect. Just four of us. Me, two Greeks and a Yugoslav who'd won the lottery in Croatia, taken a quick holiday to Italy and shot through to Australia. Day after day, month after relentless month, we stood in pairs, facing each other across a workbench. What we had to do was screw fancy gold-painted legs onto at least a hundred brightly coloured Laminex kitchen tables a day. On with the rubber feet, a quick check to make sure they didn't rock and roll, then our creation was complete. People probably still have their breakfast off my labours of love, still get daily pleasure out of what was every 1960s mother's showpiece.

All day we'd listen to Lawsey and Top 40 radio and laugh. We'd shout lewd comments above the noise. At smoko the only topics of conversation in the Namco factory canteen were sex and cars. And rugby league during the footy finals. They were exhilarating those 'New Australians', hard-working and always happy. Just overjoyed to be in the land of Oz. Each day they'd bring in strange-smelling dishes, funny cheeses and home-bottled olives in chilli. And, like them, everything reeked of garlic. They made me ditch my cheddar-and-Vegemite white-bread sambos and share their lunch. It was foreign and fantastic.

Because I spoke slightly better English than my wog mates, I was soon delegated to front the foreman and ask for a pay rise of a pound a week. We had got into a rhythm and upped our output to 140 tables a day, I pointed out. The dopey foreman didn't want to know about it. So we just dropped our production back to the required hundred a day and spent more of our time singing along with Johnny Rivers, the Stones and the Beatles on the radio.

After nine months, having paid off my education-department debt, I was getting ready to leave Namco when I was offered a promotion. The old bloke in charge of packaging, a laconic transplanted Liverpudlian, had decided to retire. He whispered to me that he'd already spoken to the same dopey foreman, who was more than happy to give me the job. It would mean an extra eight quid in my weekly pay packet. I knocked it back, telling the boss it was 'much too heavy a responsibility' for me at this tender stage of life.

The real reason was that I had actually found my escape hatch: I had just got a job in ABC radio.

If meeting Dianne had been my first great twist of fate, then joining the ABC would be my second, followed fourteen years later by *60 Minutes*. These three things changed my life, indeed *made* my life.

Chapter 5
Radio Daze

Radio was to be the passport for my magic-carpet ride – not just into the world of journalism but way beyond. It had started out as just another job interview, in late September 1965. I had no idea how significant that day would turn out to be.

The position was ABC Talks trainee. The ad in *The Sydney Morning Herald* demanded a university degree, a keen interest in current events and a wide knowledge of international affairs. Plus – surprise, surprise – a clear speaking voice. Except for the degree, I wasn't confident about meeting the job requirements. Mind you, sitting proudly at the top of my CV – almost in neon lights – was the incontrovertible fact I had 'run the Launceston High School radio station, edited the newspaper and composed the glossy magazine'. I suspect this lofty qualification was what tipped the scales and got me an interview.

The launch pad for my odyssey was the ABC offices at 181 William Street, East Sydney, an austere red-brick building. I ascended a linoleum stairway, a couple of floors above Sydney's affluent Jaguar car showroom. This 1930s-era fortress had once housed whores, gamblers and killers, when it was one of Australia's most infamous illicit gaming dens, The Forbes Club. It had now fallen on less colourful times and was the drab home of the ABC's Talks Department, complete with a brace of grey offices and a dank studio. But the department was about to revolutionise Aussie radio, with both *AM* and *PM* in the planning stages. That's why they'd started to recruit a bunch of trainees with university degrees and attitude.

I was just twenty. Clothed in my glowing white Pelaco shirt, striped tie and a suit I'd bought for a mate's twenty-first, and with a slick sheen of Californian Poppy in my hair, I fronted my two-man ABC interview panel. One of the men, an urbane silver-haired dabbler in leftist causes named Allan Ashbolt, chatted about Australian politics. Naïve and seriously out of my depth, I had little idea what he was on about. Still, I nodded with a certain sagely intent. Ashbolt was executive producer of *Four Corners* at that time and revered by his colleagues; I was impressed by his obvious intellect and erudition.

The other bloke, Alan Carmichael, the director of the Talks Department, was more your starched, imperious sort. He was tall and angular, with what I thought was a distinct military air. Carmichael had in fact been a Melbourne newspaper hack during the later years of the Depression. A couple of brown-nosing questions from me prompted him to take me down an excruciatingly long and winding road as he told me about those mean years in Australia's dim past. I seem to recall it was a yarn about a close relative – maybe even his wife, although I could be wrong – concocting Depression Soup, using swans she'd snaffled from the lakes at Melbourne's Royal Botanic Gardens.

After the enthralling monologues about politics and swans, I was escorted to nearby upper Forbes Street and into the ABC's main studios, where newsreaders once had to wear a dinner suit to read the nightly radio news bulletin. This was hallowed ground. I had to read a lengthy script into a microphone and then conduct an interview with a Talks Officer Grade 2. When I stumbled over a few of the questions, he generously erased the tape and offered me a second chance. That simple act of kindness probably salvaged my journalistic career even before it began.

*　　*　　*

Let me just pause for a brief aside. In the mid-1960s this country was still afflicted with sectarianism, the old Protestants versus Catholics nonsense. Positions in certain law firms and accountancy offices, and even council roadwork jobs, often depended on which side of the confessional you stood. At university one of my government lecturers had told us that the Treasury, for example, was predominantly Anglican, while the police force was overwhelmingly Catholic. As was the ABC, he insisted.

Well, at no stage when I joined was I asked what religion I was. Nor did I fill out a form declaring it. Yet, as it happened, I and the other bloke selected as an ABC cadet that year had both been baptised Catholic. And with names like Murphy and Raffaele, there was no doubt about the pair chosen before us. While there were exceptions, the vast majority of those who followed were left-footers, too, including Richard Carleton, Christian Brothers' alumni Jeff McMullen and Mike Carlton, whose father had been a seminarian at one stage. As if that wasn't mysterious enough, the ABC radio news boss was made a papal knight, presumably for his journalistic skills. It seemed venerable old Aunty was clearly infested with Catholics, although in all my years – I swear on the catechism – I never saw anyone make the sign of the cross before a big interview.

*　　　*　　　*

My first radio shift was 6 am till 2 pm. That meant crawling out of bed at 4.30 and coaxing my faithful Peugeot 203 rust bucket to chug 30 kilometres across Sydney to the Forbes Street studios on the seedy fringe of Kings Cross. I must admit the old grey Pug's starter handle saved my fledgling radio career a number of times.

I quickly discovered that an ABC trainee's designated duties were being a gofer and a researcher, and running up and down 'Cardiac Hill', rushing tapes between the office and the studio. I also spent mind-numbing hours observing the finer points of editing radio interviews, taking out ums and ahs by slicing the magnetic tape with a razor blade and splicing it back together again. Not that I was whingeing. I couldn't believe that people actually paid you money to have such fun. I observed studio productions, wrote rudimentary scripts and finally got to do my first interview, for a program called *News Review*, which was a quarter-hour nightly show following the prestigious seven o'clock evening radio news bulletin. In the 1960s *News Review* was an ABC radio staple.

I was sent out to do a story at the Royal Easter Show. Aspiring pre-independence Papua New Guinean political leaders, such as Michael Somare, who later would become the country's prime minister, were attending the opening ceremony of the PNG pavilion at the show. But the real story concerned an over-sized wooden penis that had gone missing from a giant Sepik

River statue, one of several statues on display in the pavilion. Apparently, the Aussie removalist who'd delivered the precious indigenous artefacts days earlier had done the unthinkable. He had carried this particular statue by holding the head with one hand and the appendage with the other. Somewhere between truck and pavilion, the penis broke off. The PNG pavilion improvised, grabbing some dependable Aussie Super Glue and sticking it back on again. Now, as every Sydneysider knows, Easter is sometimes hot, sometimes cold and often rainy. Sometimes it's all seasons at once. That year, 1966, was an especially hot and humid Easter. Unfortunately, the Super Glue stopped being so super, and the oversized penis kept drooping and falling to the floor. Passing attendants would discreetly bend, retrieve the missing organ and pop it back on the statue . . . until the next droop and drop. It became a delicate, if amusing, routine.

Then tragedy struck.

The morning the PNG pollies were due to inspect the exhibition, the giant organ simply disappeared. One mischievous attendant told me in our interview that he'd seen a very suspicious middle-aged lady slip something resembling 'the missing *objet d'art*' into her buff-leather handbag and exit the building. All that remained in the statue's naked groin area was a conspicuous wad of Super Glue.

I interviewed Michael Somare who, wearing a cheeky grin, referred to white-fella penis envy and the carving's need for an urgent organ transplant. He added that he'd never again trust Australians to keep their sticky hands off precious indigenous parts.

Not everyone in the Department of Territories was amused – but it did make for a cracker of a story.

I don't want anyone to get the impression that I went out of my way to find R-rated encounters in my early career, but when

I was sent out shortly afterwards for my first-ever interview with a star, it did seem as though a pattern was emerging. Born out in Broken Hill, John William Pilbean Goffage was much better known as Chips Rafferty, the lanky, laconic Aussie with the thick accent and the battered bush hat who became our first dinky-di film star. Renowned for his iconic depictions of outback stockmen, Rafferty had somehow pulled off a completely out-of-character role in the 1967 Elvis Presley film *Double Trouble*. That's what I went to talk to Chips about one morning at an expansive unit on Sydney Harbour he had rented. He was then about fifty-eight but looked a lot older. Maybe that was because I was just a kid. Tall and square jawed, he welcomed me at the front door, wearing a white terry-towelling dressing-gown. He laughed at the way he looked and apologised for his jet lag, just having flown in from LA. True to his reputation, there was nothing pompous or pretentious about Chips Rafferty. He was remarkably normal and friendly, making my first nervous star encounter an easy assignment.

That is, until we started the interview.

As I put my tiny Stellavox tape recorder down on the coffee table between us and quickly tested the sound level, Chips sat on his big sofa and spread-eagled his long legs. Suddenly, the terry-towelling dressing-gown fell open, dropping his full block 'n' tackle onto the edge of the sofa. It was a bit tricky for a young bloke doing his first interview with a genuine Aussie film idol to concentrate on the questions at hand. I didn't know where to look.

From memory the old Stellavox only gave you about six minutes of tape and then you had to wind it back and put another tape in. Fortunately, as we paused in our interview, Chips realised the family jewels were swinging, coughed and covered up.

* * *

These were turbulent times, with the Vietnam War beginning to emotionally divide Australians as never before, in the workplace, in pubs and at barbecues. Increasingly, we found ourselves chasing stories on the war and the growing torment it was causing back home. Nothing focused the minds of parents of teenage sons like the agony of Vietnam conscription, promoted by the dynamic, brash, horse-racing, scuba-diving, 'All the way with LBJ' new prime minister, Harold Holt. Hard as it is to believe now, Holt had won a landslide election on the strength of his commitment to the highly contentious war.

Fortunately, I missed out on the conscription lottery because my birthday fell eleven days short of the starting date. Having just celebrated my twenty-first, under the government's new legislation I was considered too old to be sent off to fight. In later years I reported on America's mass demonstrations against this unpopular war, with a million people marching on Washington, DC. I've also done a heap of stories about our Vietnam vets and was deeply involved in helping to make the long-overdue Welcome Home March in 1987 a reality. I've come to know and respect a lot of these remarkable diggers. Almost without exception these blokes, who are all about my age, still suffer terrible emotional damage from their wartime experiences. In many cases their lives and their families' lives have been devastated by divorce, suicide, birth deformities and physical and mental illness. In some sad cases the traumas run through generations. Certainly, in my experience, very few Vietnam vets went back into the world without needing psychiatric counselling and care.

Like so many things in my fortunate life, it was the luck of the draw that I missed out.

Of course, when you're in the middle of a social revolution, you don't realise what's happening. It is only much later, when someone paints the big picture, that you truly grasp it – unless you're standing on the ramparts leading it. I certainly wasn't. Still, my swinging sixties saw the end of Australia's ludicrous six o'clock drinking swill, the eruption of the pub-band music craze, the 1967 Aboriginal referendum, the relaxing of some pornography laws and the lively beginnings of the feminist revolution. Overnight, the pill became Australia's contraceptive of choice, sparking fears of rampant promiscuity. I read feverish headlines about women running amok – even nymphomaniacs – but they all seemed to be at some other party. American GIs also hit Sydney on R and R, bringing a fistful of Yankee dollars, a pocketful of marijuana and an armful of smack. Drugs would suddenly end Australia's age of innocence, radically and irreparably changing the nature of crime.

Simply being at the ABC was something of a social revolution for me. For a young bloke from working-class Aussie suburbia with barely a book in the house, it was as if I had travelled to a galaxy far, far away from anything I had known. ABC radio in the 1960s was peopled by radicals and reactionaries, political preachers and poseurs, bright thinkers and wankers. Scattered across one small department, in dingy office cubicles, were a highly educated yet frustrated science boffin, a genial philosopher/escapee from an Indian ashram, a dapper opera buff who always seemed to be lunching with Dame Joan Sutherland, a deeply melancholic book-show convenor and a veteran thespian with wild grey hair that had a life of its own, along with sundry other drama queens and would-be bohemians. There was also Mungo MacCallum, Snr. He was seriously bright and seriously eccentric, and I loved talking to him, though I sometimes struggled to comprehend what he was saying. Ernest Hemingway once said of his fellow American émigrés in Paris in the 1920s: 'They have all striven so hard for a careless individuality that they have achieved a sort of uniformity of eccentricity.' Papa Hemingway could easily have been describing the ABC Talks Department.

There was a short-fused documentary maker who became so mad with the ABC bean counters one afternoon, screaming profanities at the highest decibels she could muster, that she hurled her heavy typewriter out the open window, into the Kings Cross laneway below. It bounced off a car bonnet and smashed into the gutter, alongside a wino. Our tempestuous doco maker was convinced she'd killed him. She tore down three flights and shepherded him upstairs to the refuge of the Talks office. This high drama took place just as Iris, the ABC tea lady, was wheeling her trolley with hot drinks and a wide selection of jam-and-coconut biscuits along the corridor, a highly civilised twice-daily ritual in the office. Mortified by her senseless act of near manslaughter, the highly strung doco producer proceeded to feed our entire biscuit supply to the dishevelled and bewildered gentleman from the alley.

And there was Dan Speight, a gentle, sepulchral-voiced, crumpled-suit sort of a bloke, who became a local hero of mine and a really great mentor. Dan launched a trailblazing era of radio current affairs with *AM* and *PM*, and *Correspondents' Report* on Sunday mornings. He changed Australian radio forever. In his mid-sixties with fly-away grey hair and a big, beefy frame, Dan looked like the quintessential old-fashioned newspaper man, which he had been. As a war correspondent, in the early 1940s Dan had gone from Burma into Chongqing, China, met Zhou Enlai, interviewed Mao, marched into Yunnan with the Communist Eighth Route Army and missed the Japanese poison gas but got shot in the forehead. No matter what base metal was in his skull, Dan had a beautiful mind and he luxuriated in the English language. After a long liquid lunch down the

Journos Club, he'd sit at the typewriter and bash out for *Correspondents' Report* crisp, exquisite prose that often bordered on poetry. When Dan Speight was on fire, he wrote better words than just about any journalist I ever read. I felt privileged just walking the scripts from Dan's typewriter to his secretary's desk.

Now, riding shotgun with Speight into this brave new world of radio was a gnarled pipe-smoking curmudgeon named Russell Warner. Warner reminded me of a cross between Peter Finch and Richard Burton; he had a rich, resonant voice and was always theatrical, sometimes intimidating. There was a lot of testosterone in his swagger, but he had a charm that could be disarming. I learnt a lot from him, although he was best in short bursts.

I have no idea how the Talks Department 'odd couple', Allan and Alan, went about selecting their two ABC cadets each year, but they picked an extraordinary bunch who went on to become household names in Australian journalism, especially at the ABC. Let me pluck out a few of the star performers.

Paul Murphy was probably the best political interviewer I ever came across, along with Mike Willesee. Paul ran *AM* in its first years, was a gun reporter for *This Day Tonight*, hosted *PM* for years and became the face of SBS TV. He hung up the microphone way too early.

Richard Carleton and Alan Hogan both came into the ABC a year after me. They and Murphy became 'the three Amigo' whiz-kids of *AM*. The show would not have survived without their energy, talents and madness. When I first met Carleton in 1966, he seemed aloof (he wasn't), eccentric (he was) and difficult (he could be). Even then he was obsessed with politics and foreign affairs. Dick proved to be a unique character in both television style and talent. Alan Hogan was warmer and a superior all-round reporter to Carleton. Hogan went on to epitomise the best *60 Minutes* producer and became the founding executive producer of the *Sunday* program on Channel 9. From the outset Hogan was a class act.

Paul Raffaele was like one of those unstoppable battery toys. With his Italian heritage, his hands talked faster than his tongue. After becoming the ABC's first Beijing correspondent, Raffaele went on to write for *Reader's Digest* and *National Geographic* and is now senior correspondent for the prestigious *Smithsonian Magazine*. He's an exuberant teller of stories, and a mate.

In the years that followed, Talks trainees encompassed a range of uncommon talent, like the risible Pom Malcolm Downing; the dyed-in-the-wool Taswegian Charles Wooley; the best investigative reporter of them all, Chris Masters; and Bob Carr and Clare Martin, who each rose to political glory as New South Wales premier and the Northern Territory's chief minister respectively.

Then there was Julie Flynn, who went on from ABC Talks to burst through the glass ceiling and run Australian commercial radio, and Ellen Fanning, whose limitless skills would enable her to do anything she wanted. And she has.

Finally, along came a gifted cadet named Tony Joyce. Tragically he was shot and killed in Zimbabwe in 1979 by a deranged gunman while he sat in the back seat of a taxi with his film crew. Joyce was exceptional: handsome, charismatic and a fine reporter. Despite all the perilous, disease-ridden, war-torn, god-forsaken holes ABC reporters ended up in, Tony Joyce was the only one to pay the ultimate price. For the rest of us, alcoholism, dysentery, the clap or nightmares might be the recurring legacies of an enthralling life on the road.

Public Affairs Television, which lived in its own rarefied aerie a few flights above us, was where we all aspired to finish up. *Four Corners* and, later, *This Day Tonight* were seen by some in the

Menzies government as communist cells. Always popular and often vexing, these shows had become loose cannons in the eyes of ABC management, who had trouble reining them in. What's revealing is that subsequent Labor governments also became convinced, as things started to go pear shaped for them, that certain current-affairs shows and reporters were biased blue-ribbon Tories. Both jaundiced camps were invariably wrong. Television was all glamour, so as the staff of these shows headed downstairs to lunch we'd look at them as if they were descending from heaven.

Two floors above our Talks Department resided the puissant Sports Department, with crusty legends like Norman 'Nugget' May and Alan McGilvray. Having misspent many years with my ear pressed to an AWA bakelite radio listening religiously to ABC sport commentaries, I couldn't believe my good fortune when I'd occasionally get to share the rickety old Forbes Street lift with the likes of Nugget, Bert Oliver, Dennis Cometti or cricketing-greats-turned-radio-stars Norm O'Neill and Neil Harvey. I tried to stay cool in their presence. It wasn't easy.

I was amused to see on a number of occasions one of the great characters of ABC sports radio on the median strip in the midst of William Street peak-hour traffic, bending like a thick-trunked willow. He was trying to summon up the courage, or a momentary clear eye, to negotiate his passage across the road. He'd obviously had a well-lubricated lunch and was now three sheets to the wind. What made it truly memorable and a mark of his amazing fortitude and brilliance was that he'd just come off air, having done a fifteen-minute national sporting round-up without missing a beat. Not a slurred syllable. Yet here he was seconds later, unable to cross the road. When it came to booze and broadcasting, he was simply match fit.

Up close the ABC Sports Department in the 1960s had a slight touch of Madame Tussaud's waxworks about it. There wasn't the sort of youth and vigour that I'd imagined from the outside, listening in. None of the feisty, lively women broadcasters we hear today on shows like *Grandstand*, either. It was definitely a males-only club with strict rules – rusted on – about how radio should be done. It was a bit like a secret society, where the sporting gurus were dismissive of any blow-in who dared question their pellucid statistical knowledge. Much like the Canberra press gallery, who believe they're the only ones who truly understand politics. The irony was that years later, when I was about to leave the ABC, the general manager, Sir Talbot Duckmanton, would offer me the job of director of sports. I wasn't interested in driving a desk, but it would have set the proverbial cat amongst the comfortable old pigeons, I promise.

Looking back on these early days of my working life, I can't help but wonder: what if the September 1965 ABC job interview had faltered? What if I hadn't been granted that second shot in the studio? What if my Pelaco shirt had been crumpled? Even worse, what if I'd been born a Protestant? I probably would have ended up fronting a high-school history class. Or, if I got lucky, I would be a Sydney Uni lecturer, driving a Citroën and living in Glebe. Nothing wrong with either lifestyle, but it would have been a whole lot different from the hand of cards I was about to be dealt. And the amazing games they would let me play.

Chapter 6
Absence Makes the Heart Grow Fonder

When I first started out, Australian commercial radio still revolved around the Top 40 charts. It was all about Ward 'Pally' Austin, Tony Withers, Mike Walsh and an earlier incarnation of the great John Laws. At that time Lawsey, Alan Jones, Neil Mitchell, Ray Hadley and the rest of the capital-city opinion makers hadn't yet ascended their talkback thrones.

But at the ABC the radio-news caravan had started to move on, much like Australian society. The decision had been made to cover news 'beyond the headlines', as the slogan said. I believe it was *AM* that kick-started this radio revolution. It was always meant to be provocative and a bit cheeky, intended to shake the ABC News bulletins out of decades of BBC-style torpor, where 'balance' too often meant 'boredom'. There were plenty of sceptics massing along Aunty's plush-carpeted corridors in those early days, forecasting *AM*'s rapid demise. For about six months I was the trainee assigned to work on the pilot shows of *AM* with Dan Speight and Russell Warner.

It's hard to believe that was more than forty years ago. Suddenly there were incisive interviews, live reports from news events and livelier campaigns against injustice and bureaucratic stupidity.

AM would become an integral part of Australia's daily journalism. While John Gorton was a bit truculent about it at first, every prime minister after him, from Billy McMahon right through to Kevin Rudd, has lined up to get on *AM*.

Along with some outstanding work done by the Macquarie network's newsroom, *AM* set the bar for commercial news shows that followed. The pacy, racy style of *AM* was the template for the best of the commercial jocks who go after headlines as well as ratings. Within a decade the talk-radio kings would achieve almost oracle status. Prime ministers would soon be clamouring for a share of their precious airtime, choosing their favourite radio microphone to speak *directly* to Australians, rather than via the usual press briefing. Canberra journos, who were suddenly gazumped, squealed like the proverbial stuck pigs, claiming that by opting to speak to people such as Laws, Jones and Mitchell, politicians were taking the soft option. That was just sour grapes. The talk-radio boys often got the scoop because politicians trusted them more. They also asked the questions of interest to Australians rather than the press gallery. Oddly enough it took the Brits – and even the Americans – much longer to breed such political prophets. Talk radio was for a while a distinctly Australian social phenomenon. It was fascinating to watch it evolve.

*　　*　　*

In early 1967 I was promoted and sent to Perth, to the outer edge of the ABC empire. The weird thing is that at twenty-two, despite a nomad's life, I'd never lived away from home before. It's only since I've had children myself that I realise how heart-wrenching it must have been for my mother. To be honest, I was ready to fly and keen to take some risks. Mind you, Perth wasn't exactly a war zone.

I rented a basic flat in South Perth, shipped my car across and struck up a few office friendships. Cooking was my main burden, because having grown up with a mother and three sisters, my only real kitchen skill was washing up. Still, I never went hungry . . . especially after I bought a can opener. With a marvellous climate, lots of sport and some friendly pubs, I was immediately hooked by Perth's lifestyle. Even if you did have to drive out of town to get a drink on a Sunday and then stupidly drive home again.

But I was soon missing the love of my life.

Dianne and I had decided to try living apart and making do with just letters and a Sunday night phone call from a pay phone, which was about all we could afford. Dianne insists that she was doing fine in Sydney with work and squash and family. (Of course, I don't believe her.) I was bloody hopeless, lost without her. I lasted barely six weeks before I was pleading with Dianne to come over. Thankfully she took pity on me and made the leap, joining me in the west.

It wasn't leaving her job at the council but leaving the warm family cocoon that troubled Dianne the most. It's hard to convey what a tight, loving unit her family was. Her mother was one of those women totally devoted to her kids, who were still living at home even though they'd grown up. I knew how deeply Dianne felt about her family, so I knew what she was sacrificing. Besides, in 1967 unmarried couples didn't go off and live together the way they do today. Arrangements had to be made for Dianne to share a flat with one of the young women at the ABC. It was all very delicate and illicit. Dianne got a job at a swish real-estate office not far from where I worked. Our relationship just grew stronger.

Life was spectacular now that Dianne had joined me. Perth was so special we could easily have put down roots there, except for our families back east. Sandgropers took almost a perverse delight in boasting that Perth was not just the most comfortable but also the most isolated capital in the world. At times it really felt like it, too. Without a telephone in my flat, at a time when people still sent telegrams and airfares were ridiculously expensive, it was almost like living overseas.

Meanwhile, I was having a great time in the ABC, including reporting the occasional television story. But only occasionally. My aim was to break into TV full time; it was proving difficult, although I didn't stop trying. As well as being *AM*'s Perth correspondent, I was involved in interviewing, producing and presenting a number of local radio shows.

I still couldn't believe my good fortune at having stumbled into this journalism racket. Mind you, I had one near-miss that might easily have sent me packing, back to teaching or computers.

Under the gun one day during a gala to celebrate Henry Lawson's anniversary, I rushed out to interview the avuncular academic Sir Walter Murdoch, who'd met Lawson in Kalgoorlie fifty years earlier. I did the interview for a live news magazine show I hosted called *Out of the West*. But, embarrassingly, the tape broke on air, was fixed and then broke again. I'd been in too much of a hurry cutting and splicing. When it broke a *third* time, out of frustration and running out of time, I panicked and swore – without realising the announcer who controlled the microphones had turned mine back on. Argh! The question was: did the magic word go to air? It was too close to call, but we'd soon find out. In mid-sixties' ABC radio, if it had gone to air I was destined to be banished to one of the commission's loneliest gulags, maybe Longreach or even Burnie.

In anticipation of such a fate, and shaking badly, I gathered my papers and left the studio. Outside in the corridor I bumped smack bang into the station manager. Grim-faced and a bit breathless, he said, 'Oh, I was just coming to see you,' and handed me a blue memo. This was the ABC's equivalent of a telegram from the battlefront. There it was, in triplicate, telling me of my unacceptable breach of ABC etiquette. I had mispronounced the word 'schedule' as 'skedule'. Phew! I promised never to repeat the felony.

As a reporter I got to see about a third of Western Australia's big-sky country. I became completely besotted by the place and volunteered for any assignment anywhere. There were endless stories for *AM* as the Poseidon-led nickel and mining boom erupted, throwing the economy and politics into a frenzy, much like in 2008. Perth was the port of entry for famous visitors like the Beatles' Indian guru, the Maharishi, who was the best-known religious figure in the world at the time, even more famous than the Pope. I did an exclusive interview with him at five o'clock one morning, sent it through to Sydney and was back in bed before it went to air on the east coast.

At the end of the railway line in Meekatharra, and beyond that at Wiluna, I had my first ugly encounters with outback racism. What I saw up there was apartheid. I was shocked to see black-fellas treated like animals, excluded from pubs, shops and even hospitals, despite their appalling sickness, blindness and death rates. Ironically, this was at almost exactly the same time as the 1967 referendum in which Australians overwhelmingly voted to give Aboriginals the same civil rights as everyone else. An elderly Aboriginal man told me about police up in Roebourne chaining him to a boab tree when he was about twelve and leaving him alone for three days. A sanguine, white-whiskered bloke, he just figured that's what happened when you were a blackfella. He wasn't even angry. But I certainly was. Meekatharra would have a lasting impact on my life. Professor Fred Hollows would re-ignite my anger a decade later, but that's another story.

*   *   *

Over dinner one night, shortly after Dianne's twenty-first birthday, I asked her to marry me. It felt natural, given that we'd barely been out of each other's sight for the past four years. My mother was delighted; everybody else jokingly asked what had taken us so long. We were broke and agonising over how we could afford to have the wedding back in Sydney when the ABC came to the party by posting me back to Canberra, with a promotion! Our lives suddenly slipped into overdrive.

Funnily enough I found myself back on a train, this time hurtling across the Nullarbor, taking me to a whole new life. I'd been appointed Canberra correspondent for Current Affairs Radio, but I also did stories for the wonderful Caroline Jones's local Friday-night TV show. I revelled in the chaos of federal politics as the Gorton government fell apart – but Canberra also gave me a chance to cover offbeat stories across the Monaro, from Gundagai to the coast. There was no shortage of contrary bushies in the sheep country or rambunctious characters amongst the fishermen and the loggers down around Eden.

I did one story on a place that became known as 'the sickest town in Australia'. Delegate, an isolated border hamlet tucked away in the Snowy Mountains, was known only to trout fishermen and, I suspect, blokes running from their alimony payments. A whistleblower revealed to me that the local hospital was taking its water supply from the Delegate River – round the bend from where the town's sewage was pumped – putting patients at risk of everything from hepatitis to herpes. That news story gave me five minutes of fame.

Some time later, up in the Hunter Valley, I came across a crazed farmer who'd found a novel way to stop huge eagles swooping down from their craggy nests and picking the eyes out of his newborn sheep. This aerial daredevil had taken to the skies in his light plane to shoot the feathered pests on the wing, which, come to think of it, was probably highly illegal. I was pleased that he never managed to hit one bird in the couple of days I spent with him. Still, it again made for a colourful yarn.

Another time, back in Canberra, I was trying to scrabble something together from the national sheepdog championships out at the ACT showgrounds. There were lots of bush characters but hardly a story. Until I came across a pair of old-timers, one a cocky from Longreach, the other a breeder of border collies outside Yass. The breeder had sold the other bloke his dog some years earlier, when it was about a year old. Over a lunchtime beer, the Queenslander said he felt sure the dog – 'a real bloody champion', they both agreed – would still be able to work to his original owner's whistle commands. The breeder doubted it. Sensing a story, I urged them to put it to the test. Out in the centre of the showring, the bloke from Yass called the collie, who was dozing under a nearby gum. At the second high-pitched command the dog lifted his ear, then his head and then stood up. His Longreach boss nodded and said, 'G'won . . . g'won.' Out the dog trotted, and within half a minute he was bossing the sheep around like a drill sergeant, putting them through the race, over the bridge and into the pen. No worries. Border collies immediately jumped to the top of my animal Mensa scale. 'Ya owe me a beer,' the Longreach cocky said with a contented look, and I happily paid up.

I loved reporting and I loved radio, but television was much more glamorous and a magnet for ambitious young journalists like Mike Willesee, Gerald Stone, Stuart Littlemore, Andrew Olle and Richard Carleton. They had broken into TV, although I just couldn't crack it. I had a couple of nibbles from the ABC's flag-ship, *This Day Tonight*, but my move was mysteriously blocked each time. I had no idea, but I was being groomed for a corre-spondent's job in London or New York. Had I known, I would have stopped whingeing.

Anyway, I think to hose me down, the ABC gave me my first overseas trip. It was a radio assignment to India and Africa for a fortnight on an Air India inaugural flight, with my old Talks Department terror Russell Warner as a travelling companion. (I kept wondering: what was first prize?)

Sitting up the sharp end of the plane on my first international flight wasn't too shabby, although Warner kept reminding me not to get used to it. I never have.

We hit Bombay – or Mumbai as it's known today – on a clammy early dawn in summer. It was a lengthy walk across the tarmac to the terminal, with Warner insisting we trample over any wayward stragglers. 'Trust me, son, you've just got to forget all that polite bullshit about women and children first,' he shouted. It quickly became apparent the only taxis were a locally built basic version of the old English Morris Oxford.

The airport-terminal roads were teeming with them. Warner cut a swathe through the cacophony of drivers, pointed to one cab, clapped his hands and summarily dismissed the rest. Using his rolled Aussie newspaper as a swagger stick, he gave an impressive British Raj performance, which I could only stand and admire.

Even by the flickering glow of small roadside fires this first 'passage to India' was already delicious – the first tasty morsel of what, over many years, would turn out to be a bountiful smorgasbord. As we rattled towards our hotel, the Taj Mahal Palace, I couldn't believe so many families were out and about at four in the morning, doing their business – literally – along the route. Potholes and squatting people were my most indelible memory of that arrival. That is, until the Taj hove into view, alongside the landmark Gateway to India, which I'd often seen in photographs when Bradman and the Australian cricket team's ship stopped off on the way to England for another Ashes victory. Built just a year or two after Australia's Federation, the historic Taj Mahal Palace is a spectacular mix of Moorish, Oriental and Florentine styles, with vaulted alabaster ceilings, cantilevered stairways and Belgian cut-glass chandeliers everywhere. At least it was until the 2008 terrorist attack reduced the Taj to a blackened shell. In 1968 it was the most stunning pub I could ever imagine.

As I walked to my room, my footsteps echoing on the mosaic-marble floors, my escort was like an Indian mogul's small caravan: there were seven of them. Two lugged my suitcase, another carried my Nagra tape recorder, one had my satchel and one held my jacket, while yet another was needed to bring the *Time* magazine I'd souvenired from the plane. The other bloke just came along to keep his mates company, I think. Remember, this was my first time outside Australia.

It was bizarre. I had no idea what was happening. I certainly had no idea about tipping. But I knew I must have paid my entourage far too much money when they wouldn't stop bowing and thanking me as I backed them out the door. No sooner had I got rid of them than there was suddenly a series of gentle knocks and I was delivered a frangipani stem in a vase, some hot face towels, a plate of sliced fruit and a jug of freshly squeezed orange juice, and a boy arrived wanting to take my shoes to polish (even though I was wearing brown suede Hush Puppies). As I fell into bed, I realised I'd already blown my first two days of ABC travel allowances just in tips.

On our last couple of days in the subcontinent we decided to visit the southern state of Kerala. It held a certain fascination because it had the world's first popularly elected communist government, at a time when the Cold War dominated our foreign policy. We had a royal contact in the capital, Trivandrum – one Mr Raja, who happened to be the brother of the Maharaja. We met him for twilight gin and tonics in the pavilion of the exclusive Trivandrum Golf Club. I interviewed him and a couple of other senior politicians about the rise of Indian communism.

While we enjoyed our drinks, Mr Raja inquired which of us was 'the tennis player'. He understood that one in three Australians was 'an above-average' tennis player. I was dreaming a bit when Warner and Alan, a journalist from *The Age* who'd joined us, admitted they were hopeless, never played, couldn't even hit a ball, etc.

'Well, then. It must be you, Mr Martin, is it?'

Now, I was twenty-three, pretty fit and played A-grade squash, and I'd won a couple of tennis titles at high school. Mind you, Launceston High wasn't exactly known for producing Wimbledon champions, but sporting excellence is so often a figment of the imagination. Besides, the gin and tonics were slipping down very nicely indeed.

After about the third, Mr Raja asked if I'd perhaps like a game. I agreed, figuring that he was about sixty-five and a bit portly.

It turned out that Mr Raja was the recent captain of the Indian Davis Cup team. What's more, he told us the first thing he did whenever he went to Sydney was play tennis at White City courts, often with the likes of John Newcombe and Tony Roche. Indeed, he was such a self-confessed tennis tragic he'd spent his own family's money to have a sunken centre court and six others built at his private club, the Trivandrum Tennis Club, where the Indian Junior Davis Cup squad was currently in training. I was clearly in for a terrible hiding. I did my best to weasel my way out of the contest, pleading no shorts or shoes. It didn't work.

The next morning as we strolled to the main court Mr Raja compounded my misery by summoning a bunch of the Junior Davis Cup players to watch. 'Come, come,' he said, clapping his hands loudly. 'We have an *Australian*.' Again, I did my best to talk down my game, telling them I rarely played, but they came anyway. Once they saw how brutally innocuous my backhand was, let alone witnessed my ferociously gentle serve, the young blokes made some excuse and wandered back to their own far superior tennis.

Mr Raja played a typically Indian game on his typically Indian court. He was all spin and guile and clever placement. Cutting to the chase, he demolished me by winning six straight games in the first set, then politely let me win four games in the second. Holding his chest in mock exhaustion, he suggested we get some fresh lemon juice in the clubhouse. He didn't have to ask me twice.

I was happy to leave Kerala and fly off to Africa, far away from Mr Raja's sunken all-weather court. Warner and I headed for Nairobi and Entebbe, via Addis Ababa. Uganda was in its healthy postcolonial salad days when we got there. Our minibus driver, Hubert, was a lean, happy-go-lucky opening bowler in the Entebbe cricket team. He proudly took me out to watch his kids play field hockey at their school ground, and we all went for a family meal later at a roadside restaurant. Hubert was one of maybe a hundred thousand people who later disappeared when Idi Amin made Uganda – the 'Pearl of Africa' – his private killing field.

My first overseas reporting jaunt had given me a taste of my life to come.

*   *   *

Meanwhile, every weekend Dianne and I drove from Canberra to Sydney as we finalised our late November '68 wedding. Those trips tested the endurance and reliability of the old Peugeot 403 I'd bought when my 203 rust bucket finally seized up. Although a few years newer, the French-made reliability-trial winner had neither a heater nor a radio. That guaranteed our Sydney–Canberra safaris were cold and quiet. On the way back late on a Sunday night we'd regularly stop near Lake George so I could get out, stretch a bit to wake up and then run madly on the spot just to get the circulation going again. Dianne, wrapped in arctic clothing and topped with blankets for the drive, had decided she hated Canberra's winters. (Somehow, even in the snow, New York would seem much warmer.)

Anyway, a late spring wedding in Sydney suited her just fine.

I can't remember too much about the big day. I was in a bit of a marriage fug, quite overwhelmed by the occasion. According to the best man I ended up polishing my shoes three times. Mum was very teary and stopped ironing my suit to offer me a stiff brandy from the medicine cabinet. I think she should probably have swigged it herself to calm her nerves!

I do remember that Dianne looked utterly beautiful – elegant and classy. Her mother, Nancy, who was a stylish and meticulous dressmaker, had spent endless weeks sewing and beading the wedding gown, as well as the bridesmaids' dresses. She did the same for Dianne's brothers' and sister's weddings, which took place over the next three months. She hardly slept.

As a lapsed Catholic I didn't have any second thoughts about getting married in Dianne's neighbourhood Presbyterian church. Yet funnily enough her bigoted old grandfather took me aside to announce that he was going to ignore his antipathy towards Catholics and attend the ceremony because like him I was a South Sydney footy supporter. He meant it too. I didn't have the heart to tell him he could do a naked hand-stand in the entrance of the church for all I cared. I was marrying his gorgeous granddaughter anyway.

Our wedding reception was a pretty modest affair held upstairs in a private function room on the main street of Caringbah. I'd really like to do it again and throw a wild party with my mate Geoff Harvey and his band. Maybe for our fiftieth wedding anniversary. The first time around, a musical trio was all we could afford. I was almost broke, so Dianne cashed in her meagre Credit Union savings to pay for the honeymoon, while her parents covered the reception. Still, we had everything we needed and were deliriously happy.

We spent our wedding night in a suite in the Wentworth Hotel, courtesy of my sister Lorraine. The next morning we took off up the coast, destined for a honeymoon in Surfers. It was the first time I'd ever worn a ring, and I remember while holding the steering wheel I couldn't stop fiddling with it, feeling like I'd been branded. We'd only been driving for about four hours when a passing truck flicked up a stone and smashed the Peugeot's windscreen. Forster was as far north as we got; we bedded down for the week while we waited for the new glass to be shipped up from Sydney. It was an auspicious start to what has been a long and tender affair.

Back in Canberra Dianne and I decided we just couldn't face another ACT winter without a car heater or a radio. So, convinced that we'd be staying put for the next few years, we negotiated a loan from the bank to buy our first new vehicle, a Peugeot 404.

A week after we picked it up, all bright and shiny, I was told I'd been appointed as the ABC's North America correspondent. It was meant to be a three-year posting, but we would end up staying almost ten. Good job we sold the car.

Chapter 7
A New York State of Mind

It was the hottest movie in town. We bought tickets a day after we arrived in New York. That probably wasn't smart timing, because it meant Dianne and I first gazed upon the world's richest, most exciting city through the rheumy eyes of Ratso Rizzo and Joe Buck. They were the pair of sleazy deadbeats in *Midnight Cowboy*. Like the rest of the world, we'd laughed at Dustin Hoffman in his film debut as Benjamin Braddock, the college kid who'd climbed into the wrong woman's bed in *The Graduate*. That's why we'd gone to see *Midnight Cowboy*.

Only this time Hoffman was a down-and-out lowlife with a hacking killer-cough and a polio limp, eking out an existence on the mean streets of New York City. *Midnight Cowboy* would become the only X-rated movie to win an Oscar. In fact it would win three. Still, I have to admit that John Schlesinger's modern classic was a shock to an Aussie moviegoer's sensory perception, especially seeing it in New York. Tickets were twice as costly as they were back in Sydney, and we had to queue for a hundred yards around the block. Once inside the cinema it was every man for himself. They pushed one session out the side exits while the new mob tore in through the main doors. Then there was a manic, take-no-prisoners scramble for a seat. Welcome to America.

As the movie began, somebody must have been talking a few rows in front of us, because suddenly a formidable hulk rose from his seat, blocked the screen and threatened a chainsaw massacre unless the offender 'shut the f*** up'.

While Harry Nilsson sang his signature song, 'Everybody's Talkin' ', nobody talked.

For a couple of innocents from the Antipodes, Dustin Hoffman and Jon Voight's desperate and sordid depiction of life in Gotham City came as a rude awakening. When we headed home after midnight, along the same garbage-strewn, squalid sidewalks, every panhandling bum who hit on us looked like Ratso's brother.

*　　　*　　　*

A few days earlier on our flight across the Pacific, up the sharp end of a Qantas jet, they had served us succulent Sydney rock oysters and prize-winning lamb from the Royal Easter Show, with mint sauce. And French red plonk. ABC foreign correspondents who were heading off on so-called hardship posts flew first class in those days, just like the diplomatic corps. We could put up with that!

After only four years in journalism the offer of an overseas gig had come as a complete surprise to me. It turned out that my old mentor, Dan Speight, had manoeuvred me into the New York job to try to keep me out of television. (His plan would backfire, because the American experience would give me a direct door into full-time TV, first through the ABC and then *Sixty Minutes*.)

Career wise, accepting the job was a no-brainer, but Dianne was filled with trepidation about living in the Big Apple. Family and friends kept reassuring her 'it's only for three years!' To my surprise she instantly fell in love with the place. Almost overnight it became her kinda town. Ten years would pass in the blink of an eye.

It was May 1969, the end of the northern spring, when we arrived at John F. Kennedy airport. It was a hot 'n' steamy Saturday night that felt more like an evening in Singapore. As so often happens in the communications business, there had been a total communications breakdown. We landed without anyone in the New York office even knowing we were there.

I must confess Dianne and I were the original 'innocents abroad'. We wondered whether Manhattan was in the Bronx or Brooklyn. At the airport, when I booked us a room at the Excelsior motel in some place called Jamaica, Queens, we knew it wasn't in the West Indies, but beyond that we didn't have a clue. We saw more black people on our way to Queens than I'd seen in Uganda. The Excelsior turned out to be a neat yellow box of a building with heavy security bars on every window, which made it look more like a prison than a motel. We'd soon find out why.

There were a lot of things we would find out quickly. When I asked for white coffee, the African American waitress looked at me quizzically. I'd soon realise why I should ask for coffee with cream in future.

The next day, Sunday, we jumped the subway from Queens to 57th Street and 6th Avenue in Manhattan. We stepped from the grimy labyrinth of tunnels into a world of sparkling skyscrapers.

RAY – STORIES OF MY LIFE

We'd seen it all before on film, of course, but I'd never imagined such a magic forest of towering glass monoliths.

Dianne and I wandered down 5th Avenue then off into Central Park – in amongst the pretzel, bagel and hot-dog vendors – with, I suspect, our mouths as wide open as our eyes. We might easily have been auditioning for the Jack Lemmon and Sandy Dennis roles in the movie *The Out-of-Towners*, which they happened to be filming in the park at the time.

Our NYC home was an airy one-bedroom pad in a 1940s apartment building on Manhattan's Upper East Side. An elevator ride down from our apartment landed us at the centre of the earth every day. We kept pinching ourselves as we soaked it all up. It was hard to believe I was being paid to live there.

It didn't take long to figure out why everyone called New York 'the melting pot'. Our block was a bubbling ethnic stew of Polish delis, a German bakery, a couple of Chinese laundries and Italian barber shops. A Korean family ran the greengrocer's; there were the usual chatty black doormen and Bronx paper sellers; and burly Russian chauffeurs waiting by double-parked shiny Cadillacs. And over it all was that lusty patina of Jewish culture and spirit from a dozen European lands that makes the Big Apple so special, so sensual.

We lived on the fifteenth floor of a building without a thirteenth floor and with only Puerto Rican doormen. They all spoke Spanish, seemingly with the proviso that whenever one of them started to vaguely comprehend English he would be removed from his post instantly and replaced by someone who couldn't. Our lift, or 'elevator', was frequented by wizened Yiddisher mammas wearing genuine fox-fur jackets and excessive rouge, carrying miniature poodles they insisted were 'small people'.

We had a spectacular 190-degree skyscape out of our long

front windows. We gazed downtown, across a valley of low-rise 1880s brownstone houses, towards the Pan Am skyscraper and Grand Central. Bloomingdale's, the best department store in the world, was on our right. To our left, hanging like a string of diamonds across the Manhattan night sky, was the iconic 59th Street Bridge, which Simon & Garfunkel immortalised in their song about 'feelin' groovy'.

*   *   *

On our first Monday in New York Dianne and I stood lost in the grand foyer of the Rockefeller Center, that mammoth art-deco shrine to capitalism in the belly of Manhattan. We knew that the ABC office was somewhere nearby. A dapper silver-haired bloke got out of the lift, stopped and asked in a distinct Aussie accent, 'You don't happen to be Ray and Dianne Martin, do you?' That's how much we must have stood out.

He turned out to be Charles Buttrose, a larger-than-life ex-journo who was the boss of the New York bureau. Charlie had been exiled to another hemisphere after a highly publicised affair back in Sydney with his secretary, Margo, whom he'd since married. Americans came to see Charlie, who was a masterful PR operator, as the quintessential Australian, a funny raconteur who loved sport, fine wines and classical music. As it happened, Charlie Buttrose was also the father of Ita Buttrose. Charlie and Margo threw the liveliest dinner parties I'd ever seen, with sparkling guest lists that ranged from Gene Tunney, the boxing king, to Sir Robert Helpmann, the ballet . . . prince. They would throw any number of great conductors, virtuosos and American TV network moguls into the dinner-party mix just for extra colour.

Our ABC studio was above Radio City Music Hall, a grand, opulent theatre that was home to the famous Rockettes, a chorus line of about a hundred high-kicking precision female dancers. It was no surprise to go past the stage door on the way to work and see a dozen pairs of the longest legs in the world – in mesh stockings – out on the sidewalk as the women took a cigarette break.

Given that Australia is asleep for much of New York's daylight, the reporting team would start work mid-morning and often finish after midnight. A sixty- or seventy-hour week was pretty routine. It was a bit like working on a country newspaper, because you got to 'cover the waterfront', as the Americans say. Apart from reporting breaking news, we'd get requests from every ABC department – sport, religion, science, the arts, you name it. In the early days we mostly did radio, although the demands of ABC TV for stories would grow to be insatiable.

Wedged into our office was a cramped radio studio filled with equipment that came straight out of Noah's Ark. Still, with a few wires and a lot of ingenuity we could do just about anything, even a live debate or a music recording. There were no satellite phone connections until the early 1970s, so it would take *an hour* to book a painfully slow radio telephone line to Sydney. Mind you, that delay had its benefits. A couple of times when we'd stayed out too late – usually listening to music down in Greenwich Village – we found ourselves behind our deadline. I can now reveal that we'd 'accidentally' disconnect the radio circuit to Sydney. In other words we'd hang up. Of course, we'd blame the telephone company for the problem. That would give us an extra hour to finish our story. I don't think we ever missed any critical bulletins, but we often had Sydney biting their fingernails. It was a bugger when satellites took over, because Sydney could just ring us back straightaway!

It would take *a day* for a TV satellite hook-up, if you got lucky. We went around the corner to CBS on the rare occasions that we had to send an urgent TV news story by satellite, but most times we'd pack up the film and taxi it out to the airport ourselves. It was that primitive.

For a young newsman 1969 was an amazing time to land in America. In a matter of weeks one deranged assassin confessed to having killed Bobby Kennedy, another to killing Martin Luther King; Woodstock proved to be the counterculture's overcrowded acid trip; and Rolling Stones fans at Altamont were bashed and one man stabbed to death by Hell's Angels. A bearded lunatic named Charles Manson cut America's collective throat when he slaughtered actress Sharon Tate and her friends one night in LA. Students, gays, women and African Americans began taking to the streets, mad as hell and refusing to take it anymore. The ghettos were ablaze. At Chappaquiddick Mary Jo Kopechne drowned, along with Teddy Kennedy's hopes of ever being president. Richard Milhous Nixon had just begun his fraudulent reign, which would end with him resigning in disgrace several years later. And Neil Armstrong became the first man to walk on the moon. For a mesmerised moment we all felt like space cadets.

I coordinated the ABC's coverage of Armstrong's walk from our studio, twenty-seven floors above the clamour of 6th Avenue, in the early New York dawn. As Armstrong stepped down onto the lunar dust, it was astonishing how one of the noisiest cities on earth suddenly fell silent. I glanced out our open studio window, down onto perhaps ten thousand people below, all watching history being made on a giant screen out the front of the Time/Life building across the street from us. They spilled onto 6th Avenue and stopped the traffic. Cabbies stepped from their taxis, leaving their car doors wide open, and stared at this remarkable event. For just a glorious moment there was none of the familiar cacophony, no symphony of sirens and blasting horns. No roar of traffic, either. Barely a sound. Then, half an hour later, it was as if somebody turned up the volume knob again, and life on this planet returned to its usual ear-shattering din.

This was the golden age of space exploration for the Americans, with the excitement of lunar walks and the life-and-death drama of Apollo 13, which after a rocket explosion barely made it back home. In February 1971 the ABC's science unit, run by an energetic boffin named Dr Peter Pockley, decided to do a minute-by-minute radio broadcast from Sydney of the next moon landing, by Apollo 14. One of Pockley's producers rang asking if they could have a live chat with me, seeing this was the fourth space flight that I'd covered. I suggested we could talk about the aims of this mission and NASA's budget blow-out, and tell some stories about the astronauts, especially Commander Alan Shepard, whom I'd interviewed and who happened to be the oldest American astronaut to walk on the moon. So it was all set up that the Sydney studio would call me at home when they were ready. I remember they crossed to me just as Shepard was about to hit a couple of golf balls across the lunar surface with a six iron. I was in my kitchenette listening, horrified, as Dr Pockley read his introduction, which went something like: 'Now, in Australia we don't yet have colour TV, but the Americans have been watching the latest moon walk in colour, as has our veteran North America correspondent Ray Martin. Ray, can you describe for us all here in Australia the colours you're now seeing?'

Houston, abort! Abort!! Abort!!!

The problem was, old Ray didn't have a colour television at home. I couldn't afford one. I hadn't seen any NASA pictures in colour, ever. But we were live on radio, so I had to think of something to say. After all, in Pockley's words, I was 'a veteran', which can sometimes mean 'a professional'. Besides, I certainly didn't want to explain my financial shortcomings to the audience. When in doubt, just waffle! (While silently saying a prayer.) I mumbled something about the moon's surface being 'a greyish, silvery colour', which of course it was on my black-and-white box. As for the atmosphere beyond the moon, well, it was 'I don't know how to describe it, Peter, really a dark blue, black . . . eh, sort of colour.' I confidently told listeners that the astronauts' space suits were sparkling white and that the American flag they'd planted was in glorious red, white and blue. (No cigar for guessing that.) Then I changed the subject.

The next day – after I'd recovered from my coronary – Dianne and I went out and bought a colour TV set.

Chapter 8
Waiting for . . . Fidel

I always knew reporting from America would be different given the First Amendment protection of press freedom. I had no idea just how different until I started reading papers like the *New York Post*. Soon after I arrived, in this liberal daily I saw an astonishing column entitled 'No Sad Songs' by journalist-cum-New York folk hero Pete Hamill.

'They buried Mendel Rivers in Charleston today. And we're better off without him.'

Hamill's searing opening words were about a notorious congressman who'd been chairman of the House Armed Services Committee, a hawk, a racist and one of the most powerful men in America. The paper certainly had no sad songs for the dead congressman as it set about burying him again.

I would read this blunt tell-it-like-it-really-is journalism daily. Pete Hamill and the best of America's New Journalists, from Gore Vidal and Gay Talese to Jimmy Breslin and Hunter S. Thompson, would become powerful influences on my reporting and writing style. I'd never read newspapers with such truth, such sparkle and energy before.

That same spirit and blunt honesty was a characteristic of life in New York City, and it proved a rich vein of stories for a journalist. Soon after I came to the city, I did a story on the legend they called 'A Man for All Children', Dr Benjamin Spock. He was America's baby doctor, who'd sold fifty million copies of his paediatric bible, helping parents on every topic from colic to circumcision. Hardly the kind of guy you would expect to be a radical. But now I watched Dr Spock up on stage in a bitterly cold Times Square, bellowing at thirty thousand anti-war protestors, urging them to commit civil disobedience and get arrested if that's what it took to end the fighting in Vietnam. As big as a basketball player, this venerable doctor shouted his bedside advice to the angry crowd that they should 'get goddamn physical'.

Over seventy at the time, Dr Spock told me he'd so far been locked up in a dozen cells. 'Last one,' he cackled, 'was in Washington, DC. I spent the night with a bunch of anti-war clergymen singing hymns till three am. At least the acoustics are great in US gaols.' As I interviewed him, New York City police cars patrolled with American flags hanging from their aerials and their headlights turned on, as a way of protesting against the protestors and supporting Nixon's war effort.

'If you see any cops taking notes,' he'd shouted earlier, 'then grab 'em by the seat of the pants and runnnn 'em out of town!' The middle-class American crowd roared its approval. Mind you, the New York cops had their own fairly extreme ways of doing things, too. Their battle to control the city's formidable crime problem would become a favourite subject of my reporting for the ABC.

*　　*　　*

Along with Detroit, the Big Apple was known as the murder capital of America. There were more than two thousand murders a year, despite a police force of forty thousand officers, which was roughly the size of the Australian Army. Just after we arrived, the new police commissioner, Pat Murphy, launched a range of radical new strategies to wrest control of the streets from the criminals. One controversial operation involved anti-mugging squads, crack teams of plain-clothes cops. To trap muggers, they'd send police decoys into the most crime-ridden neighbourhoods, wait for the crims to hit, then swoop in and arrest them. 'Aggressive enticement' it was called.

The cops in these squads had to be part-time thespians. The decoys were meant to look vulnerable, appearing drunk, injured or sometimes in a wheelchair. Their backup crews were disguised as council workers, street vendors or derelicts but were armed and ready for action. It was a deadly game.

For one of my first *Four Corners* stories in New York I spent a Saturday and Sunday night filming with one of these squads, starting out at ten o'clock on the scary fringe of Greenwich Village. It was cold, dark and deserted; anybody who had a home would have long ago locked the door and taken shelter. Our decoy was a beefy cop aged about thirty wearing a bloodstained bandage around his head as if he'd just come out of the hospital emergency unit. As he staggered along the sidewalk, he would have fooled me.

It was an eye-opener just to be a part of it, because you quickly realised that this was the real McCoy, not some cops-and-robbers TV show. I knew there was a good chance somebody could get killed right there in front of us. In fact, a fortnight after we filmed, a police decoy had his throat slashed and died.

After a little while the decoy-cop shuffled past our van,

muttering as he went that things were too quiet so he was heading below Canal Street, on the Lower East Side.

'That's bad-ass tiger country,' our escort, Sergeant Luigi, said to us, with the added warning, 'You guys be goddamn careful when we hit the streets.' He didn't have to tell us twice.

About five minutes is all it took. Two young punks knocked over our decoy and then menaced him with knives. We filmed all the action, as the backup team rushed from the shadows. It was all done and dusted, with the muggers in the police car, before we got out of the van. We didn't even have time to 'be goddamn careful'!

Half an hour later it happened again. There was only one attacker this time, a big heavyweight of a bloke in a padded leather jacket. He put a knife to the decoy-cop's throat and screamed for his wallet. The cops slammed him up against the metal security grate of a shopfront and clamped the handcuffs so tight his black skin turned pink. Then they frogmarched him and wedged him into the back seat of the squad car, like they were squeezing a side of beef into a VW Beetle.

Unfortunately, our camera had jammed, and we missed the lot.

But that didn't faze Sergeant Luigi. He took a deep breath, smiled and asked somewhat patronisingly, 'Is ya goddamn camera unjammed now?' Sheepishly, we said yes.

So he dragged the felon out of the car, unlocked the cuffs and whispered something menacing in his ear. The petrified-looking thug got five steps down the footpath when one of the backup cops sent him sprawling with a rugby-style tackle, then slammed him up against the metal grating again, slapped on the handcuffs again and heaved him back into the car. Again. It was a brutal police re-enactment of the crime, purely for Australian television.

'Didja geddit that time?' Luigi asked.

Yes, thank you, sergeant, that was perfectly fine. We got it.

'Sir, we're just here t' serve,' Luigi said, smiling at us with mock conviction.

It was all a bit embarrassing, and I suspect a highly illegal breach of the bloke's civil liberties. But then the thug had held a flick-knife to their brother officer's throat. I doubt the sergeant was concerned one iota about his civil liberties.

Over the two nights the squad arrested a total of six muggers, all wielding knives except for one kid who pulled a gun, then dropped it in terror when the backup cops arrived. I couldn't believe how brazen the muggers were. Or how absurdly brave the cops were. And how unflappable. One of them, Muggable Mary, aka Officer Mary Glatzle, was just five foot two in height. The squads took over six hundred violent thugs a year off the New York streets. Muggable Mary alone ended up being involved in three hundred arrests over a two-year period.

When the World Trade Center towers collapsed, the cops from this same police station were amongst the first there. This single police unit lost over thirty officers, all killed that terrible Tuesday morning, 11 September 2001.

As I said, the city's high crime rate was a recurring theme in our TV coverage. Another time I was filming for ABC news on the squalid west side of 42nd Street, which was a favoured stretch for sex shops and drug peddlers. Two foot-patrol cops warned us to be careful and to keep a close eye on our equipment. I asked them if they would mind just walking down the street in front of us so our cameraman could get some close-ups of their guns, mace spray, handcuffs, baton and the rest of the armoury hanging off their belts.

They were seasoned performers. They walked at the right

pace – neither too fast nor too slow – never looked at the camera and talked naturally to passers-by. When we'd finished filming, we stopped to thank them. Jokingly, I said, 'I guess you guys expect full Equity rates?' One of the cops laughed and announced that he *was* actually a paid-up member of Actors' Equity, pulling out his wallet to show us his union card.

At that very moment there was a gunshot from inside a cab double-parked nearby. The cop's partner bounced over the taxi's bonnet and collared the culprit, gun and all. Meanwhile, our Actors' Equity mate zigzagged through the traffic and gently carried the wounded driver out, laying him on the footpath. A patch of blood was quickly spreading across his shoulder. As always in New York, a crowd of curious onlookers quickly gathered, about six deep.

'This man has been shot!' our Actors' Equity mate shouted to the crowd. 'I repeat, this man has been shot. Please make way for the news camera!'

The power of television.

*   *   *

I have two other quick yarns from my early New York days. These were stories I chased diligently and put a lot of time into, but for reasons beyond my control they fell over. They're what I loosely call my 'Waiting for Godot' stories. One involved an odyssey in Harlem and the South Bronx, the other meeting Fidel Castro.

It was early 1970 when an invitation came into the ABC office to meet the notorious bad boy of French letters Jean Genet at the Harlem chapter of the Black Panther Party. Long before Osama bin Laden, the FBI had called the Panthers 'the greatest threat to America's internal security'. While they were not outlawed, there had recently been a number of shoot-outs, with over a dozen of the Panthers killed as well as a couple of cops.

Against the better judgement of everyone else in the ABC bureau, I decided to go. After all, it was a chance to get three birds with the one microphone: Harlem on a Friday night, the mysterious Jean Genet and a peek inside the controversial Black Panthers.

The HQ was a refurbished Episcopalian church on 126th Street. Looking around outside, it seemed I was suddenly the only white face in the world. Inside, it was stone-motherless empty, apart from the so-called duty officer, a hugely obese black bloke with an afro as big as his belly. We waited for about two hours, but nobody else turned up.

At around eleven o'clock my new buddy informed me we had to go to the South Bronx, near Fort Apache, because that's where Monsieur Genet was. I knew from news stories that this was New York's most dangerous police district. But I was in too deep to pull out now.

So we climbed into his rusty, battered Datsun two-door jalopy, New York's fattest Black Panther with his two potent shotguns, and me with my high-powered tape recorder. Straightaway I could see that the South Bronx chapter was peopled by much more serious dudes than Harlem's. There were maybe a dozen men and women in full Black Panther regalia: blue shirts, with pants, leather jackets and berets all in black. A couple of them carried pistols in their belts, and I could see a rack of shotguns in an unlocked cabinet. There were oversized Panther insignia everywhere and slogans painted on the walls proclaiming 'The Revolution has Come', 'Pick Up the Gun' and 'Off the Pigs!'.

So, I thought to myself, this is the way American society as we know it finally blows up!

After what seemed an eternity a small, fat white man with a bald head walked through the door. This was obviously the celebrated French petty thief who had become a writer in gaol and used his novels and plays to trumpet the power of theft, murder and homosexual eroticism. I must confess, Jean Genet looked very ordinary to me.

I still have no idea what the French existentialist thought of the Black Panthers, because Genet spoke no English at all, and there were no translators. My schoolboy French was useless. So Monsieur Genet shook my hand and abandoned me.

Thankfully, at about 2 am my Datsun mate drove me – through the firebombed, dangerous backstreets where even NYC fire trucks refused to go – to the nearest 'safe' railway station, on Grand Parade, the Bronx. 'Hey, my man, take it easy,' he warned as he zoomed off. It was all a purple haze.

My other 'Waiting for Godot' moment happened a bit later. We had filmed Bob Marley and the Rasta boys in Jamaica, on our way to Cuba – where we were the first Australian TV crew since Castro's revolution. We were on the island for a promised *Four Corners* interview with Comrade Fidel.

It was 1973, and Cuba was in a fascinating time warp. It was a living museum. Somebody had turned off the lights in the late 1950s. All the paint and plaster were peeling off walls; buildings in the old city were dilapidated or falling down; and a squadron of brightly coloured 1950s Cadillacs and Buicks with big fins and chrome bumper bars roamed the streets like shiny apparitions.

There was nothing in the shops at all worth buying apart from Havana cigars and Cuban rum, if you had American dollars. The US had banned trade with Fidel for over a decade and you could see the impact. Cuba was a basket case. Moscow had pumped in billions of roubles, but the country was clearly still on survival rations. When the water pipes burst at our famous old pub – the Hotel National, where the mobsters Meyer Lansky and Lucky Luciano used to stay – the front desk simply blamed the Yanks. They weren't allowed to blame Fidel. (We bathed at the beach for a few days, quickly discovering that soap doesn't lather in salt water.) Canberra tiptoed around the embargo by selling Australian-designed Massey Ferguson sugarcane harvesters through a Canadian subsidiary. Presumably that was so Washington didn't get too upset. For some reason it was okay for Canada to trade but not Australia.

Waiting for an interview with Fidel was, like my experience with Genet, a reprise of Samuel Beckett's classic play. The Cubans kept promising, but then some crisis kept getting in the way. (Maybe his water pipes had also burst.)

While we were waiting, the Cubans took us to the various Hemingway shrines where the bearded legend had lived, worked and drunk muchos mojitos. We saw spectacular nightclub acts at the Tropicana, famous for performances by Sinatra, Ava Gardner and Carmen Miranda, and infamous for its blatant sex stage shows, portrayed in *The Godfather: Part II*. Not even Castro's regime could stop the music in Cuba's soul. An old black Cuban musician with white frizzled hair, himself a guitarist, told us how in 'the golden days' of gambling and gangsters, burlesque clubs and bordellos, he played at the ritziest Mafia-owned hotels. But because he was black, he couldn't walk through the front entrance – only through the kitchen.

A few days later we were still waiting. So we flew to the Sierra Maestra mountains, where Fidel and Che had hidden out for three years planning the revolution, and to the Castro ancestral plantation.

Finally, we got to spend a long day with Fidel. At last.

Well, not exactly Fidel, but the next best thing. It was his older brother, Ramón, who has the same beard, is about the same XXL size and wears jungle-green trousers, and whose surname is certainly Castro. He's known as the 'other Castro brother', to distinguish him from Raul, who became the new president in 2008.

Actually, we thought he looked more like Fidel than Fidel!

We spent a fascinating day with Ramón, who dispensed Cuban rum and mega-sized Havana cigars to us as if the revolution had only just begun and it was time to celebrate. (I don't even like cigarettes, let alone cigars as thick as your arm, but I admit I smoked them with Ramón.) The way he handed out these essential provisions, I could see why he had been the quartermaster for his brothers when they were in the mountains, supplying the rebels with food, medicine and arms. Ramón was an exuberant big bear of a man who for several decades ran Cuba's embryo-transplant program at over forty dairy farms across the country. After a steak barbecue with more booze and smokes he eventually poured us back onto our minibus, and we headed for our water-deprived Hotel National. As we slowly drove away from the farm, waving and loudly shouting 'Buenos días' – or some other spray of Cuba Libre-induced Spanish – Ramón stood on the dirt track and sang 'Guantanamera' in a boisterous, throaty baritone. At least, I think that's what he was singing. My brain was a bit foggy by that stage of the early morning.

Eventually, two nights later, we finally got to meet Fidel Castro himself, at a Third World university conference. His address went on for at least an hour and a half. Afterwards, he stood in a small circle of foreign journalists and talked collectively to us for another hour. And guess what? He seemed genuinely surprised to learn we had come all the way from Australia. President Fidel thanked us for the sugarcane harvesters, gave us a comrade's hug and was gone, into the night.

I don't think he had any idea we'd been waiting a week for an interview. Nor do I think he cared.

Ramón, the brother, was much more of a party animal anyway. Much more the sort of amigo you'd want to have a cigar with.

Chapter 9
Imagine John Lennon

As overseas bureaux often are, the ABC's New York office was a sanctuary for strange Aussie expats who'd stayed away from home so long they found it hard to ever go back.

The outrageously colourful Charlie Buttrose was replaced as boss by another inveterate newspaper journo, Stuart Revill. He was an elegant, thoughtful bloke who talked endlessly about the days of Eisenhower and the life of Marlon Brando, as I now bore people about the Nixon years and the death of Elvis. Stuart was a wise counsel, although as young Turks I'm sure we never admitted it.

There was an exceptionally bright woman named Carole Pierce, who'd married a wacky, clever American illustrator and worked as our researcher/producer. She devoured every written thing and had an uncanny talent for fitting news events into the bigger picture, a bit like a dot painter. She saved our bums on too many occasions.

We also had a reporter based in Washington, a mildly

eccentric veteran journo named Peter Barnett, whom Charlie Buttrose had nicknamed the Pundit, a name he was saddled with for life. In an illustrious career of reporting around the world, the Pundit's most memorable scoop occurred on Air Force One with Lyndon Johnson in 1967, when the American president flew to Australia for the memorial service of the missing prime minister, Harold Holt. Just one of two Australian reporters invited on the trip, Barnett was suddenly summoned – somewhere in mid-Pacific – for a solo presidential audience. Notebook in hand and a bit nervous, the Pundit was shocked to find LBJ sitting, trousers round his ankles, on the presidential toilet. That's where Pete got his 'exclusive' interview with the most powerful man in the world. Thankfully, it was for radio and not television.

When Jeff McMullen, a dynamic bundle of talent and passion, joined the New York office, he and I became best mates – almost brothers – sharing some unforgettable experiences reporting across America and also hanging out after hours around New York's live music circuit. In New York even the unheralded musos were bloody marvellous. We got to see Bette Midler, Manhattan Transfer, the Village People, John Denver and Bruce Springsteen in small, smoky clubs long before they cracked the big time. We watched Joe Cocker, with a bottle of vodka in his hand, tumble head first off the stage one night in a West Side theatre. We discovered that the best singer-songwriters, including Bob Dylan, hung out at a place called Kenny's Castaways in the Village, along with a new young comic named Billy Crystal.

Every great city has its moment in the spotlight. In the early seventies New York City was bursting at the seams with the shiniest stars of showbiz and entertainment. It was a cavalcade of celebrities. The legendary singer and actor Harry Belafonte had his apartment just up the block from our place, not far from the terrace house where James Taylor and Carly Simon lived. On a casual stroll there was every chance you might run into the very private Jacqueline Kennedy Onassis, Dustin Hoffman or Katharine Hepburn. Paul Simon could be discovered lurking in the corner of a neighbourhood bar, or Rod Stewart strolling 5th Avenue with his latest long-legged blonde. You might get in a lift with Norman Mailer or Streisand while shopping at Bloomingdale's, or maybe see Sinatra and his latest pack exiting a boisterous dinner at the Plaza Hotel.

All of that happened to us, at the most unexpected moments, living in New York, New York. It really was the Middle Kingdom.

It was just another wintry day when Dianne and I passed John Lennon and Yoko on West 59th Street. They were dressed in matching leather flying jackets, berets and black shades, and they were wrapped in each other, walking and talking with the soon-to-be legendary Eric Clapton. It was their Plastic Ono Band phase, and Clapton had played guitar on their recent tour. *Imagine* had just gone to number one on the American charts, and the controversial ex-Beatle was the toast of the anti-war brigades.

Almost as a reflex, we said, 'G'day, John.'

I always leave stars alone when they're in their private world. But this was different. I mean, this was John Lennon.

He must have picked up our Aussie accents, because without really breaking stride he flicked a wave, smiled and said 'G'day' back to us. Then, just as quickly, he was gone. That was our superstar vignette, our one glorious brush with fame. Within a decade John Lennon would be dead, shot four times with hollow-point bullets just a block from where we'd seen him. Twenty-five years later – almost to the hour – I was holidaying in New York with my daughter, Jenna. We stood with ten thousand other mourners in what's now called Strawberry Fields, across from the Dakota apartment block, where John lived. And died. Like everyone paying tribute that afternoon, we wondered what insightful songs we'd lost, what precious poetry we'd never get to read. 'To every thing there is a season . . . a time to mourn and a time to dance.' Ecclesiastes was right.

I remember another Sunday in the park when Dianne and I were sitting in the sun, just wasting time, doing nothing much. We suddenly realised the people around us were all nudging each other, pointing and whispering. I glanced over and recognised the man directly opposite us. It was Woody Allen, with a girlfriend.

Americans regard their stars as fair game to be stared at and ogled, as though it's a permanent hunting season. In total disbelief we sat and watched this extraordinary ritual of worship and adoration for about half an hour. Finally, one bold bloke, about thirty years old, with a girlfriend in one hand and a big Nikon camera in the other, plucked up the courage and went to speak to Woody. He confessed that he was a devoted fan and asked would Woody mind if he took a quick photo. 'Discreetly, I promise,' he assured the star.

'Okay, but could you *please* keep it cool, buddy?' Woody pleaded.

Promising he would, the fan walked a few metres up the path, then turned back. As he sauntered past, whistling in a ridiculously nonchalant way, he suddenly stopped and propped right in front of Woody. He then blocked the path as he fiddled and focused his camera. In ultra slow-motion, he went from standing up, to kneeling, to squatting in front of the cringing couple. Now everybody within a five-kilometre radius knew that Woody Allen was loose in the park. The awkward, shy genius walked quickly away, muttering 'Goddamn jerk'.

It was a scene that might have been taken straight from one of Woody Allen's own films. But then New York is like that, a picture show, the live setting for every movie you ever saw. The hot air bursting out of the street vents, the rattle of the Manhattan subway and the elevated railway to the Bronx, narrow streets filled with battered yellow taxis, fat cops and crowded diners. From the Empire State Building with King Kong hanging off it to the pageantry of a Macy's Thanksgiving Day parade it is all instantly familiar – but that doesn't water down the excitement when you get to see it with your own eyes.

New York has always boasted the cream of live theatre. We saw Pearl Bailey strut in a dynamic all-singing, all-dancing, all-black version of *Hello Dolly*; we wildly applauded Lauren Bacall in *Applause*; we watched, totally mesmerised, as Katharine Hepburn played Coco Chanel. And after falling asleep in Bernstein's *Mass* at the Lincoln Center, I reminded myself that opera really wasn't for me. Ever again.

I felt far more in my element at Madison Square Garden on a cold March night as Muhammad Ali and Smokin' Joe Frazier stood toe to toe. This long-awaited clash, billed as the Fight of the Century, earned each of the gladiators about four million Australian dollars – an unbelievable fortune in 1971 – and had the largest TV audience ever to witness a prize fight. I rate it as the greatest sporting event I ever saw, along with Cathy Freeman winning gold in Sydney.

*　　　*　　　*

With Richard Nixon in the White House a dark, sullen anger had descended on America. There were violent anti-war protests on college campuses, GI body bags coming home from Indochina, race riots setting the ghettos alight and the growing fear that all this strife would soon spread into white suburbia.

Into this cauldron of change and anxiety charged Muhammad Ali, like a glorious rogue elephant. Three and a half years earlier Ali had been stripped of his world championship and his passport for being 'an uppity nigger', a draft dodger and a Muslim to boot. A lot of Americans wanted to see Ali get his head knocked off. Certainly they wanted someone to shut his fast-motoring mouth. There was no Great White Hope to do it, so they settled instead for a chiselled black-granite street fighter from South Carolina named Smokin' Joe Frazier, the undefeated world champion.

In the lead-up to the fight Ali was remorseless in his public taunts at Frazier, calling him 'an ugly gorilla', an 'Uncle Tom' and the Ku Klux Klan's 'favourite fighter'. When Frazier and his rock band appeared on the *Johnny Carson Tonight Show*, Ali told me in an ABC radio interview, 'Joe Frazier's the only nigger in the world ain't got no rhythm, man. And he's buck ugly.'

They should have charged admission just for the weigh-in.

It was held on the day of the bout in a big exhibition hall inside Madison Square Garden, at high noon, like the classic gunfighter's shoot-out. Everybody's favourite heavyweight, the mythical Joe Louis, was there as the official greeter. The crowd was a convocation of Runyonesque characters. There were rhinestone-beaded maxi coats, mink hats, spangles and chains and jewellery, and alligator patent-leather high-heeled boots. And that was just the black dudes. There were voluptuous women in evening gowns, spilling breasts and bling at midday. Mingling with them were ex-pugs of every calibre wearing loud checked jackets with striped shirts, floral ties and shiny white shoes. With buckles. Their faces were stitched like beaten leather footballs.

When Frazier ripped off his floral-green robe, he seemed to dwarf the doctor's scales. His thighs were as thick as most men's chests. Then Ali arrived with his entourage of trainers and hangers-on, like some West African tribal potentate. He danced a mock double-shuffle, threw a few lightning bolts in Smokin' Joe's direction, and paused long enough for dramatic effect as he peeled off his glistening pure-white silk dressing-gown.

There was an audible sound – almost a gasp – as the room drew its collective breath. 'Yeah, I know. It is beautiful, isn't it? I'm the pugilistic prince,' Ali said and smirked. Everyone knew that he was, too, beautiful and a prince.

Much taller and surprisingly heavier than Frazier on the scales, Ali looked more like a champion athlete than a professional pug. More like a lithe rower or super-trim decathlete than a hardened ghetto fighter with more than 150 bouts on his record.

As we all crowded in, throwing cameras and microphones at him like spears, Ali ducked and weaved and grinned at Frazier. 'I wanna tell ya, Joe Frazier's too ugly to be champ. Ain't no man alive who can whip me. I'm too smart. I'm too pretty. I should be a postage stamp. That's the only way I'll ever get licked.'

A quick-fire round or two with his tongue and he was gone.

That night twenty-two thousand frenzied fans filled Madison Square Garden on West 33rd Street, the so-called West Side slaughterhouse. Everybody from Barbra Streisand to Frank Sinatra had turned up. Old Blue Eyes had even been registered as a *Life* magazine photographer so he could sit in the front row. No bouncer worth his tattoos would think about ejecting the Chairman of the Board.

The Garden's strict code of conduct, which was printed at the entrance and on the stairways, read: 'Guests must refrain from using foul or offensive language, fighting or obscene gestures.'

For me it suddenly turned back the clock twenty years to my childhood days when I sat way up in the bleachers at the old Tin Shed with my father and nobody took a scrap of notice of the code of conduct. This was a different time and a very different place, but there was the same old fight-night cocktail of testosterone and booze.

Ali and Frazier went the full fifteen rounds. Even twenty rows back each punch resonated with me like someone smashing a leather lounge with a baseball bat. Frazier won the fight, yet he was admitted to hospital for three days with a face so puffed and out of shape that it looked like he was suffering from a bad case of the mumps. Ali secretly visited a hospital, afraid his jaw had been broken. It hadn't; it was just badly bent.

I've got to 'fess up. The ABC paid three hundred bucks for my ticket that night, and it was worth every penny. I'd like to thank the Australian taxpayers for my seat.

Despite losing that time, the enigmatic, audacious Muhammad Ali would go on to become an American icon like Elvis and Madonna. He's probably the most famous athlete of all time. But sadly, too sadly, there would be no graceful exit from the square ring for Ali. There rarely is in professional boxing.

A couple of years ago I happened to be in New York when the great man – once an agile and lively, brave and beautiful athlete – stumbled out of a limo and stepped gingerly onto the footpath. I stopped and watched as he slowly shuffled by, mumbling and shaking uncontrollably. Ali now agrees with his doctors that it was too many punches to the head over too many years that triggered his debilitating Parkinson's disease.

I don't know what it is about the often ugly, brutal fight game that I find so compelling. I certainly don't see it as a metaphor for life's bigger battles, as some rambling social commentators like

120

to suggest. For me it's one of the great paradoxes. From Homer to Hemingway and beyond, great writers have tried to unravel its raw, repugnant, primal appeal, its mix of basic instinct and heroism. And futility.

*   *   *

Apart from a short stint at the Australian Consulate, Dianne wasn't allowed to work in America because she didn't have a green card. It meant that when I wasn't travelling for work – and even then, she sometimes came along – we spent all our spare time together. Dianne would walk the thirty blocks from our apartment to the Rockefeller Center, to meet me around midnight, then we'd stroll home, picking up the early editions of *The New York Times* and the other papers. She was a free soul, in her element and quite unafraid of New York's mean streets.

Meanwhile, there were worrying family pressures back home that had to be dealt with, only made worse by the tyranny of distance. Dianne's father, who was barely fifty, had been forced to retire prematurely because of dangerous heart troubles. He would eventually need a triple bypass. Her mother wasn't handling Dianne being across the other side of the world very well, either. I thought that a bit strange, but having had my daughter, Jenna, living in London for three years in recent times, I now understand what Nancy was going through.

We rang home regularly, although trans-Pacific calls in those days were expensive so we mostly wrote instead. Postcards were like today's emails – constant messages sent from everywhere. I discovered some thirty years later that my mother had kept every card and every letter I sent her from America, in ribboned bundles socked away in the back of a kitchen cupboard. She'd thrown nothing away and talked about what I'd written like she knew it off by heart. I suspect she did too. Mum came to visit us one summer in NYC, and we drove her all over New England, to rustic villages and seaports that we loved. I have a favourite memory of the two of us sitting on the dock in the fog, eating a feed of local Maine lobster, at a rocky coastal inlet called Ogunquit. I'd never seen Mum eat lobster before, but she got stuck into it, breaking the giant claws and sucking out the sweet meat like she had it every weekend. It was a long way from fish fingers on a Friday night, a long way from Bogan Gate. It was pleasing to have her close again, even briefly.

My sister Lorraine visited another time, as did Dianne's older brother, Brian, with his wife and baby. We loved showing them this exciting place that had become our new world, but being close to them again reminded us of how much we missed family.

We weren't yet ready to leave, though. When at the end of my first three-year assignment the ABC asked me to stay on in America, we jumped at the offer. It felt like living at the centre of the earth, and there was still too much to enjoy.

Chapter 10
Hail to the Chief

'It's useless to hold a person to anything he says, if he's in love,
drunk or running for office.'

– Shirley MacLaine

During my stint as the ABC's North America correspondent
and in the years following I travelled with and reported on every
US president from Lyndon Johnson to George W. Bush. I got to
interview most of them, usually on the political campaign trail,
before they ascended to the White House or after they'd stepped
down, because by tradition foreign journalists are rarely given
a one-on-one with the current American president. I talked to
Lyndon Johnson after he'd retired, and I remember how big and
imposing he was, with huge hands and a face that was built for
Mount Rushmore. He looked like a Texan should look. It was
Lyndon Johnson who once said the trouble with his political foe
Gerald Ford was 'he played too much football – without a helmet'. The other constant refrain we heard about Ford – the one
president I did get to interview while he was in office – was that
he wasn't even bright enough 'to chew gum and walk at the same
time'. Mind you, good old Gerald didn't help his situation with
his string of verbal gaffes like 'I watch a lot of baseball on the

radio'. Of course, George W. would later match him with gems like 'They misunderestimate me' and 'I think we all agree, the past is over'.

There are a couple of yarns about life on the campaign trail during my time as North America correspondent that still make me laugh.

It was a pitch-black February night in New Hampshire, 1972. The icy footpath was as treacherous as a skating rink, so wearing leather-soled shoes wasn't helping me. I slipped over twice in ten steps, arse over turkey as my father used to say. It wasn't a good look right outside a formal reception being thrown by the head of the granite state. Governor Peterson was his name, and I seem to recall he was an urbane bloke of Scandinavian extraction, like so many people in that mountainous north-eastern pocket of America where the first primary election is always held, kicking off the presidential race. Unlike me, Scandinavians feel at home on the icesheets and snowdrifts.

I was nonchalantly wiping a couple of wet spots off my suit – and trying to mop up a little dignity – when I glanced up and saw a beautiful redhead in a chic cocktail frock standing before me. She was grinning. In fact she was cracking up. She'd obviously seen my pratfalls, and when she'd comported herself a little she laughingly described them as 'just like the banana-skin slides in one of those old Charlie Chaplin movies'. She suggested that 'about the only thing missing was the musical accompaniment, like a piano riff or a tin whistle going whoooops . . . boyyyng!'

'Anyway, Mr Raymond Martin, I'm Shirley. Shirley MacLaine.'

She was at the entrance with Governor Peterson as the high-profile meeter-and-greeter for the liberal anti-Vietnam War senator George McGovern. Shirley had worked for Bobby

Kennedy in the last election before he was shot, and she was now campaigning for the underdog, McGovern.

I'm not pretending for a moment that Shirley MacLaine knew who I was. (Or much cared.) She'd obviously read the name tag pinned to my lapel, which the Americans put there for convenience and conviviality. I was there as one of a four-person *Four Corners* crew, just part of a small media army busting to get our teeth into some presidential-election action.

When I first met Shirley, she was in her late thirties and seemed every bit the movie star, in the wilful and deeply independent mould of a Lauren Bacall or a Hepburn. She was sassy, a bit flirtatious, had cute freckles on her face and at the time was clearly one of the most gifted actors in Hollywood.

Amongst what would become a grand parade of pro-McGovern showbiz stars, Shirley and her kid brother, Warren Beatty, beat the drum loudest. The Madison Square Garden Concert for McGovern and a number of other music extravaganzas brought together Streisand, Springsteen and James Taylor, and even reunited Simon & Garfunkel, while Dustin Hoffman, MacLaine and Beatty, legendary director Mike Nichols and others acted as ushers for the gala event. I'd never seen political razzle-dazzle like this before. It was a fascinating new American phenomenon – world-famous celebrities openly endorsing politicians – and I wanted to look at it in my *Four Corners* story. Who better to illustrate it, I thought, than Shirley MacLaine, beautiful, famous and outspoken in her political views? So later on during that icy New Hampshire night my producer, Alan Hogan, and ace cameraman Les Seymour joined me in a pincer movement to try to convince Ms MacLaine she should be the focus of our story. Looking alluring and classy, with a long-stemmed glass of champagne poised delicately in her fingers, she said she would be out campaigning early next morning at the local elementary school. She was quite happy to talk to us. But only about George McGovern, not about herself. Or about Warren Beatty.

I explained we had a momentous federal election coming up, with a candidate – Gough Whitlam – who wanted to end Australia's involvement in the Vietnam War and improve women's rights, issues I knew were close to Shirley's heart. Maybe, I suggested, we could convince Australian actors, singers and other celebrities to publicly endorse Whitlam, as she had done in America for McGovern.

'Maybe you can,' she said and smiled, holding up her crossed fingers. 'Good luck! But that's not why I'm in New Hampshire. I'm here for George.'

Someone rescued her and swept her away. Refusing to give in, we made one final bid as the night was wrapping up.

'Okay, Shirley, lovely to talk to you,' I said. 'We'll see you tomorrow at seven am at the school. We want to talk about Senator McGovern.'

'That'll be just fine, Raymond,' the movie star purred, with a touch of the sardonic about her smile. (My mother was usually the one who called me Raymond, and only when she was upset.)

'But if I could please throw in *one* question about the role of celebrities in politics, that'd be great for our documentary,' I pleaded, hoping the gravitas of the word 'documentary' would drag her across the line.

Ms Shirley MacLaine paused, smiled again, then after she emptied the last drop of champagne from her flute, she whispered, 'Mr Raymond Martin, you can go and get fu**ed.' *Gulp.*

While you hear people regularly use that word these days, it was a shock to hear it in 1972, especially from a lady. It was as

126

if the Mona Lisa – La Gioconda herself – had said it, like in one of those Monty Python skits, with a balloon coming out of her mouth. As the movie star brushed past, heading for the door, I spluttered something about looking forward to catching up again early in the morning.

The next day my attempts to ask the question, without actually asking the question, proved futile. Gough Whitlam's 1972 election campaign, I believe inspired by McGovern, would later that year get its own celebrity bandwagon rolling – including everyone from Bobby Limb and Little Pattie to Noeline Brown and Jack Thompson – for the first time in Australian politics. But it was no thanks to my efforts with Ms MacLaine.

After that Shirley was with McGovern's campaign constantly, to the point where Richard Nixon's camp floated the rumour that the senator and the showgirl were sleeping together. It was one of many dirty tricks by Nixon's fraudulent mob. The story had legs for a while, but I think finally even Republicans – who detested McGovern's 'acid, amnesty and abortion' policies, as they were colourfully described – woke up to the fact that Shirley was probably guilty of adulation but not adultery.

In later years there were persistent rumours that Ms MacLaine had a raunchy affair with a senior European politician. She finally 'fessed up to having had an affair with Sweden's leftie prime minister Olof Palme, revealing it in one of her nine books, after Palme's 1986 assassination on a Stockholm street. Shirley was, of course, also often linked romantically with Australia's Andrew Peacock in his bachelor days. All I can say is that when I later hosted *Midday* on Channel 9, Shirley came on the show at least three times, and off camera she would always ask me to ring Andrew and get him to contact her, which I always did. She never seemed to have his private number. I would have thought

Shirley's politics were very different from Peacock's. Maybe they shared a common interest in the spirit world.

McGovern's rival to become the Democratic contender against Nixon in the 1972 election was a long, lean, lantern-jawed senator from Maine named Ed Muskie. He finally pipped McGovern in that first primary, in New Hampshire. So now Muskie was heading down to Florida for the next primary, and to carry our story from snow to sunshine we needed a picture of his Learjet taking off. Manchester, New Hampshire, is a pretty basic strip, much like a regional airport in Australia, the laid-back sort of place where you don't worry too much about 'Keep Out' signs. And people were also used to seeing TV cameras in strange places in New Hampshire, so we didn't give much thought to the legalities of plopping our tripod and camera down at the end of the runway.

Les was delighted with the pictures he shot as Muskie's private plane barely zipped over our heads. He gave the big thumbs up. That was until a few seconds later, when a posse of five cars and trucks slammed to a panic stop, surrounding us, and out poured the guns. There were a county sheriff, airport security, a couple of FBI agents and other heavies. All armed, and mightily pissed off.

'What the goddamn hell are you guys doing out here?' the sheriff screamed. 'We wuz all set to shoot yez if you'd stepped any closer to the runway.'

I think he meant it. Certainly, over a few calming beers, we figured that Les, holding the big TV camera that looked a bit like a cut-off bazooka, would have been a goner. (The rest of us might have copped some stray shrapnel.)

*　　*　　*

The big American election conventions are like bizarre political fun parks. I covered a bunch of them and every time felt that I must have walked into a grand satire, some kind of political spoof peopled by raucous middle-aged fatties in silly hats. But this was the real thing, democracy on speed.

The 1972 Republican Convention in Miami was my first. And worst. I'd advance-booked a small sedan so the ABC's Washington correspondent, Peter 'the Pundit' Barnett, and I could easily manoeuvre our way through the expected gridlock along the Miami Beach strip. Instead, when we hit the airport the only car Avis had available was a gargantuan peach-coloured Chevrolet convertible. 'But I can let you have it at the small-sedan rate, Mr Mortin,' the Avis woman said apologetically.

As it turned out, the traffic was so bad only a bicycle would have squeezed through. So we wound back the convertible's white soft-top, leaving the windows up and the air-conditioning on full bore. I was at the wheel and Peter 'the Pundit' Barnett, who'd just flown in from Washington, sat in the back of his own chauffeur-driven limo like King Farouk. The only drawback was that we kept parking our outrageous topless Chevy in the Miami sunshine, only to return and find it full of water after another Florida rainstorm. We were slow learners as well as two-bob lairs. Still, the convertible was the best part of the whole Republican circus that summer.

The giant Miami Beach Convention Centre was festooned in balloons and red, white 'n' blue bunting, all primed to gloriously anoint Richard Nixon. 'Four more years! Four more years!' the delegates screamed incessantly. All this in spite of the social chaos he'd bestowed on America and the Watergate scandal, which was already stinking out the White House. John Wayne and the rest of the Republicans' Hollywood rent-a-crowd turned up to stand alongside Nixon on centrestage, while Sammy Davis Jr sang 'America the Beautiful' then embraced and finally kissed the President. Watching in the auditorium, I remember thinking that even Nixon looked embarrassed.

I was standing outside the convention centre in the middle of a huge anti-war demonstration at about noon that same day. The mob of several thousand protestors was angry and noisy, but mostly peaceful. Then, a few dozen anarchist ratbags started throwing rocks and bottles at the arriving Republican delegates, at the same time trying to break through the security barriers. That was the cue for squads of heavily armed cops, bristling with full riot gear, to charge at the mob. They knocked people sideways, belted some with batons and dragged a dozen or so off to the police trucks. I was standing clear of the front line, interviewing some protestors from New Jersey, when a police tear-gas cylinder landed not far from us, spraying its noxious fumes everywhere. Then another, and another. The wet rags the protestors generously offered me only partly stopped the stinging in my eyes and the burning sensation. It was damn painful, and I couldn't get out of there quickly enough. I felt a little odd driving away in the big peach-coloured Chevy.

It's hard to convey the chilling sense of unreality of the scene. This, after all, was the United States of America, not some tin-pot dictatorship. I remember writing a feature story in which I said that Richard Nixon's America didn't feel like 'the land of the free and the home of the brave'. It felt more like a Costa-Gavras movie, one of those political thrillers like Z, set in Greece under the generals, or State of Siege, in Latin America. In Costa-Gavras's powerful films we saw governments rotten to the core with corruption and abuse of power, where prosecutors were suddenly dismissed because they exposed the truth, where witnesses were intimidated and some even disappeared. As the truth of Watergate was exhumed – over the course of almost two years of newspaper, judicial and congressional investigations – a sinister, clandestine White House was exposed, where paranoia was rampant, out of control. This White House feared and loathed Democrats, the Kennedys, anti-war demonstrators, blacks, Ivy League graduates, Martin Luther King Jr and Jews, not to mention Paul Newman, Robert De Niro, Jane Fonda and about a thousand other celebrities. Oh, as well as *The New York Times* and *Washington Post* newspapers. Tricky Dicky's capacity to hate knew no limits.

In the 1972 campaign, if Americans didn't like Richard Nixon, they could always vote for Shirley's mate George McGovern. The pity was, as it turned out, for most voters that was no choice.

Senator George McGovern was the fifty-year-old balding son of a preacher man from the backblocks of South Dakota. I interviewed him several times and crisscrossed America covering his campaign for *Four Corners*. He was the first senior politician I'd ever come across who was honest enough to condemn old men who kept sending young men off to die in useless wars like Vietnam. As a US senator he included himself when he blamed Congress for having caused this 'human wreckage, all across our land – young men without legs or arms or genitals or faces. Or hope.' It was powerful stuff.

I saw McGovern do something quite remarkable one night in Miami, Florida. As the Democratic presidential candidate, he was invited to be the keynote speaker at a citizenship ceremony for several hundred soon-to-be-Americans, most of them Latinos, many refugees from places such as Cuba, Haiti and Guatemala. McGovern expressed his hope that all their dreams would be fulfilled in America. However, he told them he believed they brought more to America than America could ever give them.

They brought, he said, the riches of centuries of culture – music and art, food and fashion, learning and thought – which would help America be even greater, wealthier and more successful. I found it an extraordinary, enlightened thing to say to disadvantaged, homeless refugees. In all my years reporting in Australia, I'd never heard an Australian politician tell Greeks, Italians, Chinese, Lebanese or any other ethnic people how lucky the country was to have them.

On a range of issues he seemed to me to be on the correct side of the ledger. He was much more than just a soft anti-war liberal, which was the accusation you often heard. I came to believe in George McGovern and what he stood for. I have to say, that's a serious mistake for a journalist.

It was my final report for *Four Corners* on the 1972 election. I'd filmed all across America and sent the film off to Sydney to be edited. The polls overwhelmingly predicted that Nixon would win. But the more I thought about it, the more I started to believe – or convince myself – there might be a major upset, that McGovern could actually win if a number of stars slipped into alignment. So when I recorded my wrap-up, looking right down the barrel of the camera on my rooftop, with the Manhattan skyline behind me, I argued that there were some pundits (namely me) who believed there might just be a monumental upset next Tuesday. Eighteen-year-olds, who had been given the vote for the first time, African Americans, who had registered in greater numbers for this election than ever before, and those angered by the Vietnam War and the brewing Watergate scandal could all help McGovern pull off the political upset of the century. That was my final sally.

I packaged up the precious roll of film, jumped in a cab, took it to JFK airport and personally dispatched it to San Francisco, where an ABC agent collected the package and hand-delivered it to Qantas for the final leg to Sydney.

Three days after my *Four Corners* report Richard Nixon won the biggest landslide in the history of American presidential elections up until that time. McGovern lost every state in the Union except for Massachusetts and Washington, DC. But the television gods gloriously intervened on my behalf again. The film with my exclusive final prediction had never arrived. Thank the Lord! With no one the wiser about my stupid prediction I still looked politically smart.

Is there a moral to this story? If you're a journalist, always make political predictions based on your head, not your heart. Because gut instincts can leave you feeling sick in the stomach.

*   *   *

A year later I went down to Texas for a *Four Corners* assignment marking the tenth anniversary of the assassination of JFK and investigating the country's gun culture. We spent a morning filming at the infamous Book Depository building, where Lee Harvey Oswald had propped to fire on the presidential motorcade. It was a chilling experience standing at the same fifth-floor window as Oswald, looking down onto the street.

We ended up running late for our interview with the mayor of Dallas, whose office was in City Hall, right above the police headquarters, which had also figured in the tragic Kennedy assassination. As we stopped our rented car, we noticed we were adjacent to the driveway where Jack Ruby had stepped forward out of the crowd and shot Oswald dead as he was being escorted by police two days after Kennedy's assassination. What we hadn't noticed was the fat police sergeant standing on the other side of the road as our cameraman did a monster U-turn outside the cop shop. The U-turn wasn't so much the problem, rather it was the fact he'd crossed double-yellow lines to do it.

There was a pearl-handled gun in a holster hanging off the sergeant's belt, just next to his silver Texas longhorn buckle, over which protruded his mammoth gut. Taking up the remainder of the belt space was the usual arsenal of mace, handcuffs, truncheon and an impressive array of other law-enforcement essentials. As he pushed his ten-gallon hat back, we could see his unsmiling face somewhere behind a huge cigar, which cast its own shadow. Amazingly, the officer was able to chew gum at the same time as he chomped on the cigar. As he knuckled the window, he looked to me like Rod Steiger in *In the Heat of the Night*. He looked mighty upset, too.

As the window started to come down, the sergeant said in a deep, slow Texas drawl, 'Now, I gotta tell ya, son. I've seen some stupid fu**in' things in my life. But what y'awl just done, ignoring ten fu**in' big signs and crossing a fu**in' double-yellow line, outside this city's biggest goddamn pohleece station, is the stupidest fu**inest thing I ever seen. Ya hear me, boy?' Long pause. 'Licence!'

It was an astonishing opening gambit, straight out of a Hollywood script.

The sarge didn't give 'a goddamn' about our important interview with the city's mayor. He'd started writing a ticket even before the cameraman had his licence out. In fact, I think the only thing that stopped him plucking his handcuffs off his belt and locking the cameraman up was that I said we were from Australia and 'really loving our first visit to the great state of Texas'.

It's perilous to generalise about America. There's a yin and yang to everything about the place and its people. Yeah, they are noisy, brash and arrogant. But they can also be sophisticated, urbane and cultured. I've found Americans, individually, to be the most generous people I've ever come across, especially when they find out you're Australian. Maybe it's because we speak roughly the same tongue and have much the same culture. But they also see us as trustworthy, loyal friends in a hostile world where they don't have many friends anymore. They see us as a bit naïve and innocent, too, the way they fondly remember themselves in another time. Steve Irwin and Croc Dundee would later polish up our image as fearless knife-throwing crocodile-wrestling hunters. I've never tried to change that perfectly accurate picture they have of us. Why tamper with the truth?

Anyway, the fat sergeant suddenly changed tack, telling us he'd just traded up and got this flash pearl-handled pistol at Billy Bob's Gun Emporium across the road. When I mentioned what our story was, he gave us a telephone number for his best buddy, who was president of the Dallas County Gun and Hunters Club. He even suggested that the mayor 'might jest be feeling mighty generous enough to give y'awl a special kinda dispensation' and quash our traffic fine. Which the mayor indeed generously did, thanks to a quick phone call from Sgt Rod Steiger, I suspect.

We caught up with the officer's best buddy, who took us out to the shooting range that same afternoon. He told us proudly that he personally owned twenty-seven guns of various shapes and calibres – but was anxious we didn't portray Texans as gun-crazed folk just because of what happened to JFK. I reassured him that wasn't our intention, unless we found they were – which of course we did! There is an absurd tolerance for guns in the United States, the right to own them jealously protected by the

Constitution. Some of the gun-control laws were downright wacky, like in California, where you were allowed to carry a loaded shotgun – as long as you didn't actually point it at anybody. In Dallas we couldn't resist going to a shopping-centre car park to film the GM pick-up trucks with gun racks in their back windows. And one of the bank branches offering free shotguns as an incentive to take a cheap loan. And the eight-year-old boys, watched by their proud dads, blasting away at the shooting range with pistols that seemed so big and potent they threatened to snap the kids' wrists each time they pulled the trigger.

At last count Americans owned almost 200 million guns and there were over thirty thousand deaths by guns every year.

*   *   *

In the early 1970s I spent a lot of time, in fact most of my waking hours, reporting about Richard Nixon. Not just in the White House but on the presidential campaign trail and during visits to Beijing, Moscow and the Middle East, in the heady days of ping-pong diplomacy and the Soviet détente. There's no question Nixon was knowledgeable, even if he wasn't likable. He had no sense of humour at all. He lacked the powerful presence of LBJ or the folksy comfort of Gerald Ford. He had none of the warm intelligence of Jimmy Carter or the charisma of Bill Clinton. He had little of the Southern charm of George Bush Sr or the movie-star grace and style of old man Reagan, either.

Mind you, he was much smarter than George W. But then, so is a fridge. What set Richard Nixon apart was that he was the only lying crook amongst them – at least, the only one we've so far uncovered. He should have gone to gaol.

In the summer of 1974, as Nixon's presidency was unravelling, it seemed I almost lived in Washington. The capital was a sweaty, uncomfortable sauna, as usual. In June and July, when the politicians all go home, DC melts into just another Southern hothouse. But that American summer all the stakeholders – the politicians who crunch the numbers and head up all-powerful committees – stayed in town, intriguing and whispering aloud. There's no question they stayed close to their phones.

The mood leading up to Nixon's resignation speech in August was like nothing I've ever experienced. Before or since. There was an innate sense that *something* was about to happen. It was only at the final countdown during the last few weeks, when he'd played every card in the deck – and all those he had secreted up his sleeve – that the Washington political gurus started to think Tricky Dicky would really have to go.

Knowing that he was certainly going to be impeached, Nixon finally resigned in August 1974, after arranging a sweetheart deal with his replacement, Vice President Gerald Ford. Just a month after we watched Nixon helicoptered off the front lawn with the special prosecutor yapping at his heels, Ford granted him a pardon. President Ford argued that America needed to revive. I suspect Americans also needed revenge after what Nixon had put them through.

Not surprisingly, when Nixon was forced out of office there were voters proudly wearing T-shirts declaring 'Don't blame us – we voted for McGovern!'. I've still got mine somewhere.

Chapter 11
The Name's Bond . . . Alan Bond

Much as I got a thrill out of covering US politics, I really savoured the times when Dianne and I could go exploring America. As fast-paced and high-tech as it is, the United States is often quaint and deeply traditional, and is an exquisitely beautiful country. Most times we would spend Christmas with some American friends who lived just outside of Philadelphia. There were streets of spar-kling-white colonial houses with rocking chairs on wide rounded porches, giant oak trees festooned with lights, full nativity scenes in the front gardens, and children wearing flowing woollen scarves, skating on the frozen village pond. Choirs walked the suburban streets singing carols and handing out Christmas cake. It was picture-postcard stuff, very pleasant. We'd usually go to a late-night church service with a smiling congregation of honest, decent folk and come home under a light shower of snowflakes. Our friends' little boy, Chris, would take a candle and in his PJs walk upstairs to bed, followed by his golden retriever. This was a gorgeous image that seemed stolen straight from a Christmas card. We'd have a couple of hearty eggnogs and drift off to bed, first checking to see if the front yard was now under a heavy eiderdown of pure snow. It often was.

On other trips we wasted time in idyllic New England grave-yards with moss-encrusted headstones that dated back almost three centuries, shadowed by starkly beautiful white-clapboard steepled churches in neat village squares. The towns all looked like Peyton Place. We fossicked for Vermont's classic covered bridges, red wooden shelters in the snow; we saw rolling hill-sides on fire – in the fall – covered with soaring flames of birch and beech, sumac and sassafras. We traced Sherman's march to the sea, through the pungent Georgia pine forests all the way to Savannah, then wound our way back through the once blood-stained lanes of southern Virginia, to peaceful Appomattox, where the Civil War fell silent at last. We tasted sweet mountain waters as they cut through the tundra of the Rocky Mountains high country; we photographed the last rays of sunlight through the exquisite Navajo sandstone gorges of the Zion National Park.

But if Dianne and I had one truly special place outside of New York City, it was Newport, Rhode Island. It was the place where we fell in love all over again. I have to say, Newport's a roman-tic old town for a fabled yacht race. We moved into Newport for months at a time in each of the 1970, 1974 and 1977 Ameri-ca's Cup years. I had the task of setting up the technical side of the ABC's live ship-to-shore coverage, as well as going out on a rented powerboat to do the race commentaries. We adored the place so much we even took holidays there in the winter snow and visited friends in springtime, when this old seaport trans-formed into a garden.

In the overcrowded Cup summers Dianne and I roamed the lush countryside, a bit like England with its winding paths across rolling fields and long twilights. Or we took a ferry out to the beautiful islands of Cape Cod nearby. Out there we hired bikes and stopped at roadside stalls selling freshly squeezed lemonade and banana cake. It was absolute heaven. It could have been Tuscany, with endless stone fences, rosebushes dripping with blooms and freshwater lakes spotted with lilies. The seaside villages had quaint guesthouses with big porches and grey, salt-sprayed boatsheds running down to a rocky cove.

For a history buff like me Rhode Island had every era covered. As one of the richest cities in colonial America, Newport led the trade in African slaves and in the hunting of whales in the South Atlantic. In the early nineteenth century trading ships set off from Newport to China, taking in Sydney Town on the way. Captain Cook's *Endeavour* ended her days in Newport as a coastal lugger, before sinking to the bottom of the harbour. Excited archaeologists recovered part of her precious hull there. The New York Yacht Club, an exclusive clique that since the middle of the nineteenth century has boasted the richest and most powerful families in America, has a grand clubhouse at Newport. And for almost 150 years challengers from Britain and Australia had been trying to wrest the ornate America's Cup from that venerable establishment.

These days it's hard to comprehend what a huge news story the America's Cup races were for Australia. It was a challenge for a reporter, though, as the racing could be terminally dull, 'like watching paint dry', as the great Red Smith once wrote. My mission, along with Bert Oliver from ABC Sport, was to kick it in the guts. I'd never done any sailing before, so I was on a steep learning curve amongst the top-sider set. Early on, I figured it was probably safer to leave the intricacies of Kevlar sails and winged keels to the experts, while I concentrated on the colour: the sex, drugs and political shenanigans. In Newport at Cup time there were plenty of those. I quickly found that doing the daily radio broadcasts – which often meant ten hours straight out on the racecourse – wasn't always a job for fair-weather sailors. We could be 30-odd kilometres offshore when the ocean changed from a millpond to a raging sea; the sky would suddenly turn from a cloudless blue canopy to a Narragansett fog so thick you couldn't see the bow of your boat.

Captain Fred Lawton, the ABC's Cup specialist and a colourful old Yankee sea-dog, had sailed out of Newport all his life. One year when we were suddenly hit by the thickest of fogs, Fred navigated us in to shore by the sounds of the bells on the buoys, which were placed amongst the rocks. Slowly, he led a flotilla of spectators and competitors safely back to the dock. The French and Australian racing yachts followed us like lambs, as did several huge pleasure crafts including the NYYC's tender, with Jackie Kennedy Onassis on board. Jackie's family owned one of the biggest estates at the entrance to Newport harbour.

The town had been the favourite watering hole for America's mega-rich since the late nineteenth century, when industrialisation began to create enormous profits for the privileged few. Families such as the Bouviers, Vanderbilts, Astors and others with untold wealth built summer cottages as big as palaces, with hot and cold saltwater baths and private zoos. They imported Spanish stonemasons to build their walls, and marble cutters from Italy. Scenes from the classic movie *High Society*, with Grace Kelly and Frank Sinatra, were filmed in one of the Newport mansions. We were living in Newport when they filmed scenes for *The Great Gatsby*, with Robert Redford and Mia Farrow.

In 1977 it was the location for *The Betsy*, a film based loosely on the life of Henry Ford, a leviathan of the Gilded Age, played by Sir Laurence Olivier. I had a chance to chat with Olivier as we strolled through the gardens of Rosecliff, which was a full-sized replica of the Grand Trianon at Versailles. He talked fondly about a holiday that he and his then wife, Vivien Leigh, had together at Broadbeach in the unspoilt days of Queensland's Gold Coast. I'd read about their 1948 visit Down Under raising money for his Old Vic Theatre Company and for the postwar Food for Britain program. Vivien Leigh had a raging affair with Peter Finch, but I didn't expect Olivier to raise the subject. When I commented on how exquisitely beautiful she had been, he surprised me. 'Australia was where I lost Vivien,' he said. 'But I don't hold it against you darned Aussies.' Then he laughed, still very handsome in old age, and gave that enigmatic smile of his.

*　　　*　　　*

Into the genteel world of Newport crashed a succession of Aussie challengers, rattling the bone-china teacups in the hallowed New York Yacht Club. There was old Sir Frank Packer, a newspaper magnate with too much spare change who caught the America's Cup bug and threw away countless millions in reckless pursuit. In 1970, for the first time, the NYYC agreed to allow a sail-off to decide the official challenger. Baron Marcel Bich, the French aristocrat who made his fortune from Bic ballpoint pens, lighters and disposable razors, had somehow twisted their arms. Bich was a persuasive, debonair European. The night before Bich's first race against Packer's yacht, the governor of Rhode Island held a swish reception in Marble House, one of the Vanderbilts' beaux arts mansions. Baron Bich spoke in broken English about the glory of the battle. Standing on the magnificent stone staircase, flanked by priceless royal French tapestries, Bich finished his speech graciously,

'I wish the Australians good breezes tomorrow. And remember, the main thing is not to have won, but to have fought well.'

Sir Frank was up next. He was blunt and not in the mood for niceties. Sporting a gold-buttoned blazer and the Royal Sydney Yacht Squadron's striped tie, Packer thanked the governor and declared, 'Look, I think we might just let the French do the talking, and we'll go out and do the bloody sailing.' That's exactly what they did.

Earlier that afternoon, I had watched Sir Frank being interviewed beside his yacht, *Gretel II*, by a news crew from the American network CBS. To coincide with Packer's latest Cup campaign, the American media had resurrected an inflammatory editorial Sir Frank had written a few years earlier in the *Daily Telegraph*, suggesting that for every white policeman killed in the riots in Watts, California, they should hang a number of black rioters. It was against this background that the CBS interview was being recorded.

'So, Sir Frank, what kinda shape are your boys in for tomorrow's big race?'

'Oh, listen, we're in great shape. Great shape! Our skipper, Jim Hardy, has been working 'em hard – like a pack of niggers!'

I watched the American reporter and his black cameraman almost fall off the dock.

Then, of course, there was Alan Bond. As feisty as a bantamweight rooster, Bond didn't care about the Establishment. (At least he said he didn't.) During the races in 1977 he and I had a major dust-up. This was the year of his second America's Cup challenge, with the yacht *Australia II*, skippered by Sir James Hardy, one of my all-time favourite blokes. Some of *Australia II*'s gear had been held up on the Fremantle docks. Bondy, who was always impatient and impetuous, was accustomed to getting his own way. In an emotional rant during an interview with me, he accused the wharfies back home of playing 'political silly buggers'. He also called them 'a bunch of red-raggers'. It made a damn good story.

Predictably, the wharfies blew up – big time. They went crazy and threatened to lock his yacht's containers in Fremantle for months. In damage-control mode, Bond went on Perth radio denying he'd said any such things and accusing me of favouring the Sydney syndicate over the Western Australian challenge. That was absolute rubbish and he knew it.

At the next Newport press conference he refused to answer any of my questions. When I fronted him afterwards, he insisted he hadn't used the words 'silly buggers' or 'red-raggers'. Worse still, he claimed that I had made them up.

I told him I had his words on tape. A bit flummoxed by that news, he countered by saying, 'Well, no matter. The conversation was off the record.' It certainly wasn't. The stand-off continued for about a week, until – to his credit – he pulled me aside, shook hands and suggested we just get on with life.

Still, I was worried that he might not talk to me for a feature story I was doing for *Four Corners* about his business dealings in Newport. The truth is, although we'd butted heads, he jumped at the chance to appear on a program as prestigious as *Four Corners*. In 1977 Bond was desperately trying to get money from the banks and finance houses for his real-estate ventures. He never missed an opportunity. Unlike Paul Barry, who wrote bestsellers critical of Bond, I found him a likable rogue.

Decades later, when he'd bought Channel 9 and become my boss, Alan Bond rang from Perth to congratulate me on picking up a Gold Logie. In thirty years I never once got a call like that from Kerry or James Packer.

Chapter 12
Spies and Other Colourful Characters

'Deception is a state of mind and the mind of the state.'
– James Jesus Angleton

Ronald Biggs was a Cockney git. And a crook.

But he was also an incorrigible larrikin, one of those blokes who'd put his hand up for any sort of mischief. If a mate asked him, Biggsy would probably even help rob the Glasgow–London mail train and pinch five million dollars in cash. Which is what he did in spectacular fashion with a gang of crooks back in 1963.

As I write this, Biggs has just been released from his London prison hospital. He's almost eighty now, and almost dead. He's been described by Fleet Street hacks as cadaver-like, confined to a wheelchair at best. He's had three strokes and can't talk. This may be the first time in his colourful life that Biggs has ever stopped yapping.

But that's not how I remember him. The Ronnie Biggs I met was a silver-haired Lothario. Caught and sentenced to fifty-five years' gaol, he only spent fifteen months inside before organising his daring escape in a furniture van. After a bit of plastic surgery to his face he hightailed it to Australia.

'Just like the rest of my Cockney crim ancestors, my son,' he told me.

The irony is that Scotland Yard's most wanted man actually worked as a chippy for a while in the Channel 9 set department in Melbourne, just along from the channel's top-rating newsroom. Before the heist carpentry had been Biggs's honest trade. When the jig was up in Victoria, he escaped to Brazil. His whereabouts remained a mystery until he was spotted there by a Fleet Street journo in 1974.

I flew down to Rio de Janeiro soon after to shoot a story on Biggs for *Four Corners*. The only seat I could get on short notice was in first class. (I know, sometimes you just have to cop it.) I sat next to an ageing businessman who, in the time it took me to sit down, shook my hand, gave me his name and described himself as 'a Jew from Long Island who's made his fortune selling long-leaf Brazilian tobacco to China, where they're addicted to cigarettes. I do this trip so often, ya could call me a commuter!'

This dodgy character entertained me with amazing stories of survival and success. He was curious to hear about Ronnie Biggs. A bit simpatico, I suspect. It was a long journey in those days from New York, maybe thirteen hours on a sleek Boeing 707. My newest best friend was the one who insisted we should share a large plate of Beluga caviar, washed down with a bottle of vodka. Russian, of course. The alcohol-induced sleep cut the tedious trip in half.

In fast 'n' loose Rio I was treated to an incredible – and incredibly strange – week with the Great Train Robber as my tourist guide. He seemed to know everybody, especially the bronzed young bikini-clad ones on Copacabana. I didn't have to pay

Biggs a motza for his story (or his tour-guide expertise). In fact I paid him nothing. This was before the bad days of chequebook journalism. I just picked up his dinner costs and a few drinks. Okay, a lot more than a few.

He introduced me to a raven-haired beauty with lustrous black eyes named Raimunda de Castro, who was the mother of his baby son, Michael. Raimunda was a samba dancer in a disco bar when they met. Biggs moved in with her, and before long Raimunda was expecting his child. Michael's birth was unplanned – but it saved Ronnie from another forty years in gaol. Under Brazilian law foreigners who father a child can't be kicked out of the country. And when Scotland Yard detectives came to collect Biggs without going through the proper diplomatic niceties, the Brazilians prickled and refused to extradite him.

So Biggs was safe as long as he stayed out of trouble. Officially, as a felon he wasn't allowed to work. He did odd carpentry jobs and some casual handyman stuff. He also recorded a song with the Sex Pistols, 'Belsen was a Gas', which reached number six in the British charts. In later years he picked up some spare change selling mugs and T-shirts featuring his face and posed for visiting British tourists. He was even available for 'a celebrity barbecue with Biggsy' on the Lonely Planet travel website. Mostly, though, he was a kept man. I called him 'a Pommy gigolo with a licence to wander'. He laughed at that description and said he'd put it on his business card if he ever got one. Biggs had moved out of Raimunda's and was now living with a wealthy, handsome Argentinian widow of indeterminate age. She was more his speed, while I think Ronnie quietly amused her. He introduced her, with a salacious grin, as 'my patron'. It made the lady smile, too.

Biggs drove me and the film crew everywhere in his patron's sleek BMW: from the iconic Christ the Redeemer statue, through the high favelas of the squatter city, where kids kicked soccer balls to him, down to Ipanema for fruity cocktails. We even went with him for his twice-weekly parole visits to the local police station. He made the cops smile, too, with his cheeky Portuguese jokes. Rio had become his town.

My main interview was done at his patron's house, in a fashionable suburb near Ipanema. I'd had to hire a local Brazilian film crew, from the national Globo network. As the cameraman carried his tripod up the entrance stairs, he accidentally bumped a life-sized porcelain statue of a Dalmatian dog, one of a pair. The dog broke into about twenty pieces, which cascaded down the marble stairs. I had a seizure imagining the replacement cost – it must have been in the thousands of dollars.

Biggsy didn't help, saying with mock gravitas, 'Jesus, Martin, that's gonna cost ya a bloody king's ransom, my son. I hope the ABC's rollin' in it, eh?'

I made a half-hearted offer to pay for the damage, which is all I could do. To my huge relief Biggs's patron insisted she knew an artisan who'd stick it all together. Besides, she said, the statues had been a gift from her ex-husband and she didn't like them anyway.

As for Biggs, he was about as honest as you would expect a Cockney crook to be, talking about the robbery, the train driver who had been bashed during the heist, and Biggs's escape from Wandsworth. He was at pains to tell me that he was 'just a crook, my son. Just a crook.' He kept insisting he was a very different breed to the infamous Kray brothers, whom Biggs grew up with in London's East End and who were 'crazy criminals who cut people up and fired machine guns 'n' stuff. They were bloody mad. Barmy.'

Ronnie said he'd really loved his time in Oz and wished he'd emigrated years before. He said, with some tenderness, that he missed his wife, Charmaine, and their two boys, who lived in Melbourne.

Would he do it all again: the crimes, the life on the run? 'Yeah,' he laughed, slapping me on the shoulder. 'Probably. Just for the fun of it, my son. Just for the bloody fun of it.'

His only regret in life, he told me, was having the expensive plastic surgery done on his nose in an attempt to disguise himself. 'Cost me a fortune, my son. And it failed,' he said. 'I used to have a big Cockney hooter. Now I got this ski slope, and it won't even hold my glasses up. They keep slipping off my face!'

We corresponded for a few years. He wrote very amusing letters, too. Knowing he was doing it tough, I ended up sending him some clothes from New York.

*   *   *

The criminal capers of Ronnie Biggs were minor compared to the espionage stories that surfaced in the 1970s. Being posted to North America, I got a tantalising but chilling sense of what went on in the murky shadows and an insight into the way the CIA's tentacles reached into Australia's domestic affairs.

A major scoop came in 1977 when I got the chance to interview James Jesus Angleton, who had been the supreme boss of counterintelligence at the CIA for more than two decades. Angleton's job had been to identify Soviet spies, encourage defections and root out any American double agents. But he went way beyond his brief. Towards the end of his career James Angleton became known as the most dangerous, most venal man in America, even more so than J. Edgar Hoover, the bizarre boss of the FBI. In 1974 the new director of the CIA finally forced his resignation, after *The New York Times* revealed Angleton had run a vast illegal surveillance operation inside America, tapping phones, opening mail and spying on people's daily lives. The fact is, Angleton had been handed extraordinary covert powers, especially under Richard Nixon, whom we now know was clearly paranoid.

The super spy arrived very late for our interview, wearing a floor-length coat even though it was late summer, and, surprisingly, a black trilby. Actually, it was almost one o'clock in the afternoon when he eventually showed up at the ABC's office, after promising to be there by nine. But the only thing he apologised for was being a bit hung-over. He'd had a big night, he told us, a grand reunion with a bunch of his old spook mates.

He screwed his face up at the offer of a cup of coffee and asked for milk instead. Glass after frothy glass. It was for his 'goddamn perforated ulcer', he explained. The ulcer didn't stop him chain-smoking Virginia Slim cigarettes; nor did his hacking cough. I looked at this tall, gaunt ex-cryptographer with the bushy brows and the manic eyes, thinking he didn't look that scary. But I knew he was.

As the camera began rolling, one of Western intelligence's most enigmatic figures began spilling his guts about the evils of Gough Whitlam and his Labor government. He didn't actually call Mr Whitlam a Soviet agent, but he made it clear he believed Australia's PM was acting 'like Moscow's puppet', was dangerously upsetting the *esprit de corps* of the international spy game, was 'far too risky' and had thrown the intelligence partnership between Washington, London, Ottawa and Canberra into 'serious jeopardy'. He revealed quite bluntly that the sharing of espionage secrets had stopped under Whitlam, who 'simply couldn't be trusted'. It was extraordinary stuff and I couldn't believe what I was hearing.

Angleton said his feelings about Gough had nothing to do with party politics. He insisted that he didn't give a damn, pointing out that he'd personally been very close to all the Israeli Labor governments. (So close, in fact, that he'd long been accused of supplying Tel Aviv with its nuclear secrets.) Then it was Lionel Murphy's turn. The federal attorney-general came in for a huge bucketing from the former intelligence chief, who insisted Murphy had been out of order and out of control – 'like a bull in a china shop' – when he ordered raids on ASIO's offices in Melbourne in 1973. When I suggested that, as attorney-general, Murphy had the power, Angleton snapped back, 'I don't care!'

It was all highly provocative stuff about an Australian government recently thrown out of office. Each time our film ran out, the renowned war cameraman David Brill nervously changed the magazine as if in a battle zone. In a lifetime at the ABC he'd been everywhere, but he would say later that he'd never heard anything to match this. Brill's hands were flying in the camera bag, afraid that The Kingfisher, as Angleton was known – this super spy who knew all the CIA's top secrets – would take flight.

I was more afraid we were going to run out of milk for his ulcer.

Dave and I ended up recording well over an hour of Angleton's wild accusations. The interview was a gem, a round-up of Cold War chicanery and cozenage. Maybe after all those decades of staying silent, James Jesus Angleton was busting to talk. Maybe he was really quite mad. Either way, once again I believe we got our exclusive interview because he had a genuine soft spot for Australia. As he described it, the United States and Australia were part of a tiny, exclusive English-speaking intelligence club. Besides, Angleton said with a kind of knowing certainty, Australia always did what the Americans told them.

Incredibly, Angleton invited us back to his home in Langley, Virginia, just down the road from the CIA headquarters. He showed us his two Leica spy cameras and his darkroom, where he'd processed some of the magnificent photos that now hung on his walls – strange, evocative still lifes and portraits in shadows, every one of them in black and white.

He took us through his garden to his orchid house, where he'd pollinated tribes of rare and exotic plants. 'Orchids,' he explained, 'use colour, shape and odour to deceive insects into landing on their pods and spreading the pollen.' Angleton's whole life, it seems, had been about deception.

He went on to regale us with stories about regular fly-fishing forays outside Canberra with Colonel Spry, the long-time head of ASIO. He laughed as he told us how Spry had been instructed by a ruthless J. Edgar Hoover, the FBI boss, to personally deliver to Washington the Australian Royal Commission Report into the Petrov spy scandal. According to Angleton that's what Spry dutifully did: 'On all fours, pushing the pile of volumes to Hoover's desk – with his nose.'

I think he was speaking figuratively.

I scripted what I knew was an explosive story, packaged Brillo's precious film and despatched it off to *Four Corners*, which had a few days to get it to air for the following Saturday night's show.

The acting executive producer, Brian Davies, contacted both Gough Whitlam and Lionel Murphy, telling them of Angleton's accusations and asking them for a comment. Murphy, who was now a High Court Justice, threatened to 'sue the pants off' the ABC. So, incredibly, *Four Corners* dumped the whole story. No part of the Angleton interview would ever be used on television, which is extraordinary given all the subsequent stories about the CIA's involvement in Gough's dismissal. It wasn't even aired on television after Murphy's death.

However, I had also sent the full Angleton interview through to ABC radio current affairs to be broadcast on the program *Correspondent's Report*, on the Sunday morning after *Four Corners* was supposed to go to air. Remarkably, it was run in full, without any editing. Neither Murphy nor Whitlam took any legal action – we never even heard from their lawyers.

After some frustrating and futile attempts to get an answer as to why *Four Corners* had been so cowardly, I was sent off to Newport to cover the 1977 America's Cup showdown by Alan Bond, expecting the interview would eventually be run, but for some inexplicable reason the eight rolls of film, my script and transcript of the full Angleton interview never saw the light of day.

I don't normally believe in conspiracy theories, but a few years later a highly experienced journalist and mate, Bruce Stannard, rang me with some startling news. Along with Richard Hall, Stannard was doing a Channel 7 documentary about the latest allegations that Nixon and Kissinger had engineered Gough's downfall. Bruce approached the ABC, asking to buy a copy of my Angleton interview. The ABC, which has easily the best archive in Australian TV, routinely sells such material. But this time Stannard was informed that the film shot so breathlessly by David Brill in our New York office had mysteriously disappeared. The ABC's impeccably thorough archivist, Wendy Borches, says she has no idea what happened to the interview. They were never even logged in the ABC film library, which is standard procedure. Just as intriguing is that all the archived ABC News footage of Gough's 11 November dismissal speech on the steps of Old Parliament House, and surrounding events, disappeared from the Canberra film library. It's never been seen since either. It remains for me one of life's great mysteries.

*   *   *

As it turned out, I ended up doing a number of interviews about alleged CIA meddling in the affairs of the Whitlam government. One was with a man named Victor Marchetti, a career spook who had risen to become the executive assistant to the CIA's deputy director. Appalled by the agency's brazen interference in friendly countries whose governments they didn't approve of – namely Australia and Chile – Marchetti resigned from the agency. He wrote a sensational bestseller called *The CIA and the Cult of Intelligence* and became a valuable contact for me, as much as I could ever trust a former spook.

It was thanks to Marchetti and his spy connections that I suffered the only migraine of my life.

In September 1977 Indonesia launched an especially brutal attack on rebel forces in the mountains of East Timor. There was widespread, indiscriminate killing. Malcolm Fraser's goverment turned a blind eye to Jakarta's savagery, just as Whitlam's had before it. All the bravery shown by the Timorese who gave their lives for Aussie diggers in the Second World War was once again forgotten by our leaders.

I went sniffing for a 'Washington reaction' story. I didn't really expect to find much because, like Canberra, the American government was bending over backwards to keep President Suharto and his cronies happy. Half a dozen phone calls to congressional staffers, a couple to state department desks and the Pentagon all came up cold. Then an old military officer at the Pentagon, who'd been a valuable source of mine for a few Vietnam stories in the past, told me he'd heard the CIA had been handed 'something new' about East Timor. But he didn't know exactly what it was.

Ringing around again, I discovered that the Indonesian military had been trying a new tactic against the East Timorese: napalm and saturation bombing, plus chemical sprays. What's more, I learnt that for the first time they were using Agent Orange defoliant, which the Americans had deployed in Vietnam so controversially. Villages and mountain gardens in Timor had been devastated. I was also told the Indonesians had used Bronco counter-insurgency aircraft, recently supplied by President Jimmy Carter, to do their dirty work.

If it was true, it was a huge story.

Then a second CIA contact confirmed the information, saying it had actually come via Australian intelligence sources, from a top-secret communications base in the Northern Territory.

So I wrote the story.

Close to deadline I stood by the phone in the tiny kitchen of our apartment and sent this scoop through to *AM* in Sydney.

Dianne was sitting on the lounge listening. When I hung up, she looked at me and asked, 'Are you sure about that?' I told her I was. After a moment's thought I realised both my sources were inside American intelligence agencies. My wife had made me question myself, especially as her instincts are too often correct. We talked about the story over dinner, and our discussion didn't ease my niggling concerns. Quite frankly, by now I was starting to fear that I might have been set up.

Anyway, I went to bed, only to be woken by a phone call from Sydney at about 4 am.

'Eh, Ray. Sorry to wake you. This is Talbot Duckmanton,' the voice said. Still half-asleep, I thought it was an old journo mate of mine pretending to be Duckmanton, the ABC's high priest. He'd done it before.

'G'day, cobber. What's hap'ning?' I asked.

'Ray, are you awake? This is Talbot Duckmanton.'

In one perfectly executed move, I sat up and swung my legs off the bed. Now I was awake!

It really was the ABC general manager, who'd never, ever rung me at home before. He was also one bloke whom you never, ever called 'cobber'. I'd always maintained a good relationship with Duckers, as everybody secretly referred to him, but I can't pretend he was a friend.

Right now, that was the least of my problems.

'I'm sorry to say,' Duckmanton continued, 'your story on *AM* this morning has caused us quite a problem.'

Deciding that offence was probably my best defence, I replied, 'How about saying it was a good story?'

That slowed him up for a second.

'It *was* an excellent story . . . but the Indonesians deny it. In fact they're so upset they're now talking of closing the ABC's Jakarta bureau. And our correspondent Peter Munckton's family is under siege, with protestors outside their house.'

Wow. That news gave me pause. Munckton was a hardened war correspondent and could probably handle a mob of protestors, but I was worried about his family. Duckers went on to explain he was flying to Canberra that morning to try to pacify the Indonesian ambassador. One of the problems he faced, he said, was that no other Australian news organisations had carried the story. He asked if it was possible to convince the Washington correspondents for *The Age* or *The Sydney Morning Herald* to confirm the story in print. Sir Talbot Duckmanton's ABC was always pleased to get a news scoop – but only if it didn't upset the government of the day.

Clearly, I had to fly down to Washington.

Once there, I had an early-morning coffee with an old mate named Creighton Burns, who was *The Age*'s man in Washington and would soon return home to edit that august paper. He was also a crack journalist and was happy to hunt down the story to confirm it for me.

Then I arranged to meet my 'Deep Throat', who worked at the CIA, in a local park, like a scene out of the movie *All the President's Men*. My second source, who worked at the Pentagon, wasn't answering his phone, which worried me.

It must have been late summer, because I can remember the park seat was surrounded by bright flowers and kids were playing nearby on the lawn, oblivious to my impending disaster. My contact was late arriving, and I feared that I'd been double-crossed, but he finally turned up and confirmed what he'd told me the previous night, with some extra details.

I still couldn't find the second bloke, so I called the Australian ambassador, Alan Renouf, who agreed to see me. He didn't need to ask why I was calling. Renouf was an impeccable, highly skilled diplomat. I hoped desperately that he'd be able to confirm my *AM* story.

By the time he was free, I had the worst migraine in the history of headaches. Mind you, it was the *only* migraine I've ever had, so I don't have much to compare it with. I just knew there were two blokes with large hammers trying to beat their way out of my skull. And I felt quite nauseated.

At the Australian embassy, we shook hands and the ambassador offered me a seat. I started to tell him about my story, stumbling a little over my words. Alan Renouf said, a bit sternly, 'Yes. I heard your report on Radio Australia this morning. I've spent much of the morning talking about it with a couple of my colleagues here.' He paused. I waited. Then, he smiled.

'If you're asking, I have no problem with the accuracy of your story, Ray,' the ambassador said. 'None at all.'

I could have kissed him – except I was distracted by the realisation that my migraine had suddenly gone.

Chapter 13
Tick. Tick. Tick . . .

Dianne and I came back home in December 1977 for a visit. It was only our second in almost nine years. The first time it had been a dreary winter, but this was a sparkling Sydney summer, a reminder of that special light you only seem to get in Australia. The Heidelberg artists painted it, and my camera sees it every time I come home. You have to wind back the aperture, it's so bright. Dianne and I found everything fresh and friendly. Apart from catching up with family, there was a whole new bunch of nieces and nephews to get to know, and Christmas Day was loud and memorable. We suddenly felt like we'd been away too long.

Strangely enough, while I was in Sydney the boss of the Seven Network, Ted Thomas, rang and invited me to lunch. He said he had plans to launch *60 Minutes* in Australia and wanted me to be a part of it. That ratings-busting show had gone to air on CBS just as Dianne and I arrived in New York. I doubt we ever missed it. Every Sunday night I watched American TV heavyweights Mike Wallace, Morley Safer and Harry Reasoner zip around the world, and I thought 'How good would that be?'. From Nome to Nairobi, Kabul to Copenhagen – just find a story, get an airline ticket and go. And then do the same thing next week! For a reporter the *60 Minutes* concept was magic, the stuff of dreams. Now suddenly here I was, sitting at lunch with Channel 7's top dog, being offered a role in the Aussie version. Thomas informed me it would be Mike Willesee, me and a yet-to-be-named third reporter. He certainly made the offer sound exciting, but after a boozy lunch I never heard another word. Nothing. Either the Seven board knocked it back, or Ted Thomas lost interest.

Anyway, Dianne and I headed back to New York, where maybe five months later, out of the blue I got a call from Gerald Stone. I knew him from his ABC glory days in the 1960s, but he was now a Channel 9 news boss. Gerald announced that he was starting an Australian *60 Minutes* show, with some crack ABC journos, covering the world, with a pretty much unlimited budget. Was I interested?

I laughed and told him I'd had the same offer from Channel 7. But Stone insisted Kerry Packer had just bought the CBS rights and *60 Minutes* now belonged to the Nine Network. I couldn't have known this at the time, of course, and maybe they wouldn't have done it as well as Nine, but *60 Minutes*'s runaway success would help Seven lose the ratings for the next twenty years.

When I told Stone that I was certainly interested, he asked me for a recent story so he could show Kerry Packer who I was. I sent him my *Four Corners* yarn on Alan Bond in Newport, figuring that was probably the way to go given Sir Frank's America's Cup infatuation. I couldn't have been more off the mark. Many years later, at the time he sold the network to Bond, Kerry told me that although he loved sport he couldn't stomach the America's Cup, which he called 'as boring as f***ing batshit'. Packer couldn't remember ever seeing my Bond story either. So I'd clearly left an indelible mark on Kezza!

I must say I had some deep reservations about leaving the cloisters of the ABC. Dianne, along with her father and my mother, was nervous. All three believed it was a bit reckless to risk a promising ABC career on a commercial show that had no guaranteed future.

But the decision was mine. To me *60 Minutes* felt instinctively right. I liked the team Stone was assembling, and, besides, Dianne and I were both ready to go home. As much as we still loved the unbridled hedonism of New York, our month in Sydney had been an exhilarating reminder of how much we'd missed our families and how good the Aussie lifestyle was.

Oddly enough, while putting clothes away when we'd returned to New York after Christmas, at the back of my sock drawer I had come across a crumpled letter from Dan Speight, my old Sydney radio boss and mentor. Three or four years earlier, he'd written to offer me the prized Canberra correspondent's job, which I'd promptly knocked back. Dianne and I were still having too much fun in the Big Apple at the time. But Dan was a wise old codger. As I sat on the edge of the bed and reread his letter, I was taken by how astute he had been:

If you want to stay on in New York, well that's all right. But I promise you, there will come a time when 'home' – and all that encompasses – will become more important. It will take over. It may be in a year's time or ten. But it will happen, believe me.

I remember thinking at the time: 'What would silly old Dan know? This is not war-torn revolutionary China [where he'd been a correspondent]. This is New York, New York – a helluva town.'

He was right: it had happened, even in this helluva town. It was time.

But after a number of calls from Gerald Stone, updating me with plans and promises, the phone went quiet. I began to smell a repeat of the Channel 7 experience.

So, as New York turned into a summer furnace and knowing I faced a pretty hectic ABC schedule in coming months, I went on holiday.

Dianne and I had discovered a tiny Caribbean-island hide-away called St Martin. It's a half-French, half-Dutch paradise that specialises in sunburn and pina coladas. We were indulging in both when an old-fashioned cablegram arrived, hand-delivered by a courier on a bike, asking me to 'CALL PETER MEAKIN URGENT'. I had no idea who Meakin was, but I called as urgently as I could.

On a balmy Caribbean night we drove our rented topless Citroën down to the island's telegraph station, handing Meakin's number across the one-man desk. Then we waited outside for a couple of hours for somebody to switch me via Kingston, Miami, Paris and London to Sydney. I stood in an outdoor phone booth, shouting at the starry night, with all the locals tuned in to my strange conversation across the world. Meakin informed me that Stone was meeting with Kerry Packer and the Nine board that afternoon to get the final green light. So, he asked, was I in or out?

Take a deep breath, Raymond.

Yep, count me in!

The die was cast. Commercial TV here I come.

*   *   *

I gave the ABC three months' notice. Dianne and I had just returned from Edmonton, Canada, where I'd been covering the Commonwealth Games, when Talbot Duckmanton swanned through the New York office. It was a perfect time to talk to him about my decision. After thirteen amazing years in which I'd been privileged with opportunities I could only dream about, it wasn't going to be easy. Duckers had once told me I could stay in New York reporting from North America indefinitely. It had seemed like a rolled-gold offer.

I must say I felt a bit like a deserter, if not a traitor. The GM took me downstairs for a coffee and quietly listened to my reasons for leaving. He puffed his pipe and calmly offered me a job on executive row back in Sydney. Knowing the kind of sporting tragic I am, he dangled the position of director of sport in front of me. It was worth more money than the *60 Minutes* contract, which I hadn't yet signed. But living amongst the carpet strollers was of absolutely no interest to me. 'We all get offers from the commercial stations,' he said. 'Some people accept them. But when the winds blow cold, they usually come back to the ABC, knocking on the door.'

Any lingering doubts I may have had suddenly disappeared. That instant I made up my mind that no matter what happened, no matter how cold the winds blew for me in commercial TV, I would not come knocking on Duckers' door.

*   *   *

Commercial television was a whole different galaxy from my old world at Aunty ABC.

Don't get me wrong, I loved the change from day one. It was just very, very different. It was fast and exciting and great fun. It had none of the public-service feel of the ABC, where you still had to fill out blue forms in triplicate and where there were strict demarcation lines about who did what job. At Nine, people just did it.

But probably the biggest difference was that commercial TV was impelled by a rampant publicity department. (I didn't know if the ABC even had a publicity department; if it did, I'd never heard from anyone in it.) At Channel 9 they were mostly young, glamorous women full of ideas and adrenaline – and with an unquenchable thirst for champagne. Months before the show was even launched, I found myself in the epicentre of a swirl of newspaper articles, radio interviews and spreads in all Packer's glossy mags. The full catastrophe. His weekly news magazine, *The Bulletin*, had a racy cover story on how the network's reputation was riding on three virtual unknowns, the Three Musketeers, Negus, Leslie and Martin. Gerald Stone kept insisting our status as unknowns would soon change, and it did. Clearly KP wanted *60 Minutes* to work. If it didn't, well, look out! There were more than fifty jobs riding on the show. Like me, George Negus and half the team had burnt their bridges with the ABC.

Although Dianne was an integral part of my decision to move to commercial television, from the outset she was a reluctant media performer. She loathed the limelight, resenting any intrusion into her private life. She got even more protective when our children, Jenna and Luke, arrived. I doubt the publicity department had come across anyone quite like her; they were more accustomed to one or two notorious wives who hogged the spotlight almost as much as the stars. It took publicity a while to get the message that my contract didn't include Dianne. Still, she would occasionally acquiesce to a photo or an interview. More often she'd find herself snapped at an opening night or some social event that I'd dragged her along to. She was constantly amazed when somebody in the grocery aisle at Woolies would recognise her from a magazine photo published months before. She wasn't bothered by the pictures themselves – she usually looked great, anyway – she just hated the attention.

In years to come, even when I was up for a Gold Logie, we would avoid the red-carpet parade – with all the flashing bulbs and adoring crowds – and instead make our way through the side doors of the casino where the event was held, or occasionally through the kitchen. Dianne thought it was hilarious to stop and talk with the chefs about the night's meal rather than smile for *TV Week*.

Ian Leslie and his vivacious wife, Jan, had two small children, which was a rarity in the early years of *60 Minutes*. We'd occasionally join them in one of those 'at home with the family' spreads for *The Australian Women's Weekly*. George Negus was much more likely to feature in a Sunday paper with his shirt buttons undone and his cowboy boots propped on a stool, or cooking up a pasta storm in his kitchen.

Negus, who started his career at *The Australian*, was your quintessential newspaper journo, born for television. The medium maketh the man. He was the New Age, male-feminist Balmain cowboy, with an opinion on everything from football to Philadelphia cream cheese. With a distinctive moustache that seemed to drip down into his chest hairs, and his loud, nasal, Aussie voice, he was an easy target for satire and comedy, like Paul Hogan's iconic George Fungus character. Yet it was this instant recognition, along with his remarkable reporting skills, that I believe made him the most valuable asset to *60 Minutes* in the early months, when we struggled to establish the show's identity. Had it not been for Negus, I sometimes wonder whether we'd have survived and gone on to become arguably the most successful Australian TV show ever – along with *Hey Hey It's Saturday*. As well as spending thirty years at the top of the ratings, *60 Minutes* has pulled in about 300 million dollars in revenue for the Nine Network. It's no wonder Kerry wanted it to work.

While I knew and liked Negus from my ABC days, having been in New York I had no idea who Ian Leslie was when I joined *60 Minutes*, except for reading that he'd been an award-winning news reporter at Channel 10. He proved to be much more than that. Amongst other things, Ian would become a legend at *60 Minutes* for buying carpets and marble coffee tables overseas, and getting his wife to put the phone alongside the radio so he could listen to his beloved Parramatta footy team win the Grand Final. Leslie was in Russia, I think, at the time, but he heard every minute of the game in Sydney.

He also pulled off some great *60 Minutes* yarns. It was in a Philippines jungle that rebels held a pistol to Ian's head and pulled the trigger. Thankfully, the gun was empty. (Rumour has it that Leso had to take time out to change his daks, though.)

The other key to *60 Minutes*'s success was American-born executive producer Gerald Stone, a veteran reporter who left Ohio to cover the Vietnam War and never went home. Stone was simply the best. He was certainly the best executive producer I ever saw in television, and was an impeccable judge of stories and staff. He pulled together an amazing amalgam of producers, camera crews and editors, better than any program in Australia had seen before. I have no doubt about that.

With *60 Minutes* Stone wanted to achieve something quite special, something very different in Australian public-affairs television: the best pictures, from the most exotic places, and interviews with the newsmakers themselves, in a storytelling style that was simple and straightforward. As Gerald used to say,

'Let *Four Corners* tell the tedious story of the Great Flood – we'll do a riveting profile of Noah.' It was a formula that Stone stuck to rigidly, and it proved to be tremendously successful.

You didn't want to be around Stone when something went wrong or somebody stuffed up. We called Gerald's temper his force-nine gale. But his temper wasn't the reason people worked so hard for Stone. It wasn't fear, it was total respect. He was without peer.

*　　　*　　　*

Channel 9 had paid CBS big bucks to buy the rights to produce *60 Minutes* in Australia, paying for the name, the format – even the stopwatch. So expectations were high.

When you look back on it now, the first show, which aired in February 1979, was pretty darn ordinary. A bland story about a multimillion-dollar cigarette-smuggling racket across state borders by Ian Leslie; my dull report from Ohio about future shock, with homes wired for computers; and a George Negus yarn called 'Primal Scream', about emotionally disturbed people.

The show rated poorly and was panned by most critics. The front page of *The Australian* carried the prediction that Australia's most costly, most trumpeted current-affairs show wouldn't be current for too much longer. Besides that, *60 Minutes* ran up against Peter Luck's juggernaut *This Fabulous Century*, on Channel 7, which for some months seemed unbeatable.

Suddenly, Talbot Duckmanton was looking prescient. We were all living on borrowed time.

Kerry Packer called in the show's producers for a 'Pull your fingers out, stop wasting my money' pep talk. The reporters weren't invited. When one bold producer suggested to Kezza that

60 Minutes would soon win the Sunday night 7.30 spot, Packer snorted and informed him he was 'a f***ing imbecile'. He bet them all it would take much longer.

Fortunately it didn't. Over the next month or so the show seemed to find its rhythm, and we started to climb in the ratings. Then, early one Friday night, we got word from the Channel 9 gatehouse that the Big Fella had driven in and was heading towards our cottage. Beer and wine bottles miraculously disappeared – seemingly evaporated – into bins and desk drawers and holes in the wall.

Packer charged in with the network's diminutive CEO, Sam Chisholm, in tow. It was a bit like Schwarzenegger arriving with Danny DeVito. After some idle chatter Kerry announced that he'd come to pay up on his debts to the producers. He made a big deal of the fact he never welshed on a bet – at which point he smiled, turned to Sam and said, 'Righto, Chizo, pay 'em the money I owe 'em!' Which Sam did, in cash – out of his pocket, not Kerry's.

A few weeks later Negus, Leslie and I were summoned to Packer's Park Street parlour for lunch, along with Chisholm and Stone. Kerry Packer used to serve up the finest wines, even though he hadn't touched a drop of alcohol himself since his late teens. Kerry told us he was very happy with the show. With the fine wines and the approval of the Big Fella, our debut lunch was going along fine – until Kerry asked us if we were happy in the service. It was a question that probably didn't need an answer. Nevertheless, Negus chimed in: 'I'll tell you what I appreciate, Kerry. It's the way you obviously make your complaints known direct to Gerald and let us get on with our job.'

Ohhh. Wrong answer, George, wrong answer.

The excessively large bloke who owned the network paused for a moment, then he rose to his feet.

They were really big feet.

Standing directly opposite Negus, he blocked out the light from the window – in fact, he blocked out the world – casting a shadow across our tomato 'n' leek soup. He pointed at Negus's heart as he spoke.

'Listen, son, the truth of the matter is' – that's a phrase Kerry Packer used a lot, meaning 'the truth according to me is' – 'if I ever want you to f***ing know what I think, son, *you will be the first to f***ing well know*. I promise you.'

It was a bit like Clint Eastwood saying 'Read my lips'. Kerry's explosive temper was tantamount to a .44 Magnum anyway.

*   *   *

In the first few years feeding the demands of *60 Minutes* with three new stories every week meant that Negus, Leslie and I would often be on the road for six weeks at a time and away from home for half the year.

Dianne settled easily into life back in Sydney and didn't seem to mind my itinerant pack-the-suitcase, see-ya-later lifestyle. That surprised me a bit. I feared she might have serious withdrawal symptoms after our decade in New York. The Big Apple stint had given us the space to grow, together and individually. She had delighted in the freedom and anonymity of such a stimulating place. Living next door to eight million people, it's no problem getting lost.

By stark contrast, back in Sydney we moved into a suburban brick-veneer house we'd bought a few years earlier as an investment, on the edge of the northern-suburbs bush. And I mean bush. Our backyard stretched for thousands of hectares of gum trees and rocky gullies. And the silence at night was deafening,

169

after the din of New York City. To her credit Dianne lasted there for a couple of months, much of the time on her own, as I whisked around the world. I wouldn't have stayed there for a week. So the moment we could, we shifted to a rented apartment in North Sydney, overlooking the busy harbour, and our lifestyle went up a notch or two.

Dianne had resumed relations with her family, back in that warm cocoon that offered unconditional love and comfort. She and her younger sister, Susan, had had little in common as teenagers, sharing a small bedroom and fighting like the proverbial Kilkenny cats. But as women they complemented each other in style and personality and are impossibly close. Suzie had three children, as did Dianne's elder brother, Brian. My sisters produced ten children between them. They were all lively, interesting kids, and we loved being with them. Dianne and I happily adopted the role of favourite aunt and uncle. You know the routine: buy 'em presents, take 'em on holidays and then hand 'em back!

There was no expectation from our families that we should have children ourselves. Having been married and away in New York for so long, it seemed the pressure was off. Besides, life was hectic and I was away more than I was home. Apart from having six weeks off at Christmas, which Dianne and I seemed to fill with still more travel, she also managed to come overseas with me on several *60 Minutes* trips. (For some strange reason she tended to favour London or Los Angeles over Lahore.)

Our Aussie bias was confirmed daily: Sydney is the most beautiful city in the world, and we were lucky enough to live there. I caught blue swimmer crabs with Dianne's dad from his 11-foot tinny in Port Hacking, and I watched my Mighty Rabbitohs footy team in vain. Only a premiership could possibly have made life any better than this.

As a job *60 Minutes* was made for me. I was getting paid to roam the world with a great bunch of mates, wining and dining at Kerry Packer's expense, and tell stories to a weekly TV audience. Locked deep in my DNA is the spirit of a journeyer. As certain as brown eyes or a gap in the teeth. I'm the best tourist I know. Around the block or across the world. Maybe it's my wanderlust Sagittarian soul, or maybe it just became a habit, given my itinerant childhood. Whatever the cause, I figure I've clocked up more than a million air miles, across a hundred borders. And a few hundred thousand kilometres more riding the roads and rails. Just hand me my trusty camera, an airline ticket and a glass of something frothy, then you can send me to hell and back.

So imagine my thrill at crisscrossing the globe with *60 Minutes*, one day flying higher than migrating birds in a bulky tin can of a B-52, the next jumping in a Cessna in a tropical thunderstorm, or sipping Turkish mud coffee on a dilapidated ferry out of Gallipoli. Once I'd been happy in the luggage racks of a dogbox on the rusty New South Wales country railroad tracks. Now I could say I'd been treated to a bed, a valet and gourmet fare on the legendary Orient Express.

Let me tell you about the Orient Express for a moment, because it sums up the best – yet simultaneously the most frustrating – aspects of reporting on a magic-carpet ride like *60 Minutes*.

A trip on the Orient Express is a retro journey, harking back to an age when it was not just the fastest but also the most luxurious train ride of all time. We were travelling with the ghosts of Mata Hari, Greta Garbo and Agatha Christie. We climbed aboard the antique sleeping carriages behind the big blue and white locos at the fabulous old Sirkeci Station, in Istanbul. A Sufi dance troupe of whirling dervishes farewelled us, spinning themselves almost into orbit across the ornate tiled floor of the Customs Hall. It was all fantastic colour and movement, a spectacular start to our story. Our backdrop was one of the world's most exotic cities, with the Blue Mosque and a skyline of minarets.

As a *60 Minutes* yarn, it went downhill from there.

It was only the first day. Heading into Bulgaria, towards the setting sun, we began planning our very own *Murder on the Orient Express*, targeting some of our absurdly wealthy fellow travellers. Let me set the scene for you. There were about forty high-paying customers on this elegant trip from Istanbul through Sofia, Belgrade and Lucerne, down into Paris. Now, our strict deal with the sponsors, American Express, was that we wouldn't film passengers who didn't want to be on camera. It was non-negotiable.

From the outset a group of seven of them made it perfectly clear they didn't want 'any goddamned cameras any place near us'. And this irascible, annoying septet went out of their way to mix with everybody else, every time our lens appeared: when the vintage French champagne bubbled, during the five-star dinners, at the telling of war stories in the state room, amidst the singalong round the grand piano and the jitterbugging on the dance floor. We simply couldn't film or get close to the rest of the passengers without the obnoxious ones deliberately getting into shot.

Like a gambler reaching into empty pockets, we kept trying to find a way to salvage the story. By now we were skint and flush out of ideas.

I guess the last hurrah came when a magic storytelling moment was blown for us.

Our millionaires' express stopped at a dismal grey terminus

just outside of Belgrade. Heading in the other direction, right alongside us, was a proletariat all-stations commuter train. It was dangerously overcrowded with a mob of straphanging Yugoslav factory workers going home. Through their grimy-windowed despair they spied our wealthy pleasure seekers quaffing genteel afternoon cocktails, in reefer jackets and cravats.

It was one of those 'capitalism meets communism' encounters that a journalist dies for. The picture was worth the proverbial thousand words.

But as our unflappable cameraman, Nick Lee, panned from the sullen workers – who looked about as happy as caged animals on their way to the slaughter yards – he found our 'magnificent seven' dopes waving at the camera. Or reaching forward to put a hand over his lens. I thought Nicholas was about to job somebody. Maybe *seven* somebodies.

Anyway, that was *it* for the luxury train tale. Unlike us, the yarn was going nowhere.

We had little option but to grab an expensive cocktail, select a canapé or three and mingle with the bourgeoisie as if we belonged. It was no good trying to film.

Actually, what Nick did was reach across the ideological abyss. It was like a classic melancholic scene from a Charlie Chaplin flick. And it cracked me up. He handed two cut-crystal glasses filled with the vintage French champers to a couple of our working-class straphangers. They smiled, saluted and swigged the grog. They also souvenired the expensive glassware as the train pulled out of the station and we waved goodbye.

So often, filming a *60 Minutes* story would be a variation of that rail-journey experience, with rich images of places and characters, moments of panic and joy and frustration.

*   *   *

In Warsaw, the endurance of the human spirit snuck up and unexpectedly took my breath away. It was a decade before the Soviets' Iron Curtain was lifted off the Eastern bloc, and the dour Russian presence was pervasive. There were severe food shortages in the capital of Poland and endless queues, even for the most basic stuff. But believe it or not, I interviewed a lady who was queuing up for . . . chocolates! She was an elderly woman in boots and a heavy coat. As we filmed her, the line slowly wound its way past a magnificent monument to Frédéric Chopin, musical genius and fellow countryman. It was a stark reminder of Poland's rich past, in the midst of the present gloom. When I asked her why she was standing in the bitter cold for two or three hours just to buy some chocolate, she looked at me kindly, as if I was a halfwit.

'I stand here for my grandchildren,' she said.

'I could understand it if you queued for bread or meat,' I suggested, 'but isn't chocolate a bourgeois luxury?'

Again she smiled at me, almost condescendingly.

'Oh no, sir,' she explained, 'chocolate is an essential part of being a child. The Russians may destroy our culture, but we must never let them destroy our children.'

I suspect Chopin heard that Polish grandmother's cry from the heart and smiled approvingly.

Later in the old city of Warsaw, in a beautiful medieval square that the Poles rebuilt brick by precious brick after the Germans blew it up in the Second World War, we witnessed one of those magical Hollywood moments. We were going off to dinner at a restaurant that specialised in wild boar and other game. From one side of the elegant snow-covered square ran a handsome Polish soldier boy in uniform; from the other ran a beautiful young woman in a boot-length coat with a high fur collar. They united in the middle, and he swept her off her feet, twirling her as they kissed.

It was a classic film reunion, which they were happy to repeat for our camera. It was young love, as pure as the falling snowflakes. Yet as warm as a fireside embrace. We offered to pay for them to go to dinner, minus the camera crew. They smiled, thanked us and suggested they had other things to do. I can't think what. Incidentally, the driver of our small TV van – a true Polish patriot – once told me of his dilemma about invaders. 'If I had the choice,' he said over a vodka, 'I guess I would kill the Russians for duty and the Germans for pleasure.' He meant it too.

Another of my many memorable postcards for *60 Minutes*, in terms of the sheer beauty of the pictures we got, was Romania. We were doing a story about Australians flocking to try out the totalitarian state's spas, mud baths and mystery chemical concoctions that were all supposed to be the elixir of youth. It had become a booming geriatric industry. We were desperate for an opening picture sequence for the story, from our wonderfully eccentric cameraman Phil Donoghue. On our way back to Bucharest from the countryside we spied a gypsy caravan coming towards us, clip-clopping along the narrow causeway. It had all the magic ingredients we needed.

A stallion pulled the brightly painted wagon, which was driven by a bare-chested, dark-skinned man in a pair of jeans with long boots and unkempt hair. Beside him sat his two naked kids, while a voluptuous woman stood at the caravan's window, breasts swaying. It was straight out of a Fellini movie, with the gypsy waving to the camera as he passed, flashing a dangerous smile.

But wait, there was more.

Behind the fast-moving caravan the camera panned to a mother goose and her goslings, which stepped onto the road in front of us and stopped to look at the passing parade. It was a magnificent shot, but in those days of 16-millimetre film you couldn't be certain the focus and lighting were perfect until the film was processed. We looked at Phil as he punched the air, saying, 'Yeah, I got it.' (Pause.) 'I thiiinnnk . . .'

He had it all right.

*　　　*　　　*

The appeal of *60 Minutes* was its unpredictability. One minute the menace of a shirtless gypsy, the next Paul Newman, decked out in a soft-pink terry-towelling tracksuit. Still, the macho heart-throb was ready for action.

We met Paul Newman outside Atlanta, Georgia, for a *60 Minutes* profile. He was in his late 50s at the time and was spending the weekend driving ridiculously fast in his Datsun 280ZX turbo racing-machine.

Newman, who'd become capriciously shy with the media, agreed to talk to us because his spaghetti sauces and salad dressings were about to go on sale in Australia. (Newman's food ventures ended up handing out an incredible two hundred and fifty million dollars to his various philanthropic causes – a reflection of his brand-name value.) On the day of the big race, Paul and his wife, Joanne Woodward, the Academy Award-winning actress, were encamped just down the corridor. Paul came by after an early-morning jog wearing the aforementioned pink tracksuit. It was a look that only Butch Cassidy could possibly get away with. He stopped to say g'day, told us a couple of lurid jokes about racing-car drivers and waxed on about the weather. We had to remind ourselves that this was a Hollywood legend and not just the bloke next door.

Even more unlikely was seeing Newman and his co-driver dressed in their knitted Kevlar, fire-resistant suits standing behind the mammoth Pantech Racemobile transporter, as they played with electric-controlled *toy* cars for about two hours.

(I just couldn't imagine Hombre or Cool Hand Luke indulging in such small boy's antics.)

Newman continued to be full of surprises. When one of our crew appeared with some ice-cold Foster's cans, the macho star's eyes lit up. 'Hey, I wanna try one of those. Get your cameras out: this is the first time I've ever drunk a Foster's beer.' We filmed his first taste of genuine Aussie culture and he gave it the thumbs up!

Late that afternoon Newman rolled his Datsun – hopefully nothing to do with his swig of Foster's – and had to abandon the race. On his walk back from the track a couple of besotted female fans ambushed him for an autograph, or anything else that was on offer – like a kiss. Joanne Woodward was holding his hand at the time, obviously relieved he was okay, but nonetheless upset to have seen him crash. She turned on the women, guarding him like a Tibetan mastiff. You could almost hear Tammy Wynette telling her to stand by her man. They got the message and quickly backed off.

*   *   *

My best memories of *60 Minutes* over thirty years are of the crews I travelled with even more than the stories. Gerald Stone's selection of producers and camera teams was extraordinary, in both their talents and their temperament. Despite the pressure-cooker lifestyle, blow-ups were rare. I got a bloke named Andrew Haughton as my producer. Talk about the daily double. Andrew and I did a hundred stories together over the first six years. Working with Andrew Haughton was as smooth as a Swiss chronometer. He was a canny Scot (I always wanted to write that) from Stirling, up in Braveheart country. After an early flying career, being launched off British aircraft carriers, he married an Australian lady, had a couple of Aussie kids and put down his roots here.

When you spend years together working crazy hours, eating indigestible food and sleeping standing up, it has to be fun or else it gets too damn hard. With Andrew it was always fun. He was smart, skilful, good company, and a wonderful raconteur.

When *60 Minutes* first started, a typical overseas trip with Haughton might include a story on the Yorkshire Ripper, in Leeds; saving elephants in Kenya; the Sydney String Quartet playing beautiful music in snowy Salzburg; the eruption of political turmoil in Poland; a salacious yarn about the porn business in Sweden; a succulent tale about La Tour d'Argent in Paris, one of the world's most famous restaurants; and maybe on the way home a report about Beirut being blown up. It was that kind of amazing journalist's smorgasbord. We'd have a week for each story – to get there, film it, script it and ship the film back to Sydney. When Jana Wendt joined the team, we added an extra camera crew, and life was supposed to become a little less hectic. It didn't. Although Jana would become a huge asset.

Chapter 14
That Was a Bit Close

I once waded across a waist-deep billabong as clear as pea soup somewhere in a swamp outside Darwin with Professor Graham Webb, who is the foremost expert on Australian crocodiles, walking out to a small grassy island to collect their eggs. It was, I still believe, the most stupidly dangerous thing I've ever done.

And I've done a few.

I once burst into a rat's nest of a house in the highly volatile Los Angeles barrio district about two o'clock in the morning with a modern-day bounty hunter. That was pretty silly, too. The bounty hunter and his three accomplices, who were licensed and heavily armed, were there to arrest some Hispanic felons and collect the rewards – like in the days of the American Wild West. I've never felt so guilty as a journalist, or so scared. As the bounty hunters broke open the front door and burst in brandishing their pistols and shotguns, followed by us wielding our TV camera and bright lights, women suddenly appeared in dressing-gowns, screaming abuse, children shrieked in terror and half a dozen blokes in nothing but jeans or underwear jumped through open windows heading for an alley. The LA police chief told us later that we might easily have been machine-gunned to death, or at least hacked with machetes. The things you do for love. Or work.

Over the years I've been in the middle of a few civil wars, from El Salvador and Panama to Iran and Afghanistan. They can all be a little hard on the adrenal glands, too. Driving through the empty streets of Kandahar in an open truck with Soviet-friendly Afghan soldiers looking for snipers was scary. As was refusing to hand over our secret film to an angry Russian colonel in Kabul, who pulled out his pistol and threatened us.

But it doesn't always have to be a war zone. Just walking through the dank alleyways of west Belfast with Gerry Adams, the alleged boss of the Provisional IRA, made me feel like a target. Only weeks after we filmed with him, he was badly shot up outside a Belfast courthouse.

I was once sitting on a plane from Heathrow to Belfast when Adams's arch-rival, the fanatical Protestant Ian Paisley, staggered down the aisle. With his fat, snarling lips, his manic eyes and his wild shock of grey hair, he looked like one of those ugly gargoyles you see hanging off medieval buildings. It wasn't how he looked that frightened me, but who he was. For the rest of the short flight I expected a bomb to go off. It's the totally unexpected that can really set the pulse racing.

*   *   *

One afternoon in Iran under Ayatollah Khomeini's repressive regime it nearly all turned horribly wrong for me. A blizzard had closed Tehran airport, so we were diverted and held in the exotic southern city of Shiraz, known for poets, wine and nightingales.

After endless hours of flying and delays Shiraz somehow didn't seem quite so romantic to us. It was tense.

When we finally did make it to Tehran, the Persian minibus driver who collected us at the airport had a 'Best of Fleetwood Mac' tape playing loudly. Tehran, with its snow clouds, sleet and chill winds, was as cold as any place I'd ever known. Fleetwood Mac's 'Don't Stop' seemed like the perfect anthem, the mantra for Khomeini's Iran: 'Yesterday's gone, Yesterday's gone'. The Islamic fundamentalists had kicked out Shah Pahlavi and his corrupt family. Yesterday was surely gone. Now every time I hear Fleetwood Mac's enduring song on the radio, the images of that trip come back to haunt me.

It was early 1980, and we were there with the hope of interviewing the sixty or so American diplomats who were being held hostage in the US embassy. The country was prickling with fears of an impending US Special Forces strike, so the Ayatollah had kicked all Western journalists out of Iran, except for one Canadian TV crew in the south of the country. And now us. The Iranian embassy in Canberra had suggested we might be allowed in to meet the hostages, and they had told us they'd certainly support us in our efforts. An interview with the Americans would be a world exclusive.

The Iranians did allow us inside the US embassy to film what could loosely be called a press conference. Afterwards, a couple of the student militants who'd stormed the embassy agreed to be interviewed. But they offered us no American hostages to interview. 'Not today, I'm sorry,' the scruffy khaki-clad ringleaders apologised. 'Maybe tomorrow.' Again I heard Fleetwood Mac in my head: 'Don't stop thinking about tomorrow.'

What I got instead of an interview with a US hostage was one of the scariest moments of my life.

A noisy, angry crowd had gathered in the square outside the embassy compound. As we left the building, we encountered maybe ten thousand people – most of them men – with placards in English saying 'Put the Killer Shah on Trial', 'Death to the Shah' and 'Death to America'. The usual diatribes. Some of them burnt US flags, while mobs of students chanted 'Die America' to the cameras. These were the antics we expected, approved by Khomeini because they would make it onto Iranian TV, then guaranteed to be shown in America and Europe. But this mob was angry, volatile and unfriendly towards us, thinking we were Americans.

In the crowded square, which was now sombre as day had turned to night, I suddenly found myself separated from everybody: crew, interpreter and driver. I was being shouted at in Farsi and I had no idea what they were on about. But I did have a sense it might soon turn ugly. Two or three blokes bellowed something at me and slapped me on the shoulder. They laughed at each other, but there was nothing amusing about their mood. Each slap was a bit rougher, harder than the one before. Now I knew I was alone and probably in a bit of strife.

Suddenly, two young men pushed their way through the protestors and shook my hand. They had broad Aussie accents. Australian Iranians, they were back in Tehran to visit their families. As luck would have it, they were dedicated *60 Minutes* fans. In all my travels I don't think I've ever been so happy to hear an Aussie voice. They explained everything to the mob and even argued with a couple of non-believers (probably SBS viewers). Having turned the tide for the moment, like a couple of lifesavers my two new mates put their arms around me and escorted me about a kilometre to the safety of our minibus.

Over the next week or so I got a rare glimpse into the aftermath of the Shah's reign. We went to the cemetery, where hundreds of families grieved for loved ones who, they told us, had been killed by the Shah's secret police. I interviewed a man who had formerly been the Shah's dog handler, at the Shah's magnificent Summer Palace just outside Tehran. He was a delightful old gentleman, cultured and with excellent English. 'The Shah would come every day,' he told me, 'to play and talk with the dogs.'

'Did he talk to you?' I asked.

'Oh no, sir. Never. Only the dogs.'

A shantytown spread for several kilometres below what had been the Shah's glittering palace on a hill overlooking Tehran. The huts and lean-tos of the desperately poor families were linked by paths of frozen mud. The residents fossicked in the garbage piles. They were rural workers, we discovered, thrown off their land when the Shah nationalised the farms.

It was bitterly cold, with a raw wind that cut to the bone. We filmed two little girls playing with a toddler, a boy of about two who had no pants on despite the freezing temperatures. He slipped on the icy mud and hurt himself, his cries bringing an anxious woman from one of the nearby huts. When she saw us, she went berserk, letting her head covering slip from her face as she screamed like a banshee at our camera. The woman's face was lined and worn out. We figured she was about fifty, maybe a bit older, and probably the little boy's grandmother.

Our feisty interpreter, Rasa, quickly intervened. She explained to the enraged grandmother that we were filming a story about the excesses and cruelty of the Shah. Rasa said we'd been filming the palaces and prisons and empty fields, and that we'd spoken to the mullahs and many grieving families. The peasant woman lowered her voice, speaking in Farsi, the Persian tongue.

I asked Rasa what she'd said.

She explained that the woman was in fact the boy's mother,

and barely twenty-four years old. She guessed the woman must have married at thirteen or fourteen. An uneducated farmer's wife with six children, she and her family had been driven off their family plot by the Shah's soldiers.

Rasa went on, 'She says, "If you truly wish to film the truth about the Shah, then you must film our hearts. You must film our hearts." '

I was stunned by her answer. 'You must film our hearts.' Where did that come from?

It is as if millennia of classical poetry lie in the Persian DNA.

> Indeed the Idols I have loved so long,
> Have done my Credit in this world much wrong;
> Have drown'd my Glory in a Shallow cup,
> And sold my Reputation for a song.
> *The Rubaiyat of Omar Khayyam*

*   *   *

I had just come off that ten-day foray in the dangerous vortex that was Khomeini's Iranian revolution when I found myself in a very different high-adrenaline real-life TV melodrama, this time in Spain. In Tehran I had stood a good chance of getting bashed by angry mobs just for being there. In Spain I faced a prison term for kidnap.

The story was essentially this. After a bitter divorce from her Spanish husband, Jose, a Tasmanian mother named Kayleen had been granted custody of their baby son, Guido, by the Australian courts. Kayleen, who was in her late thirties, figured Guido was probably the only child she'd ever have. But in Barcelona, where Jose had fled with twenty-month-old Guido, the law gives the father automatic rights to the baby. Kayleen, who'd been apart from Guido for many months, was desperate to get him back.

A craggy old investigative journalist from Adelaide named Dick Wordley had left the newspaper game and turned his hand to hunting down children who'd been kidnapped, usually by their fathers. Wordley was one of those police roundsmen who end up thinking and acting like the cops they cover. Over just a few years Dick had managed to return fourteen children to their rightful parents. Kayleen's dad, a big raw-boned Tassie publican named Len Thorne, hired Dick to try to recover Guido. Dick called this case Operation Snatchback, because that's what would happen if things went according to plan. It was too good a story to miss, so off we raced to north-eastern Spain.

For a few days nothing much happened, except that we secretly filmed an uncomfortable meeting between Kayleen and Jose, who had turned up without the baby. Then things got interesting. When a lunch was arranged in a local café, Jose surprisingly turned up with Guido in his arms. The elements suddenly fell into place, as if everybody was reading Dick Wordley's script: father, mother, baby and rescuer all at the same restaurant, while Dick, Len Thorne and I lay in wait outside. Len, who'd been an Aussie Rules ruckman, was big enough, and quite prepared, to physically look after his daughter and grandson if he had to. It was such an emotional wrangle, we all knew it might come to that. When Jose went to the bathroom, Kayleen snatched her baby boy and ran to my rented Peugeot, which happened to be parked round the corner. I drove through tiny back lanes until we hit the freeway, heading for Madrid hundreds of kilometres away, running on adrenaline and the excitement of the chase, yet realising this was a deadly serious game. The plans were all fluid, because we didn't know what might happen next. Once

Jose sounded the alarm, the police might intercept one or all of us. I knew I had to get away from Barcelona quickly and had to get off the freeway, where I suspected the police would be looking. Dick, Len and the rest of the *60 Minutes* team split into two other cars and took different routes. The plan was to rendezvous the next morning in central Madrid, switch cars and drive to Málaga, on the coast, where a speedboat was waiting to zip us to freedom in British Gibraltar. It was Boy's Own adventure stuff – except this was real. These were the days before mobile phones, so we had no way of getting in touch until our planned breakfast meeting. For the next twelve hours I was on my own with the fugitive mother and her stolen child.

Upset by all the drama, Guido cried most of the way as I sped to Madrid. Still, the getaway had worked like a precision military operation.

Figuring police wouldn't look for us there, I booked into a sleazy truckies' overnight motel near the airport. It turned out to be a cheap brothel, with a lot of bargaining going on in the corridors. Nobody even noticed us. Guido refused to settle and kept crying until I went to a nearby canteen to get some milk for him and takeaway paella for Kayleen and me. Like truck stops everywhere, the food was excellent. Kayleen had packed clothes, jars of baby food and nappies.

The motel room had a double bed, a tattered couch and some essential paintings of matadors. When Guido finally dropped off, I sat on the floor in the dark, drinking a Spanish beer. I listened to heavy steelcapped boots pound up and down the concrete walkway outside our room and thought, 'Here come the Federales.' They were probably only truckies going back to work.

When we regrouped the next morning over omelettes and coffee, Dick – our very own 007 – called for a sudden change of plans. It was decided that I should dump the incriminating getaway Peugeot in Madrid and hightail it out of Spain. So I was gone. Pronto. At least I got my exit visa stamped. The others all did a runner, zipping round the corner to Gibraltar.

Within four days everybody was safely back in Tassie, including Guido, who'd finally stopped crying. Dick Wordley had pulled off baby rescue number fifteen. It made for a good story, too.

*   *   *

There's a frightening randomness about death in Beirut. Andrew Haughton and I went there a couple of times during the eighties, when Lebanon was the Middle East's bubbling hot spot. Our crews seemed to be always in and out of the place.

Beirut had the livid scars of a once cosmopolitan city that had been pulverised; its landscape reduced to rubble in many places. But in the remnants of its high-fashion shops and café society you could still see why it had been known as the Paris of the eastern Mediterranean. It was quite surreal. You could be sipping an espresso on the sidewalk, reading a copy of that day's *Herald Tribune,* and hear the thump of heavy guns and the rat-a-tat of submachine guns a few streets away.

Death could come casually, out of nowhere, in Beirut. On one trip we were in a taxi coming from the British Army base on the city's outskirts. It was a quiet, sunny day. Suddenly the areas we began to pass through seemed *too* quiet. We noticed the shops had all closed their shutters, the roadside car mechanics had quit working and the streets were deserted. That's when submachine guns started pumping, the sound echoing down the laneways. Our driver screamed something that sounded like panic in Arabic and flattened the accelerator. As we turned left, all hell broke out to our right, with militia hurtling out of the side streets, firing at an unseen enemy. I think it was instinct that turned our driver left even though our hotel was in the other direction. No matter what, it was a bit close.

Filming another story there in 1984, I was standing on a high ridge inside the fortified American military base. I was with a US colonel who was dressed in a heavy flak jacket and helmet. I was armed with a notebook. As he pointed out which militias controlled which part of the city below, I became conscious of a rustling in the trees above us. It sounded as if there were birds squabbling.

'I think we better take cover!' the colonel barked. 'Somebody's shooting at us.'

He didn't have to tell me again. The sniper wasn't missing us by much. We spent the next hour inside a giant concrete bunker, as heavy shells landed inside the base. Our camera crew were stranded out in the open, cowering behind sandbags.

Late that night Druze militiamen raided our hotel. We were staying in the Commodore, famous for being the residence of a parrot who whistled Beethoven's Fifth and now as a temporary home for dozens of journalists from around the world. I'd just gone to bed when a band of hooded gunmen shot a couple of alleged Lebanese drug dealers and smashed all the liquor bottles on the bar. Then they left. The surviving patrons, an American and two Polish freelance photographers, finished their beers and departed too. A few hours earlier those same drinkers had fronted the bar, visibly shaking after getting caught on the wrong side of an urban battle outside. We bought them each a stiff Scotch to calm their nerves, while they regaled us with details of the action photos they'd taken. Now the madness had come inside their pub. It was that sort of city.

It was becoming clear that Beirut was on the verge of collapsing. We knew that if we didn't get out soon, we might not make it out for a very long time – or at all – so we made plans to evacuate. The night before, the consul from the Australian embassy had taken us to dinner. Beirut was deserted, as there was a strict curfew. Only diplomats, journalists and bakers of bread were allowed on the streets at night. In the consul's yellow pock-marked Peugeot 403 sedan – the same model I'd driven on my honeymoon – we drove through total desolation surrounding the bombed American-embassy compound. He parked near a little Italian restaurant, which I seem to recall was named Mamma Maria's, and gave a couple of teenage kids a handful of dollars to make sure his car wasn't firebombed. It worked every time, he told me.

Now, the specialty of the house that night was written in chalk on a blackboard that Mamma Maria herself brought to our table. I did a double-take: 'Fresh Rabbit – Neapolitano'. Savage warfare was going on just a few blocks from us, and here was a restaurant serving fresh rabbit, Neapolitan style. I had to ask Mamma if the bunnies really were fresh.

'Si, si. Of course, signor. They bring them from the mountains this afternoon.'

I had no choice. I had to have rabbit, didn't I? If only out of respect for the rabbit hunters who had braved death just to deliver them to Mamma Maria's kitchen door.

The next afternoon we hired two old London cabs to take us to the airport. We still didn't know if we'd make it out, as the conflict was closing in. When we stopped at the passport checkpoint, directly behind the American military base, I noticed a peasant woman from the nearby refugee camp standing on the median strip in front of us. She was alone, carrying bundles of clothing and an armful of plastic bags. Her head was wrapped in a bright scarf. Then came a mighty roar. A mortar shell. One second she was standing there, then pieces of her bags and clothes exploded through the air. A mortar fired from somewhere deep in the valley had missed the American base and hit her. It was a direct hit. The checkpoint guards screamed at us to '*Go, go, go,*' so we hurtled out to the terminal. It was like a ghastly scene from a war movie. Twenty-five years later I can still remember the chaos and horror of the moment.

We spent our last hours that Saturday night standing in the airport car park watching the big guns and mortars on the hillsides fight it out – to the death. Like a macabre fireworks display. That night the insane civil war tore open the city's heart and closed Lebanon's ports and airports for five months. We got lucky and hitched a ride on the last plane out.

Three hours later, with the gory image of that poor woman still fresh in our minds, we were in a fancy hotel in Bahrain, safe and showered and sitting down to a silver-service dinner. It's a strange, strange world we live in.

* * *

The eighties are also remembered as an especially hazardous time along Israel's border with Lebanon. Late at night on one of my trips to Israel, Haughton, the crew and I drove from Tel Aviv to Nahariya, on the Mediterranean coast. The fear was palpable. That morning before dawn PLO terrorists had landed in inflatable boats and shot up a housing estate. We spoke to a still terribly traumatised South African émigré family named Shapiro who had been innocently caught in the middle of the killings. The father, who like all men in that Jewish community was armed, had actually killed a couple of the terrorists. Tragically, his wife had accidentally suffocated their baby daughter. When the terrorists burst into the apartment, she was hiding in a cupboard with their three children. Fearing for their lives, she'd held her hand tightly over the baby's mouth to stop her crying. The little girl stopped breathing. Hearing that mother's agony was one of the most terrible moments I can remember.

The next day we drove along the border and filmed heavy Israeli guns blasting into Lebanon at Metula, the location of the misnamed 'Good Fence' erected by the Israelis as protection. There was ominous talk of a Lebanese incursion that night in retaliation. We visited women and children who'd been moved to the safety of underground bunkers. We had dinner at Kibbutz Manara, a hill settlement where Leon Uris had once stayed while researching his novel *Exodus*. The young men who lived there arrived at the dinner table with a girlfriend on one arm and an AK-47 assault rifle on the other. If you looked across the Hula Valley into Lebanon, all the lights were switched off in densely populated Arab towns. There was an eerie feeling of uncertainty.

Driving back to our motel, the man we had hired as our escort, Rafi Horowitz, ex-Israeli Special Forces, asked us if we knew what to do in the event of a Katyusha rocket attack from across the border, which was now very much on the cards. We said we didn't have a clue.

'Grab your pillow and blanket, wait for a break in the firing sequence and then *run* from your motel room to the nearest bunker! Understand?'

We certainly did. Nevertheless, when we arrived back at our motel, we decided on one small drink before bed – just to take the edge off our anxiety. The building was a simple fibro affair, much like an Aussie bush motel, except it sat next to the electrified wire fence that separated us from the hill country of southern Lebanon. The woman who ran the motel said there had been regular incursions by the PLO through the fence. Just last week two locals had been killed in a night-time raid.

'You know what to do if the rockets come tonight?' she asked kindly. Without giving us time to reply, she answered the question herself: 'Don't leave your room! You have heavy wooden beds. Sleep under the beds, they'll protect you. And make sure you fully open your windows so they don't explode with the concussion from the rockets.'

We were in deep trouble. Go to the shelter? Or stay in the room? To be or not to be?

Totally confused, we decided on another small Scotch to calm the nerves. This time the woman's husband brought us the drinks. His advice was crystal clear.

'Open your windows!' Okay, so far they were in sync. 'And when the rockets start dropping, take your pillows and blankets and sleep in the bath. The bathroom is reinforced.'

Now I was really rattled.

My options were pretty limited. Unlike the other three members of the team I was staying on the ground floor. I figured that if a PLO raiding party cut their way through the electrified fence, they'd come straight in my window and slit my throat first. So I kept the window and heavy curtain tightly closed. But I did put some of my spare bedding in the bath, just in case. I figured it would be more comfortable there than under the bed if the rockets started falling. Mind you, I also thought of a quick sprint to the town bunker, which I knew was probably safest.

I barely slept all night, waiting for the first signs of attack – but mercifully it never came. Around sun-up, I was showered, dressed and sitting in the breakfast room drinking freshly squeezed Jaffa orange juice. Miraculously, I'd survived the night. Andrew wasn't far behind me. Nick Lee, the cameraman, was another mightily relieved survivor who joined us for breakfast.

What was curious was that the soundman, Peter Frager, didn't surface for at least another hour. When he did, he looked remarkably fresh and revived, saying he'd slept like a babe. When we asked how come he was so chirpy, his explanation floored us: 'Oh, I turned on my bedside radio when I got back to the room. The BBC news was on, and they announced there's been a forty-eight-hour truce declared.'

Onya, Pete! Thanks for telling your mates.

Later that day, after making our way through the Golan Heights battle zone, with its fields of blood-red poppies, we arrived at a glorious spot above the Sea of Galilee. Peter, who is a devout born-again Christian, asked Rafi if this really was the spot where Christ had once walked on water.

'Yeah, that's right,' said Rafi, with his thick Israeli rasp and Yiddish sense of humour. 'Look closely. You might still see the footprints!'

For lunch we sat at an outdoor café and ate fresh John Dory – the type of fish associated in legend with Saint Peter – at the spot where the Jordan River runs into Galilee. It was yet another *60 Minutes* magic moment, despite the night before.

*   *   *

Perhaps one of the reasons we all put our necks on the line occasionally – apart from the adrenaline rush – was that under the benevolent dictatorship of Sam Chisholm, Channel 9 was simply the best place for a journalist to work.

I'll give you a quick example. In our second year producer Anthony McClellan and I embarked on an investigative piece about the 1979 coalmine tragedy at Appin, in New South Wales. Our story pointed the finger at BHP management for gross neglect and complacency, which had resulted in a methane gas explosion that killed fourteen miners. We didn't think it mattered that BHP kicked in five million bucks a year as the major sponsor of *60 Minutes*. Channel 9 didn't flinch. Chisholm's attitude was to just do the story and let the chips fall. That's how much journalistic freedom we had in those days: we could even slam our corporate sponsor for negligence. That wouldn't happen today. Incidentally, to their credit, BHP copped it and signed up again as sponsor the next year.

Samuel Hewlings Chisholm, formerly of Auckland, New Zealand, is a larger-than-life character who flaunts bright-red socks, a chiselled haircut and all the feisty swagger of a bantam rooster. Whip-smart and occasionally flamboyant in his ideas, Chisholm has a stare that would cut through kryptonite. It's also been said that Sam's speaking style is – at best – droll. He was simply unique.

Whatever enthusiasm we showed for stepping into hairy situations overseas was more than matched by his loyalty at the helm. I remember coming back from Lebanon or Afghanistan – somewhere dangerous – and being summoned to Sam's office, which overlooked the helicopter pad. Chisholm said to me, shaking my hand to seal his promise, 'You have my word, if anything should happen to you – heaven forbid – I will immediately pay Dianne a million dollars' compensation. If that's any comfort.'

It was a comfort, Sam, believe me.

I was on thirty-five thousand dollars a year at the time, so a million bucks seemed bigger than the GDP to me. I have no doubt Sam would have paid up. He was always a man of his word.

Mind you, it helps when you're winning. Ours was consistently the top-rating show on television and year after year won the Logie for Best Current Affairs Program. I think we won it for six straight years at the start. After its initial stumble the program has been an absolute runaway in the TV ratings, taking on everything the enemy has thrown at it. And more.

Our cameramen can take a big part of the credit for the show's success. I filmed a heart-wrenching story in 1982 about a baby racket in Taiwan. Babies and toddlers were being snatched from apartment blocks, shopping centres and even temples, and sold to foreign couples, including Australians, as orphans. It was a compelling tale, but what made it special was that it was the first story ever picked up and run by the American *60 Minutes* program.

The feedback we got from the CBS end was a well-deserved compliment to our cameramen: 'Hey, you guys shoot great pictures.' Our guys certainly do. I happen to believe the Australian *60 Minutes* film crews are way better, certainly more versatile, than the Americans. Every Sunday night the pictures are exceptional. I wouldn't be brazen enough to compare reporters, but I also think our best producers would play the Yanks off a break.

I've dipped in and out of the program for thirty years. Here a pilgrimage to Fromelles, there a profile on Rolf Harris in London. Or maybe an amazing little bloke named Connor, who holds the record for the greatest number of operations – forty and counting – at Westmead Children's Hospital. And all Connor does is make you feel happy.

When they pay you to do a job like that, you grab it by the throat.

Chapter 15
Death Row and Other Fun Places

I was actually inside San Quentin Prison in California when the joint got hammered by an earthquake. We were interviewing the warden at the time. All the alarms clanged and boomed, gates slammed shut and a couple of photos fell off the warden's wall. For a moment I wondered if our story was suddenly going to be about the mass breakout of murderers, rapists and hijackers.

Over the years I have spent too much of my time inside gaols talking to killers and unlucky losers. You find a bizarre sort of camaraderie inside. It's palpable. But even when they're cracking jokes, you can feel the prisoners' hatred – of the system and, too often, of each other. It numbs your brain just walking the noisy corridors, past the caged animals. In my experience most of them are misfits who've been beaten up by life, by parents and by drugs: booze and chemicals. They shouldn't be there.

But I've also met some psychopaths who should never be let out.

*   *   *

Thirty-year-old drifter John Spenkelink was Hollywood B-grade handsome, with a stylist's white streak through his thick black hair. Robert Sullivan was thirty-six and grossly overweight, and seemed a likable sort of a bloke for a convicted killer. I interviewed both men for *60 Minutes* in a prison at Starke, an ugly neon-and-billboard strip of a town in Florida. Later the state put 2300 volts of alternating current through each man's skull. For thirty seconds. That's usually enough. But not always.

Spenkelink and Sullivan were both shotgun murderers. Their executions marked the return of capital punishment in America, which was why we were doing the story. They would be the first of well over a thousand executions.

I have to say, the interviews gave me the weirdest feeling as a reporter, and as a human being. It was lights, camera and action as usual, like so many other interviews. The difference was these two men had been sentenced to death by electrocution. What would I talk about? These men both had a past and a present but no hopes, no dreams, and they were about to be violently killed. Over the years I'd interviewed a number of people with terminal illnesses, people with not much time left. They seemed to have a serenity about them as they faced death. However, there was nothing serene or calm about these two killers in their last hours. Indeed, according to horrific news reports after his execution, Spenkelink actually died with a broken neck because he'd fought so wildly with prison guards to avoid the electric chair.

A few months before he died, Spenkelink talked to me about the inequity of capital punishment, saying, 'Them without capital get the punishment.' While he admitted killing a man, his travelling companion, he claimed it was only because the older man had forced him at gunpoint to commit a homosexual act. None of the evidence supported that claim.

Robert Sullivan, on the other hand, looked me in the eye many times and insisted he was innocent. He had been convicted of murdering a grocery-store manager, but he kept saying he was nowhere near the store at the time of the killing. Still, in ten years of trials and appeals, his attorneys could not convince either judge or jury of his innocence. I interviewed Sullivan twice in Starke prison's media room, a cell especially set up for TV interviews, usually with blokes on death row. I also filmed Sullivan with two dozen other death-row inmates in the exercise yard as they worked out with barbells and sank baskets, like they were in some local gym. Starke prison officials tell me every one of them is now dead. In Florida very few come out of death row alive.

Believe it or not, the prison warden let us film in the empty execution chamber in the weeks before Spenkelink's death. He let me sit in Old Sparky, the chair in which they'd electrocuted more than three hundred men since the early 1900s. Only in America, I thought to myself, would they allow a TV crew to do that.

As I sat in the wooden chair describing for viewers what would soon happen to Spenkelink and Sullivan, there was a chilling sound from the cells nearby. It was just after lunch, and one of the death-row inmates kept beating his tin plate against the bars of his cell. Like a mournful metronome, it just kept banging, and echoing. He kept it up for at least an hour. Bang! Bang! Bang! Sullivan told me later that it was him, knowing we were filming inside the execution chamber and wanting to make his presence felt as the day of his death drew near.

While he was banging away, we had a serious editorial stoush in the execution chamber. The cameraman and sound recordist thought it was a bit ghoulish of me to sit in Old Sparky while I talked to the camera. So, to soothe their sensitivities, we filmed an alternative piece with me standing behind the electric chair.

I must confess that when we finally looked at the footage, they were right. It had been in bad taste, so we used their suggestion instead. Still, it was a macabre experience.

Sullivan even wrote me letters over the next year, recalling his childhood in Massachusetts and telling me about the snow and the fall colours, which he'd never see again. His parents and civil-liberties lawyers wrote, too, pleading his innocence while clutching at straws that the Australian *60 Minutes* might have some connection with the influential American *60 Minutes* show.

It didn't help. They killed him anyway, about two years later.

From Starke we moved on to Huntsville, Texas, where prison authorities were experimenting with what was then a newfangled technique, a lethal injection, to replace their overworked electric chair. Texas was the only state in America that executed more men than Florida did. Indeed, when George W. Bush was Texas governor, he ordered the execution of 131 convicted killers, more than any other governor in American history. At Huntsville the warden refused to let us speak with the next prisoner due for execution because – he told us somewhat apologetically – the death-row inmate was 'emotionally unstable'. I could understand that.

We did, however, interview the local newspaper correspondent who'd been the news media's eyewitness for 187 executions at the Texas prison. He told me that long ago he'd switched sides, becoming an outspoken critic of capital punishment. 'It's no deterrent,' he insisted, 'just barbaric.'

I wholeheartedly agree.

*   *   *

Californian Christopher Boyce was an intriguing rogue with an IQ of 140. Boyce was imprisoned in maximum security, but not because he murdered anybody. Rather, they put him in Fort Leavenworth because he stole American secrets and sold them to the Russians. He was the Falcon of the award-winning book *The Falcon and the Snowman* fame.

In fact Christopher Boyce was the most famous American spy in decades; in thirty years of *60 Minutes*, interviewing him remains one of our greatest coups. At the age of twenty-two Boyce got a job as a telex operator in a top-secret wing of the Californian aerospace giant TRW, because his father was in charge of security. Boyce insists that when he started reading highly classified cables about the CIA's deception and interference in the affairs of the Whitlam government, one of America's closest allies, he decided that Washington was a threat to democracy, indeed a threat to world peace. So he set out to try to destabilise America's grip on power, he said, by selling the Russians secrets that relied on information gathered by satellites at the Australian bases. After two years he was arrested and sentenced to forty years' gaol for espionage. He subsequently escaped from his Californian prison, conducted a spree of bank robberies to survive, was recaptured and sentenced to an extra twenty-five years, and was transported to Fort Leavenworth in Kansas.

Former CIA man Victor Marchetti first paved the way for me to talk to Boyce back in 1977. When I was still the ABC's North American correspondent, I had interviewed Boyce on the telephone after he was first arrested for spying. For several years after that one of *60 Minutes*'s gun producers, Anthony McClellan, pestered Boyce and his lawyer for a TV interview. McClellan was absolutely relentless, and in 1984 Boyce finally agreed. He had knocked back all the big American networks clamouring to interview him and agreed to talk to our show, he told me, because we were from Australia. He wanted to explain to us that he betrayed his country and turned to espionage . . . for Australia!

To get the interview, we had to fly to Kansas City and then drive to the old limestone behemoth of Leavenworth. It looked as forbidding as you'd expect a maximum-security gaol to look. They locked up Bugs Moran there, the man who tried to massacre the Al Capone gang. And the crazy James Earl Ray was incarcerated in Leavenworth after he killed Martin Luther King Jr.

To get inside, they put us through more metal detectors and body searches than it takes to get *out* of the Fort Knox gold vaults. The prison warden sat with us through the whole interview, shadowed by a guard with a double-barrelled shotgun.

Boyce was articulate, personable and cheeky in our interview. He had sold US secrets to the Soviets as a vengeful protest, he said, at an American dirty-tricks campaign against Australia. He clearly believed that Washington had played a crucial role in bringing down the Whitlam government.

Boyce was a highly principled traitor. 'Washington double-crossed you guys. They dishonoured my country,' Boyce told me in our exclusive interview. 'You were supposed to be our best buddies. One of our oldest allies.' He accused America of 'shameful hypocrisy' in its dealings with Australia.

When I told him the CIA had called him a traitor and one of the most damaging spies since the Second World War, Boyce just laughed and said, 'Serves them right.'

He laughed at what he derided as the Keystone Cops level of security that had allowed him to escape from his previous federal prison. Worst of all for his own safety, when he autographed my copy of the book *The Falcon and the Snowman* – based on his exploits with his spy accomplice, Daulton Lee – he wrote, 'Next time bring a chopper!'

As we stopped at one of the many security checkpoints on our way out, the warden read what Boyce had written in my book. 'Smart-ass sonofabitch,' he snapped.

McClellan and I were delighted with the interview. We knew we had a cracker of a yarn. What we didn't know until the next day was that Boyce was savagely bashed within half an hour of us leaving. A group of white racists called the Aryan Brotherhood had put him into the prison hospital. They knocked out one of Boyce's front teeth, smashed his face and gave him two black eyes and two broken ribs. The brutal attack was sparked by one of the screws baiting the prisoners, telling them that the 'pretty-boy spy' was a show pony and had 'ratted to the Australians' about the location of an illegal liquor still. He hadn't, of course.

Boyce never did get his chopper, but he got out early on parole, after spending twenty-five years in gaol for his crime. These days he lives quietly in Washington state.

I still shake my head wondering why Boyce's scandalous allegations – which clearly backed up earlier stories I had done suggesting secret US involvement in Whitlam's dismissal – caused so little fuss in Australia. It was almost as if we just took for granted that the CIA interferes and removes governments that Washington doesn't like. Maybe nobody cared because Aussie voters were sick of the madcap antics of the Whitlam government anyway.

*   *   *

There were many blokes *60 Minutes* did stories on who should have gone to gaol but didn't. Alan Bond certainly copped it sweet, although he didn't volunteer. But Christopher Skase and a whole bunch of crooked businessmen went free.

As did the men behind the scandal at Chelmsford Private Hospital in Sydney. At least twenty-four innocent Australians were killed by electric shocks and drugs there. Killed not by an executioner or a murderer but by doctors' cruelty. Psychiatrists, to be accurate, named Bailey, Herron and Gill.

The men administered Deep Sleep Therapy, which involved inducing coma to treat depression and a range of other disorders, including alcoholism and drug addiction. The radical treatment had long been abandoned – or outlawed – everywhere else in the world. Stevie Wright, the lead singer of The Easybeats, who had undergone this toxic therapy for drug and alcohol dependence, told me that he had finally fled, naked and disoriented, through an open window one night. Rock legend Johnny O'Keefe was admitted suffering depression, as was television star Bobby Limb, whom I knew very well. Bobby said to me he'd been heavily drugged at Chelmsford and couldn't remember the details of his treatment, although he described the whole episode as 'a terrible time in my life'.

A lot of victims weren't as lucky as Wright, O'Keefe and Limb, who at least escaped Chelmsford with their lives. We would discover that many patients who didn't die at the hospital committed suicide soon after being released.

My producer, Anthony McClellan, had initially been tipped off about the story by a branch of the Church of Scientology, who vehemently campaign against psychiatry. This time they were spot on, because our investigation revealed a startling range of physical and psychological side effects, as well as the twenty-four deaths.

The extraordinary *60 Minutes* findings helped spark a royal commission, which concluded that medical practices and events at Chelmsford were both deplorable and criminal. The commissioner found evidence of fraud, obstruction of justice and serious medical negligence, and he condemned all the doctors involved. This helped lead to the awarding of $5.5 million in compensation payouts to 152 former patients.

Yet, despite all this evidence, a decade later the Director of Public Prosecutions in New South Wales decided to drop all charges against the psychiatrists. It was an absolute disgrace. The survivors and the victims' families still live with the human wreckage caused by Dr Harry Bailey and his medical mates.

So we did a follow-up story after the DPP's deplorable backdown. The moral of our story was painfully simple: don't sue doctors, especially if you happen to be a mental patient. The Establishment – the bureaucrats, lawyers and doctors – will beat you, or just wear you down.

For these Chelmsford stories *60 Minutes* won more awards than for any of the other three thousand plus stories we've put to air, including four Logies, for Best Public Affairs Report (twice) and Reporter of the Year (twice). I do feel some satisfaction that we were able to bring the outrageous criminal behaviour at the hospital to public attention. But nobody went to gaol. And that's a medical scandal in itself.

Disgraced New South Wales detective sergeant Roger Caleb Rogerson was one bloke who did time, but many people question whether he has ever been held to account for the full scope of his misdeeds. In the early days *60 Minutes* made headlines when the girlfriend of a thug named Warren Lanfranchi broke down on camera and told me that Warren had in fact been executed. Not in an electric chair but by a fearsome cop named Roger Rogerson. Now, there's no question that Rogerson shot Lanfranchi. Even he admitted to that. It's just that Roger and the New South Wales Police Department praised it as 'an act of self-defence'. But in an extraordinary interview with me late one night in 1981 Warren's girlfriend, Sallie-Anne Huckstepp, who was both a prostitute and a drug addict, accused Rogerson of acting as 'judge, jury and executioner'. It was a sensational accusation, one that quite frankly worried me at the time. But Channel 9's learned QC, who sat in on the interview, insisted it was defendable. So we went ahead and broadcast the accusation.

It ended up a huge story, one of many that helped spur a royal commission into widespread New South Wales police corruption. It gave *60 Minutes* credibility, even amongst newspaper journalists, who had been slow to praise the program. It was also one of the grittiest stories I've ever reported, involving heavy drug deals and dangerous criminals, some of whom would go on to be core figures in the TV series *Underbelly*.

This was the first of three occasions in my Channel 9 career when we would have armed guards at my house. I'd received a couple of anonymous death threats, which *60 Minutes*'s police contacts suggested I should take seriously. It's all a bit spooky and intimidating, let me tell you, when instead of the next-door neighbour's cats there's a security guy with a gun patrolling your yard. For a moment it does make you wonder whether the story is really worth the risk, but you know that's exactly why the threats were made in the first place.

Sallie-Anne Huckstepp was the one they were really after. But she was so full of anger and revenge she didn't seem to care about her own safety. Sadly, she'd also just miscarried Lanfranchi's baby. The task of *60 Minutes* went beyond getting the exclusive interview with Sallie-Anne: it included protecting her life, as death threats were repeatedly made against her at the time of our story.

The incomparable Wendy Bacon, now a professor of

journalism at the University of Technology, Sydney, was the researcher-cum-fixer for *60 Minutes* on that Lanfranchi story. It wouldn't have happened without Wendy's diligence and dogged determination. For days she hid Huckstepp in an upper-floor suite of Sydney's Hilton Hotel, caring for and protecting her while the world was trying to locate her.

In 1986 Huckstepp was finally murdered, found face down in a lake in Sydney's Centennial Park. Sundry police and known criminals such as Neddy Smith were randomly accused, but nobody was ever charged. I must say that given her dangerous lifestyle and all the underworld secrets she claimed to know, I'm surprised she survived as long as she did. A couple of times in the year or so before she died, Sallie-Anne rang to offer me exclusive stories, but she'd become a sad, pathetic figure.

(Incidentally, for her heroin addiction, Sallie-Anne had also been drugged and electrocuted at Chelmsford by the notorious Dr Harry Bailey, without any success.)

About the same time as her death Roger Rogerson agreed to an interview with me when I was filling in for Mike Willesee on *A Current Affair*. I forget what the interview was about but it certainly had nothing to do with Huckstepp's murder. It was probably about yet another police-corruption scandal.

After all those years since I'd first interviewed Sallie-Anne Huckstepp, I was looking forward to finally meeting Roger-son. By repute he was cold, calculating and clever. But when he walked into the studio, Rogerson, the most scandalous cop in Australia – and one of the most highly decorated – looked more like the captain of the local bowls club, in a blue jacket and striped tie. He was very affable, almost charming.

'Thanks for the fifty thousand,' he said and smiled as we shook hands before the interview.

'No worries, you're welcome,' I replied, pretending I knew what he was talking about.

Then the penny dropped. At the time of our *60 Minutes* story in 1981 Rogerson had angrily talked about suing Channel 9 for defamation because we'd broadcast Sallie-Anne's 'judge, jury and executioner' allegation. I was told by Gerald Stone that legal action had begun, then some years later I recall Sam Chisholm saying it had been settled. I had no idea of any fifty-thousand-dollar payout until my studio interview with Roger.

Roger was not so appreciative after the interview. He would later say that it was an answer he gave me in this interview that finally got him sacked from the New South Wales police force, in April 1986. I can't even recall the answer he was referring to.

Now, there's another postscript to this story, a kind of full stop. In 2008 I was the MC for a charity dinner raising money for intellectually disabled kids. For the silent auction Roger Rogerson had donated a copy of his official police report to the coroner on the shooting of Warren Lanfranchi. So, twenty-seven years later, here it was, framed along with a newspaper photo of him standing over the dead body. Rogerson had even gone to the trouble of autographing it. I found it a strangely macabre memento, almost ghoulish, especially at a children's charity night, sitting amongst the usual array of donated wine and sports paraphernalia. The dinner organiser, Max Markson, explained to me that he'd included it in the silent auction because he knew there would be lawyers and cops in the room, so somebody might find it fascinating. I certainly did. When I left that night, Max presented it to me as a gift. Today, as I write this book, it hangs in the stairway to my study, amongst a bizarre collection of the flotsam and jetsam of my journalistic life.

Chapter 16
Food for Thought

It stands to reason that if *60 Minutes* takes you to so many weird and wonderful places, you have to sample the local tucker. Whether you want to or not. It doesn't always go down too smoothly, either.

I'm not talking about haggis or ultra-hot curries. I can handle the heart, lung and liver of a highland ruminant; I can handle Johnny Cash's burning ring of fire. No probs, I've got a strong stomach.

I've eaten whale blubber with Inuits at the North Pole and dugong with Aboriginals in the Northern Territory. They both tasted like a slab of Dunlop retread. I've tried nine-banded-armadillo stew and fried possum pieces in Grenada. They were all right.

I have a bit of trouble with China and the monkey-brains dish, though. I realise it's a delicacy, but I had to walk away from a plate of primate grey matter. It was even worse than raw sea urchin.

And then there were the sheep's eyes, out the back of Mecca, in Saudi Arabia. There wasn't even any beer to wash those beady morsels down with.

We had given our Saudi car drivers some money and asked them to go into the souk and buy some traditional takeaway so we could sit up in the rugged hill country late that afternoon, watch a magical sunset and feast on Saudi food.

Which we did. We had platters of lamb and chicken, with rich scents of turmeric, cumin and cinnamon. And a hot flat bread they call *kimaje*, which you use to scoop up the food. There were fresh fruit juices to drink, *zinzibil*, a sweet, heavily gingered tea, and, of course, pots of Bedouin coffee flavoured not with sugar but crushed cardamom. And dates. The drivers had even produced beautiful Persian carpets from the boots of their cars for us to sit on. It was magnificent.

Until they served up the *pièce de résistance*.

The highlight.

The bloody sheep's eyes.

There had to be a butcher's dozen, like a tray of black marbles, all staring up at us. As were our drivers.

They'd been fantastic over the previous couple of days, getting us out of some sticky moments with Saudi officialdom. For this meal we were their honoured guests. Or, at least, I was! That was according to Nick Lee, the cameraman. Nicholas suddenly bestowed on me a title and a rank I'd never had before. Usually I was left bringing up the rear, lugging Nick's tripod. Now I was suddenly Aussie royalty. And, of course, as such it would be a grave offence if I turned away this special treat.

I had no choice but to swallow the sheep's eyes.

As I reached for the plate, I heard some fatuous prattle from Nick: 'Matey, they taste just like oysters. And you love oysters.'

He was half-right. It's true, I do love oysters. But, as I knew, he had no damn idea what sheep's eyes really tasted like.

So let me tell you. They taste like nothing. A rubbery texture and a fluid explosion. By whatever description . . . they're not good. I was in need of the *kimaje* bread to sop it up and some thick Bedouin coffee to wash it down. Mind you, eating a couple of sheep's eyes does give you bragging rights. Once the sludge disappears, that is.

Still, every dog has his day. There would come a perfect pay-back time. It was inevitable. I just had to be patient and wait.

Well, that day came. It was in the backblocks of Taiwan, on a flower farm. Before we could film this vast floral vista, we had to meet the board of the Flower Cooperative over dinner one night. They were all farmers and all blokes – in very bad suits. Still, they had dressed for the occasion, and again we were the honoured guests. We had to respect that.

Fortunately, I still had food in my rice bowl when they brought out the specialty of the house. This was a mystery dish. It was a veritable mountain of fried something – on a large platter. We thought it was animal, maybe mega-insects, but more probably small birds.

It turned out to be a flock of starlings, plucked of their feath-ers but complete with eyes, beaks and wing bones. There were dozens of them. They were also staring at us.

By way of sign language, given that my Mandarin is a little rusty, I made it clear to our hosts that my friend sitting beside me – namely Nick – had an empty plate. And he was as keen as mustard to try some.

As they pushed the large platter towards him – all waiting proudly for Nick to dig into Mount Starling – he mumbled to me in Fast Aussie Tongue, 'Matey, what are these li'l buggers, and how do I eat them?'

Over the years I've found that Fast Aussie Tongue cannot be understood by people who have learnt English as a second language. So, smiling, I replied in the same lingua Aussie, 'Nick. Just eat the bloody things. This is embarrassing.'

I had no idea how they should be tackled.

Nick struggled, and the starling fell off his chopsticks three or four times. Finally, in panic, he picked the fried bird up in his hand and stuffed it into his mouth. The crunching sound of beak and bones and eyeball echoed through the small restaurant. It was like eating soft-shell crab, except this wasn't soft.

This was chicken-bone-resonating loud.

For some reason I kept thinking 'sheep's eyes'.

Guarding the small pile of rice on my plate, I watched how the Taiwanese, who after politely waiting for Nick to start, were now helping themselves to starlings. These blokes didn't bother about the chopsticks, as Nick had tried to do so manfully. Instead they picked them up with a thumb and forefinger and delicately picked the meat from the bones with their teeth. They placed the scraps back on the plate.

Nick was too far into the procedure to change course now. He was busily eating all his.

'You're disgusting, Nick,' I told him quickly. 'David Attenborough will be looking to film you for one of his BBC Primal Man series.'

He was clearly appreciative of my comments. The rest of us nibbled away at three or four of the succulent starlings while Nick was still frantically crunching away on his mouthful of eyeballs and stuff.

Poor Nick. How embarrassing for him.

Even Australia offered extraordinary culinary experiences, which were, thankfully, much more palatable. Out of Nhulunbuy, in the Gulf of Carpentaria, I flew with a wonderful character named Galarrwuy Yunupingu to collect some blackfella bush tucker for a bit of a Saturday-night feast for his mob. Galarrwuy, who was made Australian of the Year in 1978 for his work on land rights, is a Yolngu lawman, a respected senior leader a bit like a tribal king. He's also a larrikin with whom I spent many years on the Council for Aboriginal Reconciliation.

I'd gone up to Nhulunbuy to do a story about John Howard's initiation – if that's the right word – into Aboriginal culture, NT style. The prime minister had some key decisions to make about reconciliation and land rights, and he was proving to be a slow learner. Or maybe just stubborn.

Anyway, after the PM had fled back to Canberra in his private jet, Galarrwuy offered to take me up in his company's chopper, which I figured was going to be pretty exciting, seeing as both back doors had been removed. His pilot flew along some of the most breathtaking, pristine coastal country I've ever seen. There wasn't another human being for three hundred clicks or more. We were enveloped by big blue skies and crystal-clear turquoise water. In fact it was so clear and so isolated that we passed maybe six giant manta rays just sunning themselves in the waters below and at least a dozen sharks.

We landed and collected giant clams on the rocks, saw crocodile eggs in a nest and watched hundreds of mud crabs scrabbling on a mangrove bank. He picked them like strawberries off a bush. Then Galarrwuy stood alone – like an ebony warrior – in a shallow estuary and speared stingrays the size of dinner plates. He was a big man with a sizeable gut, but as he balanced on one leg, with the other one tucked up, he looked lithe and athletic. When he speared a ray he'd place it on another sharp stick, which he had in his left hand, stacking them like pancakes. When he had about seven or eight stingrays, he'd put them on the riverbank and then go back for some more. Amazingly, I never saw him miss one when he threw the spear, despite the way flowing water distorts your vision. It was uncanny.

Later, from inside the back of the chopper, he took a 12-gauge and shot a giant bush turkey on the wing, then we landed on an empty beach to retrieve it. When he held it out for my camera, the bird's wingspan was greater than his arm span. That's a big turkey. I couldn't help but think this helicopter safari was a long way from his dreamtime concept of traditional hunting and gathering of food. But, for me, it was an unforgettable day at his local markets.

Chapter 17
Two-and-a-half Men

The Aussie bush stories remain my *60 Minutes* personal favourites, filled as they are with larger-than-life characters and pictures that take your breath away. We've shot the droughts, the floods and the bushfires. And we've met some marvellous, memorable bushies.

Like seven-year-old Normie and his kid brother, Wayne, who was four. I knew he was four, because Normie told me. In no uncertain terms. We'd just driven two hundred dusty kilometres out the back of Derby, Western Australia, packed into a Land Cruiser. We were there to do a story about the culling of wild donkeys in the Kimberley. As we unfolded ourselves from the Land Cruiser in front of their parents' station house, the two kids collared us. 'What's your bloody name?' was Normie's opening gambit.

'I'm Ray. What's your name?'

That's when he hit us with the facts. 'I'm Normie, an' I'm seven. He's Wayne, an' he's four.'

Foolishly, I suggested Wayne looked more like . . . maybe five?

'Look. I jest bloody told yez. I'm seven, and he's f***in' four. Right?'

'You can't swear like that,' I chipped him.

'Yeah, I bloody can. 'Cos there's no women around.'

Both kids were skinny blood nuts with freckles, and they were wearing nothing but underpants – with hula-girl and palm-tree motifs on them. They'd been running crazy under the sprinkler when we arrived. (Crazy was the only way they knew how to run!) They directed us to an open shed under a big old eucalypt, where their father, Lionel, was working under the bonnets of a pair of mud-caked station Toyotas. Lionel was long and lanky, wearing a blue singlet; he had red hair too. As we tried to sort out the plan for the next few days of filming, the two kids screamed and swung from the metal framework of the shed like monkeys.

'C'mon, you bloody li'l mongrels, piss orf,' shouted their old man.

'Don't tell us to pizz orf, Lionel. Settle down,' said the seven-year-old.

'No, youz settle down, ya' annoying li'l bastards.'

Despite their choice language they were funny kids. They were fearless tearaways, too, into everything. They took their lessons through School of the Air and got involved in farm activities with the blokes, including mustering and kangaroo shooting. They even drove their own battered ute, with Wayne steering, while Normie somehow changed the gears. They proudly told me, 'One arvo we drove the bastard into the dam!'

The crew and I went bush for about three days with a team of shooters and a bubble-helicopter pilot. I absolutely love helicopters. Mind you, with choppers my strict rule is that if the pilot doesn't look old enough to have flown combat missions – under heavy enemy flak – I don't go. I once saw a bubble chopper carrying a CBS film crew covering the America's Cup yachting races simply fall out of the sky into the waters of Rhode Island Sound, just in front of our ABC boat. The pilot died and the cameraman was broken to bits.

In the Kimberley we flew with Reg, a grizzled Vietnam vet, and a team of crack riflemen, who were shooting herds of feral donkeys on the run. Eradicating these pests, which were left over from earlier mining camps and have threatened the outback ecology for decades, seemed a good thing.

We were in big-sky country, camping under the stars, eating from open fires and washing off the red dust in billabongs frequented by pretty harmless Johnston River crocs. How did we know they were harmless? Well, a local Aboriginal bloke, who also happened to be the best of the shooting team, told us they were 'pretty harmless'. But just in case he was pulling our leg, we only went in for a tub whenever he went in. And we shadowed him like limpets.

When we returned to the station house, Lionel put on a barbie for everyone.

'G'day, you old bastards. Where yez bloody been?' was Normie's greeting.

As we sat around in a semicircle drinking cold beers, the two marauders ran up behind everybody, attacking with flying feet and karate chops. They were addicted to kung-fu shows on video. Reg, the chopper pilot, had been subjected to their antics before. As he locked his hat in his truck, he explained to me, 'Them li'l bastards will start hurling it around like a bloody frisbee if I don't.' Half an hour later, after assaulting most of the bushies, Normie got a bit too close to Reg. As the kid flicked his foot, the chopper pilot – without even looking – reached back, grabbed Normie by the leg and flung him up against the chicken-wire fence. It knocked the stuffing out of him, too. Four-year-old Wayne was mortified. Normie was Wayne's idol and he'd never seen anybody take him on before.

'Didn't 'urt, ya bastard,' Normie spat at Reg, this time staying safely clear.

As he brushed off the dust from his shorts, looking for a little solace, he said to me, 'Ay, ya know Reg, the chopper pilot?' Before I could answer, he whispered defiantly, 'Well, Reg is a c***.'

'Normie, you mustn't use that word,' I told him.

'Well, ya saw what he did ta me. Reg is a c***.'

Just then his mother appeared at the flyscreen door, a red-headed baby in her arms, and screeched, 'Normie. Wayne. Get in 'ere. It's ya bloody bath time.'

'Righto, Mum. Comin'. See ya, Ray.'

And they were gone. Obedient – if not humble – when the boss cracked the whip.

*   *   *

I first met the legendary bushman R. M. Williams in 1982 in the Queensland outback on another *60 Minutes* shoot. And I'm glad I did. In a jam-packed, colourful life, RM had gone from swaggie to multimillionaire, losing and gaining fortunes along the way, without too many ulcers. He was as wise as anyone I've ever met; he had, as they say, sorted out the chaff from the wheat years ago, which made him worth listening to.

At the age of seventy-three Reg Williams was competing in the Winton to Longreach Endurance Ride, truly one of the toughest of horse races. He told me it would be his last great ride, although he clearly wasn't about to pack the saddle away.

Over the years I got to know RM because he'd often ring up to yap about politics and life. Especially politics. He once invited me up to his Darling Downs property for a weekend, to get to know Pauline Hanson. 'We'll knock off a few bottles of rum,' he suggested. 'When you get a chance to talk, away from her Rottweiler minders and the cameras, I think you'll like her.' I told RM that I thought he was right on most things, but not Pauline. He just laughed.

There were about sixty riders who started from the Winton Showgrounds in that big endurance race one dark Saturday night. The horsemen thundered off across the stony scrub, riding all through the night, till late the next afternoon. In spite of his age RM was one of only a handful who made it to the finish line. It was amazing to watch this tough old bushie, still sitting high in the saddle, caked in red dust and wearing a pair of the iconic elastic-sided boots he'd designed and begun making half a century before. He also had on his trademark blue shirt with Longhorn insignia.

At the end RM was gnarled and knotted, and at times a short-tempered old bastard, but he was still a great man. I'd put him up there with Don Bradman and Professor Fred Hollows. He belonged to another age; he was almost the last of the great bushmen. I went and saw Reg in hospital at Toowoomba a day or so before he died. He was decked out in the same blue shirt, wearing it like a pyjama top. A loyal R. M. Williams company man to the end. He was mellow, in the mood to reminisce about how much he'd learnt from black stockmen in his early days of driving cattle; he spoke of hoarding gold near Tennant Creek with his Chinese partner and the risky business of selling the bush ethos to modern Australian city slickers who would never really understand. He had a book of Lawson poems by his bed and read me some, although he never looked at the book. RM just knew them off by heart, from another lifetime. He handed me the book and told me to keep it. It's one of the treasures of my library.

> And the creek of life goes winding on,
> Wandering by;
> And bears for ever, its course upon,
> A song and a sigh.
> – 'The Song and the Sigh', Henry Lawson

*   *   *

By his very nature R. M. Williams was quiet and considered, and never crass. Reginald Byron James Pilbeam – better known as Rex – was quite the opposite. But, like RM, Rex Pilbeam was a classic Aussie bushie. Rex came out of that wild-west Queensland town of Longreach and found his way to Rockhampton, where he had been mayor for almost thirty years when I first met him.

Let's not mince words, because Rex Pilbeam certainly didn't. He was a sexist, racist political dinosaur who was about as physically imposing as Kerry Packer. He once resigned as mayor after being caught having an illicit affair in a local motel. But he was so popular in Rocky that he was duly re-elected – with a bigger majority. From a television point of view Rex was an absolute gem, the most politically incorrect politician I ever came across. Even worse than his fellow Queenslanders Joh Bjelke-Petersen and Russ Hinze, if that was possible. There's no way you could make up some of the outrageous things he said to me on camera, such as, 'Our public toilets are so clean, some races actually sleep in them.' Tick the box marked 'racist'.

In the 1970s, with the women's movement flourishing, Mayor Rex decided that married women who worked at the council had to quit their job if they fell pregnant. He said 'working mothers cause a litany of social evils'. Now tick the one marked 'sexist'.

Rex raised all the money to build a cultural centre that included one of the finest regional art galleries in Australia. He had to personally approve every new painting they purchased, which meant there could be 'none of that impressionist or avant-garde crap', as he so eloquently put it. As he proudly walked me through his gallery with the camera rolling, I asked him why, for example, there was no Brett Whiteley. 'Nahh, that's not art,' he said, with all the certainty of a respected curator. 'All Whiteley paints are blokes standing on their head, with their dick in their mouth.' This time, tick 'philistine'.

Come to think of it, a certain physical heftiness wasn't the only thing Rex shared with Kerry Packer, who certainly held his own in the ribaldry stakes. I recall a dinner once when KP had decided on a little celebration to mark some bumper ratings for *60 Minutes*. It was just Kerry and the four reporters. Jana had flown in that morning from Paris, where she'd been doing a pro-file on Mick Jagger. 'As we were about to start the interview, I noticed Mick was wearing a pair of those long, thin winklepicker shoes. I told him I'd never seen shoes that big before,' she said.

Kerry was listening intently.

'Anyway, Jagger laughed that wicked laugh of his,' Jana explained, 'then he announced, "Yeah. They're size 12. And you know what they say . . . big feet . . . big *willy*!"'

We all laughed.

'Ohhh, is that right?' Kezza quipped, pulling one monster foot out from under the table. 'Have a look at these, then . . . size bloody 16!' There was nothing shy or retiring about KP either.

One afternoon we filmed Rex in his council chambers. He was dressed up in the mayoral robes, with all the mayoral chains, the mayoral medallions and sundry mayoral awards hanging off him, like a knight in a suit of armour. The occasion was an official meet 'n' greet with the mayor of Osaka, Rockhampton's sister city in Japan. It was meant to be a very formal occasion. It was also meant to happen at three o'clock in the afternoon. At 3.15, Rex's Japanese counterpart still hadn't shown up, apparently delayed on a flight from Brisbane. Again with the *60 Minutes* camera rolling, Rex turned to me, pointed to his watch and quipped, 'They weren't bloody late for Pearl Harbor, were they?' And a last tick in the box marked 'totally insensitive', please.

They don't make pollies like Rex Pilbeam anymore. Not even in Queensland. He was so outrageous and so unapologetic. Yet his remains one of my all-time favourite *60 Minutes* yarns.

Chapter 18
And Baby Makes Three

It was early 1984, and I had no inkling my life was about to change so drastically. I had gone off for a month to Central and South America with my favourite *60 Minutes* mate, Andrew Haughton.

We started out with a colourful yarn on the tiny Caribbean island of Grenada. In 1984 there had just been a brief Marxist coup in Grenada, and President Reagan expressed grave fears of another Castro regime in their backyard. So Uncle Sam sorted them out with a lightning strike, which went under the ridiculous codename of 'Operation Urgent Fury'. After a four-day curfew, during which the US forces rounded up a few of the ringleaders, life quickly returned to calypso and cricket. It was a storm not so much in a teacup but in a tropical fruit punch. Those trouble-in-paradise stories are always fun to tell.

We then moved on to El Salvador, one of the most dangerous places on earth. For the locals living there, if the police death squads didn't get them, then gangs of political thugs or drug lords might. Kidnappings and murders and bashings were a daily occurrence. But Ronnie Reagan didn't seem to be bothered by this nation's terrifying right-wing regime, which was also shooting priests and flooding America with heroin and cocaine. Some of the people of San Salvador, the capital, had a special loathing for foreign media, who were now shining an unwelcome spotlight on the city's drug trafficking. Just driving around the streets, you could sense the menace and fear.

One morning we were taken to a popular tourist lookout, where the locals told us that the previous day police had arrived in oversized four-wheel drives with the windows all blacked out and thrown a few political 'troublemakers' over the cliff to their death. In a tiny church nearby, terrified villagers had taken refuge when a crime gang had shot up the main street. One young boy, whom we found praying, still had a graze on his cheek from a bullet that almost got him. When we returned to our hotel that night, we discovered that my old camera pal David Brill, who was there for the ABC, had chalked up his own near-death experience. He'd been held up at gunpoint by a couple of highway bandits. With a pistol cocked at his head, Brill was forced to hand over his wallet, his watch and cash – but thankfully not his life.

The next evening I played tennis with the Sheraton's manager on the enclosed hotel courts. Midway through the match I noticed two armed guards standing nearby in the shadows. When I asked what they were doing, the manager calmly explained that his last tennis partner – a Brazilian journalist – had been shot dead a fortnight earlier. On the same court. It turned out the hotel boss was on a death squad's hit list, and they'd mistakenly shot the journo. This was a seriously scary place.

From El Salvador we flew to Argentina, where we spent a week talking to mothers, wives and sisters of the *desaparecidos*, the 'disappeared'. Maybe thirty thousand people – most of them men – had been executed under the orders of the ruthless military junta that took control in Buenos Aires in the late 1970s. Many of the bodies had been dumped at sea. Some people had been tortured – many even had their hands cut off – and were then piled into mass graves. Talking to these ordinary women was deeply disturbing, and there was a pervasive sense of danger about the place. It was clear that the military and police didn't want TV crews digging up the skeletons of Argentina's 'Dirty War'.

I have to say it was a relief to get home after what had been a pretty harrowing assignment. I'd only had a chance to speak to Dianne on the phone briefly over the previous month, and always on the run.

The news she had for me was best suited for a quiet, private moment anyway.

I remember Dianne took me into our lounge room and sat me down, saying she had something to tell me. She had a certain look on her face, like she was about to tell me that while I'd been away she'd bought a new house. Or that we'd won the lottery. (In a way we had.) It was clear from her confident smile she knew something that I didn't.

That's when Dianne told me 'we' were pregnant. After sixteen years of marriage it was unplanned and totally unexpected.

I was thirty-nine and had packed a lot of living into those first four decades. But suddenly I felt that everything I had done was insignificant compared with having a baby. (It didn't matter that ten billion other couples had been through the same 'miracle experience'. It never does.)

Quite frankly, even in her mid-thirties, Dianne hadn't been distracted by the biological clock ticking madly in her ear. In fact she's the first to admit that I was usually the one besotted by other people's babies, far more than her. Besides, we loved our freedom and wanderlust lifestyle, so we'd never decided either way on a family. Suddenly, the decision had been made for us.

Once she'd let me in on the secret, I was hopeless, could think of nothing else. In my own head I'd become Father of the Year. Of the Century, in fact!

I knew straightaway that this was the end of my *60 Minutes* travels. Much as I loved living life out of a suitcase, it didn't matter to me anymore. My colleague Nick Lee and his wife, Suzie, were also about to have their first baby, so for the next few months he and I trotted around the world nattering on like a pair of midwives. We came across a hilarious book called *Good Morning, Merry Sunshine*, witty Chicago columnist Bob Greene's diary of his wife's pregnancy. Nick and I both decided to write our own version, which of course we never did.

Over the whirlwind of the next few months Dianne and I discovered the baby was healthy and due about mid-November 1984. We had no idea whether we were having a boy or a girl.

On a *60 Minutes* trip to Hokkaidō, in the far north of Japan, I bought our baby's first stuffed toy, an impossibly soft red fox. A week later in Memphis I couldn't resist collecting one of the world-famous Peabody Hotel's stuffed toy ducks. The toy is a near life-sized replica of the mallard drake – with white-feathered collar and green head – that every day leads a line of four ducks as they waddle from the hotel's penthouse, down the elevator, to the marble fountain in the foyer. It's a Memphis ritual, almost as famous as the hallowed walk around Elvis's tomb. When I got the stuffed toys home, Dianne put an instant ban on me collecting any more, at least until the baby arrived. Of course, that embargo was a waste of time. I was on a roll. The duck and the fox still sit pride of place in our daughter's bedroom twenty-five years later.

In the meantime, beyond the wonders of the toy department, I had to somehow tell Gerald Stone that I was leaving *60 Minutes*, the first reporter to do so. As it turned out, I shouldn't have worried. Gerald was tickled pink for us both. What's more, the timing was perfect because Sam Chisholm, Channel 9's irrepressible boss, had a big job offer for me. After owning daytime television for thirteen years as host of *Midday*, Mike Walsh, one of Australian TV's true legends, had decided to move on to host his own weekly *Tonight* show. He'd had enough of his so-called blue-rinse set, even though they had made him a veritable fortune. Chisholm informed me that Walsh wanted me to replace him.

'So, what about it, Raymondo?'

I must admit, Sam's offer took my breath away. I'd been a guest on Mike's show a number of times. I really liked the variety of his guests and topics. I also knew some of his crack production team. But the *Midday* show would be ninety minutes of *live* television a day, before a screaming audience. And it was basically showbiz, rather than news or current affairs where I'd spent all my working life. Even though it would mean I'd be at home and would get a hefty jump in salary, Dianne wasn't convinced, either. (That was a worry: maybe she'd come to like her independent lifestyle too much!)

I spent a few weeks umming and ahhhing. Chisholm kept insisting this was such a great television opportunity that I should 'walk over broken glass to grab it'. Jokingly, I told him I wasn't prepared to bleed for any show – except maybe *60 Minutes* in a war zone. With *60 Minutes* about to wrap for the year, I started to paint the baby's bedroom. The more I thought about *Midday*, the more I liked the idea, especially when Chisholm and Walsh said they'd expect me to steer the show in a more newsy direction.

In those days of TV overindulgence Channel 9 used to throw an extravagant Melbourne Cup party every year in the Sydney boardroom. Now, it's no secret that I have the racing nous of a five-year-old child. But for some reason I backed the Robert Holmes à Court gelding Black Knight to win the 1984 Cup. And it did. In fact, it beat the unbackable Cup-holder Kiwi across the finish line. Figuring it had to be a good omen, in the euphoria of victory I finally told Sam Chisholm I would host *Midday*.

Sam promptly escorted me to his office, plonked a generous contract in front of me to read and sign, and then went back to the Cup party, telling Walsh it was a done deal.

But there was one more hiccup.

Close to six o'clock at night and after buckets of Bollinger a very merry Mike Walsh, along with his good mate and executive producer, John Chapman, carted me down to the show's production cottage for a little orientation. As we walked through the door, their talented team applauded me. That was reassuring.

Walsh and Chapman wrapped their arms around each other, and like a couple of chorus girls from the Rockettes started a high-kick routine. Others joined in, madly clapping and mincing between the desks. It was all in good spirits, primed by a big afternoon of Cup alcohol. I knew that.

But. Somehow I felt I was in the wrong circus tent.

I rang Dianne and told her of my worries. She suggested I ring Gerald Stone for a little wisdom of the Elder. Gerry and his wife, Irene, invited us out to dinner. During the meal Stone said that if I was having second thoughts and wanted to stay with *60 Minutes*, he was prepared to adjust the filming schedules so that I could do mostly Australian-based stories. That'd mean not being away from home much. I realised that was a bit unfair on others at *60 Minutes* – although admittedly there were some who couldn't leave home quickly enough. Anyway, Stone said what we all knew: that Chisholm would probably have the last word.

After a fitful sleep that night I made an early-morning appointment with Sam to sort out my *Midday* dilemma. When I walked in, Chisholm was at his most charming, persuasive best. After listening to my qualms, he suggested that I 'go forth and ruminate', while finishing my paint job on the nursery walls.

'Just have a rethink, Raymondo. Talk to a few people on the show, have a beer with Harvs,' he said, referring to Geoff Harvey, the *Midday* band leader. '*Midday* has you all over it. I know it has.'

Chisholm had called it right, once again. From the outset I would love hosting *The Midday Show*. I would front the show for nine years and never even take one sickie. In fact it was to be the most fun I would ever have in television.

*   *   *

Our baby, a girl, was born in November 1984, three months before I started *Midday*. We decided to call her Jenna Angeline. Dianne and I honestly thought we had made up the name Jenna. Dianne's family has close links to the English medical pioneer Sir Edward Jenner, who developed the smallpox vaccine. Traditionally the men in Dianne's family, including her father and two brothers, all have Jenner as their middle name. As Dianne was in her mid-thirties when Jenna was conceived, we wondered whether there'd be any more babies for us. So, doubting that we'd be lucky enough to have a boy ourselves, we decided to change the old family name from 'Jenner' to 'Jenna'. A year or so later we learnt that we didn't invent it after all, because it's actually a traditional Welsh Christian name. Still, I know from all the letters I've received over the years that there are many girls called Jenna in Australia who owe their name to the fact their mums were fans of *Midday*.

One night while I was writing this book, Jenna stumbled across an original TV promo for *Midday*. It's now on YouTube, like every forgotten hit. Jenna cracked up. She couldn't stop laughing at how daggy it is.

> You've dined with kings and beauty queens,
> You've made us laugh and made us cry.

There are the iconic *60 Minutes* pictures of me with Prince Charles, Bo Derek and sad-eyed babies in Afghanistan. Then the tempo switches to an upbeat chorus:

> Ray, you're making my day. Every day.
> It's good, so good to have you home.

I'm suddenly bouncing out of a convertible, into studio rehearsals with long-legged dancers and a laughing pianist. I'm even wearing a Gene Kelly-style straw boater.

> *The Midday Show* with Ray Martin!
> Coming soon to Nine!

For an old newsman like me, being the centre of a TV commercial like that was a bit embarrassing. And a rude shock to my self-image. Still, as Paul Keating used to say, it was time to flip the switch to vaudeville! Sam Chisholm had hired Mojo, the same advertising geniuses who made 'C'mon Aussie, C'mon' part of the culture, to create my catchy jingle. Unfortunately, this time they didn't have Lillee and Thommo dancing down the pitch, just a journo with two left feet.

You know, there's a certain irony about my daughter's derision. After all, Jenna was the reason I made the switch from Beirut to Broadway in the first place. And that *Midday* jingle was first run on television the day that she came home from hospital as a newborn baby.

I was excited – yet still a bit anxious – about taking on something as different and as daring as *Midday*. I actually love the adrenaline rush that comes with risks, which was one of the reasons I'd left the safety of the ABC job in New York. But this was way out of my comfort zone: a band, an audience and live TV, with no safety net. However, I liked what the excellent journalist Michael Parkinson had done on British television, and I felt I could match what Mike Walsh had done, albeit in a different style. I must confess, I always thought it would work.

My only worry was that I wouldn't enjoy the show-business side. I was wrong. I would in fact love the close encounters I had with stars. And I would also get the chance to fill in for Willesee on *Today Tonight* and host countless network news specials. Audiences would have no problem accepting *both* Ray Martins, as the ratings would clearly show. It was mostly newspaper journos who'd struggle to decide which box I should go into: news or showbiz? That was a question that would keep coming at me for the next twenty years.

Chapter 19
High Noon

Midday felt like a highwire act with no safety net.

I remember the great American singer Tony Bennett asking before we went to air one day, 'Ray, you mean "live to tape", don't you? Like prerecorded?'

I had to tell him, 'No, Mr Bennett. This show is *live* live.'

Tony pretended to reach for his heart pills.

Midday was live television. About as live as it gets.

I have a habit of clearing my throat when I'm under pressure; it's almost a nervous cough. Dianne used to laugh about it every time I'd have to get up and go on stage at the Logies. Cough. Cough. Well, the first lunchtime, in February 1985, when I stepped out into the packed *Midday* studio, there were a few coughs, let me tell you. Cough. Cough. Cough. I was terrified. I think I was more nervous that afternoon than I was at our wedding. In fact, I'm convinced it was sheer terror that somehow got me through the opening monologue, feeling all alone out there, like the boy on the burning deck. I told the audience that it felt worse than sitting in a bunker in Beirut and copping incoming shells!

I know Rowena 'Pat the Rat' Wallace was one of our guests, along with raconteur Stuart Wagstaff and the feisty Democrat Don 'Keep the bastards honest' Chipp. The colourful show-biz entrepreneur Michael Edgley also brought on some chimps from his *Moscow Circus on Ice* show. But I have no idea who sang that day or who the comic was, because it's all just a purple fug.

Whatever we did on that first show, the reviews were all positive, so we turned up again the next day. And a few after that.

On the morning of that first *Midday Show* Kerry Packer had rung to wish me well, which had never happened to me before and never happened again. It seemed there were good-luck messages from everybody, including Prime Minister Bob Hawke. I would quickly discover that the *Midday* audience was 'middle Australia', making the show the perfect floor on which to dance the Macarena or any other political twostep.

It was a marvellous show to work on, at times quite intoxicating. I was only frustrated on the rare occasion that I missed covering a presidential election or some other major event. We covered most breaking-news stories on *Midday* anyway.

'Make 'em laugh, make 'em cry, make 'em gasp.' That was the *Midday* creed, and it would be for almost a decade. Each day we served up five or six live interviews. One minute I'd go head to head with the PM, the next have a sad chat to a child with a terminal illness. We'd have three songs, usually with our live band, never with a backing tape. There'd be a stand-up comic, and performing live meant they had to instantly get the laughs of the studio audience or else they'd bomb. We had regular overseas interviews via satellite, live crosses to reporters scattered around

Clockwise from top left: My grandfather, Fred Lamey. By repute he was a gun shearer and a hot fiddle player.

My grandma, Mary Jane Betteridge, was barely five foot tall but gave birth to eleven children, including my mother.

My father, George James Grace, joined the RAAF as a mechanic but moved on to a bomber crew. The only action he saw was in the local pub.

My mother at eighteen, looking like she was auditioning for a role in *Bonnie and Clyde*. She always boasted she was a crack shot with a rifle.

Left: Dad holding baby Joyce, with Kay, and Lorraine on his right. I didn't show up for another couple of years.

Below: Young teenagers Lorraine and Kay flank Grandma Lamey and her country sisters on a wild Saturday night at Luna Park. Joyce is in the middle. The old girls loved The Big Dipper.

Right: 'The kid' with big sisters Kay and Joyce. This was in Wellington, New South Wales, where Dad and Mum made the strange decision to run a milk bar. We didn't last long there.

Below: Me and Joyce at Tottenham, New South Wales. Obviously I wanted to hold the border collie rather than the damn ginger cat.

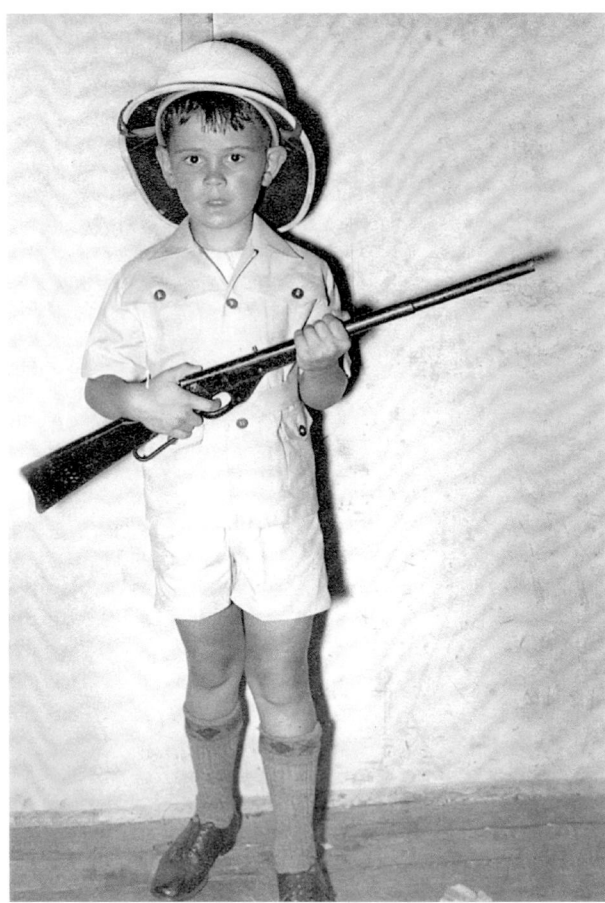

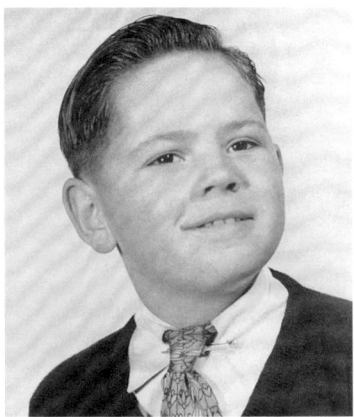

Left: The great white hunter.

Above: A door-to-door photographer talked Mum into having this portrait taken for my tenth birthday present. I would have much preferred a cricket bat.

Below: At Launceston High. Sport was my priority, well clear of girls or books. With my best mate, John Honey (kneeling in front of me), I had fun running the school radio and newspaper.

Top: Me at seventeen. Elvis had a lot to answer for.

Above: At fifteen, my first public speech before the Lord Mayor. I was nervous; Mum (in glasses) was proud.

Above: The ABC's new Canberra correspondent. Short shorts and long socks were de rigueur in 1967.

Left: Dianne was born elegant and classy, with impeccable taste – in most things.

Dianne and I were married in November 1968. We planned a drive to the Gold Coast for our honeymoon, but a smashed windscreen stopped us at Forster. It didn't matter, we were in love.

Left: My first publicity shot when I joined the ABC in 1965. It mortifies my son, Luke, because everyone says I looked a bit like he does today.

Below: Our last Sydney supper for four years, with my sister, Lorraine, and her husband, Des. We were off to 'look for America', as Simon and Garfunkel sang.

Right: Hard at work as the ABC's North American correspondent. I couldn't believe I was being paid to live in the States.

Below: An innocent abroad. On the roof of our apartment block, which looked out on downtown Manhattan.

Above: America under Richard Nixon was beset by civil strife and the Vietnam War, but we found some peaceful places.

Left: Dianne didn't really want to go to New York. But before long it became 'her kinda town'.

Top: Hard at work with my mate and ABC colleague Jeff McMullen on the island of St Martin.

Above left: Ronnie Biggs, the larrikin great train robber, nabs the *Four Corners* camera.

Above right: Notorious American spy Christopher Boyce, who said he 'did it' for Australia.

Left: In Cuba, waiting for Fidel and smoking Havana cigars with his brother, Ramón.

Below: In the Caribbean on holiday in 1978. It was here that I took a deep breath and told Kerry Packer I was joining *60 Minutes*.

Left: With Gerald Stone up front we looked more like the cops from *Miami Vice.*

Below: The original three musketeers. How come I got all the hair jokes?

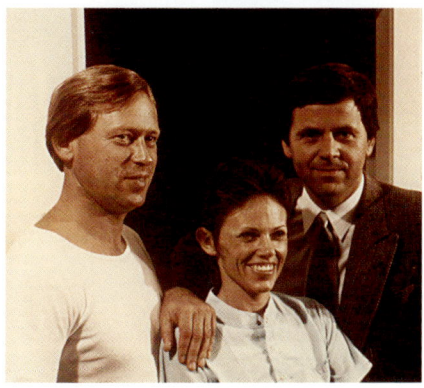

Left: Reporting for *60 Minutes* meant lugging countless bags and boxes to war zones and some strange places.

Above: I don't know how the Chamberlains survived the outrageous public stoning – especially Lindy.

George Negus and Roy Martin head the Channel 9 election team of political experts. With special guests: Bob Hawke, Andrew Peacock, Don Chipp and Fred Daly. **Live, as it happens from 8.30 tonight.**

Top: Another day at the London office – with camera genius Phil Donoghue (left) and my favourite producer, Andrew Haughton.

Above left: Jana Wendt was bright and beautiful. She was an asset to *60 Minutes* when she joined.

Above: George Negus and I hosted the 1981 Federal election. For me it was the first of around 20 election nights and great debates.

Left: Paul Newman about to drive at 300 kph around an Atlanta racetrack.

Right: Filming in Lebanon; in the eighties there you could sip coffee at an outdoor café, read the *Herald Tribune* and listen to mortars dropping.

Below right: The Beruit cab that probably saved our lives.

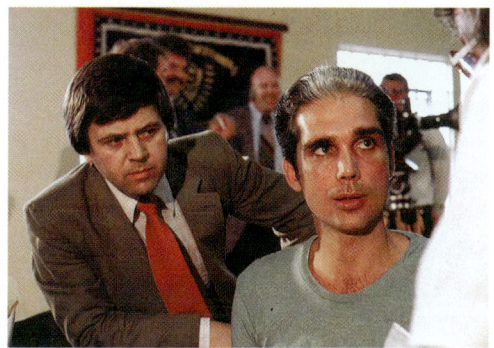

Left: Old Sparky, the Florida electric chair that has killed more than 300 men.

Above: John Spenkelink, the convicted murderer who opened the execution floodgates in America again.

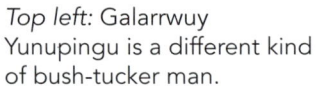

Top left: Galarrwuy Yunupingu is a different kind of bush-tucker man.

Top right: Jenna was too young to read a stopwatch, but she loved her T-shirt dress.

Above: Thirty years on, it was an honour to be presented with the original *60 Minutes* stopwatch – the symbol of Australia's most successful TV show – when I left Channel 9.

Left: Nick Lee, the original *60 Minutes* cameraman, who made me eat sheep's eyes and paid for it later.

Above: Baby makes three. Jenna came into our lives and *60 Minutes* left. At least for a few years.

Right: Jenna shadowed my mother whenever she came to stay and Mum loved the attention.

Top: There's only one Geoff Harvey . . .

Above: The Ron Casey–Normie Rowe punch-up on *Midday* made headlines around the world.

Left: Gary Burns, my *Midday* executive producer, spent years trying to get me to finish the show on time. He failed miserably.

Right: Harvey at the end of my last *Midday* show. He still makes me laugh.

Middle: The only time Hawke and Keating were interviewed together. Their body language gives it away.

Below: A smiling Paul Keating. After the *60 Minutes* 'piggery storm' he loathed Channel 9.

Left: Gretel Killeen and Ross Daniels try to save me from actors' suicide, in another appalling episode of 'A Town like Dallas'.

Middle: My great mate Peter Wynne produced a top-rating *Midday* special with Tom Cruise, so the Hollywood superstar offered to repay us by taking our photo – with my camera.

Bottom left: John Denver flew me 'rocky mountain high' in his stunt plane and somehow I survived to tell the story.

Bottom right: The things you do on a tedious magazine cover shoot. Jana Wendt was always fun.

Left: Mike Crufferd, also known as Michael Crawford, can sing, dance and tell stories wonderfully. Warm and funny, Crawford's the complete package – the perfect guest.

Below: Sam Chisholm's mock letterhead. He was the best boss I had.

Bottom: Just another cup of coffee at Sam's place, as depicted by the brilliant Bill Leak. Lawsie, Hendo, Jonesy, Jana, Sam and myself – in the 'golden days' of TV.

From the desk of ...

THE MOST FEARED MAN IN TELEVISION

Right: Jenna meets baby Luke . . . twenty years later they're still inseparable.

Middle: Get 'em early and they follow Souths for life.

Bottom: He still gives me as much joy today, although he's now six foot five.

Below: For twenty years I called *Carols by Candlelight* 'the loveliest night of the year'. Now it's no longer part of our Christmas, I miss it.

Above: I was in the Canberra studio in 1966 when Mike Willesee first auditioned for a television job. He quickly became one of the best political interviewers in the world.

Left: Bruce Gyngell was more than just the first face on Australian television. He was a class act.

Top: The last *Midday* team in 1993 – incredibly talented, its members now run most of the top-rating shows on commercial TV.

Above: Never believe the headlines. (I had to wear that ridiculous shirt to become one of the few men to go solo on an *Australian Women's Weekly* cover!)

Top: The cartoonists had a field day when I left *The Midday Show.*

Above: Professor Fred Hollows, the hard-swearing, whisky-drinking eye doctor, was the most remarkable man I ever met.

I've been fortunate enough to interview some very beautiful women. *Clockwise from top left:* Sarah Murdoch, Elle Macpherson, Claudia Schiffer, Audrey Hepburn, Joan Collins.

Nov. 8, '93

Clockwise from top left: Linda
Evangelista, Bo Derek, Jane Fonda,
Olivia Newton-John, Nicole Kidman
and a special kind of woman, Dame
Edna Everage.

Top: A fundraising dinner in Sydney, 1989. Sir Donald Bradman promised me that night that if he ever did a TV interview, he would do it with me. Seven years later The Don kept his word. It's my most cherished interview.

Above: After our interview The Don patiently signed our bats – as he did for countless people around the world.

Left: A stroll across Bradman's beloved Adelaide oval, holding his priceless world-record-breaking Sykes bat. I should have been wearing gloves.

Top: Da boys – a crack *Current Affair* unit. Producer Steve Bibb, sound recordist Jason McCawley and camera ace Mark Munro. Together we covered the Sandline civil strife in Papua New Guinea and Diana's funeral in London, standout stories among many.

Above: Me, Munro and McCawley with our PNG army mates, who helped us weave our way through roadblocks and all kinds of trouble.

Left: Dame Edna, dressed down for Prince Andrew and Fergie's Royal wedding.

Below: Maggie Tabberer adds a touch of class to everything – even Royal weddings.

Above: Bronte Cullis, who beat those deadly anorexia voices and today is fit and cheeky.

Right: 'Kerry Packer at play' with Don Burke, Daryl Somers, Jana Wendt and KP's favourite newsreaders, Brian Henderson and Brian Naylor – another fantastic illustration by Bill Leak.

Above: Alec Campbell, the last man alive out of a million soldiers who fought at Gallipoli. At 104 he didn't have a lot to say to us on camera, but he and Luke had a great chat about life and luck. 'Make sure you have a go,' was his advice to Luke. Alec had certainly taken his own advice.

Left: Long-time Channel 9 CEO David Leckie, who, along with Sam Chisholm, turned Nine into one of the world's great TV networks. His sacking by Kerry Packer was a disaster.

Below: Dianne, Jenna, Di's sister, Susan, and her husband, Brian, with whom we've travelled the world, like the Griswalds. They long ago became second parents to our kids.

Left: Luke and me splashing around before he became old enough to have a beer with me.

Below: Years ago, after watching South Sydney lose game after game, the Rabbitohs finally won. Russell Crowe grabbed Luke and took him down to the players' dressing room for the long-overdue celebrations. Luke's never forgotten Russell's kindness.

This is the team you want when the story gets almost unbearable. In 2004, when the tsunami devastated Aceh in Indonesia, Tim Hawkins, Paul Jolly and producer Hugh Nailon went north with me to cover the tragedy. Together with a dozen other Nine news teams, we slept on the concrete floor of this half-finished building. An amazing local family cooked for us, while their beautiful children kept us all sane.

Top: An oil tanker twisted inside out by the tsunami's wave and hurled onto a house roof.

Middle: The Acehnese fisherman whose terrible story almost broke my heart, when I thought I'd heard it all.

Below: The army had to wear gas masks and collect the tens of thousands of bodies in black bin liners.

Top: An old friend – veteran *ACA* producer David Hurley
– and a new find – TV wizard Jo Townsend.

Above: Completing the circle – Les Seymour last shot
a story for the ABC almost twenty-five years ago. It had
been thirty years since I left the ABC for *60 Minutes*. We
joined forces in July 2009 to film a special report on the
old Aboriginal gulag of Palm Island for *The 7.30 Report*
– fifty-five years in the making.

Top: The loves of my life, at Coolum
on the Sunshine Coast.

Above: Mum surrounded by me
and my sisters, Lorraine, Kay and
Joyce – together again for her
eightieth birthday.

Jenna and Luke at the wedding of Geoff Harvey's daughter, Eugenie. As sister and brother they laugh together a lot.

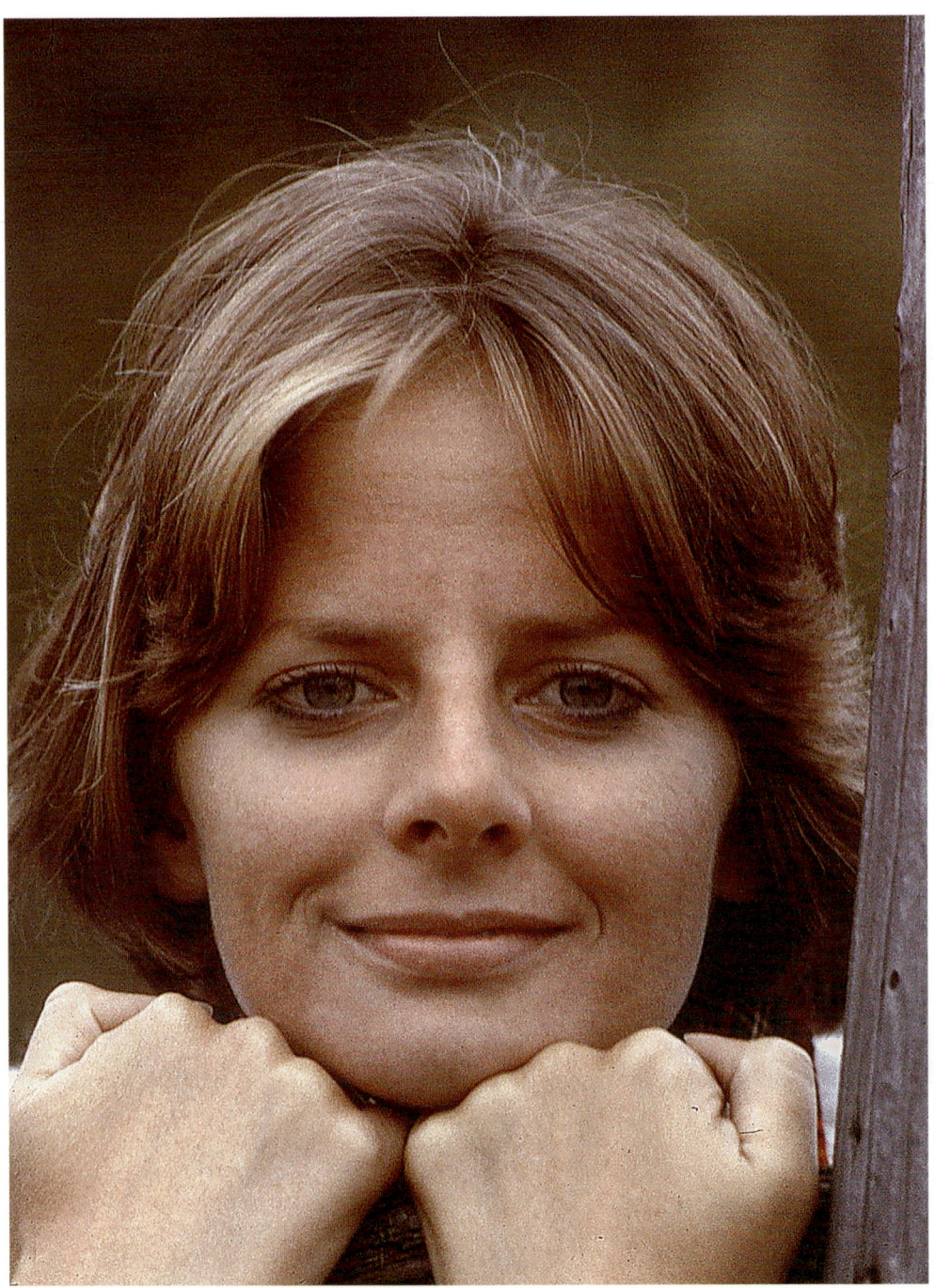

The story of my life –
Dianne. This was taken
during one of our odysseys
to Newport, Rhode Island,
in our New York days.

the country and the world, and regular *Midday Show* experts on everything from genealogy to horoscopes and colic.

And it seemed there was a superstar in our studio every other week. For a boy who grew up in the bush, to be sitting talking to a Hollywood icon like Jack Lemmon, the renowned Beatles producer George Martin or a legend like Peter Ustinov was astonishing. I was often starstruck. I mean, here I was some-times co-hosting my own TV show with the likes of Jane Fonda, Michael Caine or Tom Jones. Throughout my journalistic life I'd reported on showbiz. Now I was a tiny part of it, and it was a buzz.

It was successful too. Exactly how much a TV show makes is always a network trade secret, guarded the way the CIA or Kremlin guards its dossiers. The only way I ever found out was by running into one of the advertising sales executives after an especially long lunch. That's when he or she might reveal the ad rates for a particular program, and then – usually on the back of a wet drink coaster – work out how much a show might be worth.

A senior executive once revealed that *Midday* was making about ten million dollars a year profit while I was hosting it. Sam Chisholm would tell me much more about his private life than he'd ever reveal about *Midday*'s profits. I remember one long night in a bar Sam summed it up this way: 'Raymondo, news, current affairs and sport are the bread and butter of the Nine network. *Midday* is the jam. *Hey Hey It's Saturday* is the cream.'

Whatever the exact figure, it was obvious that 'the jam' was extremely sweet. That's why Chisholm hadn't really flinched when he had to fork out seven million dollars to buy *The Midday Show* rights from Walsh. Clearly, Sam knew he would recoup that in no time.

It took about forty people to do *The Midday Show*. We had a team of reporters, camera crews, studio teams and musicians – but I have to say it was the producers who really drove it, day after day, with no time for leaning on the shovel. To be a producer on the show, it didn't matter if you were a bit eccentric (as some were) just as long as you hated to lose in the ratings, though ironically, in those days it was only Channel 9 shows competing against each other: *Midday* against *A Current Affair* against *The Today Show*. Channel 7 hadn't really entered the game of live television. Channel 10 had long ago lost the plot.

During my years at *Midday* I managed to burn out three executive producers: Paul Melville, Gary Burns and Virginia Hodgson. The EP needed to be a whip-cracking captain, a nanny and occasionally the resident comic. Before and after every show there was a production meeting that was part military debrief, part vaudeville. It was often hilariously funny as beforehand the producers ran through everything that might go wrong and afterwards told behind-the-scenes stories of their encounters with the weird and famous guests. There should have been an entry fee for the *Midday* production meetings. I remember Paul Melville screaming late one afternoon about how 'dull and lifeless and colourless' the next day's show looked.

'Can't somebody find me a f***ing nun who used to be a stripper, with fingernails dragging along the ground?' He wanted 'the gasp factor'!

Somebody eventually found a woman in Louisiana with ridiculously long talons, who read palms. (I don't recall if she was also a nun.) She appeared on the show via satellite and predicted my future. She got it all wrong, of course, but she certainly cranked up the show. Over the years there was no shortage of bizarre sideshow-alley acts. One bloke swallowed a handful of twenty cent coins and then regurgitated them in sequence according to their date; another spat a dozen ping-pong balls, like a cascading waterfall. Lithe young women in bikinis wrestled in a bath of baked beans. Other wackos had me walking across a bed of hot coals. (Maybe I was the wacko for doing it!)

We didn't just have eccentrics. There's a long and sparkling line-up of TV stars who launched their careers on *Midday* – Ernie Dingo, Gretel Killeen, Angry Anderson, Don Burke, Amanda Keller, Lisa Forrest and Rachel Friend. Shane Bourne, the host of the top-rating *Thank God You're Here*, was our warm-up man in Melbourne and a regular guest. Stephanie Kennedy, the ABC's London correspondent, was a junior researcher. The producers of a range of top-rating shows, from *The Footy Show* to *Big Brother*, *Talkin' 'bout your Generation* to *Dancing with the Stars*, all got their stripes as *Midday* producers. It was a marvellous training ground in television.

*　　*　　*

The Americans and the Brits had long ago abandoned live variety television. With the exception of *Midday*, the Australian networks had given it away as well, because quite frankly it was too dangerous. The potential for disaster was too real. When Glen Campbell broke two strings on his six-string guitar while warbling 'By the Time I Get to Phoenix', he just had to keep singing. When Michael Crawford forgot the words to a song, he had nowhere to crawl but under Geoff Harvey's piano. When the leader of the Canadian Ladies Marching Band slipped and landed on her hefty derrière, she had to struggle to her feet and march on. After all, this was live, no-second-chance television.

There was also a live studio audience of a couple of hundred people every day. It gave the whole station a frenetic buzz. In the car park there'd be buses unloading mothers' clubs or ladies' bowls teams from the bush and lines of stretch limos with stars stepping out of them. In the background there'd be the raucous snarl of Meat Loaf's rock band rehearsing one day, the sweet strains of Nigel Kennedy's classical violin the next. Or both together if they were appearing on the same show!

The studio mob was an integral part of *Midday*, but occasionally we'd get a busload from a Sydney nursing home, out for the day. It was a challenge to keep them awake. Or quiet. One day I was about two minutes into what promised to be a lively show when I heard an old lady in the front row ask her companion, 'Is it time to go home yet, Maureen?' She'd *already* had enough, and we'd barely begun. I remember after one visit Whoopi Goldberg did a whole routine at her State Theatre show about the *Midday* audience. It was hilarious, too.

Sometimes we had just as little control over our guests. Live on air I almost lost my trousers to Billy Connolly's crazy missus, Pamela Stephenson. She ended up sticking her tongue in my ear instead.

I'd interviewed Pamela once before. This time when she bounced out onto the stage she was like a harlequin on speed, wearing a canary-yellow jacket, red Robin Hood shoes, checked slacks and every imaginable colour in her hair, face and lips. I kissed her and quipped, 'Hey, thanks for dressing down!'

That seemed to kick-start her mania. 'You like my jacket? Okay, let's swap,' she challenged me. So we did.

But it didn't stop there.

She ripped off my tie, along with three buttons from my shirt, and then we swapped shoes, leaving me trying to squeeze my toes into her minuscule size fives. Suddenly, she jumped into my lap and lunged, screaming, 'C'mon, the trousers. Let's have the trousers.' She meant business. The audience erupted with laughter. Pamela is such a tiny woman that I just wrapped my arms around her, a bit like a straitjacket. That's when she stuck her tongue in my ear, as a kind of counterattack.

I was just about to go to a commercial break when out of the corner of my eye I spied Geoff Harvey leave his piano and hurtle towards me. I feared he was about to join forces with Pamela. Instead, he undid his belt, dropped his daks and said, 'C'mon, I'm taking mine off.'

Harvs had saved the day (as he so often did) and given Pamela a great tag to the joke. Off they headed, out the back of the set, and I was left to try to pick up the remnants of a *Midday* show.

Once when I was taking a week's break, George Negus filled in as the host. Unbeknown to Gorgeous George, one of his guests wasn't wearing any knickers under her dress. She swung her legs at one moment and flashed her bare essentials. Our director was quick to switch cameras, but the truly dedicated viewers caught a glimpse. Before the show went to air in Perth, the editor had to do a quick nip 'n' tuck, so to speak. That's the only time I think *Midday* was ever censored!

It shows how naïve – or innocent – we were in those days of live TV. We never had security checks on people's bags when they came into the studio, even if we had an international celebrity or the prime minister on the show. There was one bloke who came into the audience carrying a large sports bag. When our burly Italian-Australian security guard known affectionately as 'Black Ronnie' asked if he could store it someplace, the bloke said, 'Yeah, mate, thanks. Keep an eye on it, though, 'cos it's got a gun inside.' When Ronnie opened it, sure enough it was a shotgun, without the bolt. Or bullets, thankfully. Thinking back, I can't believe that in more than two thousand shows we never had a flasher run through the studio and no one ever shouted obscenities at a politician. Or me.

Of course, our most famous punch-up was when radio shock jock Ron Casey jobbed the sixties pop idol Normie Rowe live on national television. That memorable mayhem put *Midday* on news shows right around the world. It all happened in the middle of a heated debate; Ron was for an Australian Republic and Normie against it. Casey made a loose crack about Rowe and other Vietnam vets 'hiding behind the flag'. Normie lost his temper and charged across the studio floor, only to be stopped by a swinging roundhouse punch from the much older former sports commentator, Casey. That's when Black Ronnie moved in to separate the pair.

The funniest line came from Casey and didn't make it on the air. I went straight to a commercial break, and a gasping Ron said to me, 'Thank God the security bloke came in. I didn't have another punch in me.' And he meant it. It made me laugh.

On the other hand, Geoff Harvey excoriated the formidable Black Ronnie. 'You silly fool,' the Maestro screamed in mock rage. 'Why did you stop them? Imagine how much free publicity we'd have got if there was blood on the floor.' The bandleader was joking, I think, but he did have a valid point.

Because the fracas was such big news, we had their wives on the next day, and they were just as mystified – and mortified – as anyone. Hot-tempered Casey had, of course, famously thrown a glass of water on the floor in a studio debate with Jana. But that's a lot different to swinging a haymaker at another guest. Studio floors don't hit you back.

Apart from punch-ups and singers forgetting their words, another major hazard of live TV is that you have no real control over language, in particular defamatory comments and swear words. What's amazing is that in almost a decade of free-wheeling talk and gossip we only ever had to settle one lawsuit, when Angry Anderson defamed one of our top Olympic Games officials. As for swearing, that was a more regular threat. Sam Chisholm, who indulged in the occasional colourful Shake-spearean epithet himself, used to go off his skull when stand-up comics said 'bloody' or 'bastard' in their routines.

These were only mild indiscretions, but in my nine-year stint on the show there were two howlers we had no chance to censor. At the time I feared they might even put us off the air. The first involved a handsome white-haired bloke with a silver tongue. He spoke Latin fluently, as he did several languages, especially English. He was Frank Galbally, a QC widely regarded as the best criminal lawyer in Australia, having defended more than three hundred men charged with murder and getting most of them off. It was said he mesmerised juries with his oratory. At one stage of a rich and colourful life Galbally had studied to be a priest.

He came on the show to promote his new autobiography, *Galbally for the Defence*. I'd read the book before the interview, as I always did. So, in the commercial break before he walked on, I asked him if he would tell the story about the pet-shop parrot who told the judge to 'Get f***ed. Get f***ed' in the middle of a criminal trial about animal cruelty. It was a very funny story.

'Can I use those words on television?' Galbally asked, somewhat naïvely.

'No, of course you can't, Frank!' I warned him. 'Just say, "Get what's-a-named, get what's-a-named"; the audience will laugh and then we'll move on to another story.'

'Yeah, that's a great idea. Thanks. That's exactly what I'll say.'

Everything was going according to plan when halfway through our interview I asked him to tell the parrot story. 'Oh, can I tell that on television?' he asked. Like the master thespian lawyers often have to be, he sounded perfectly sincere.

'Of course you can, Frank,' I replied with a wink. 'We're all adults here, aren't we?'

The audience of mostly old ladies urged him on, shouting 'Yesssssssssss. Go on.' So he did. Except when he came to the punchline, the trainee priest cum Australia's greatest legal word-smith forgot what he'd agreed to say.

He blurted out, 'And the parrot squawked, "Get f***ed. Get f***ed."'

To say I was flabbergasted would be a gross understatement. You could hear the *Midday* audience suck the air out of the studio in one collective gasp.

As I quickly asked Galbally for another story, I glanced past him at Gary Burns, the executive producer. I figured we were both out of a job. Burnsy was frantically scratching something on a large cue card. I thought it had to be his resignation. He held it up when he'd finished. It read:

WE HAVE A BOMB THREAT! MUST GET EVERYONE OUT OF THE STUDIO!!

He flipped it over to the other side of the card, on which he'd written:

BUT DON'T PANIC!!

I was panicking all right, from the bomb that Galbally QC had just dropped on my show. Somehow we survived both explosive situations.

The other incident was even worse. It involved the c-word. I know it's been used on *Sex and the City*, but this was back in

1988. I'm certain the word had *never* been heard on Australian television before.

It was the Week of the Disabled, and we'd flown in a guest from Adelaide who had long suffered a degenerative illness and been confined to a wheelchair. She came on with her husband and their two children. As it happened, the younger child was celebrating his ninth birthday, so we had a cake ready to bring on.

In our interview I suggested to the woman and her husband that Australians had in recent times become much more sensitive towards the disabled. They agreed with me. But the perfectly proper husband – an accountant in a sober tweed jacket and tie – lamented that some Aussies were dragging the chain. He explained that the previous weekend they'd been at Hahndorf, in the Adelaide Hills, and the owner of a craft shop asked the family to leave because the wheelchair was clogging up the aisles. *The Midday Show* audience's reaction was audible. 'Ohhh, that's terrible.'

The father explained that as they walked across the street to their car, a truck roared around the corner and barely missed them.

'The driver stuck his head out the window and screamed at us as he drove past, "Get out of the way, ya stupid *–U–N–T!" How bad is that?'

I couldn't tell him how bad it was. I just couldn't speak.

He hadn't *said* the word. He'd *spelt* it. Somehow, that made it even worse. Like a blowtorch across the studio audience's faces. I simply could not believe he'd said it. He was a nice sort of a bloke who I don't think would normally even say 'damn'.

To move on from this appalling live moment, I called for the birthday cake. (What else could I do?) The cake and candles came out, the band played 'Happy Birthday' and we went to a commercial break.

The producer, Pat Lavelle – one of the best in the business – who'd arranged for the family to come on *Midday*, couldn't stop shaking. When I got downstairs to my office, Sam Chisholm had called. So had my wife. So had six viewers. That's all. Believe it or not, only six viewers bothered to phone. One predictably would 'never watch again', two were 'highly offended' and the three others thought it was 'hilarious' and 'bloody funny'.

*　　　*　　　*

Maybe because we weren't a current-affairs show, all the politicians – even prime ministers – loved to wander onto *Midday*. They gave us plenty of free headlines, because you could delve into personal as well as political issues with them. Somehow *Midday*'s live audience made the pollies relax and seem a bit more human, almost vulnerable. Joh and Flo Bjelke-Petersen always brought a plate of Kingaroy scones. Gough and Margaret were invariably witty. John Howard readily appeared, with Janette – before his remarkable makeover – in a daggy tweed sports jacket, with his eyebrows still unplucked and his teeth not yet capped. I once bagged Kim Beazley's boring tie, saying he'd never make it to the Lodge looking that drab. So he borrowed my psychedelic tie, which he then sported in Question Time, looking as proud as Joseph did in his Amazing Technicolor Dreamcoat. Alas, the tie didn't maketh a PM!

I think the most revealing political encounter on the show was in 1990, when Bob Hawke and Paul Keating came on together. Their body language was brutal, like that of a couple at the marriage-counsellor's clinic with irreconcilable differences.

Mind you, at the time nobody was aware of their 'Kirribilli Pact', which they'd made at a meeting two years earlier. Hawke had agreed to step aside for his ambitious Treasurer, yet by the time of their appearance on *Midday* Hawke had apparently welshed on the deal and things had turned sour. But nobody knew this was the reason for the tension.

Keating was surly, looked away and fidgeted a lot. Hawke was supercilious, ensuring that viewers were left in no doubt that he was the PM.

Keating had just won a radio contest naming him The Sexiest Man in Australia. A bit embarrassed and desperately trying to downplay the tag, he made a vulgar riposte that being over forty and having had four kids meant it was 'time to put the cue in the rack'. He even noted that he wore 'flannelette shocker' PJs to bed. So at the end of our interview I presented each of them with a boxed pair of silk pyjamas. It was so clear Paul didn't want to be there with Bob that one of our producers quipped in the following production meeting it was like I 'had handed them a steaming turd each'!

I have to say that I found Paul Keating probably the most interesting Australian politician of my lifetime, along with Gough Whitlam. What's more, given what was about to happen politically, that interview remains one of my favourites at *Midday*.

In June 1991, not long after that studio episode, Keating challenged Hawke for the ALP leadership and lost. I wrote inviting him to become one of our *Midday* regulars, like Angry Anderson, Dr Karl and Richard Neville. I have no doubt *Midday*, on which he could have talked about everything from antique clocks to climate change, would have helped soften Keating's image a lot. He told me he kept my letter on his bedside table and thought about it for a fortnight until finally deciding not to join the show. 'Politics, like life,' he said to me, 'is all about timing.' He wanted to be free to launch his next strike against the Honourable R. J. Hawke when the time was right.

*   *   *

Now, there's a sting in the tail of my dealings with Paul Keating that's worth mentioning because it says a lot about the bitterness of the bloke. I did a couple more interviews with him after he became prime minister, including the last he ever gave as PM, in 1996, the night before John Howard kicked him into the political scrapbooks. The fact is, because I had such respect for his intelligence, we always got on pretty well – although for what it's worth I thought his speeches about Aboriginal injustice were much tougher than his actions. But it was the so-called Piggery Affair, a fascinating political sideshow, that turned out to be contentious for me and Keating.

In March 1999 Paul Lyneham did a damaging investigative report for *60 Minutes* in which he alleged that Paul Keating had suspect dealings with the Commonwealth Bank over a piggery investment with his business partner, Al Constantinidis. Keating was understandably left frothing at the mouth. The Howard government held an inquiry into the very serious allegations and found no wrongdoing at all on Keating's part – but *60 Minutes* never reported that finding. After that Keating applied the blowtorch to Kerry Packer and Channel 9 at every opportunity.

The controversy died for a few years, until June 2009, when the retiring *60 Minutes* boss John Westacott went public, insisting that Kerry Packer had nothing to do with the Lyneham story.

That's simply not true. Packer was up to his ears in it. I know, because in July 1998 I attended a dinner at the Packer family house in Bellevue Hill, in Sydney, along with Paul Lyneham, Peter Costello, Laurie Oakes and David Leckie, the Nine Network CEO. After dinner Kerry Packer was to climb aboard his private DC-8 aircraft, which was fitted out as a flying hospital, and head for New York City for a heart bypass operation at the hands of the world-renowned cardiothoracic surgeon Dr Wayne Isom.

Standing by a crackling fire, the last thing Packer said to us was, 'The dogs are barking about Paul Keating and this piggery business. Why aren't you jokers doing the story?' He was looking straight at Oakes, whom Packer somehow knew had been secretly handed a pile of documents about Keating's financial activities. Oakes, who still wonders how Packer found out he had the documents, told KP that he'd certainly heard the rumours and looked into them, but the story didn't hold up and he didn't want a legal fight with Keating. As always, Laurie wanted to get it right. That's why he never went ahead with the story.

Packer replied, with considerable gusto, I might add, 'Leave the legal problems to me, son. Just go and get the f**king story.'

What's interesting is that the next day another set of the same documents mysteriously landed on Lyneham's desk at *60 Minutes*. Unlike Oakes, Lyneham and his producer, Peter Wilkinson, went ahead and did the story.

In 2008 I was asked to chair a dinner forum for the Oxford University Alumni, with Malcolm Turnbull, Chris Patten, the last governor of Hong Kong, and Paul Keating. I hadn't had anything to do with the former PM for almost a decade – but Paul Keating promptly informed the organisers he wouldn't participate if I was involved. I sent him an email asking why I was suddenly off his Christmas card list, given that the piggery allegations had nothing whatsoever to do with me.

His lengthy emailed reply was classic Keating speak, with loony logic, but still worth framing. He conceded that I had nothing to do with the piggery story:

But the fact is, Ray, you lent your good name, reputation and general kindliness to that sleazy outfit for nearly a quarter of a century . . .

You are one of the people, one of the decent people, I might add, who provided an acceptable face to that deeply evil, cynical and, I believe, corrupt organisation Channel Nine . . . If John Alexander is truly the reason for the inadvertent demise of Channel Nine, in my opinion he deserves an AC with a kewpie doll thrown in.

How good is that? True to form, the ex-PM finished by giving me a clip across the ears, suggesting that I needed:

. . . a reasonably lengthy stay in the detox shower to remove . . . any vestige of that truly rotten culture. Regards, Paul Keating

I had fun replying, pointing out that Mr Keating had lost none of his persuasive charm. It was vintage Paul Keating, as I say, and I treasure the correspondence.

Chapter 20
Maestro, Music Please . . .

Comedy and music were a huge part of *Midday*. In Geoff Harvey the two strands came joyously together.

I worked alongside Geoff every day for almost a decade and have enjoyed his company in the years since *Midday*. He's a genuine maddie who makes everybody around him laugh. That's a rare talent. His many friends call him 'The Maestro' or 'Harvs'. His wife calls him 'Jack'. He convinced his four beautiful little granddaughters that rather than call him Pa or Gramps, they should instead call him Soldier. Which they do, as if it was perfectly normal.

By whatever name, he is a marvellously talented musician.

If you're unlucky enough to travel overseas with Harvey, you'll be amused to find that he variously writes 'Llama Farmer', 'Inventor' or even 'Chicken De-sexer' on his immigration forms. And he gets away with it.

In Chinese restaurants he'll ask for 'spaghetti bolognaise, please'; in fish cafés he will predictably order 'a bloody big sirloin, please. No? What about a porterhouse then?'; at a sashimi bar it'll be something like 'I'd love a nice hot nasi goreng, thank you'. Then, he'll pretend to be surprised when the waiter explains that dish is Indonesian. 'Oh, really?' he'll say with his eyebrows raised. 'I'm sorry, how about a tandoori masala then?'

He could easily have been one of The Goons on radio, or a lunatic in those Monty Python television sketches. And there's a tiny bit of Chaplin, a touch of Mr Bean, about his simple-minded lunacy.

Years ago, when mobile phones were the size of small house bricks, only a few VIPs in airport lounges had them. They'd walk the floor and always talk loudly. Harvey would take off his shoe and, like Maxwell Smart, speak into it, laughing away and holding a rip-roaring conversation as if he really was phoning somebody. Other times he'd sit across the aisle from me on a plane, alongside some poor unsuspecting passenger. While they'd be reading *The Financial Review* or *The Australian*, the mad musician would suddenly whip open a Chinese newspaper he'd bought in the airport shop. Flicking the pages – starting from the back, of course – he'd cackle away to himself and point stories out to his fellow traveller, pretending he understood what it said. On some flights he'd appear with a copy of *Bodybuilder's Monthly* or *Quarter Horse Digest*, and he'd say he was a licensed breeder.

I remember on one particular flight I took with Harvs, the former PM Malcolm Fraser sat near me, wearing a tweed jacket and matching tweed tie, as befitted a wealthy grazier from Victoria's Western District. Harvey happened to be a few seats behind. As I walked off the plane, he rushed up alongside and said, 'Why don't you tell Mr Fraser what you said about his tie?'

'What are you talking about?' I protested.

'Oh well, if you don't want to repeat what you said earlier on board, that's fine.'

Fraser looked at me a bit strangely. I assured him I had never even mentioned his tie and that Harvey was insane. The ex-PM laughed. But when he'd collected his bag from the carousel, before he headed off with his driver, Fraser paused and asked, 'What's wrong with my tie?'

I've seen Geoff suddenly put his arm around my wife Dianne's shoulder as we've walked into a charity function. Then he stops, smiles for the cameras and tells the snappers it's his wife, Katrina. Next Sunday's social pages there's the photo of the happy couple with the totally wrong caption. Harvs will ring up, cackling with delight.

He also makes a habit of chewing – and even swallowing – the airline boarding passes of people travelling with him, just as they're about to get on the plane. Or your ticket in a shopping-centre car park, as you drive up to the exit booth. Then he'll deny it and watch with glee as you try to explain what happened. 'Oh, don't be so ridiculous,' he'll say. 'Nobody would do that. Just pay the lady, please.' He never cracks.

I once stopped my car outside a building site to let a semi get through the narrow gates. It was the biggest Mack truck, with a humungous driver. Blue singlet, no neck and gigantic arms all squeezed into the cab. He was doing a great job edging out, until Harvey reached over from the passenger seat and blasted my horn. The bloke stopped, glared at me, put his slab-of-beef arm out the window and then gave me the bird with his enormous middle finger. I feared he was about to come over and smash my bonnet and my face. Angry, he went back to driving the truck. As he did, Harvey lunged again, aiming for the horn. In panic I grabbed his long, delicate piano-playing fingers and threatened to crush them.

'Go on. You can handle him,' he laughed.

I promise you, I couldn't.

'How much are these hands insured for with Lloyd's of London?'

'Oh, at least a dollar fifty,' he quipped.

I've got to say, he makes *me* laugh.

On *Midday* he'd do things like hang a string of sausages from his zipper. He'd wait till he could see the live studio camera was on him, then he'd spin around like a deranged flasher, hoping to catch the director and the audience off guard. He often did.

We would regularly have blind guests in the audience and on the show. The extraordinary triathlete and bubbly bloke Ched Towns would always have his guide dog with him. Harvey would wait until midway through the interview, when the highly intelligent animal had settled nicely and was nodding off under his master's feet. Suddenly, the dog would get all agitated, fidget around and stand up. Ched was mystified and would have to work hard to calm him again.

'Sit down, mate. I don't know what's upset him today,' he'd say to the audience.

It took me a few shows to realise Harvey was to blame.

'What? What did I do?' he would ask innocently as I turned to him.

What he would do was play barks and whistles on his electronic synthesiser at a pitch that only the dog could hear. When I apologised to Ched, he just laughed.

'Hey, Geoff, that's really funny. You're a mad thing, aren't ya?'

Roy Ainsworth was a brilliant sax player and for many years a much-loved regular in Channel 9 bands. Just a little bloke, about the size of a jockey, Ainsworth had contracted polio as a kid, which meant he walked with a stick and a noticeable limp. No one cared for him more than Geoff. You'd think that might stop Harvey's tasteless practical jokes. It didn't. Polio was never a handicap for Roy in his life or his work. Harvey was the handicap.

Like the time Roy, Geoff and a couple of band members were in the city, heading from a local pub to a recording studio. While they waited at the lights to cross, an old builder's ute came slowly around the corner in front of them. Without warning, Harvey picked a startled Roy up in his arms and tossed him in the back of the truck, which sped off down the road. It was a couple of kilometres before the builder discovered he had some squealing human contraband on board, in the middle of his toolboxes and ladder. As he was helped down, Roy found it useless to try to explain to the astonished bloke what had actually happened. When Roy finally arrived at the recording studio, Harvey chipped him for being late.

Most days after the show a bunch of these musical desperates would head down the local pub. Roy was one of them. He would sit on the last stool at the bar, where it was easiest for him to get up and down. But that made him an obvious target for Harvey, along with one or two others. They'd bump him on their way to the toilet. Occasionally he'd be knocked off his stool, and he'd cackle and call them all 'a bunch of bastards'. It was just mates horsing around. Roy would get his own back by tripping Harvey with his walking stick.

Well, one lunchtime, it was a different pub but the same old stunt. However, sitting in the corner of the bar happened to be three big bikies. All leather jackets, bushy beards and quaffing Jack Daniel's. Annoyed at first, they then started getting angry about the mistreatment of the bloke with the walking stick. It was just bad luck for Harvey. Because, making his toilet run, he gave Roy a nudge and walked straight into the biggest bikie's belly.

'Why don't you pricks leave the cripple alone?' he demanded. 'Let him just have his beer.'

Geoff smiled and explained they were all mates, they played in a band together and they were just having a bit of fun. When the bikie asked Roy if it was true, the sax player denied it.

'I never seen this smart-arse until today. He says he's on television.' He pointed to Geoff.

The bikie grabbed the piano player by the throat and told him to 'leave the little bloke alone and piss off out of the bar'. Which Harvey did. It's a famous story the old band members love to tell at Harvs's expense.

*   *   *

Geoff was born in the London working-class suburb of Wood Green. His parents were musical, and his whole life has been music, music, music. He played the church organ at eight and piano while he was at the Westminster Cathedral School. By the time he was twenty, he'd graduated from the Royal College of Music. After that he played in jazz clubs for a few years and then became a cruise-liner pianist. In 1960 he jumped ship in Sydney to become musical director at EMI records and then at Channel 9, where he played piano, arranged music and composed the network's theme songs, for everything from *The Sullivans* to *Sunday*.

For over thirty years he was in charge of the music for the Logies telecasts, *Carols by Candlelight* and every entertainment special broadcast on Channel 9. He swung the baton, played fall guy and regularly rescued the station's TV stars, including

Graham Kennedy, Bert Newton, Daryl Somers, Don Lane, Mike Walsh, Kerri-Anne Kennerley and myself. Not to mention the extraordinary Irish wit Dave Allen, Bobby Limb, Brian Henderson and Barry Crocker.

It wasn't just the quantity of Harvey's musical output that was phenomenal. So was the quality of what he did. At times it was breathtaking. For his work as a pianist, composer and arranger, Geoff has earned plaudits and praise from musicians ranging from Sinatra to numerous symphony orchestras, and was awarded an Order of Australia. In recent years he's been studying the church organ at St Mary's Cathedral, reaching the highest levels of excellence.

Musically, there was nothing quite like what he did on *The Midday Show* anywhere in the world. He actually had three different bands, which he rotated weekly. In a good year they would play well over five hundred musical numbers. Five hundred. The band each day featured Harvs and eleven superb musicians who were regarded as the very best session players in the business. You'd regularly find them featured on a new album, a movie soundtrack or commercials; they performed in all the musical comedy shows and travelled with visiting superstars like Sinatra, Shirley Bassey and Tom Jones. On *Midday* they played everything from rock to blues, jazz, soul and the classics. Quite often Geoff would add extra strings or brass, or sometimes a full symphony orchestra. Neither Letterman nor Leno could match that output. Johnny Carson never did, either. Remember Michael Parkinson was only on once a week, for a limited season.

Under Harvey *Midday* was also the television launch pad for Anthony Warlow, Keith Urban, guitar virtuoso Tommy Emmanuel and country idol James Blundell.

Young and handsome, with a shock of blond hair, Anthony

Warlow had left the Australian Opera and was on the way to becoming the most talented musical comedy star in Australia. Anthony became almost a regular on *Midday* and was a delight to work with, without ego or tantrums. Just a most wonderful voice and a quirky sense of humour. It was actually after singing on *Midday* in Melbourne, as he tried to put on his tie, that Warlow discovered a suspicious lump on his neck. It turned out to be non-Hodgkin's lymphoma, which kept him out of the original *Jesus Christ Superstar* production and even threatened his life. During his rehab period he came on the show and promised to sing with one of our regulars, Simon O'Donnell, who'd played cricket for Australia and had recovered from the same cancer. Anyway, going from the sublime to the ridiculous, Warlow eventually joined O'Donnell in a painful version of 'Billy Don't Be a Hero', the only song in Simon's sad repertoire.

The good news is that Anthony managed to recover and returned to being a music superstar – minus the blond mane, which he'd unfortunately lost to chemotherapy. Not that it's held him back at all.

Keith Urban was discovered by *Midday*'s sassy music coordinator, Lesley Moy, when he was only about eighteen. Lesley had no doubts that the sexy guitar wizard from Caboolture with the shaggy peroxide hair was bound for glory. The truth is, he was bound for Nashville. I remember speaking to Keith at the time of his first appearance, and even then his was a single-minded pursuit: to get to Nashville and play guitar with the country greats and write some hit songs. Maybe because of his tight jeans and his good looks, his incredible guitar-playing talents went a bit unnoticed here at home. But with the Grammies and 'the girls' – Nicole and Sunday Rose – he's racked up the success he deserved. Again, like the best of them on *Midday*, Keith was a delight to work with behind the scenes. Funny how the good ones are usually easy.

For an old journo like me, sitting next to the *Midday* band every lunchtime, listening to them play and enjoying their company was probably *the* most special part of the show. Time after time I watched in astonishment when a guest would suddenly mention a song and the band would just rip into it. There wasn't any song that they didn't know. I was taken by surprise once during an interview when the classic crooner Johnny Mathis, who was in Los Angeles, stood up and started to sing. Because of the satellite time delay, Mathis's voice was a second or so behind the band. Harvey and his musos somehow adjusted their tempo to fit. To this day I don't quite know how they did it. It was extraordinary.

Another time the great Tony Bennett was rehearsing with his piano-playing musical director, Ralph Sharon, and an expanded *Midday Show* band. (There was no expense spared when a music god like Tony was on the show.) I went across to the studio just to watch rehearsals. At one point Bennett called Ralph over and whispered to him. A worried Harvey checked to see if there was something wrong. 'No, on the contrary, Geoffrey,' said Sharon. 'Mr Bennett was just asking if he could have your band for the rest of our tour.'

Incidentally, our director was told that Bennett didn't want any close-up camera shots from the side. In other words strictly *no profiles* of Tony's prominent proboscis. Having heard that request, I was surprised during the show when, towards the end of 'I Left My Heart in San Francisco', one of the cameras inadvertently slipped into the no-go zone. Bennett, the old pro, saw it coming. As he reached his big finale, he raised his right arm up and blocked out the whole side of his face. The director had no choice but to cut to another camera.

Julio Iglesias was another super-singer with a camera no-go zone. I forget which side Julio's was, but the Spanish lady-killer insisted the cameras stay on one side of the studio. That was so they didn't show his bald spot.

Of course it wasn't only musicians who could be vain. Sylvester Stallone came out in his high-heeled boots, shook hands and asked if he could swap seats. Why? 'Because that's my best side,' he told me. But Bob Hawke probably ranks as the most vain *Midday* guest ever. We had to turn off the TV monitor with Hawke, otherwise he'd spend the whole interview looking at himself on the box, preening and stroking his silver locks and talking to himself.

The music phenomenon Tom Jones was a *Midday* favourite. Once, he arrived with a bleached-blond, hyper-muscled bodyguard who stood just at the edge of the studio. In the commercial break he came out and asked Tom if he needed water. Tom nodded. The bodyguard grabbed a bottle of chilled Perrier – which Sir Tom's entourage had specifically requested – then he broke the seal, had a swig and gave it the thumbs up.

'Yeah, that's okay, Tom,' he said, assuring the Welsh coal-miner's son there was no poison or nuclear waste in it. I'd read about medieval potentates and mafia kings having official taste testers, but I'd never seen anything like this before.

Another musical knight of the realm, Sir Cliff Richard, co-hosted *Midday* one lunchtime. A delightful old lady in our audience had come to the show with her family, to celebrate her 104th birthday. So Cliff and I asked her a couple of questions about the secret to long life, which she answered with great humour. But in mid-sentence the lady suddenly stopped, looked at Cliff and said, 'Now, I know who Ray is, but what's your name? And what do you do?' For a bloke who'd sold more than

250 million records and may be the best-known British pop star after the Beatles, this was quite a reality check. But Cliff didn't mind. He almost fell off his stool with laughter.

*　　　*　　　*

Somehow managing to corral all this musical talent five days a week was the incorrigible Geoff Harvey. Who knows, maybe it was that insane sense of humour that gave him his energy. I'd like to finish with a final story about Harvey's lunacy, plucked from our many perilous air miles together.

The piano player and I were flying back to Sydney after a week of *Midday* shows in Melbourne. Sitting in the aisle seat, Geoff yawned as the stewardess came along with the tea trolley.

'Oh, I see we've been burning the candle at both ends, have we, Mr Harvey?'

Silly question. Silly move, really. (It's safer not to engage Harvey on a flight.)

'Well, no . . . er, Janice,' the piano player replied, reading her Ansett name tag. 'Actually, I didn't get to sleep at all. I've been staying at my sister Maureen's house out at Moorabbin.'

I figured Janice was now in deep trouble. Harvey has no sisters and wouldn't have the foggiest idea where Moorabbin is. Out of his alcohol-soaked labyrinth of a brain he'd somehow fossicked this fraud of a story.

There'd be worse to come, I just knew it.

'My little nephew Trent, who's almost three, had a terrible bout of the croup. I was staying out there while Maureen's husband, Wayne, was away. He's a ship's captain. We carried Trent up and down the corridor all night. It was exhausting for us; imagine what it was like for the little bloke.'

257

I had to turn away. I mean, Trent? . . . and Wayne, the ship's captain? Where had they come from? The croup?

I thought I was going to be ill. Janice was clearly upset.

'I'm so sorry, Mr Harvey,' she said. 'Is the little darling all right?'

'I don't know, Janice,' Harvey replied with agonising sincerity. 'I dropped him at the Royal Melbourne Children's Hospital and then caught the plane.'

'Oh dear,' the deeply disturbed Janice said. 'Can I get you anything to drink?'

It was coming up to 11 am, and the rest of the plane was getting warm tea and cold finger sandwiches.

Harvey asked for 'a blizzardly cold Foster's, with a small cognac, if that's possible. Just to settle my nerves.'

Of course it was possible. Janice was so upset by Trent's condition, anything was possible.

'You're a low act, Harvey,' I scolded as Janice went to get his booze.

'She'll be all right,' he laughed, 'but what the bloody hell is the croup?'

By the time we got to Sydney, the piano player had scored another round of Foster's, with the cognac chaser. His nerves were starting to settle.

'G'bye, Mr Harvey,' Janice said as we left the plane. 'I hope Trent's feeling better.'

'I'm going to ring the hospital immediately, Janice. But I must say, I fear the worst.'

I do hope that Janice never reads this book.

Chapter 21
Flying High

After *60 Minutes* I put the passport away for a while, except for the occasional quick trip. Strangely, my life had a set routine. That had never been the case for me before, at least not since high school. Now every weekday I had to be in the same studio at the same time – wearing a loud tie and colourful socks.

Incidentally, I can't tell you how many calls we received from women asking where they could buy my ties. Nadia Benussi, the fabulous *Midday* stylist, had all the natural-born taste that comes with Italian blood. We had offers from local manufacturers for us to endorse their socks and ties, but we knew they'd never match the artistry of the Milanese silk numbers Nadia chose for me.

But if my private life suddenly had a calm rhythm, my television world was a bit crazy.

In a sense I became 'the face of Channel 9', following in the footsteps of Graham Kennedy, Don Lane, Bert Newton and Daryl Somers. In the early nineties, Dianne started to complain that I was always on the TV, and when she turned it off . . . I was still there. At home. I think she was joking.

David Leckie, the Channel 9 boss at the time, once sent me a newspaper cartoon. It showed a TV repairman and a woman standing in front of a blank TV screen. The caption reads: 'The reason the screen's blank is that Ray Martin has been on holiday for a while!' I must admit, for a period it *was* hard to avoid me on Channel 9. As well as hosting *Midday*, I continued to fill in for Willesee and then Jana on *A Current Affair*. I hosted the Commonwealth Games and even World Cup cricket, headed every election telecast, moderated the Great Debates, and fronted *Carols by Candlelight* and an endless stream of network specials, including the Bicentenary Spectacular with Jana and Clive James. That was the most extravagant one-off special in Australian TV history.

It was these specials, probably thirty of them over a decade, that gave me the chance to work with an amazing, creative bloke named Peter Wynne. In the television game an exceptional producer, cameraman or editor can make all the difference. In my career Wynney has made the difference. He's probably the best special-events TV producer Australia has ever had.

Peter Wynne's a big bear of a bloke with a mop of salt-and-pepper hair. I sometimes think he resembles a Hollywood movie director rather than a TV producer. He's colourful and can be loud when he feels the urge. He luxuriates in telling amusing stories. If he's in the mood, after a few choice reds, he'll try to 'out-Cocker' Joe with an unaccompanied rendition of 'You Are So Beautiful'.

Pete and I recorded one-off specials with Michael Douglas in Cannes, Jim Carrey in Atlanta, Madonna in the Hollywood Hills, Ben Elton in London, Billy Joel outside Miami, Tony Curtis inside our Melbourne studio and Stevie Wonder in crime-ridden South Central LA.

But perhaps my most memorable journey with Pete was to a place high in the Rocky Mountains of Colorado, with John Denver. It was for a prime-time special that ended up rating its socks off. We had no way of knowing that this show would also be Denver's last hurrah.

Denver laughed a lot as we strapped on our parachutes and flying helmets and jumped into his stunt biplane, his beloved Pitts Special. Standing on the tiny Aspen tarmac, against a backdrop of America's most spectacular snow-covered peaks, I was listening hard when he said, 'If I say "Eject", Raymond, let me tell ya', it's non-negotiable.'

The folk-singing superstar had grown up an Air Force brat, with a dad who was a US test pilot. Denver was himself a highly rated pilot, cleared to fly everything up to and including Learjets.

We'd spent the morning filming Denver singing a few of his favourite songs, at Maroon Lake, a spectacular glacial valley up in the White River National Park. It's been called the most-photographed spot in all of the Rockies. We had the wilderness to ourselves. Along with the elk and bears. Denver's perfect-pitch tenor voice had sounded crystal clear in the high country air.

I'd interviewed him many times on *The Midday Show*. I was a huge fan of this complex man and his beautiful music. Still am, over a decade since he died. This time he was deeply distracted. His relationship with his Aussie-born wife, Cassandra, had turned worse than sour. It was curdling his emotions.

Wynne took me aside at the Aspen airport and said he didn't want me to take off. He just didn't feel good about it. Pete was seriously worried that John Denver was too depressed, maybe even suicidal.

Anyway, after tossing it around, I opted to go flying. I'm so glad I did.

I sat up the front of the Pitts Special as we skipped across a sparkling blue sky, along the jagged, rocky filigree of the mountaintops, twice as high as Mount Kosciuszko. Unbelievably, I had John Denver laughing and singing 'Rocky Mountain High' for me live in my earphones. He was showing off this world that had inspired so many of his favourite songs.

He suddenly seemed exhilarated again, free and full of joy. It was one of the most awesome moments of my life.

'How 'bout we go flying, Raymond?' he asked rhetorically. I figured we were going flying whether I liked it or not. Anyway, it sounded like fun. 'Hang on, here we go!'

And straight up we went. Vertical, till the engine seemed to peter out and stall. We hung for a long moment high above the highest peaks. Then we backflipped and corkscrewed down towards Maroon Lake, flattening out at the last moment and skimming across the aspen and birch forests, like Jean-Claude Killy zigzagging down a ski slope.

Wynne and the camera crew, in another plane, asked if we could do it all again. So we did. Just as fast and just as exhilarating; it seemed to suck the oxygen out of my brain.

So often in life, after the highs come the low points. Even for the rich and famous.

That night Denver invited us for a barbecue at his beautiful ranch up on Starwood Ridge, high above Aspen. A few days earlier he'd caught some wild salmon in Alaska, and he wanted to share it with us.

He was an amazing bloke with an extraordinary range of talents. As well as being a world-renowned singer-songwriter, he played half a dozen stringed instruments and the piano. He had a scholar's knowledge of astronomy and space technology, of religion and poetry. He also took exquisite photographs.

In fact, now that his estranged wife and daughter were living out in California, all that remained of his broken family life were the photographs. Painful portraits of Jesse Belle, his darling daughter, were everywhere, hanging on half-empty walls, like incandescent candles scattered around a gloomy cave.

Long paspalum and flowering weeds had grown up through the floor of the little girl's faded cubby house, which sat forgotten in the garden. Denver's big, empty dwelling was in desperate need of a coat of sunshine. It sadly missed the music of laughter and play. I kept thinking it would probably never come again. Worth maybe twenty million dollars on Aspen's hot real-estate market, it was no longer the warm hearth and home that the happy troubadour had so often sung about. Rather, it reminded me – in a strange, enigmatic way – of those final black-and-white scenes from *Citizen Kane*.

His wife, Cassandra, he told us, 'was a heartache waiting to happen'.

He said things much worse than that, too. It was hard for us to reconcile this toxic, torn heart with all those tender, sweet songs that still bring hope and happiness to lovers everywhere.

We drank some Coors beers with Denver, guaranteed him good times on his upcoming Australian tour and wandered onto his huge wooden deck. In the rarefied Colorado darkness you could see the wonders of the universe.

He seemed happier as we left, thanking him for a generous day, his hospitality and the Alaskan salmon. We wished him peaceful dreams.

Back in my Aspen hotel room I opened the blinds to look out on the grandeur of his beloved Rocky Mountains. Sitting in the darkness, I played a CD he had just given us, which included one of his favourite songs, 'On the Wings of a Dream', which was a requiem to his late father.

Denver came to Australia a few weeks later for what would be his final tour. We did some more filming in our GTV Melbourne studio, which was filled with dewy-eyed adoring fans, and he flew us back to Sydney in a Learjet. That's the last time we spoke.

Sadly, this wasn't long before John Denver crashed to his death flying an experimental Long-EZ plane off Monterey, California. The official investigation concluded that it was 'probably an accident' when he ran out of fuel.

I hope that's what happened. We'll never know.

*   *   *

As I mentioned, our special with John Denver was just one in an incredible galaxy ranging from Tom Cruise, the world's biggest movie star at the time, to the legendary *Star Wars* producer George Lucas. We got to spend time with some of the most famous faces in the world of entertainment.

But you can't kid yourself. A star's availability for an interview always depends on whether they have a movie or concert to promote. Paul Hogan put the relationship between stars and the media pretty succinctly to me one day. (Hoges is always honest!) When I asked him why he put himself through the media wringer after being bashed up over his love affair with Linda Kozlowski, he smiled and said, 'Listen, no offence, Raymond, but I wouldn't have anything to do with you jokers if I didn't have a movie to flog!' Fair enough too.

Despite the fact that they all rated fantastically, getting network specials on air at Channel 9 didn't just happen. There were always arguments and horse-trading with the almighty program directors. Wynne and I would have to offer our souls; it was like selling them to the devil. I remember having a punch-up about a Michael Crawford special because the program chief asked, 'Does anyone care about Michael Crawford anymore?' We argued loudly that he had an enormous rusted-on Aussie fan base, his albums always sold a hundred thousand plus and the TV special was a guaranteed smash-hit. But we kept our fingers crossed when it finally went to air, especially as it was slotted late on a Saturday night, which was not exactly Michael's demographic. (It seemed our friendly program director was out to sink us again.) So it was high fives all around when a million plus viewers were still laughing along with Michael at 11 pm. Phew.

Michael Crawford is a remarkable showman, and if I had to single out the best show-business star I have ever interviewed on TV, it would be Michael. I know that's a big call, but Crawford has got the lot. If you combine the comedy brilliance of Frank Spencer in *Some Mothers Do 'Ave 'Em* with his exquisite voice in *Phantom of the Opera*, the circus skills he displayed in *Barnum*, his matinee-idol good looks and his natural warmth, along with his hilarious storytelling ability, then Michael Crawford is pretty much the complete package.

Crawford's funniest laughs are always at his own expense, which makes him all the more endearing. Michael says, for example, that he was the last choice for the role of Frank Spencer; the BBC wanted the legendary comedian Norman Wisdom or Ronnie Corbett instead, but they both turned it down. He insists it was the same with the *Phantom* role. Others turned it down. 'So, really, I have been the last choice for everything,' he laughs, with a shrug of the shoulders. 'My mother didn't even want a child.' Audiences crack up at that story. His vulnerability is part of his charm.

Crawford is always at pains to prove that he's not like Frank in real life, that it's just a TV character he played, that he's not really a klutz. Then you'll watch him walk into a closed door or miss the chair when he sits down at lunch. Or he accidentally drops his tie into his soup. Or his trousers fall down. Just like Frank Spencer.

But what I find extraordinary is that such an amazing, multi-talented star as Michael can be painfully shy, totally lacking in self-confidence one minute, then the next he bursts onto the stage and rules the world.

The first network special Wynne and I did with Crawford was the highest-rating show of 1991. Yet when we first talked about doing it, Michael insisted that he didn't have enough amusing anecdotes for a one-hour show, even if he performed three songs. So we went to dinner, and he started telling us about his plane flight from America. It seems that somewhere over the Pacific he lost the button on his trousers, and, without a belt, the zipper wouldn't stay up. As he tried to step across the lady lying in the seat next to him in first class, she woke up in shock. Just like Frank Spencer, he breathlessly tried to explain what had happened. And why his fly was undone as he straddled her. I couldn't stop laughing.

That story set him on a comedy roll, and out came a dozen similar hilarious anecdotes. My stomach was aching by the end of dinner.

Still, when we came to record the special before a huge live audience, I noticed that Michael had biro scribbles on the palm of his hand. He explained that these were cheat notes in case he forgot any of the stories. He was like a kid in an exam. I couldn't believe an international mega-star could be so brilliant yet so insecure.

The truth is, the only thing he ever forgot was the final words to one of his favourite songs, 'Since You Stayed Here', when he was a guest on *Midday*. It was just Michael and Geoff Harvey together at the grand piano, and a studio filled with Crawford tragics and high expectations. When Michael and Geoff came to the big finale, there was a breath, a pause . . . and then silence.

'And . . . I forget the words . . . Da daaaaa,' Michael sang as he collapsed to the studio floor and crawled under the black shiny grand.

I remember one other embarrassing but hilarious crawl across the floor by Michael Crawford. He was co-hosting *The Midday Show* with me, and we were interviewing Tanya Blencowe, the eleven-year-old girl who had played a major role in Sydney's bid for the 2000 Olympic Games by delivering a speech during the final presentation to the International Olympic Committee at Monte Carlo in 1993. Tanya explained that in the lead-up she had to keep her involvement a secret from her Bangor Primary schoolmates. She explained her absence from school by saying that she had to go to England to see her sick grandmother.

'Oh, I see, the old sick grandma trick,' said Michael. 'And any-way, Tanya,' he asked, smiling, 'how is your grandmother, eh?'

There was a momentary pause as Tanya looked towards her mother, who was off camera.

'Oh, well . . . er . . .' Tanya mumbled.

'No, c'mon, Tanya. How is Granny?' he asked again.

'Well, actually, Mr Crawford, my grandmother died. She really was sick.'

There was a gasp from the audience, while Michael fell to the floor and crawled out the door. He returned to cuddle the little girl and apologise. She was fine; it was Michael who was morti-fied. But that's the sort of mishap that befalls Mr Crawford.

A few years later I saw Michael in Las Vegas in his seventy-million-dollar casino tour-de-force show *EFX*, at the MGM Grand. It was a box-office smash-hit for a couple of years but was so physically demanding that Crawford had to quit and have a hip replacement after a heavy fall. As it does to all of us, Father Time was catching up with him.

Then, in December 2002, I paid up on a promise to spend a week in New York with Jenna after her final high-school exams. We saw Broadway shows every night, including Crawford in the lead role of a short-lived musical-comedy flop named *Dance of the Vampires*. I'd rung Michael after we bought the tickets and he invited us back to the dressing room after the show. We ago-nised over what to tell him. He clearly knew he had a disaster on his hands, so we just said to him, 'You were great!' (which he was), and we did a runner. Not even Michael Crawford can win 'em all.

Chapter 22
A Dad for All Seasons

Midday gave me time to be a dad. In my 'spare' moments I also wrote a weekly column for about thirty suburban and country newspapers. Jenna was invariably the subject of these weekly musings. As her tediously besotted father, I recounted the miracles of her amazing life – like walking and talking. I was hopeless, and realise I must have bored everyone with my latest Jenna stories till there was blood coming out of their ears.

The truth is, when Jenna was barely crawling I wanted five more baby girls just like her. Immediately. (I suspect Dianne would have committed herself to a mental hospital if a genie had granted us that wish.)

One wintry morning when Jenna was about three, I raced out to the front gate to collect the papers. She got upset because I usually carried her out with me for this daily chore. I explained that I'd left her inside because it was so cold that even the azalea bushes were shivering. (Thankfully, when she looked out the window they were shaking – from the wind.) Anyhow, when I left for work an hour later she walked with me to the car, carrying all her dolls' blankets, and proceeded to stretch them over the azalea bushes. 'There you go, flowers,' she whispered, 'now you'll be nice 'n' warm.'

She also used to talk to the Sydney Harbour Bridge as we drove across it.

'Hello, bridge,' she'd chirp every time. 'How are you today?'

I would pretend to be old man bridge. 'I'm very well, thank you, Jenna. And where are you going?'

She'd tell me that she was off to Grandpa's, Auntie Suzie's or taking Mum shopping. Whatever. The conversation would stop as soon as we drove off the other side – with 'Goodbye, bridge' – until the next time.

This routine went on for a couple of years, till she was almost five. Then one day I picked my mother up from the airport. Mum visited us quite often, even though she was in her seventies now and living up in Gunnedah again with her elder sister, Annie. She sat with Jenna in the back of the car as we returned home across the bridge. That was Jenna's cue to start our familiar routine.

'Hello, bridge, I've got Nanny with me in the car. She's come to stay with us.'

Then, as we got to the end of the bridge I heard her whisper to Mum, 'It's not really the bridge talking, Nanny. It's just Dad, but I humour him anyway!'

Sadly, that was the last time it ever happened. She'd obviously outgrown that phase and moved on to studying astrophysics or some other higher endeavour.

As a child, Jenna quite often came into *The Midday Show* and would sit in a corner of the studio with a couple of her favourite producers. One special day when the full complement of the Sydney Symphony Orchestra was on the show, performing Leopold Mozart's 'The Toy Symphony' live, Jenna was given the task of tinkling a tiny bell. Jenna, who was only six, had practised her two-second performance for weeks.

In those early years, when I could steal her away from her mother we'd go to nearby playgrounds and parks for hours. She loved to race her brightly coloured plastic tricycle down a grassy hill, and then do it a hundred times more. She'd hurtle back and forth on 'the big swing' until darkness drove us reluctantly home. Every Thursday evening she and I would sit on our local railway platform in the shadows and 'surprise' her mother as she returned from late-night shopping in the city. It was our Thursday-night ritual, no matter what the weather. We used to sit there making up our own scary stories about the people behind the faces that stared, like zombies, out the lighted train windows.

On Saturday afternoons Jenna and I would often adjourn to Luna Park, where for about three hours – and costing the rude sum of three dollars – she'd wear out the merry-go-round and the other toddlers' rides. She'd wave as she glided past me and I'd endlessly take her photo. She was always laughing as a child. Still is today, although it's harder to get her to agree to a photograph now. The bribe of fairy floss no longer works.

We were on vacation in a grand old railway hotel in Edinburgh for Hogmanay when we gave five-year-old Jenna the wonderful news that her mum was having a baby. Dianne was almost four months pregnant, and we were overjoyed. The early hours of a brand-new year seemed a perfect time to reveal news of the brand-new baby. Jenna had long been pestering us for a baby sister or brother. It was about two in the morning, and we'd seen in 1990 with Dianne's mum and dad, who had come on holiday with us. They'd danced through the midnight hour in the hotel ballroom spotlight, like a couple of young lovers. Jenna burst from our room and raced down the old hotel corridors, brimming with the hot news to tell Dianne's parents. They affected surprise. It was one of those delicious family moments.

Unlike when Dianne was pregnant with Jenna, we were anxious to know this time whether it was a boy or a girl. That way we would be able to deviously manoeuvre Jenna into a state of mind where she had her fingers crossed for a baby brother. Mind you, there was an uncomfortable moment when the specialist first told Dianne that we were having a boy. Dianne wasn't confident she'd be able to handle a tearaway adolescent son with muddy footy boots and an excess of testosterone. Her mother, Nancy, who had raised two boys, and her sister, Susan, who'd survived three boisterous lads (who all fitted the tearaway description), reassured Dianne that they'd help her through the journey. And they did. Anyway, Dianne's fear was just a momentary distraction: Luke, like Jenna, is the absolute light of her life.

Luke came along early one Tuesday morning in May 1990. The night before, I was scheduled to be the MC at a fundraising dinner for schizophrenia research, organised by the late and legendary Jack Gibson, who was perhaps the greatest rugby-league coach of all. Jack's adult son had long been troubled by schizophrenia, and the disabling mental disorder had finally led to his tragic death. The afternoon of the dinner Dianne went for a checkup and the obstetrician warned her that the baby was ready to drop. So her parents slept over while I did my MCing duties for Jack, keeping my mobile phone handy. Fortunately, I made it home in plenty of time. I was sound asleep when, at about 2 am, Dianne woke me. We headed for the hospital, where Dianne comfortably gave birth to our son later that morning. We liked the name Luke, and as that had also been the name of

Jack Gibson's boy, it seemed like a good choice. Jack, a man of few words, told me later that he was honoured.

As Luke was born just after eight in the morning, I was able to go on *Midday* – unshaven, with the kindly John Mangos hosting – and announce that we now had a boy. I'm still astonished by the number of former *Midday* viewers I meet who recall, to the precise hour, when Luke was born. As well as handing me a fat cigar on camera, Geoff Harvey played the beautiful 'Song for Luke' he had composed, then handed me the original score, which we still proudly have. Geoff would later plant a deciduous tree for Luke in his gorgeous country garden. That followed an apple tree he'd planted for Jenna across the other side of the paddock cum cricket pitch.

Our darling boy, Luke, was the missing piece in the family jigsaw puzzle. He got his fair share of my newspaper columns, too. And just as I had wished for five more baby girls the instant we had Jenna, so too I would have also loved five boys! The simple fact is, in another lifetime I think I was meant to raise a huge family.

Because Luke came later, his Channel 9 experience was more often at *A Current Affair*, which of course was never as much fun as Jenna had at *Midday*. He got to go to Kirribilli House several times, when I was doing the show live from there or an interview with the PM. John Howard gave him a private tour a couple of times. I have to say Mr Howard was kind and gracious, and, like a consummate politician, he never forgot Luke's name.

From an early age Luke started going with me to cricket and football games, something every father dreams of doing with his son. I used to smile as he would quite comfortably chat with sporting legends such as Ken Rosewall, Johnny Raper and Richie Benaud, as if that's what every kid did. At his age the closest I ever got to such heroes was a newspaper photo stuck on my wall. At the Souths games Russell Crowe would always console Luke after yet another defeat, although Luke came to doubt the word of the Gladiator after he'd gone to twenty-three games without seeing one victory. That can sorely test your footy faith when you're only eight. As luck would have it, the Mighty Rabbitohs finally won a game, and that's when Russell grabbed Luke and Tom Cruise – who was in the box at the game – and raced them down to the celebrations in the dressing room. Luke dumped me that day.

My mum doted on Luke, who was the last of her grand-children. She was able to see even more of him once she left Gunnedah to live in Sydney in her own apartment.

It warmed my heart to see her contented and serene after such a turbulent and tough early life. We laughed out loud one day, just the two of us having a glass of wine together on the back verandah as we contemplated life in our suburban 'castle'. Dianne and I now owned our house, with a swimming pool and a nice car. The kids had never changed schools and each had their own bedroom, with a spare bedroom for Nanny. My sweet old mother shook her head almost in disbelief and chuckled about the spiders in the church at Scone, all of us crowded together in the Salvo hotel's double bed, and the nights we spent sleeping at Central Station. Still, they were overwhelmingly good memories for me, because of Mum's selfless devotion.

One day Jenna hid behind Nanny's bedroom door, waiting excitely to jump out and surprise her. But Mum came in chattering away to herself, which shocked Jenna, so she stayed silent till Mum had gone again. Talking to herself was her only sign of mild dementia, and Mum remained physically quite strong almost until the end. As I said, she was country tough.

*　　*　　*

My *Midday* routine was to start my research and reading for the next day's show after the kids had had their bath and gone to bed. I used to take home a pile of notes and clippings from magazines and newspapers for each of the next day's interviews, which had been pulled together by a producer. I read at least three books a week, often more. Australians are avid book buyers, so we gave them a chance to meet the face behind the words they loved. It was about people, not books. I'd work till about one o'clock in the morning and then be in my office at Channel 9 by ten.

I would end up hosting *Midday* until Jenna had almost finished primary school and Luke had just begun, which meant that I was there to read bedtime stories, take them to preschool, and pick them up from primary school, sports carnivals and music lessons. Not to mention watching their artistic talents in sundry stage productions. Unlike their parents, they can both sing and act, and show little shyness. On the contrary, they have grown up besotted by the world of theatre and showbiz. I don't know whether I can blame *Midday* entirely for the fact that I have not one but two offspring who want to be actors, but as kids they were always surrounded by entertainers. There weren't many accountants or scientists, let me tell you.

Carols by Candlelight was our special Christmas Eve delight when the kids were young. Dianne and the kids would travel down to Melbourne with me a few days prior for rehearsals, and we'd return early Christmas morning, after a fleeting late-night stopover from Santa at our hotel room when Jenna and Luke were still true believers. For the first ten years or so of Luke's life he and I had a pre-*Carols* 'mystery tram' routine, which he loved. Dianne and Jenna would go shopping in the Melbourne CBD, while Luke and I went down to Flinders Street. Luke would choose a tram for us to ride. I'd try to steer things so we'd go out to St Kilda or Port

Melbourne, where we'd grab a fish 'n' chips lunch or get some rides at Luna Park, but it was his call and there were times when the colour of some rattler would take his fancy and we'd end up out at Coburg or Maribyrnong, eating pizza or a cheap bolognaise. Then he'd come out to the Myer Bowl for rehearsals and he'd get to eat with all the music stars and the crew of about a hundred, wearing his 'entry all areas' dog tag. Talk about King of *Carols*.

I was first invited to host *Carols by Candlelight* in 1988, when Melbourne's popular newsreader Brian Naylor stepped aside after eight years. Peter Wynne was the creative brain behind the telecast and Geoff Harvey was the maestro, so when the job fell vacant it seemed natural to join them. I would host *Carols* for twenty years, even after Peter and Geoff were no longer involved, although it was never the same without the team.

I used to call *Carols* 'the loveliest night of the year'. It really is the most enchanting television gig of the lot. As Debra Byrne once told me, you can feel the warmth radiating from the crowd of fifteen thousand people when you step on stage. You look out and there's a sea of families, all smiles, rugged up and huddled together, waving their candles and singing along; wide-eyed babies in their mothers' arms, destined to fall asleep; teenage girls in their Christmas ribbons and Santa hats, swooning over the latest pop idol; thousands of faces stretching way up the grassy slope, captivated by the colour and movement and by the performers.

For the regular pilgrims who stretch out blankets and put down their picnic baskets in the same spot every year, and the three million plus Australians who sit at home wrapping their presents and singing along, it's an integral part of Christmas, almost as much as the tree and the turkey. I used to think that those Aussies who are lonely or separated from their loved ones are all brought together by the ritual of *Carols* on Channel 9.

Believe it or not, we used to get six thousand people turning up the night before to watch rehearsals. Actually, rehearsals were a bit like watching a goof reel, as some of Australia's finest singers missed their cues, resorted to a 'la . . . la . . . laa' mumble, slipped down the steps on their bums or occasionally chucked a tanty about the music tempo. On the big night it would be faultless.

As lovely as it is, I believe *Carols* is the toughest TV gig of all, for the whole production team. It's one of the last remnants of the Nine Network's culture of excellence. With about fifteen cameras scattered around the Bowl, a couple of hundred microphones and a staging extravaganza and lighting rig that would put most rock concerts to shame, it's a technical disaster waiting to happen. And because it's Christmas Eve there's no question there's something spiritual, almost sacred, about the *Carols* telecast, compounding any mistakes that do happen. Because it's mostly outdoors you're always at the mercy of the weather, too. The pressure's mind-boggling. I think it's a much scarier telecast than any other live show on television.

Directors and producers have coronaries or go bald when they do *Carols*. For the music director it's simply terrifying. I think he has the toughest job of all. There's months of rehearsals with a choir of over two hundred, a sixty-piece orchestra and the Hi-5 song and dance whiz-kids, along with a selection of Australia's finest performers, as varied as John Farnham, Anthony Warlow, Olivia Newton-John, Marina Prior, John Williamson and Hugh Jackman.

Geoff Harvey had the task of somehow pulling it all together, dealing with egos, temper tantrums, singers with sore throats, *Australian Idol* stars who forget the words to the most famous carols, choirs who just want to talk and old musicians who've heard it all a thousand times. One year, the orchestra's pianist had a seizure during our live broadcast, so Harvey had to take over the piano playing, while at the same time conducting. Another year, the director was talking in Geoff's earpiece one minute and the next there was just the sounds of silence: he had collapsed on the floor of the broadcast truck and been taken off to emergency.

In one of my first years hosting *Carols*, I unintentionally managed to get back at Harvey for some of the pranks he'd been playing on me for years and all the near heart attacks he'd caused. We'd been lucky enough to get the legendary Seekers back together for the event. As well as singing a couple of traditional Christmas songs, Judith Durham and the boys sang 'Morningtown Ride' – by popular demand. It absolutely brought the house down. As the applause thundered through the Royal Botanic Gardens, I stepped up to the mistletoe-covered podium and asked the Bowl, 'Would you like one more verse?' One hundred thousand people, it seemed, screamed *yeeeessss*.

Harvey's look could have killed me. In my innocence – call it musical ignorance – I had apparently offered the stupidly impossible. Through the deafening crowd noise, Harvey had to communicate with the choir up the back, the musicians and The Seekers to decide which particular verse to perform, while the director was screaming in his ear at the same time, telling him we were already way over time.

But I had an army of screaming Yuletiders on my side! Somehow, the musicians all managed to stagger through 'just one more verse', and we went to a commercial break. It took four beers and a couple of cognacs long into the evening before the piano player had recovered sufficiently to suggest I probably shouldn't do that again.

Chapter 23
Gold Rush!

In 1986 I was nominated for the Gold Logie, the award for Most Popular Personality on Australian TV. Daryl Somers won – but Mike Willesee and Paul Hogan congratulated *me*, saying winning the Gold Logie had notoriously been the kiss of death for TV performers such as Graham Kennedy, Bert Newton, Don Lane, Tony Barber and Mike Walsh.

Neither Willesee nor Hoges had ever won Gold – which they insisted had saved their television careers.

Well, as it turned out, from 1987 to 1996 I won five Gold Logies, including four in a row, and was a finalist every other year. It seems it took more than a decade after that for the dreaded Curse of the Gold Logie to kick in!

I've honestly lost count of the Silver Logies, but I guess I received more than twenty in my time with *60 Minutes*, *Midday* and *ACA*. The network won the Best Sports Broadcast Logie for the 1998 Kuala Lumpur Commonwealth Games, which I hosted, but for some reason Eddie McGuire got up and made the speech. It didn't really matter, but it was highly unusual.

My most embarrassing and last Logie experience was in 2007, when my interview with Terri Irwin won Most Outstanding Public Affairs Report. I was specifically asked by the Logies executive producer, Pam Barnes, not to talk about Steve Irwin because Steve was already getting two posthumous Logies, including the Hall of Fame award. Barnes didn't want the Logies to become 'The Steve Irwin Show', as she put it.

But in choosing an excerpt from my interview to be beamed across the country on awards night when they read out the nominees, Pam had selected a part that showed Terri at her emotional low point, crying and clearly distressed. Terri was sitting in the Logies hall at the time and was still very brittle after her husband's death. I was told later that she had never watched the interview before, because she thought it would upset her. Well, Terri Irwin actually lost it, leaving the ceremony and heading to her hotel suite quite upset.

In my speech I thanked my producers and camera crew, and as promised I avoided mentioning Steve. It had been my intention to present the Logie to Terri, because she'd been the star of my hour-long special – but the moment had been lost.

I had thought it was really poor taste on Channel 9's part to screen that footage at the awards ceremony, but in the wash-up I was the one who copped flak in the newspapers and on talkback radio for being totally insensitive towards her. I had no idea.

*   *   *

Every year there is a chorus of complaints about the way the Logies are run. Who votes? How many people vote? Is it rigged?

Is the voting now dominated by kids with mobile phones? And so on . . . Again, I don't know.

But the Logies are still the only TV awards we have, so until somebody comes up with a better idea, the Logies are worth winning.

That I was awarded so many while working on *Midday*, beating heavily promoted prime-time programs, showed how capable the team was and brought home to me the place our show had in people's lives. And it reinforced something I had realised my very first day on the show: *Midday* belonged to its audience, more than any other show on Australian TV.

Midday got up to six hundred phone calls a day and regularly received a thousand letters a week. That's a lot of stamps. My devoted and brilliant PA, Lisa Danson, helped me reply to every single viewer; in some cases it started up a correspondence that went on for years.

There were letters of appreciation for the show, but people would also write and tell me the most intimate stories of their lives, from horrendous experiences of incest or rape to the fact that they had abandoned their children in the past. One old lady sent me a handwritten letter, sixteen pages altogether, detailing how she'd been sexually abused by her grandfather as a child and teenager. She'd never told anyone, not even her husband or daughters, keeping it bottled up all her life until now.

It was heartbreaking to think that this woman and many others like her felt there was nobody else they could trust and speak confidentially with. I always treated viewers' secrets carefully and avoided playing family shrink. I would usually suggest they talk to their doctor or a community counsellor, but I made follow-up phone calls in a couple of exceptional cases, when I feared a viewer might be on the edge of a serious crisis. On occasions, *Midday* even arranged for family welfare or social workers to discreetly pay a visit. Thankfully they were always professional and maintained confidentiality.

I received one extraordinary letter from a middle-aged man who revealed he was a bigamist and had three wives and families. I thought he was kidding, so I rang the number he'd given me and spoke to him several times. Suffering terminal cancer, he now wanted to salve his conscience and come clean with all of them. He asked me if I'd go with him, which was a bit tricky. He died before I had a chance to tell him he was on his own.

Another devoted viewer, a lovely kind-hearted woman from outer suburban Melbourne named Anne, came to the first and final show of every year. She'd catch a train or a bus to Sydney and then return home the same day. She also wrote regularly, told us about her kids' school activities and always sent Christmas cards. Many others would come to the show a dozen times or more each year, some because they were desperately lonely.

At the end of every *Midday* Geoff Harvey and I would stay behind and talk to the audience for at least half an hour, usually longer. We never once missed doing that over the whole nine-year period. Altogether we spoke to more than seventy thousand people in person and answered their questions. I doubt that happened anywhere else in the world and I think it was a major reason people were so loyal to the show. I found it a great way to gauge the audience to find out what they liked and didn't like. They'd certainly tell us. Geoff would always play the piano if someone in the audience was having a birthday and usually tell them a heap of lies, but they'd all laugh and head home happy. Quite often they'd be facing eight hours in a bus after the show. It was the least we could do to repay that kind of devotion.

*   *   *

In 1989 Channel 7 launched Bert Newton against us, with his own variety show. Bert and I had worked together – quite amicably, I thought – for about ten years when he was at Nine. I had great respect for everything he'd done in television. But speaking of the coming battle, Bert told a Melbourne newspaper reporter, 'I'm glad I'm not taking on an old friend.' There's no love lost in the TV business.

In the bush, Prime TV broadcast *The Midday Show*. Then Prime, who had a tie-in with Channel 7, suddenly switched to Bert's show. There was outrage. One Tamworth woman spent three thousand dollars to get a satellite dish so that she and her mates could still watch *Midday*. 'I can't stand the Bert Newton show,' she told the local newspaper. 'Nothing personal. It's just not as good.' We felt like sending her a bunch of roses. Another woman rounded up sixty *thousand* signatures on a petition of complaint to Prime TV.

The big-city newspapers trumpeted it as the midday match-up between Bert and Ray, calling it 'High Noon' and 'The Lunch-Box Shoot-Out', with cartoons of the two of us as gunslingers. But it turned out to be a fizzer. A no contest. Bert's show survived only one season. We were getting seven or eight times his ratings. The powerhouse *Midday* team, with its superior production values and music, was much too strong.

Migrants told us they learnt their English from the show. Schoolkids wrote saying they watched it in their classrooms. ('We turn down the sound on the boring bits,' one teenager said.) Farmers would refuse to get back on the tractor until Harvey's last band number, and blackfellas gathered daily to watch the show in their community halls. Shiftworkers were avid fans. For the lonely, it was the one constant in their lives, as we visited them every lunchtime and made them laugh. Pensioners made it part of their meal break; people stranded in hospitals and air-ports always tuned in; and mothers fed their babes and children while they caught up with the day's events.

A woman wrote in once and told me a funny story. Visiting her mother every day around midday in a Sydney nursing home, she got to watch the show on a regular basis because the lady her mother shared a room with had a handwritten note plastered with sticky tape on the side of her portable television: 'Attention, nurses. This TV must be tuned to Channel 9 at 12 noon EVERY weekday. Or else.' In all her visits my correspondent had never seen this lady awake. Still, as they say on Broadway, the show must go on! Every weekday at 12 noon, in fact.

I often told that story, suggesting that the comatose old lady in the nursing home was the quintessential *Midday* show viewer. (It was a joke, Joyce.)

The fact is, 40 per cent of the *Midday* audience at home was male, and the bulk of the viewers were under fifty-five, with very few sporting a blue rinse through their curls.

Chapter 24
Housewife Superstar, and Other Truly Beautiful Women

'So, who's the most beautiful woman you've ever met?'

The funny thing is, that's the question *women* most often ask me.

After I splutter something about my wife, my daughter, my sisters, they always say, 'Yeah, sure. Apart from them?' It's a tough one to answer, honestly. It really is a bit like picking your favourite movie or your favourite meal. There are too many to choose from, and often it depends on what mood you're in. And everyone has their own definition of beauty.

If it sounds like I'm copping out, I'm not.

Over the years I've certainly met an array of beautiful women, mostly when I was hosting *Midday*. They were part of the colourful tapestry of the show. It was usually a brief encounter: a chat before the program and then an interview in the highly artificial confines of a TV studio. So all I have to base my judgement on are their physical beauty and quick impressions of their personality. But when I did stories for *60 Minutes* or *Four Corners*, I sometimes spent days getting to know a beautiful star. Some, such as Olivia Newton-John and Nicole Kidman, I've interviewed many times over the course of many years and have come to know quite well.

Anyway, here goes . . .

Let's begin with a trio of movie legends: Jane Fonda, Joan Collins and Lauren Bacall, who at different times co-hosted *Midday* with me. Jane Fonda was hard to imagine as either her famous character Barbarella or in her real-life persona as the strident protestor sitting on a North Vietnamese anti-aircraft gun in Hanoi. She was razor sharp and witty. On the other hand, Joan Collins was incredibly vain. She demanded make-up, hairdressing and the wardrobe lady during every commercial break, even though she looked great. I guess when your career depends on how you look, vanity kicks in.

It was hard not to get a bit starstruck, especially with Bacall. I had only recently moved to lunchtime when she co-hosted, and I was nervous enough about doing a live variety show, without sharing a stage with a movie icon like her. She was easily the most playful of the three. When we put up some old black-and-white pictures of her, I commented on what a classic beauty she had been in those early films with Humphrey Bogart. She gave me that trademark Bacall stare – with the chin drop and the sultry eyes – and purred, 'Are you married or just available?' The *Midday* audience cackled at that opening gambit. She talked openly about Bogie, her second husband, Jason Robards, and even her fling with Sinatra. I didn't want to ask her for her most famous line, but she volunteered it anyway: 'You know how to whistle, don't you, Ray? You just put your lips together and blow.' Ever the comedienne, Bacall still had that distinctive husky voice and loved to tease, even at sixty.

Admittedly these actresses were at the end of their film careers when I met them, but they were timeless beauties loved and nurtured by Hollywood as screen goddesses. By any definition you'd have to call them beautiful.

I found the feline British actors Jacqueline Bisset and Charlotte Rampling, who were in their late forties when I met them, to be ageless and quite beguiling. English reserved and English sexy, with 'great cheekbones'. Jacqueline Bisset agreed to come on *Midday* only if we let her set up the studio lights beforehand. She transformed the studio, giving it a moody, almost nocturnal look. She explained to the audience, 'When we women reach a certain age, we need all the soft lights and pampering we can get.' The audience gave her a standing ovation for that bit of wisdom. When I suggested she looked amazing anyway, she gave the siren smile and said, 'You should see me first thing in the morning sometime.' Mmmm.

At various times Bisset and Rampling had both been voted the most beautiful women in the world, and it was easy to see why. They were so elegant you had to think they were born that way. Their grace and class were, it seemed, qualities that must be in their DNA. They both denied it, insisting they were·gawky, daggy and unbearably self-conscious.

Every beautiful woman I've ever met says that, by the way.

Delta Goodrem, Elle and Olivia Newton-John are quintessentially Australian beauties. They're warm and natural, and fresh. They're also amongst the loveliest women I've ever met. I think Sarah Murdoch is extra special too. I remember when she first came on *Midday* as a gorgeous twenty-year-old model, back in the early nineties. She was almost perfect back then, but when I watched her walk on stage as a Logies presenter in 2009 and when she hosts *Australia's Next Top Model*, it's hard to imagine any woman in the world being more elegant or more striking.

Not all great beauties are as immediately apparent as Sarah Murdoch, though. Bo Derek was a case in point. When Bo burst onto the world stage with Dudley Moore in the movie *10*, she was on everybody's Top-10 list, and for a *60 Minutes* story I spent some days with her on her northern Californian ranch. She was very pretty but certainly not drop-dead gorgeous. Until we put her in front of a camera. It absolutely adored her, in a way I've never seen. By some further optical twist the lens also made her look tall and long-legged. She was neither.

Bo Derek's husband, John, said to us during a break in filming, 'If you want to see the bone structure of a really beautiful woman – her cheeks, her eyes and the shape of her face – then you have to film her in the shower or throw her in the water.' John Derek probably should know. A B-grade movie star turned professional photographer, he'd taken all those exquisite pictures of his wife for *Sports Illustrated* and *Playboy* magazines that had left the world gasping. He'd helped make her a 10. Still, I wasn't about to chuck Bo Derek into the water.

As it happened, Bo was a damn good sailor. I found that out the next day when she took me skimming down some inland canals on her fast-flying catamaran. But edging back into the jetty, where our cameraman was standing, Bo 'accidentally' fell into the water. I'd just stepped onto the dock, so it wasn't my fault. With her long hair and face dripping water, she looked better than a 10. Climbing up the jetty ladder in her wet T-shirt, smiling at the camera, Bo was simply sensational.

Supermodels Claudia Schiffer and Linda Evangelista also were 10s. They were physically perfect – from their sparkling teeth to their buffed toenails – with much longer legs than Bo, but without her innocent charm or gentle naïvety. As catwalk models, Claudia and Linda had the inner toughness and survival skills of gladiators. Beauteous Maximus.

Madonna was never going to match the other women as a 10. Never in her life. But if a woman's beauty is more than just her physical charms, Madonna would have to be on my Top-10 list, for having 'the total package'. When you meet her in person, she is quite compelling. I must confess she's not my kind of woman; still I found it hard to take my eyes off her.

We did an hour-long special with Madonna up at her house in the Hollywood Hills, when she was in her late thirties. Now, while she wasn't what I'd call a classic beauty, what surprised me was how delicate and finely chiselled Her Madgesty was in person. The other thing that surprised me was how poised she was. Madonna was thoughtful, even measured, in her answers, without any of the profanity she's famous for. But there was one pop-icon moment worth mentioning. My producer, Hilary Innes, had gone to Bergdorf's department store in Beverly Hills the previous day to buy Madonna a gift. Hilary chose an exquisite bottle of Fracas, a French perfume that set Kerry Packer back more than three hundred dollars. I presented it to Madonna shortly after our arrival. I suspect she might have shown more interest if I had sneezed. She didn't even bother opening the chic wrapping paper, depositing the gift on a nearby side table instead. Anyway, I seem to recall that our cameraman 'accidentally' tipped the perfume box into the light case later, as he was packing up. It wouldn't have been missed. But I'm still left wondering what you give a lady who's said to be worth half a billion dollars. I'll probably never know.

In the flesh (so to speak) Jennifer Lopez was prettier and more voluptuous than Madonna. The same age Madonna had been when I first met her, Jennifer arrived in a five-car motorcade for our *60 Minutes* interview in the South Bronx, where she grew up. She had an entourage of about twenty, including a hairdresser, make-up artists, manager, personal assistants and hangers-on. With four bodyguards, you'd have thought she was being inter-viewed by Osama bin Laden.

In her impossibly high heels, J. Lo was much taller than Madonna. She walked like an athlete and had the taut, muscle-toned body of a professional dancer. Having learnt from the empty experience of the French perfume for Madonna, I pre-sented J. Lo with a single long-stemmed red rose. I knew that flamenco dancers love them, and, besides, the Packer empire was no longer as opulent as it once was. At least J. Lo put the rose between her teeth for a picture!

Talking about Hispanic beauties, I have to say that Pene-lope Cruz is an absolute stunner. With her dazzling smile, her dark eyes and pure-white skin, she has the baroque beauty that Spanish painters from Goya to Picasso all adored. She was quite enchanting at a dinner we had in Sydney for her and Tom Cruise, when they were an item.

Now for my top three. Bronze, Silver and Gold.

Sofia Villani Scicolone. Sophia Loren. I was in Miami doing a *Four Corners* story about the film industry when Sophia came into my life. In a storytelling sort of way, that is. The powerful Ameri-can Motion Picture Association was holding its own version of the Academy Awards and Loren had won Best Actress, for her Oscar-nominated Italian movie *A Special Day*. It also starred the veteran heart-throb Marcello Mastroianni, who played her homosexual lover. (What do I know? It was an Italian movie, with subtitles.)

The organisers had assigned a young Miami University student as our liaison person. She was about twenty, buxom, beautiful and of Italian extraction. Let's call her Maria. She told us excitedly that her family and friends often said she looked 'a lot like Sophia Loren – only much younger, of course'.

Sophia was forty-two at the time. Dressed in haute couture – a cocktail frock with a high neck and a high price – she moved like she was born for the camera. She was dazzling. After the awards press conference the Italian goddess agreed to a photo with Maria. The only trouble was, the beautiful young thing couldn't resist telling Sophia what her family and friends had said. (Oh, Maria, too much information.) That's when Sophia suggested Maria share the same small plastic chair for the photograph, sitting cheek to cheek. Suddenly Ms Loren had turned the simple family snap into a showdown, and there could be only one winner.

The bunch of TV camera crews and photographers fiddled and focused their lenses.

'Gentlemen, pleeease tell me when you're ready,' Ms Loren instructed. Somebody finally said 'Ready', and that's when the real Sophia lifted her chin, deftly tossed her hair back and took total control, as she'd done with every camera she had faced for the best part of two decades. The young pretender disappeared into the floral wallpaper. Sophia simply erased her from the picture.

Now it's true confessions time. I fell in love with Audrey Hepburn in *Breakfast at Tiffany's*. As a young bloke, I couldn't imagine a woman more delicate, more gamine sexy and more stylish. Audrey Hepburn was pure fantasy in *Roman Holiday* and *Sabrina*, and as Eliza Doolittle. But especially as Holly Golightly. I found Audrey irresistible.

She was sixty-two when I interviewed her on *Midday*, and I must say I was still smitten by her beauty. She had wrinkles, as you're supposed to after six decades of life. And laugh lines around her sparkling eyes. But those high sculpted cheekbones were still on display, along with the elfin chin and the smile that had conquered audiences around the world.

I found myself blurting out something the likes of which I'd never said in an interview before, and haven't said since. 'Miss Hepburn, can I just say – at the risk of embarrassing you – you're as beautiful as I thought you would be.' Or words to that effect. I know it was something asinine and schoolboyish.

'Why, thank you. You're very kind,' she said with a warm, coquettish smile as she dipped her gaze to the studio floor. I've no doubt Bogie would have been much cooler. (He'd have at least offered her a cigarette.)

This leaves me to mention only one other truly beautiful woman. Nicole Kidman. I first met Nicole when she came on *Midday* to promote her chilling breakthrough film *Dead Calm*. She was just nineteen. She was also breathtakingly beautiful, with porcelain skin that had never seen the scarring of a suntan.

A couple of years later, when she and Tom Cruise were doing the publicity circuit for *Far and Away*, their Irish-immigrant epic, they both came on the show. Separately, as they always preferred. In fact they *were* the show for two days in a row.

They were generous guests, easy to talk to and full of fun. I have seen Nicole on American TV shows, and she ends up giggling, almost lost for words. Apart from her natural shyness I can only think it's because they ask so many dopey questions. She's a highly intelligent woman. Tom came on *Midday* first and Nicole kept ringing up to playfully correct things he was saying. She denied that in the movie's great race across the prairies Tom had ridden faster than her. She even called him a wimp.

Mind you, that's not the word she used the next day, when she appeared on the show and I asked her about the scene in which Tom's character is sleeping on the bed naked, with just a bowl covering his private parts. I asked her why her character in the movie is so shocked at what she sees when she lifts the lid – literally. And then has a second look.

'Oh, Ray. What's under there is very impressive, let me tell you.' That brought a howl of laughter and a huge round of applause from all the *Midday* women. (They were obviously taking Nicole's word for it.)

The day Nicole appeared, there was a little girl in the audience who had been in hospital for a serious operation. She was in love with Nicole, so the Children's Hospital had let her out for the day as a special treat. It happened to be her birthday, so Nicole asked her what she was hoping to get as a present. She mentioned a special doll, which everybody in the audience – and especially her mother – knew cost much more than they could afford. It was simply out of the question.

The next day the girl's mother rang us to say Tom and Nicole had quietly bought the doll and had it delivered. No fuss, no publicity. I believe they also made a substantial donation to the hospital.

Because I've done a lot of interviews with Tom and Nicole, people are always asking me if their relationship was the real thing. Given all the scurrilous rumours and innuendos, especially about Tom, was it a fair-dinkum romance or a marriage of convenience? Well, let me tell you, from everything I ever saw they were madly in love. While Tom was in Europe doing the publicity tour for *Jerry Maguire*, in 1996, I met him in Paris to record a one-hour special. He revealed that when he and Nicole were filming in London, they would sneak away for romantic interludes in Paris. He even recited love poems he'd written for her and told me and the crew about a private film he'd shot of the two of them as young lovers wandering through Paris.

We went out to dinner with Nicole and Tom, his *Jerry Maguire* co-star Cuba Gooding Jr, Tom's sister and her husband, the film's director and the chief make-up artist, Noriko Watanabe, who happens to be the wife of Kiwi actor Sam Neill. The drive from the Ritz Hotel to the restaurant on the other side of Paris was a precursor of what would happen to Princess Diana and Dodi Fayed. A horde of paparazzi on motorbikes and in cars raced alongside Tom and Nicole's black Mercedes limo, taking ridiculous risks. They shone lights into the car and filmed as the limo reached well over 100 kilometres per hour. I was in a car two behind hers, just watching it all unfold. It was frightening stuff.

At the restaurant Tom cuddled Nicole and talked about the little things he loved about her. Later, the party moved on to a fancy dance club. As the host, Tom fussed around all his guests – but Nicole remained the centre of his attention. Holding a bottle of beer in one hand and Nicole in the other, he danced so close to her they should have been arrested.

As she matured, Nicole just seemed to become more confident in interviews, more and more stunning in person. I had flown with a crew to Atlanta for the *Batman Forever* publicity circus in 1995. Knowing she hadn't been back in Australia for quite some time, my producer got in touch with Nicole's mother, Janelle, and asked if there was anything Nicole would like from home. Janelle suggested some Aussie sweets and jars of relish, would you believe? You'd have thought we had brought gold bullion, Nicole was so excited. She kissed all our crew, asked for some gossip from home and relaxed in the middle of what had been a crazy nonstop round of interviews for her. 'It's great to hear some Australians. Just great to hear your voices,' she said. Wearing a pair of jeans and a simple white blouse, she looked a million bucks. She jumped on the bed, tucked her legs under her and joked about how different this was compared with her previous grilling, which was by a perfectly proper BBC film correspondent. 'Nothing fancy about Channel 9, is there?' she joked. Nothing fancy about her, either. Everything about Nicole is stylish, cool and classy. But there's no pretence.

*   *   *

See, this is why I've always been reluctant to answer the old 'Who's the most beautiful woman you've ever met?' question: there's bound to be someone I overlook. How is it that I could have failed to rank perhaps the most beloved Australian icon of glamour and style in my list of favourites? I suspect that Norm would be rolling in his grave right about now. Norm Everage, that is, of Moonee Ponds, Victoria.

Over the years I have had many funny, funny encounters with Dame Edna Everage. What I find interesting is that when you chat to Dame Edna, you have to change your interviewing style. She gets on a roll, into a certain comic rhythm with her answers, and as the audience laughs at each hilarious line it spurs her on to another. And another. It's a bit like a dripping tap of comedy. You never quite know when to turn it off and move on to the next question. (Interviewing Robin Williams can be much the same.)

One of my most memorable encounters with the Housewife Superstar was in 1986 when I hosted Channel 9's coverage of the wedding of Prince Andrew and Sarah Ferguson, along with the truly beautiful Maggie Tabberer. We three were perched on an open-top red London bus directly across from Westminster Abbey. The first royal wedding in a decade was meant to be one of those classy, respectful TV events. Fergie's spectacular designer wedding dress could have just about filled the nave of the abbey. Maggie and I were dressed accordingly, she in something exquisite and me in a serious suit and pearl-grey tie. Dame Edna, filling the role of what is known in TV as a 'colour commentator', had the job of adding a little flair to our coverage, especially when there was a lull in the action. She was wearing a creation that was peacock bright and predictably over-the-top. Every royalist amongst our viewers that day was appalled.

She was hilarious, explaining how she'd knocked back a personal invite to sit with Her Majesty – to be 'inside the dark and dank of Westminster Abbey' – just so she could appear on our broadcast and pass on her 'intimate knowledge of the royal moment' to Australia. Edna told us how she'd helped 'that pretty little Sarah' with everything: the dress, the cake and the protocol, all the way through to 'a few tips about the wedding night itself'. When Fergie finally arrived at the abbey, standing in an open carriage, Edna waved a huge bunch of gladdies and screamed at the top of her lungs. Fergie saw her, almost fell over laughing, and waved wildly back to Edna. It was a great moment, a great coup for Aussie royalty.

I have to say, it was an amazing experience to work with Barry Humphries. He is a unique talent, an absolute treasure. We shared a trailer nearby, where we changed into our clothes before the telecast. As Barry pulled on his girdle and high-heeled shoes, he suddenly morphed into Edna. The voice, the walk, the complete, marvellous absurdity.

The next year, at the Logies, Dame Edna came on stage to present me with my first Gold Logie. With the awards having run way over time, host Don Lane then wrapped up the show, as Dame Edna waved to her TV millions. She kissed both Don and me. Don laughed, scraped his cheek and screamed, 'Oh God, that's the first time I've been kissed by a *bloke*! Goodnight, Australia!'

Downstairs, still dressed as Dame Edna, Barry went absolutely berserk, screaming at Don for breaking 'the unbreakable comedy convention' by calling her a bloke. 'I've spent forty fu**ing years creating this character,' he yelled, 'and you've destroyed it in one fu**ing night.' Humphries had every right to be mad.

Besides, truly beautiful women are allowed the occasional tantrum.

Chapter 25
Three Women and a Funeral

Apart from being asked about the most beautiful women I've met, I've also been asked frequently over the past thirty years, 'Who's the most remarkable person you've ever met?' That's a hard question to answer, but there are four people who come to mind.

I can't go past one bloke – Professor Fred Hollows, the remarkable eye surgeon. His craggy face is still recognised on bus-stop posters, asking for twenty-five dollars to fix blindness, even though Fred died years ago from renal cancer. Thankfully, his legend lives on.

And there are three women I'd like to mention: Terri Irwin, Bronte Cullis and Lindy Chamberlain. Until they hit the headlines, they were just ordinary, extraordinary women. Each of them withstood devastating personal trauma and then the blowtorch of public scrutiny. I don't know how they did it, but somehow they survived the ordeal.

*   *   *

We buried Fred Hollows on the edge of Bourke in February 1993, in the red dirt that he loved so much. He was only sixty-three.

A mob of blackfellas came down the rough track from Enngonia for the funeral and they howled. I remember it rained that sad day – the first drop along the Darling in over a year. 'God's cryin' for Proppiter Pred,' the wizened old mission lady in her faded floral dress told me. It didn't worry her that the world-renowned eye doctor was an atheist. Like every blackfella in Australia she knew that Professor Fred had devoted his life to trying to fix the appalling neglect of Indigenous health in 'The Land of the Blind'.

That's what we called our *60 Minutes* story in 1981, when I first met Fred way out the back of Katherine – 'The Land of the Blind'. It's when I first discovered that Aboriginal people are five times as likely to go blind as white fellas. 'If animals were neglected like this,' the irascible old surgeon used to say, 'you'd call the f***ing RSPCA.'

Mind you, Fred had quite a few choice quotes. 'What makes humans different from every other f***ing species,' he used to say, 'is that we have the capacity to care. And rich c***s should care a bit more f***ing often!' Recognising the immensity of the Aboriginal health disaster, he'd say – with crystalline logic – 'Yeah, well the alternative is to do nothing! And that's no f***ing alternative.'

Frederick Cossom Hollows was probably the most remarkable bloke I ever met. Even today he remains a huge influence on my life. He was the most profane saint I ever met, too.

I first came face-to-face with him by the flickering light of a campfire on Wattie Creek cattle station, after Fred had spent a long day in a makeshift tin clinic treating the eye epidemic called trachoma. I'd just arrived that afternoon. 'So, you're the f***ing superstar, eh?' were Hollows' opening words to me. It was a rocky start to what would become a great friendship.

Gabi Hollows was there as his orthoptic assistant, the nag who made him put on clean socks and the woman who loved him to distraction. 'Fred, don't be so rude to Ray, you cranky old bugger!' Gabi chipped him.

He just cackled with laughter, with a dry-tobacco pipe in one hand and a wet, four-fingered Scotch in the other. 'F**k him. He'll learn not to take offence,' Fred said. And I did. Ten years later he asked me to be the first chairman of the Fred Hollows Foundation. I stayed in the highly rewarding voluntary job for another decade.

I learnt a lot from Fred. Like the fact that trachoma was eliminated from white Australia over a century ago; that access to clean water, basic hygiene and even sunglasses would wipe out the disease amongst indigenous people; that blackfellas think going blind is just a natural part of ageing; that 'surgery' too often meant removing the eye; and that Aboriginal kids start out with spectacular vision, much better than white kids. It's all downhill after that.

It's the same scandalous story with indigenous health generally. Researchers at the Menzies School of Health Research in Darwin tell me that they're now discovering new diseases in overcrowded Aboriginal communities that don't exist anywhere else in the world.

I've watched Hollows tear strips off prime ministers, public servants and corporate presidents – and they still made him Australian of the Year. His humanity and his good work were irresistible. He'd take on Joh's hired henchmen and any other thugs who didn't like his medical practice or his politics. He'd never back away from an argument or a brawl. He lost a bit of blood on occasion, the odd tooth, and even spent one night in gaol after trying to cut through the Sydney Cricket Ground's safety wire at a Springboks rugby protest rally. Even as a university professor he loved a scrap.

Fred's political blowtorch fired my passion for reconciliation, which had lain dormant during my decade in America. After meeting Fred, I would spend the next three decades trying to get Federal governments to deliver social justice to Aboriginals. Not just lip service.

Fred had been born in icy Dunedin on New Zealand's South Island, had studied religion in a seminary for a while, then jumped the fence, moved into medicine and membership of the New Zealand communist party, as he began his lifetime journey of care. When I met him, with his voice like a blunt buzz-saw, his impatient temper and truculent manner, he was part rough diamond, part Renaissance man – with a love of poetry and the classics, mountain climbing, woodwork, sculpture, surgery, philosophy and arguments. And good whisky.

As a final inspiring moment for our *60 Minutes* story in 1981, Hollows brought a blind seventy-year-old elder named Vincent Lingiari to Sydney and fixed his left eye. Vincent – who was arguably the most senior lore man in Australia – smiled as wide as The Territory when Fred pulled off the patch and said, 'Touch my finger, Vincent.' There before our cameras a black bushman's finger reached out and connected with Fred's steady surgeon's index. Symbolically it said it all.

'This job is too f***ing good to be paid for doing it,' Fred said smiling. It's a declaration I heard him make over and over – especially when fixing cataract blindness.

In the late 1980s, dying from renal cancer himself, and with five young children, Hollows came up with the cock-eyed idea to eliminate cataracts, which is the main cause of blindness in the Third World, inflicting suffering and in many cases death to over three million people. 'Just get off your arse and do it' was Hollows' no-nonsense formula for success, and his acolytes have done just that.

The Hollows Foundation had to beg, steal and borrow to get under way, targeting cataract blindness around the world and indigenous eye health back home. At last count the foundation had restored the sight of well over 1.2 million people. Every year Hollows' factories produce tens of thousands of low-cost lenses and the foundation has broadened its reach into Aboriginal Australia. Generous Australians have also dug deep to keep Fred Hollows' work alive, raising more than thirty million dollars.

I remember that Hollows' university office was total chaos. There was a circuitous walk from door to desk through canyons of books, stray folders and boxes scattered like landmines every step of the way. On one wall behind his broken leather chair was a half-naked poster of Elle Macpherson, stretched out and smiling, with a handwritten message from her: 'Onya, Fred. Love Elle xxx.' On the only other vacant wall was a huge photo of a smirking Mexican counterfeiter, wearing a double-breasted white suit and a panama hat rakishly pushed to one side. A super-sized cigar dangled from his mouth. It was a brazen picture of defiance, because in the foreground you could see an army firing squad opening fire – a puff of gunpowder escaping from the barrel of a gun a millisecond before he would cop the bullets. Fred loved it. 'What a way to f***in' go,' he said, as he explained that it was a classic *Life* magazine picture from 1914. It's the way Fred would have gone, I suspect, if he'd had the choice. With flair. He was a truly marvellous, rich and colourful character. An absolute one-off.

I sat with him at his colonial stone house in South Sydney just a couple of nights before he died. It was a Saturday night and everybody had left, except for Gabi and the kids, who were mostly in bed. The downstairs dining room, which looked towards Coogee Beach, had been turned into Fred's bedroom. There was a forest of Scotch bottles on the table, brought by an endless string of visitors, along with a clutch of medicines. Feeding tubes protruded from every corner of Fred's now-frail body. We talked about serious issues such as East Timor, the oil cartels and Brett Whiteley's paintings. Fred had an opinion on everything.

'Get ya'self a f***ing Scotch!' he instructed. Before I could pour it, he added, 'And get me one, too.'

I figured his surgeon wasn't going to object at this stage of the game. As I eased him up into a sitting position, Gabi, ever vigilant, silently appeared from the kitchen with a small drinking straw. In what I suspect was the last defiant act of his life, Fred hurled the straw across the other side of the room. 'Ya don't have f***ing straws in Scotch . . .' The words trailed off as we eased the crystal glass to his parched lips.

A few days earlier I had interviewed him again for *60 Minutes*. It was Fred's fourth appearance on the show. I asked him about his crazy, colourful life, and his love of the kids and Gabi. 'She's the most selfless, beautiful, decent human being I ever met,' he gasped, meaning every word he uttered. He always meant what he said.

In 1990 it was Fred who insisted that I accept a seat on the Council for Aboriginal Reconciliation – first under Bob Hawke and two further terms under John Howard. The Council was an extraordinary collection of black and white commitment, but it was never matched by governments. Over the space of ten years the CAR crisscrossed the country visiting isolated communities, shanty towns and inner suburban slums, listening to indigenous Australians and working to find a national strategy to bring about true reconciliation.

But the Howard government barely read the Council's reports. I think the political ghosts of One Nation had frightened the PM into avoiding an apology or taking part in the historic walk across the Sydney Harbour Bridge with three hundred thousand fellow Australians. Howard watched it from the verandah at Kirribilli House. I spent a year of my life organising the details of that great march of unity, and the historic corroboree the previous day at the Sydney Opera House. With every Federal, State and Territory leader there, plus prominent women and indigenous Australians, it was better attended than Federation in 1901.

We had to wait seven years until Kevin Rudd did the decent thing and said 'Sorry'. It was so easy in the end.

The truth is Howard baulked at every reconciliation hurdle he faced – from land rights to a formal apology, from the demand for basic amenities like water and electricity to the cry for protection from women and children in violent communities. The weird thing is, in early 2000 I arranged for two senior women on the Council for Aboriginal Reconciliation, including the Howard-appointed chairperson Evelyn Scott, to tell the PM about the appalling degree of sexual and physical violence in Aboriginal Australia – especially in the Northern Territory and Cape York. They spoke from personal experience. For an hour Howard and the assisting minister, Philip Ruddock, listened aghast to the women's harrowing stories of constant and widespread abuse. Both the PM and Ruddock also said they had seen my earlier *60 Minutes* story about sexual attacks on schoolchildren in the New South Wales town of Wilcannia.

But it was another *seven years* before the Howard government acted, with its heavy-handed Northern Territory intervention. I doubt they would have waited *seven days* had such heinous crimes occurred in leafy North Shore electorates.

John Howard stands condemned for his gutless, blinkered neglect of Australia's poorest and most disadvantaged – like every other Federal government before him.

In 1998 Bryce Courtenay invited me to launch his new novel *Jessica*, which is set along the Murrumbidgee. A lot of people from the Murrumbidgee Irrigation Area attended the Sydney launch, including a local librarian. She told me that during a recent NAIDOC Week celebration she had hung many old black-and-white photos of Aboriginal people around her library entrance. She said that a regular borrower – a man in his late sixties – had told her a shocking story as she stamped his library books. He claimed that as a young boy, perhaps six or eight, his father and uncle had taken him as part of a shooting party one Sunday morning down to an island on the Murrumbidgee River. There he said he had heard the adult men shooting Aboriginal people. She said two things appalled the man – most of all that the men had shot the Aboriginal people, but also that they would think it proper to take a young boy along. As if such criminal bastardry was part of the country culture. The librarian worked out that, given the man's age, he was probably talking about an event that happened as recently as the 1930s. Unbelievable.

Although Fred Hollows died in 1993, his influence on my life has stretched almost three decades. Long before the CAR had completed its ten-year term in 2000, and while I was still Chairman of the FHF, I became patron of a non-profit entity called the Aboriginal Employment Strategy. Originally based in Moree, New South Wales, this innovative and highly effective Aboriginal jobs program has now spread across Australia, with well over a thousand Aboriginal traineeships on offer in banks, food chains, Telstra and Australia Post. The brainwave of an amazingly dedicated cotton farmer called Dick Estens, the AES is already changing the lives of a great many young indigenous people, at the same time helping to resuscitate dying town economies.

More recently I've become the chairman of a new non-profit organisation called the Australian Indigenous Education Foundation. Given a commitment of twenty million dollars from Kevin Rudd in 2009, we have to find matching corporate and private money to provide full-time high-school scholarships in some of Australia's finest boarding schools. The target is 2000 scholarships for Aboriginal boys and girls. It will soon start to turn out badly needed leaders and role models to Aboriginal communities across Australia.

Every time I feel like easing off the pedal on my drive for Aboriginal social justice, the grizzled voice of old Fred is quick to remind me that 'the alternative is to do nothing. And that's no f***ing alternative'.

When we buried Fred out at Bourke, Frank Hardy, the iconic Aussie writer, penned a poem, which he gave to me. Fred and Frank had been card-carrying commies and non-believers in God. Despite that, Gabi Hollows invited Father Frank Brennan – a family friend – to conduct the funeral service. In the last interview he gave me days before he died, Fred admitted that he might have been wrong about religion. So, on the basis of that possibility, Frank Hardy wrote this poem for his old mate:

Belief with me is out of season,
As the tears that beckon to my eyes.
But, if an afterlife confounds my reason,
I will seek you in *the kind men's ward* of Paradise.

*   *   *

Terri Irwin was quite amazing in those agonising days in the world spotlight after Steve's tragic death on the Great Barrier Reef.

I flew to Australia Zoo to interview Terri shortly after Steve died, and American ABC flew out their seventy-seven-year-old mega-star Barbara Walters. Steve Irwin had been an American phenomenon long before he really caught on back home, and ABC had forked out a lot of money for their exclusive. Out of courtesy, really, Nine's hottest Brisbane producer, Sean Walsh, was on hand to help our New York visitors. He discovered he wasn't really needed, and we stood with our mouths agape as Babs and her 'crew' seemed to keep coming – a director, producers, writers, cameramen, sound engineers, an autocue operator, personal assistants and finally the highly coiffed Ms Walters herself. Hollywood had arrived and was about to swallow Queensland. The Americans even built their own 'sound stage' for Barbara, with koalas hanging from nearby trees and elephants strategically tethered. Rather than an interview, it looked like they were shooting a feature film.

But Terri took it all in her stride. She had jumped on crocodiles before, so I figured Babs in her hipster jeans and her six-inch heels probably wasn't going to faze her.

I ended up watching both interviews and think we did just fine with our skeleton TV team.

Terri Irwin is highly intelligent, capable and very professional. Still, it was one of the trickiest interviews I have ever done. That's because she was also terribly brittle, emotional and, I sensed, on the edge of collapsing. So we kept it all simple. We took Terri well away from the crowds, in a back corner of the zoo, alongside a shady billabong.

Two or three times Terri seemed about to lose it, starting to shake visibly. All I could do was lean forward and reassure her that we could stop if she was too upset, although I feared that might be the end of the interview. I got the impression that Terri had made up her mind and wanted to tell her story – especially the story of their love affair.

And that's what I remember most from our interview: Terri, with her almost brash, up-front American confidence, revealing that Steve gave her a strength she didn't know she had.

'You can do it, Terri. You can do it, darlin'.' That was Steve's approach, whether it was picking up a deadly desert snake, a promotion campaign or the zoo accounts. And it worked. Terri found herself way out of her comfort zone, taken to the edge – and then beyond – because Steve believed in her.

A 'you can do it' from someone who loves you is a huge endorsement. And she did do it. But now, with Steve gone, Terri seemed to be wondering aloud whether she could do it alone. Ever again. It was honest, raw and quite revealing.

*　　　*　　　*

Bronte Cullis was barely sixteen when we first met in 1995. She was confined to her Melbourne home, with bones poking through her parched skin like tent posts. Yet Bronte kept insisting that she was fat and ugly, and she really believed it. The screeching voices in her head were beating her to death and she couldn't switch them off.

I really liked Bronte from the moment we met. She was special – bright and sensitive – but just weeks away from death.

Bronte's story was Australia's first look at the deadly disease called anorexia. It made us all wake up to just what an epidemic it is. Psychiatrists, doctors and the health system didn't know how to stop her decline and had all given up on her. But Jan and Graham Cullis never thought of giving up. That's the only reason she's alive today.

In her madness Bronte took her devoted parents to hell and back, with all her screaming, her violence, her tantrums and the regular post-midnight panic runs to hospital they had to do when she'd ripped out her feeding tubes.

With her parents' permission we secretly filmed Bronte pouring food and life-saving drinks into the pot plants. She refused even to enter a room where someone had been eating.

We ended up doing a couple of hour-long specials and a long series of reports for *ACA* on Bronte's terrible journey here and in her Canadian clinic. We had more TV stories about Bronte Cullis than anybody I can remember. Every one of them was a runaway ratings winner. Later we did stories about the remarkable success Bronte and her irresistible mother, Jan, had in counselling and treating dozens of fellow anorexics.

The Cullises were never paid a cent for their story. Not a penny. From the outset they argued that if telling what had happened to Bronte could help save another family from the horrors of anorexia, then it was worth it. They're a very decent family.

Bronte recently celebrated her thirtieth birthday. She's in love and is a qualified high-school art teacher. She eats anything she feels like. She and my daughter, Jenna, have been great mates for years now, and Bronte stays with us when she's in Sydney. I just shake my head when I watch her tuck into a hamburger or a big dessert. It must amaze Jan and Graham Cullis even more.

*   *   *

Lindy Chamberlain was my first news-breaking exclusive TV interview, and in 1986 probably the biggest story in Australia since Gough's dismissal. Lindy must be the most remarkable survivor of all. I can't think of anyone I've ever met who suffered worse, given the unbelievable way baby Azaria was taken, Lindy's unjust conviction for murder, along with the brutal public condemnation and pillorying. Not to mention being sent to gaol when she was totally innocent, and then having her newborn baby girl, Kahlia, taken away as well.

I simply do not know how Lindy Chamberlain survived.

I had been at *Midday* for over a year when I received a call from Gerald Stone, my old *60 Minutes* boss. He wanted a cup of coffee in the canteen. That's when he revealed that Channel 9 and the *Australian Women's Weekly* had done an exclusive deal with Lindy's agent, Harry M. Miller. I congratulated Stone on the coup. The only trouble was, for some reason Lindy wanted me to do the interview, which I knew wouldn't sit too easily with George, Ian and Jana back at *60 Minutes*. (I never did find out why. Maybe she'd been a *Midday* viewer while in her Darwin prison cell.) Of course, I was ecstatic about getting the chance to talk to Lindy, Michael and their children because it was such a huge story. In August 1980, when Azaria disappeared, *60 Minutes* had just started to win the Sunday-night TV ratings, so I was always on the move and hadn't followed the Chamberlain trials closely. Still, it was impossible to go to a barbecue or dinner anywhere in Australia at the time without

310

people giving their opinions of what had really happened that night at The Rock.

I hit the story without any firm opinions either way on Lindy's innocence or guilt.

As with Bronte, I liked the Chamberlains the moment I met them. When I got to know them, I liked them even more. Poring over the details of Azaria's disappearance and reading the transcripts of their trial, I couldn't comprehend how or why they had ever been convicted. It was an absolute travesty.

Lindy told me to ask her anything and everything. But when I asked that inevitable opening question – 'Did you kill Azaria?' – I thought she was going to collapse. Her pitiful answer – 'No, I loved that little girl'– still rings in my head almost a quarter of a century later.

Long after our *60 Minutes* special went to air, I kept running into people – total strangers – who would say, 'I think she bluffed you. You know she did it, don't you?' All I could do was shake my head.

In subsequent years I became good friends with the Chamberlains – especially Michael. I remember as we stood in their Cooranbong kitchen, having endless cups of tea before we started filming that *60 Minutes* special, both Lindy and Michael wondered aloud whether their marriage could really survive all they'd been through. It couldn't. But after their split Lindy would often ring me and arrange for her and some girlfriends to sit in the *Midday* audience, and she was always great fun. I remember one Friday she even asked if she could be 'the guest' on a ridiculously stupid 'soapie' we did once a week called 'A Town Like Dallas'. We loved the idea and wrote her into the script, with the proviso from Lindy that there were no dingo jokes. We were bad, but not that bad!

A bit like Fred Hollows, the Azaria story never seems to leave me. I revisited it for a 20th anniversary special, again for *60 Minutes*. I spent a few days with Lindy, her second husband, Rick, and the now grown-up Chamberlain kids on their farm. Then I went back to Uluru with Michael, his new wife, Ingrid, and their beautiful daughter, Zahra, who was just a toddler. It was an emotional journey for all of us.

I find Michael to be a spiritual, deep-thinker and a good, decent man. Talking to him, as I often do these days, just compounds the crime that the media and public opinion inflicted on them all – not to mention the misnamed Northern Territory justice system.

In 2003, shortly after I did a story for *ACA* on Michael and Ingrid teaching Aboriginal kids out in the New South Wales wild west town of Brewarrina, I received a very strange phone call. It was from a Melbourne pensioner whose name was Frank Cole, although he wouldn't tell me his name at the time. Cole said that back in 1980, while travelling through the Uluru national park with some mates, he had shot the dingo that still had the dead baby Azaria in its mouth. I took about twenty pages of notes, quizzing Frank all the time and trying to trip him up on his unlikely story. I was totally sceptical at first, but the more he talked the more it seemed to have a ring of truth about it. Frank refused to meet me but promised to ring me back.

I told Michael about the call and we both laughed and dismissed it as improbable. But then, a year or so later, the story broke in Melbourne's *Herald Sun* newspaper. We tracked Frank down to his little suburban home and he apologised for having 'dudded' me by not ringing back as he'd promised. He insisted that a mate had leaked it to the *Herald Sun* without his permission.

Once again, twenty years later, the Azaria story had come into my news orbit. It's a story that never stays away for long. I won't bore you with the details, which are probably worth a book, but in subsequent weeks Frank Cole successfully passed a lie-detector test and he met Michael Chamberlain with his high-powered legal team. They left believing, as I do, that Frank was basically telling the truth, although Lindy still disagrees.

It was no surprise to Michael Chamberlain that the Northern Territory police, who found time a month or so after *ACA* to finally question Frank, decided that there was not enough new evidence to re-open their investigation. The Northern Territory performance in this whole Azaria saga has been scandalous.

And there the story ends. For the moment. But my admiration for Lindy continues.

Chapter 26
The Best of Times, the Worst of Times

'And the winner is . . . *Sydineeeeee!*'

A beaming Juan Antonio Samaranch made the historic call, making twenty million sports-crazed Aussies jump with joy. Within seconds I had raced down the aisle of the Monte Carlo Casino to interview the tiny Spaniard who ruled the multi-billion-dollar Olympic empire as if it was his private fiefdom. Which it was. That afternoon in September 1993 I remember thinking as I held the microphone to his lips that Samaranch was like some little Caesar in the Colosseum, giving the thumbs down to Manchester and Beijing, and selecting Sydney to herald in the new millennium.

In the wild front rows of the Monaco audience I could see Gough and Margaret Whitlam leaping up and down. They were like teenagers in a mosh pit, hugging and kissing Liberal politicians Bruce Baird and John Fahey, along with Australia's Olympic tsar, John Coates. It was a most unlikely political liaison.

Just as strange was the fact that Channel 7's ace sports

commentator Bruce McAvaney and I were co-hosting the live television broadcast being seen by crowds in pubs, clubs and kitchens back home. I'm a huge fan of McAvaney, yet commercial TV rivalries are so fierce it was a bit like sleeping with the enemy!

The next day the Channel 9 team organised a celebratory lunch. There were only a few of us, but it turned into a 'long day's journey into night'. We took over a little harbour-side café down below Grace Kelly's toy-town castle with its guards that look like chocolate soldiers on parade. Monaco is one of the world's great gambling dens and society playpens, and Mike Willesee was ready to relax, along with the rest of us, after a gruelling week. Sometime during the celebrations that night Mike quietly told me he was ready to pull up stumps at *A Current Affair*. He'd had enough. That decision would change the course of my career. And my life.

Willesee and I had a long history together. I was in the studio back in 1966 when he first auditioned for the job of Canberra reporter on the groundbreaking ABC show *This Day Tonight*. It was *TDT* and Willesee who set the bar for all the nightly current affairs TV shows over the next four decades.

After quitting the ABC, Mike moved on to become the best current-affairs host in television. Bar none. For many years *Willesee*, the program he spearheaded – which would later be called *A Current Affair* – dominated the ratings and set the political agenda. Now he had become disenchanted with his own iconic TV baby.

Mike admitted to me that he felt there were disturbing changes in the very core of the program: it was moving away from hard current affairs, especially political stories. He feared, even back in 1993, that *ACA* was in danger of losing its sting. The program had given Willesee the chance to snare the big interviews, usually out of Canberra. These were Mike's specialty, but the opportunities to do political interviews had gradually disappeared over the years, killed off by the pressures of ratings.

In fact the dynamics of the lucrative 6.30 nightly spot, which Channel 9 had dominated for a quarter of a century, had been transformed forever. There were two determining factors in this sea change. The first was ACNielsen's replacement in 1990 of its fortnightly diary books, which viewers filled out when they remembered, with far more accurate daily-ratings meters connected directly to TV sets. The meters meant that for the first time network bosses knew minute by minute which shows audiences were watching and when they turned off. For commercial current-affairs shows the new system revealed that many viewers turned off during interviews with politicians and stories about politics. Though there were only a few thousand such ratings machines in selected homes in the capital cities, they determined the fate of programs, and the jobs, pay packets and mortgages of everyone in television – except for most in management, who seemed oddly immune to ratings failures.

The other alarming change for Channel 9 at 6.30 pm was the start of a new current-affairs show on Channel 7, run by the formidable Gerald Stone of *60 Minutes* fame. Called *Real Life,* the show was hosted by a promising young ex-ABC reporter named Stan Grant. The new Channel 7 rival had a stuttering start in 1992 but was now a serious threat.

So, with two commercial current-affairs shows going head-to-head, the ratings that Willesee and Jana Wendt had monopolised in the so-called good old days were now split. In fact, by the end of 1993, when Willesee quit, *Real Life* was consistently beating *ACA*. It made you wonder why Seven hadn't tried it before. They achieved success, as Gerald Stone wrote in his book *Compulsive Viewing*, by 'tapping into a new range of consumer stories more appealing to female viewers'. That meant diets, bras, supermarket rip-offs and where to buy cheap toasters. It was a portent of things to come when *ACA* foolishly started looking over its shoulder and then copying its Channel 7 rival.

In the early nineties *A Current Affair* had become the target of carping media criticism, with accusations that it had gone tabloid. The momentum of these attacks had built following a number of controversial stories, including the notorious one about the Cangai siege, in which Mike Willesee spoke live on the phone to a young boy who was being held in a farmhouse by a crazed killer. Interviewing the child hostage brought the wrath of police and politicians. In hindsight it was probably a mistake, but one that even the most experienced journalist might have made. Newspapers, of course, have never been a friend of commercial television, which had stolen much of their advertising revenue, and they were certainly never kind to the Packer family. So they went to town on *Willesee* and *ACA* over the seige coverage, as did the talk-radio jocks. And that controversy sparked *Frontline* into production, which meant the current-affairs kitchen was about to get even hotter.

Outraged academics joined in the sideline chorus, jumping on talk-radio and newspaper criticisms of *ACA* at every opportunity. Mind you, most of these critics, who lectured in media or journalism at unis and colleges, were either unemployable ex-journos or old lefties who'd never even covered a car crash. They cavilled, without comprehending. They also ignored the range of consistently strong news-breaking stories still being reported by *ACA*, because it wasn't part of their ideological brief. For instance, a defining moment in the 1993 federal election campaign was Willesee's forensic questioning of John Hewson over the planned introduction of the GST, centring on the infamous birthday cake that Hewson was unable to calculate the cost of under his proposed tax system. There were plenty such moments on *ACA* over the years.

Willesee didn't give a damn about what the academics or newspaper TV critics thought. After all, he'd originally learnt his craft on a tabloid paper in Perth. He knew tabloid journalism wasn't a sin if you were doing it right. As Channel 9's former head of news and current affairs, Peter Meakin, once snarled to a reporter from *The Age*, 'Just because you're a tabloid program, it doesn't mean you're not capable of good journalism.' At its best *ACA* had always been more tabloid than gravitas, more *Herald Sun* than *The Age*. The simple fact is that the tabloids have the biggest circulations because they live in their readers' world; they understand what troubles them. I well remember Rupert Murdoch saying to me, 'Show me an intellectual newspaper and I'll show you a dead newspaper.' It's the same with television. What concerned Willesee was that at *ACA* the hard-nosed investigative yarns and 'keep the bastards honest' type campaigns that characterised the best of tabloid TV journalism were becoming less frequent. I suspect he was also tired of the daily slog of nightly current affairs, which he'd been living for the best part of two decades.

Still, *ACA* remained a dominant card in Channel 9's pack, and it was recognised that winning the 6.30 pm spot helped kickstart the night-time ratings. It was expected that I would move into the chair if Willesee quit, because I'd always filled in for him and because that's what David Leckie, the Nine boss, wanted.

*　　*　　*

There was a fascinating background to all this.

Back in the seventies Willesee had actually been sacked from his 6.30 show by Kerry Packer, with the legendary caveat: 'Son, don't cross my door again . . . unless I f***ing need you, that is.' Which, of course, Kerry did a few years later. Mike returned to Nine to host the imaginatively named *Willesee*, until he quit in 1987. Oddly enough, the Nine supremo at the time, Sam Chisholm, asked me if I was interested in taking over as host of the 6.30 spot. I was having too much fun at *Midday* to want to switch – and I don't know what he would have done if I had said yes to his offer, because he'd also offered the gig to Jana Wendt, who took the job. (TV executives play strange games.)

Incidentally, that same year, the media wrangler Steve Cosser offered me and my team a bucketload of cash to take *The Midday Show* across to Channel 10. I had no interest in defecting anywhere, because we were never going to get better backing than we had with Sam Chisholm. A few years after Jana accepted the role of *ACA* host, Channel 7 then enticed executive producer John Westacott with even greater riches to move *ACA*, with Jana Wendt, across to them. Seven subsequently withdrew their offer – but these examples demonstrate that in those days there was certainly no shortage of money in TV for pinching successful shows. And they raised some real questions about network loyalty, too. Incidentally, it remains one of the great mysteries of TV how Westacott kept his job and was even promoted to run *60 Minutes* a few years later.

While I was hosting *Midday*, I also filled in for Jana during her five-year stint at *ACA*. There was one memorable night in 1991 when Westacott summoned me because she was 'unavailable', he said. He didn't reveal that Jana had stormed out in high dudgeon because the program was running a tasteless story about topless salesgirls in a Melbourne hardware store. It was Jana's way of protesting. She returned a day or so later, a bit bruised by the whole experience. I suspect that was one of the final straws for her: there were changes under way at *ACA* that she wanted no part of. She left the show the next year.

Strangely enough, the prospect of me hosting *ACA* had actually been on the cards for some time before the fateful day in Monaco when Willesee told me he was quitting. In 1990, while I was still at *Midday*, Packer had bought the Nine Network back from Alan Bond, for a fraction of what he'd sold it to him for three years earlier. Some months later I rang and asked to see KP. When I went to see him, he was sprawled across a four-seater lounge at his Willoughby office, in his shirt-sleeves, with his arms outstretched. He was a bit like a giant white octopus encompassing most of the couch. He was recovering from his near-death experience on the polo field, when a last-minute whack from an ambulance defibrillator had kick-started him back to life. We chatted about football, cricket and politics before he asked me what I wanted. Concerned about his recent sacking of Sam Chisholm, I told KP that I wanted to know what my future was at Nine. He sucked the air out of the room and exploded into laughter. 'Your future? Your f***ing future? I don't know what my f***ing future is. Why would I care about your f***ing future, son?' It was one of the funniest lines I'd ever heard.

Five minutes later, when I was leaving his office, Kerry staggered to his feet and walked me to the door. Wrapping his arm round my shoulder, he said, 'Don't you worry, son. We have plans for you, hosting *A Current Affair.*' I always wondered whether Jana or Willesee knew about that long-range plan. I doubt it.

*   *   *

Looking back now, that period seems a bit mad and chaotic. At the end of 1993, when Willesee quit, I was happily ensconced with the 'make 'em laugh, make 'em cry, make 'em gasp' team at *Midday*. We were rocking along, winning Logies for the show and occasionally pulling night-time-sized ratings – at lunchtime.

I had mates inside Channel 9 warning me against making the switch from *Midday*, because like Willesee they could see *ACA* ditching serious current affairs and heading down the path of what was even then dismissed as 'consumer crap'. They had an insight I didn't share at that stage. But others, including some ex-colleagues at the ABC and an award-winning reporter for *The Australian* newspaper, rang asking if they could join me on a revitalised *ACA*. Like me, they all believed the program could return to its former glory days despite the changes in the TV landscape. Richard Carleton, who'd started with me in radio back in the mid-sixties, suggested we have a coffee in the Channel 9 canteen. He volunteered to do live interviews with me for *ACA* from any trouble spot he happened to be in for *60 Minutes*. 'I wouldn't bother for your predecessors,' he said, 'but I'll happily do it for you.' I felt flattered by this warm endorsement from Dick, who was eccentric, even cold sometimes, but a man of his word.

I was in two minds about leaving *Midday* to front *ACA*. I felt a similar uncertainty to when I'd given up my NY correspondent's job to go commercial, and when I'd left *60 Minutes* to host *Midday*. I was excited about getting back into daily news stories again, especially political ones, but I still loved the TV smorgasbord of *Midday*, and the team. It was just about the most fun I'd ever had in television. Yet the timing of the change seemed right to me. I figured I'd been at *Midday* for nine years, and *ACA* was a natural step back into prime-time TV again. I mightn't get another chance like this. Plus, I was about to turn fifty. The *Australian Women's Weekly* had run a cover story to match, with the words 'Ray's Mid-Life Crisis' splashed across the cover. The stars were in alignment.

Dianne was happy either way, though this time she thought it was probably time for a change. Jenna had just turned nine, and Luke would soon be four. Except for when I had to cover breaking-news stories interstate or overseas, we figured I'd still be home before they went to bed each night. And I'd probably be able to juggle my schedule to catch their important milestones, like birthdays, swimming carnivals and school concerts.

What made the prospect even sweeter was that David Leckie was offering to appoint a new executive producer, Neil Mooney, to work with me at *ACA*. At the time, Mooney, who had been a top-notch newspaper man, was running the *Sunday* show. I had worked with him on days I'd filled in for Jana on *ACA*, when he ran the show's Melbourne bureau. I liked what I knew of him. As well, Leckie was planning to bring back to *ACA* a superb word-smith named John Muldrew, whom I respected enormously. Still do. Finally, we were to be joined by ex-ABC foreign correspondent Paul Lockyer, who'd reported with me at *Midday*. He is as good as any TV reporter I've come across. So, with this fresh trio – and the existing excellent *ACA* team whom I already knew – I took a deep breath and said yes.

My last *Midday* show, in early December 1993, was about the eighteen hundredth episode I'd hosted. That's almost three thousand hours of live TV, or, as one viewer added up, 'more than four months of nonstop, live *Midday* shows!' That's an awful lot of variety TV. It's more than five thousand songs, two thousand stand-up comedy routines and almost ten thousand interviews. The mind boggles. We'd done the show from

Melbourne, Perth, the Gold Coast and London, but mostly from the familiar surrounds of Studio 2 in Sydney, which had been home over the years to *Bandstand*, Bobby Limb, Barry Crocker, Don Lane and Mike Walsh, and in more recent times has been the set of *The Footy Show*. Studio 2 is where we held our last *Midday* extravaganza, with a huge cast on stage, some favourite guests, mega musical numbers, and our biggest audience ever, including my mother, my sisters and my wife. Mum, who used to watch the show every day with Auntie Annie in Gunnedah, cried. We went over time by a record seventeen minutes that final day, but nobody cared. Not much they could do about it, anyway.

Although *Midday* would continue, hosted by Derryn Hinch, my final show sparked a number of cartoons of housewives jumping off window ledges or confined to bed with depression. It was the end of an era for me, too. After almost a decade of fun, leaving *Midday* was a bit like leaving the familiar comfort of home. Even sadder. It was all very emotional for me and Geoff Harvey. I'm not very good at farewells.

*   *   *

I went into my new role at *ACA* firmly believing we could get commercial current affairs back on track again. The whole team felt the same.

I don't mean to be flippant, but it was a bit like the battered wife who believes that with love and hard work she can change her partner's brutal, drunken behaviour. She rarely can. In the long run night-time commercial current affairs would prove to be about as recalcitrant and ornery.

But none of us had the benefit of hindsight. Having made the decision, I was really excited about returning to daily journalism. I love the wild adrenaline rush of deadlines and the unpredictability of breaking news. There's nothing quite like it. I felt that all of my experience chasing same-day stories in New York and Washington, and all the months I'd spent filling in for Willesee and Jana, had primed me for *ACA*. I would quickly discover it was like nothing I'd done before.

I didn't know that my move back into prime-time television would be a maelstrom, an absolute whirlpool of awards and abuse, of headlines and headaches, of sensationalism and satire. The next five years would be, to quote Charles Dickens, the best of times and the worst of times for me. It would easily be the busiest, the most challenging and the most frustrating time of my life.

Chapter 27
The Saddest Man I Ever Met

A Current Affair began the new ratings year in February 1994 lagging way behind *Real Life*. Within a month we'd overtaken it. Within six months *ACA* would be close to number one nationally, just like in the old days. Only Channel 9's disastrous affiliate station in Perth, STW9, would keep us out of the top spot. What's more, by the end of the year Channel 7 would haul up the white flag and take *Real Life* off the air. It was to be replaced by *Today Tonight*, which unlike its predecessor was not a national program but rather had separate hosts in most of the capital cities.

Our executive producer, Neil Mooney, unfortunately only lasted a couple of years before quitting. He was committed to achieving a mix of hard news and colourful feature stories, some consumer stories and even the occasional diet or backache yarn. We regularly interviewed politicians – and not just the prime minister either. I'm still convinced, and I think we proved it, that if you want to be considered a legitimate current-affairs program, you have to cover politics. Any ratings hit you cop is only temporary, and viewers respect you for it in the long run. We set out to capture much of *The 7.30 Report* audience, without boring people to death. And we did.

We also launched full-blooded populist campaigns such as Farmhand, which ran for several months and raised nineteen million dollars for drought-ravaged farmers. We began an astonishingly successful series of stories in which Angry Anderson, the former head-banging rocker from Rose Tattoo, gave a helping hand to charities and individuals who were down on their luck. Angry and his team rebuilt playgrounds, community centres, houses and backyards with the help of volunteers and equipment given by hardware stores and businesses. Angry, who was an outstanding TV talent, ended up being awarded an AM and was even nominated for Australian of the Year. His segments became the prototype for makeover shows such as *Backyard Blitz* and *Random Acts of Kindness.* We had earlier set about reuniting long-lost family members, and those stories became the template for the high-rating *Find My Family* program on Channel 7 today.

We had a crack team of reporters, producers, editors and camera crews who I believe were a match for *60 Minutes, Four Corners* or any other program. In those days we routinely chased stories overseas, and over the next five years I hosted *ACA* from as far afield as Washington, London, Jakarta, Hong Kong, New York, Los Angeles, Ho Chi Minh City, Rabaul and Port Moresby.

That's why we won the ratings: because we stayed staunchly in the current-affairs tradition. The biggest news story of the day, either here or overseas, was covered on *A Current Affair.* You could count on it. Not anymore.

Still, *ACA* is an insatiable beast. It devours everything you throw at it. It's never satisfied. Pumped up by adrenaline and nervous energy, it's an absolute pressure cooker. When you've got an exclusive story, the show sizzles. Or it just fizzles if things don't break your way. Every now and then it explodes in your face. Maybe that's why some journos get addicted to it, while others can't get out of the studio quickly enough. I must confess that I was addicted to it. Having started out as an on-the-road reporter, that's where I've always felt at home. That's my forte: telling stories by making words fit great pictures. The trouble is, it's hosting a TV show that brings the kudos and the cash.

At *Midday* I'd missed packing a suitcase and going places with a favourite film crew, so at *ACA* I kept busting out from behind the host's desk. It helped me keep my sanity, but it sometimes made for an awfully long day. I might have to get up at 4 am and fly off to a bush town to film a story, then be back in the chartered plane by early afternoon to return to Sydney airport to take a helicopter to the studio for, say, a political interview at 5 pm, then front *ACA* at 6.30. After the show there'd always be a beer and a shake-out of the day, till maybe eight o'clock. Like a rock and roll band coming off stage, we couldn't just turn off the lights when the juices were still pumping.

We regularly took the show around Australia, which was like a military manoeuvre. It cost the network a lot of money but paid off in ratings. I hosted *ACA* from far and wide: from Karratha to Cooktown, from Hobart to Darwin, from the lookout high above Albany to a dusty dry paddock outside Emerald, in central Queensland.

I think Dianne could sense that the journeyer in me needed to get away again. She had the family routine under control, with the backup of her parents. As Luke grew up, she'd occasionally remind me that our boy badly needed his dad to roll around on the lawn and wrestle and fall into the pool with. That was easy.

I craved quiet time with Jenna too. She and Luke had become inseparable and adored each other, as they still do today. Nothing pleases me more than to see them laugh together.

I had most weekends free, and most nights I made it home for dinner, which we had a little later than most families with young children. We spent at least a month on holiday together at Christmas, and I managed to escape for another week in the middle of the year during a non-ratings period. Our family time was non-negotiable.

Yet you can never really switch off when you work on a program like *A Current Affair*. Every news bulletin or CNN story you watch, everything you see when you're surfing the net, every late-night phone call is about the show. That's the nature of the beast. Nobody cares *why* a cameraman missed a vital shot. (Mind you, they rarely miss.) There were countless times when I walked into the Sydney studio and Marty King, a veteran star reporter in Melbourne, was still editing a story about something in the news that day. I'd introduce it live on air, fingers crossed that the tape would roll on cue. It always did. Or Laura Battistel, our editing genius in Sydney, would cut one of my political interviews in the space of an hour though it really should have taken half a day. The next morning when I went in to thank her, she'd waggle her finger and remonstrate about those last six questions I'd asked. But she'd always smile.

In television, outside of management – who pay the bills – it's the executive producers who have the ultimate power. And probably the greatest pressure. It eats away at them. Over the years I saw one hard-arse EP who normally swallows razor blades for breakfast end up blubbering like a babe one night; another became so paranoid that he organised for a senior cameraman to write secret reports on every member of *ACA*, including me. That EP subsequently had a nervous breakdown. Yet another was confined to bed for weeks with an outbreak of shingles. One of the most capable EPs we ever had, who was a chronic asthmatic, doubled his nicotine habit. He finally walked away from television altogether. Just as there is a constant turnover of hosts on *A Current Affair*, the EPs don't have a long lifespan at the show, either.

EPs are a bit like directors on feature films. They run the show, creatively and otherwise. The EP needs to stay abreast of every breaking-news story, and has a twelve-million-dollar annual budget to manage and a team of about forty egos to stimulate and stroke, including that of the often intractable host. For the show to prosper, the EP and host need to work in partnership, even if they don't always see eye to eye. It's a bit like a marriage, without the sex or the mortgage payments.

It's the EP, in cahoots with his senior producers, who decides what stories will run. It was only in the days of *Willesee*, when Mike owned the program himself, that the host had the final say. Of course the host usually has 'persuasive input'. Still, when I was at *A Current Affair*, the EP's name was rarely mentioned by the critics when a controversial story blew up or a show tanked. Then it always seemed to be Mike, Stan, Ray or Jana's fault. During my years as host, *Media Watch* and Phillip Adams went on an obsessive, half-cocked rampage against *ACA*. Yet the EPs, who had been responsible for what went to air, were pretty much ignored. It was the reporters and hosts who were singled out for most of the brickbats. But then we occasionally got bouquets too.

*   *   *

I hosted *A Current Affair* for eight years altogether and I can honestly say it is where I did some of my favourite stories. We comfortably won the ratings much of this time, and we did it with some outstanding TV journalism. The program exposed a wide range of issues, from outrageous politicians' perks to the lack of safety on building sites, the looming waterfront wars, hospital waiting lists, the high suicide rate in the sugar industry and the crisis in dental care for pensioners. We also covered the political resurrection of John Howard, the collapse of Labor in Canberra and the 1996 election, the highlight of which was the Great Debate between Keating and Howard, which I was lucky enough to host. That's when I asked them both if they knew the cost of a loaf of bread. Stumped by the question, Keating was not amused.

Amongst several hundred stories I did in the nineties for *ACA*, there were some especially memorable yarns that I reported with producer John Muldrew. One almost broke my heart. It was probably the toughest interview I ever did, along with Terri Irwin's.

It was down near Port Arthur, in Tassie, two days after the gruesome massacre in 1996. Tasmania was numb, and the rest of Australia grieved with the island state. What had happened in this lovely place with such a brutal past was too cruel to comprehend.

Walter Mikac had lost the love of his life, Nanette, and his darling daughters, Alannah and Madeline. The local family chemist, Walter had been on a golf course when the monster came calling at Port Arthur in his yellow Volvo with the surf-boards on top and with semiautomatic rifles inside his sports bag. Lani was six, 'a dancing queen', in Walter's words. Three-year-old Maddie had blonde curls that giggled down her cheeks. Their mother, Nanette, worked at weekends as a tourist guide at Port Arthur. Their faces festooned the fridge, in family snaps from happy times. Martin Bryant, with the manic stare and the low IQ, didn't even have the decency to spare one of Walter Mikac's beloved girls.

It's true what they say: the eyes are the windows to the soul. Walter's were puffed and circled by dark rings because crying had become his habit in the days since the madman had gunned his family down amidst the fir trees.

Thirty-two other innocents had also died that morning. The horror of Port Arthur – Australia's deadliest mass killing – was probably the biggest news story of the decade. At that moment every journalist wanted to talk to Walter Mikac. His terrible tragedy was as agonising as any human could imagine. A media mob armed with telephoto lenses and mobile phones had bivouacked outside the Mikacs' high gates since Sunday, when the murders took place.

Normally I'd have given anything to get the interview – but what I gave was a simple shoulder to cry on.

In an eerie coincidence I had been on the same plane flight from Melbourne with Walter's parents, Milka and Danny Mikac, the Monday morning after the shooting. I ran into them at the airport security checkpoint, after getting off a plane from Sydney to pick up the latest newspapers. Having never met them before, to me they were just two sad-eyed strangers. They greeted me like a long-lost relative. Born in faraway Croatia, Milka told me that for years she'd learnt her English and had often laughed along with the antics on my *Midday Show*. However, on this day she couldn't stop crying for Netty and her 'beautiful, beautiful baby girls'. She broke down and wept on my chest.

Grandmothers don't just cry. They bleed.

Milka and Danny sat in front of me on the bumpy flight to Hobart, constantly turning around to talk and sob. A Victorian policeman was sitting next to me. As it turned out, he had been best man at Walter's marriage to Nanette, so I gave him my phone number. It was this accidental meeting that prompted Walter the next day to ring Channel 9. He invited me to come down from Hobart with a camera crew and listen to his painful cry for his lost loves. Being in the cutthroat news business, I would normally have punched the air at getting such exclusive access. But this was too sad. I truly wished there was no story to tell.

It was late in the day when Walter phoned me, so in order to make that night's *ACA* program we hired a chopper and landed it behind the Mikac home, on the playground of Alannah's school. An angry headmaster ordered us off, until I explained that Walter had asked us to come. He then drove us up the hill, through the phalanx of waiting newsmen and women.

I felt honoured that Walter had trusted me to tell his story. He shook my hand and then cried on my shoulder, just as his mum had done the previous day. Milka generously offered tea and cake, as you might offer a house guest in normal times. I thanked her but declined. These were not normal times.

Walter led me from room to empty room. He laughed at the fridge picture gallery with the smiles and twinkling eyes. Then he sobbed as he picked up the girls' favourite dolls and kissed them. His voice was high-pitched with emotion.

He took me to the intimacy of his bedroom. The bed he had shared with Nanette was still crumpled, untouched since they'd last slept there, the night before he'd gone to play golf. The night before the awful massacre. Walter reached across and plucked Nanette's grey flannelette pyjamas from her side of the bed. He hugged them to his chest for what seemed like minutes, sighing heavily yet saying nothing. He gasped, a bit like someone hyperventilating. Then he started wringing the pyjamas out, searching for something.

I felt like an intruder in a very personal, private place. I had no chance to film any of this, because my camera crew were waiting outside. I'm not sure I wanted it recorded anyway. It was all too raw.

Now, I've seen enough trauma over the years that I can usually offer words of comfort. On this occasion I had nothing to say. So, silently, I just wrapped my arm around his shaking shoulders.

Outside in the yard, with the crew, Walter said, 'Film my thoughts.' He wanted us to film the emotion he was trying so hard to put into words. His pitiful cry reminded me of the Persian peasant woman I had met in the bitter-cold slums of Tehran who'd asked us to film her heart. I wished I could do it for Walter. I'm afraid George Eastman never made Kodak film that transparent.

Sitting beside the children's empty sandpit, Walter lifted two half-grown pumpkins, which he said the girls were growing for Thanksgiving. 'We'll have to carve some funny faces in them,' he said, speaking in the future tense without thinking.

Then he suddenly remembered some snapshots of Alannah and Maddie and Nanette that he'd taken at this spot, only hours before they'd gone off to Port Arthur. The pictures were still in his camera, unprocessed. 'They're the last precious memories I'll ever have . . . of the way we were,' he murmured.

He laughed and cried and laughed again, shaking in spasms.

He had wrapped Alannah's blue velvet headband around his wrist, and without realising he was doing it he tightened the thick cloth, as you might a tourniquet against a snakebite. 'How can I possibly live without my girls?' Walter Mikac kept asking, looking deep into my eyes, searching for an answer. He twisted the velvet headband still tighter and sighed. 'He's put a bullet through my heart.'

And Bryant clearly had. It was much too sad for me. I remember later asking Muldrew whether we should issue a warning before the *ACA* story that night, saying that this next interview would almost certainly make viewers cry.

To this day I can still see Walter's bloodshot eyes. I can still see his pain. I had no possible way of feeling it. My Luke was the same age as Alannah, and Jenna was not really much older. I can't begin to imagine how empty Walter must have felt. It was like I was trying to console what remained of him, just the shell of the man.

After our interview we all hugged him and said goodbye. As we drove through the agitated bunch of journalists at his front gate, we stayed silent. There wasn't much any of us could say.

The next day the police allowed us back into the Port Arthur Historic Site, though understandably we were kept well away from the crime scene. All afternoon technicians and crews from the networks' giant outside broadcast trucks battled against the clock trying to get a satellite signal out. Down in the misty valley, probably 50 kilometres from Hobart as the wedgetail flies, it looked like we were all out of range.

The deadline for the 6 pm news bulletin came and went, with the newsreaders and reporters silent and out in the cold. Literally. On the telephone I was talking to Mike Munro in the Sydney studio. He'd suddenly been called back to fill in for me and was now praying for a miracle. Poor old Mike had been away for three days working on a completely different story for *ACA*. There was no way he could have been across the details of this one, but if we couldn't hook up the satellite link he faced the prospect of having to do three live interviews about Sunday's appalling events at Port Arthur.

Then, during the last seconds of the *National Nine News* closing theme, a technician on the roof of the old sandstone building behind me screamed out, like a sailor high in the crow's nest, 'Hey, fellas, I think we got a signal.' Muldrew waved me in and we started the show: 'Hello and welcome to Port Arthur. I'm Ray Martin.' From Eaglehawk Neck, way down on the bleak Tasman Peninsula, I swear I heard Mike Munro's sigh of relief back in Sydney. Covering a different story, I might have celebrated our good fortune – but it had been a harrowing, terrible time for everybody.

Walter Mikac would soon become a powerful, impassioned anti-gun campaigner and would turn John Howard's heart, much to the chagrin of Nine's boss, Kerry Packer. At a dinner one night I was alongside Kerry, and the Treasurer, Peter Costello, was sitting on the other side of him. The gun-loving Packer asked Costello what he thought of Prime Minister Howard's 'stupid new gun laws'. Costello, who at the time seemed destined to be our next PM, replied cautiously. 'Well, Kerry, you have to remember, Martin Bryant killed thirty-five innocent people and wounded another twenty-one. Howard had to do something.' It was a reply that displayed sense and logic. But it made not a scrap of difference.

'The truth of the matter, Peter, is that you are f***ed in the head,' said Australia's richest man.

Packer then turned to me and asked the same question.

'Actually, I don't think he went far enough, Kerry,' I replied, knowing I was going to get both barrels myself. 'I think they should now go ahead and ban all handguns as well.'

Packer looked at me aghast for a long moment, shook his

head in utter disgust and said, 'Martin, you are a complete idiot. You're f***ed too.'

I wondered at the time whether Kerry Packer would have been quite so bawdy, so outrageously certain, if he had seen Walter Mikac the way I'd seen him, and if he had seen what a carload of guns had done to Mikac's three darling girls and all those other innocent victims who had been left dead or injured.

Chapter 28
Sir Don's Last Innings

In television the daily ratings come in just after nine o'clock each morning. It's like waiting for your exam results to arrive every day. It can put you off your coffee and croissant, let me tell you.

At *A Current Affair* you'd often see Rob Carmody, the chirpy chief of staff, slump down in his chair, give a shake of his head and utter the sad refrain, 'Oh, bugger. A tale of two cities, again.' What the indefatigable Carmody meant was that the previous night Sydney had rated well and Melbourne was a heartache. Or vice versa. There usually was no logic to it. For no good reason, a story – or even a whole show – would work in one capital city and bomb in another. Brisbane could be just as erratic. They were the three Packer-owned stations, the key cities in the Nine Network. A disappointing result at any one of them would give us all more than just a bad-hair day.

Perth, on the other hand, was as predictable as the 'old Fremantle doctor'. The Channel 9 affiliate there had long been a ratings basket case. It had been back in Willesee's and Jana's days, and it still was. The city's TV viewing is dominated by Channel 7. *Today Tonight* regularly beats *ACA* in Perth by one hundred thousand viewers a night, just as the Channel 7 news trumps Nine's.

We had to keep a close eye on Adelaide. Although *ACA* won comfortably most nights, we still made sure we had plenty of South Australian stories, and I visited regularly, hosting *ACA* from our Adelaide studio when there were events like the Formula One Grand Prix, arts festivals, even big footy games. We went across to cover major news events like the Hindmarsh Bridge debacle and the funeral of local cricket legend David Hookes.

In 1996 I spent a week there hosting *ACA* while I was in town on a special assignment: to interview Sir Donald Bradman, easily the best-loved and most-respected Australian then alive. There's no question that scoring the interview boosted our standing with every South Australian. Along with a few million others I'm an absolute cricket tragic. I would have given anything just to talk to The Don for five minutes, let alone get the last interview. And The Don made it clear this would certainly be his last interview. Michael Parkinson tells me he had been after this interview for years. But Parky understands that we couldn't possibly have let a Pom get *the* interview with our Don Bradman.

It was Hazel Hawke who had first introduced Dianne and me to Sir Donald and his wife, Jessie, at a function at the Adelaide Oval, back in 1989. Jessie was warm and vivacious, much more at ease with strangers than Sir Donald. She recounted how the two of them often sat at home eating a lunchtime sandwich and watching *The Midday Show*.

The next time I saw them was later that same year, in Sydney, when I was the MC at a raucous fundraiser for the Bradman Museum attended by about seven hundred well-heeled cricket nuts, including Prime Minister Bob Hawke. (As it happened, Hawke would keep popping up in my pursuit of Sir Donald.) Before leaving, the ever-polite Don came across and thanked me. I invited him and Jessie onto *Midday* when next we did the show from Adelaide. (Up to that time we'd never actually done *The Midday Show* from Adelaide, but we surely would if he'd ever agree to appear.) Don flashed me a 'yeah, good try, son' look. Shaking his head, he told me he and Jessie had had 'more than enough publicity' in their lives. He explained that the incessant media spotlight and idolatry had been the main reason their son, John, had decided years earlier to change his name from Bradman to Bradson. He'd done it to escape getting the same predictable questions and embarrassing hagiography of The Don every time he mentioned his iconic surname.

'That was a sad time for us,' Don said wistfully, looking me straight in the eye. 'So, you see, we've had our publicity.' Offering his hand, he said, 'But I give you my word, if I ever do a television interview, I'll do it with you.'

Amazingly, that promise reverberated years later. Six years after the fundraiser, in 1995, I got a call from Bob Hawke. The ex-Labor PM invited me for a latte in a swish Rose Bay pub. Coffee had only recently become his drink of choice. That's when Hawke told me he had a problem.

'Ahhh, Hazel and I were in Adelaide last week. We had a couple of dinners with Sir Donald and Jessie Bradman. Ahhhh, anyway, he's not getting any younger, and he's the greatest cricketer the world has ever seen, as you know, ahh, I'm sure. He finished with an average of 99.94, ya know . . . ahhhh . . .'

I really like Hawke, and I have great respect for his intelligence and his talents. But I've found over many years that Bob makes a habit of telling you what you already know.

Anyway, over another round of lattes he explained that he'd finally convinced Sir Donald to do a TV interview with him for *Wide World of Sports*, on Channel 9, who would give him a handsome fee and give Don an equal amount of money for the not-yet-completed Bradman Museum, in Bowral, New South Wales. But Bob Hawke had run into one major hurdle.

'Ahhh, Don says he once made a promise to you, mate, that if he ever did a TV interview, he'd do it with you. Will you let him off the bloody hook so I can interview him?'

I figured it was important for Australia, and for the whole cricket world, that this grand old man told the stories and answered the questions about his glorious life, before the colours faded. But I told the Silver Bodgie that if Don was now willing to be interviewed, I was back in the game. I wanted to do the interview myself – without a fee.

Mr Hawke wasn't very happy and used words like 'double-cross', but he's a big boy.

As it happened, The Don backed away from an interview with either of us. He became quite ill with pneumonia, and his beloved Jessie had heart troubles and then was diagnosed with leukaemia, so it seemed there would be no interview. Ever.

But, out of the blue in early 1996, I got a phone call from Bob Mansfield, the prominent businessman who's run some of the biggest companies in Australia, from McDonald's to Telstra. A close friend of Sir Donald, he and a couple of mates had decided to fix a million-dollar shortfall and finish the Bradman Museum while Sir Donald was still alive.

Mansfield had met with Kerry and James Packer, who'd agreed to hold a national telethon but only if Channel 9 scored the long-awaited interview with The Don. 'If it's going to happen,' Mansfield told me, 'then you have to do it.'

So, within a few days I was in a cab with Peter Wynne, my producer mate, driving to the modest Bradman family home in Kensington Park in Adelaide to do our best to try to persuade him. I was as excited as I'd ever been about any meeting in my life.

When we arrived at the Bradman home, it was as if we'd stepped into a time warp, in the nicest sense. We had entered a drawing room frozen in the 1940s, with fine prints, floral wallpaper, period furniture, good manners – the lot. There was a polished wood traymobile on rocky rollers, a present from a cricket club. Lady Bradman served us tea and biscuits, the fine china she used probably a gift from some English baron. The drinks cabinet, well stocked with Scotch and a crystal brandy flask, was presented to Don by the South Australian Cricket Association when he retired. A Brinsmead grand piano sat in the other corner, where it had been for almost half a century. Sir Donald, reputedly a player of concert standard, explained how on The Invincibles 1948 Ashes tour he tried to buy a Steinway three-quarter grand – 'the most beautiful piano I ever played in my life', he called it – but it was made in New York and at that time the British government wouldn't allow exports in US dollars. So he had to settle for this English one instead.

'It made a lovely sound, when I used to be able to play it right,' he said. Would he play it for me? 'Oh no, I've had a stroke down my right side and the fingers aren't as supple as they used to be. It's a bit sad actually. I used to play every day. I miss playing a lot.'

At eighty-seven Don Bradman had that distinctive high-pitched voice and accent of a man who'd grown up in an earlier time, when Australia was a different place. Over the next three hours Wynne and I were enthralled by this grand old man wearing a pale blue cardigan, who instead of the piano played graceful cover drives and savage square-cuts, without even needing a willow in his square, nuggetty hands. He moved around on tiny size-six feet with the grace of a dancer. I never saw Don Bradman bat, and I'm sorry about that. It must have been something special to watch him in full flight. But I did get to see him play a 'cover drive' right there in his lounge room. The cover drive is my favourite shot in all of cricket. The Don hammered that imaginary ball so hard, I swear I heard the pickets rattle. I know I felt the hair on the back of my neck stand up. And I remember thinking to myself, 'You lucky bugger, Martin. Fancy being paid to do a job like this.'

He talked about playing cricket as far afield as Hollywood and Philadelphia, the hands-in-the-pockets controversy as he walked the Balmoral lawns with King George VI, his passion for Chopin sonatas, his stockbroking near-disasters, the need to encourage Aboriginals to play cricket, and apartheid. (Incidentally, one of the first questions Nelson Mandela asked upon his release from his twenty-seven-year purgatory in prison was 'Is Sir Donald Bradman still alive?')

Sir Donald also told us a very funny yarn about getting booked for speeding one Saturday afternoon. When the Adelaide traffic cop realised he'd pulled up the national icon, he still wrote the ticket but had the gall to ask for an autograph. 'Yeah, sure. It'll be on my cheque,' The Don told him gruffly. It must have been the only time in half a century that Don Bradman said no to an autograph request. Don had another endearing tale, too, of digging up some spuds in the backyard one day and finding Jessie's long-lost engagement ring, a link with love she'd accidentally thrown out with vegetable scraps thirty years earlier.

The anecdotes just rolled on as another pot of tea trundled in. Wynne and I were absolutely mesmerised.

It was a joy to listen to him. Without a television camera staring at him, Don laughed easily and talked honestly and humbly about his long life of fame – with some misfortune – and his eternal love of Jessie.

Bradman promised that if he *did* eventually agree to the interview, he would be happy for us to film anything and ask any questions – with two exceptions. Jessie, who was still recovering from her cancer treatment, didn't wish to be filmed, and Don would not talk about their two children, John and Shirley. A senior lecturer in law at Adelaide University, John still had some issues with his father, which the two men were trying to reconcile. Shirley had been born with cerebral palsy. Sheltered from the media's gaze, she had long lived under nursing care. Sir Donald's conditions for the interview were reasonable, especially for a reclusive character with such a deep distrust of the media.

As we were heading for the door, Peter Wynne asked what colour clothes Sir Donald might like to wear – should he agree to the interview, of course. 'Oh, look, I don't know what I've got,' he replied, looking to Jessie for an answer. 'I'm sure we'll find something in the cupboard. Maybe a sports jacket, if it still fits me.' Pete pointed out that Kerry Packer's budget for this particular interview could probably extend to a new suit if need be. Sir Donald wasted no time smacking that loose delivery right out of the park, saying bluntly, 'No, I don't think that sort of largesse will be necessary. Mr Packer needs every dollar he's got, I'm sure.'

Heading for our waiting cab in the misty Adelaide moonlight, we edged past the Bradmans' ageing silver Holden Sigma standing polished in the driveway. There was nothing pretentious or extravagant about this local hero. Wynne and I hardly spoke as we drove back to Adelaide airport. We were still trying to take it all in. Trying to comprehend what we'd just experienced.

Early the next Saturday morning my phone rang, and a deep drone issued from it.

'Ehh, Kerry Packer here, Ray.'

'G'morning, Kerry.'

'Listen, son, I've got you the interview. So don't f*** it up.'

'I take it you mean Don Bradman, Kerry?'

'Of course I f***ing mean Don Bradman. Who else would cost me a million bucks? So, like I said, don't f*** it up, okay?'

'I'll do my best, Kerry.'

It turned out that Kerry and Bob Mansfield had flown to Adelaide in Packer's private Falcon jet for lunch at the Bradman home on the Friday. Even though Don and Kerry had been the two most influential men in Australian cricket, they'd never met before. Each man thought the other hated him, because of the war that erupted over Packer's World Series Cricket in the 1970s. Mansfield told me that it quickly became 'an absolute bloody love-in' between this very odd couple.

'So, Kerry, how was it? Did you enjoy meeting The Don?' I asked Packer.

'I loved it, son. It was truly one of the great days of my life. He had answers for everything.'

'Did he stand up and play those amazing phantom cover drives for you?'

'Yes, he did, he did. It was absolutely bloody marvellous.'

Having had enough of the small talk, Packer cut to the chase.

'Now listen, son. I promised him, when the show is cut and before we put it on air, he can have a look at it. I told him that if he doesn't like it, for any reason, then we'll burn the bastard. Okay? *So don't f*** it up, son.*'

Packer laughed as he hung up the phone. He had a certain dignified charm about him did Kezza.

The Bradman interview was one of the trickiest I ever did, because of who and what he was. Apart from being the greatest living Australian, Sir Donald still remembered every innings, probably every stroke he'd played since he was about eight. I knew I had to get every detail correct. I also knew the interview had to appeal to everybody, not just cricket fanatics like me.

Adding to my anxiety, Jessie Bradman had rung the day before to warn me that Don had experienced a few sleepless nights thinking about the big event. 'He's quite happy talking to you,' she explained, 'it's just the cameras. He wouldn't worry if it was radio. He says television can make you look silly.'

That made me a bit nervous.

Sir Donald drove himself – in the old Sigma – to the Adelaide Oval, where we had set up a makeshift studio. He was wearing a plain grey suit of a certain vintage, a well-worn white shirt and a simple South Australian Cricket Association tie.

'This is the absolute last interview I'll ever give,' he said, smiling nervously as the cameras rolled into our countdown. He clearly didn't want to be there.

First question coming up.

'Sir Donald, thank you for talking to me. I've spoken to princes and presidents and prime ministers. Why am I nervous about talking to you today?'

It seemed to ease the tension, a little.

'No, you're not,' he answered, with that country smile that won over a nation. 'I'm the one who's nervous.'

He certainly wasn't nervous scoring 300 runs at Lord's or facing the bodyline barrage, so why would I make him nervous?

Bradman always tried to duck the hero 'palaver', as he called it. The glare and glory of being the greatest, the most loved, the most respected Australian of all time sat uncomfortably on

Bradman's small shoulders. It always had. It's hard to believe it today but during the Bradmania of the Depression years crowds followed Don everywhere, like a rock star. A huge mob gathered, stopping peak-hour traffic in lower George Street, just to see him return to his job in the old Mick Simmons sports store after the 1930 Ashes tour. My father-in-law, Bruce, worked in a Sydney film theatre as an usher in the 1930s. His job was to stand at the edge of the screen, write Bradman's score in chalk on a black-board and shine a torch on it. Otherwise, movie fans would stay home and listen to the radio. When I told Sir Donald about what Bruce used to do in the movies, he politely said, 'Well, do me a favour and please thank Bruce for me, would you?'

In England, on the 1948 tour, Don had to have a driver with a separate car so that the swarming fans wouldn't block the team bus after a game. During that tour, after a match he'd spend three hours a night in his hotel room opening and reading six hundred letters a day. Then he'd reply to all those who had enclosed a stamped envelope.

That sort of hero worship is a fascinating phenomenon. I wanted to hear Bradman's personal take on fame. 'I think it's been a bit exaggerated,' he suggested, twisting in his seat as if he was undergoing some sort of torture. 'Besides, there wasn't much I could do about it, was there?'

The secret to a good interview is to try to make it seem natu-ral, as if the viewer is listening in on a private chat. But unless he was talking cricket the great man was not a natural-born, relaxed storyteller. I found myself pulling back, changing tack, sometimes even moving on without a complete answer, just to keep him involved. I figured if he clammed up, then all would be lost.

Don was much happier talking about modern-day cricket controversies – from mega-salaries to sledging. He made news when he called Shane Warne something of a genius and the best leg spinner ever. Who was the greatest batsman? Oh, maybe Brian Lara, maybe Steve Waugh. He revealed that he thought the wonderful Indian wizard Sachin Tendulkar was the closest to Bradman himself in style. Or so Lady Bradman told him. (She knew her cricket and was usually right.) I asked him why he didn't crack more sixes, and his simple reply was, 'I could hit sixes if I wanted to, but you get caught if you hit the ball in the air. That's a silly risk to take.'

Cricket – and life, I suspect – was really pretty basic for Don Bradman: if you practise a lot and stick to the rules, you'll do okay.

We talked for close to two hours, ranging far and wide, and then we filmed out on the Adelaide Oval. I carried Don's record-breaking 1930 bat, which he had used earlier to illustrate a few of his strokes. As we walked across the grass, I found myself swinging it freely, like it was some old hickory golf club rather than a priceless national treasure. What little remained of the ribbed rubber sleeve on the handle after sixty-five years was flaking off in the palm of my hand. I quickly passed the bat back to the curator – after having a few photos taken with it, of course.

Don had certainly relaxed now that the TV inquisition, as he saw it, had finished for the day. For me it was all too surreal, as the great man chatted about moments that were part of cricket history, like the time he hit 452 not out against Queensland, a score that held the world record for ages.

'How big were you seeing the ball on that day, Don?' I asked.

'Oh, like a big beach ball,' he laughed.

'Could you have scored 600? More?'

'On that day,' he said, quite matter-of-fact, 'I could have scored anything. I was young and had my eye in.'

Don agreed to talk again the following day, to answer

questions about The Invincibles tour in which Bradman's Australians went unbeaten – something that had never happened before and hasn't happened since. I really did want to ask him about that 1948 tour. But I also had an ulterior motive, and to pull off my plan I badly needed Lady Bradman's help.

We were filming at the Bradmans' house that day, and when we arrived in the morning The Don was upstairs getting dressed. Over yet another cup of tea Jessie told us he had been very happy with the previous day's filming and had even had a good time. She asked if we were happy with what we got. I assured her we were, except for two missing sequences. 'What are they?' she asked.

'Well, Don's told us a great love story, but we only have *one* of the lovers. We haven't seen you.'

'Mmm,' Lady Bradman said and smiled, 'so what do you want me to do?'

'I want you to walk through the garden with Don.'

'And what else are you missing?' she asked.

'I want Don to play the piano, because, after you and the children, he says the piano has been the love of his life.'

Jessie finished her tea, smiled and said, 'Why don't you set up the lights at the piano, and I'll have a quiet word with Don?'

Now, the one consistent thing you hear about Donald Bradman from those who knew him best is that once he'd made his mind up he never changed it. Unless, of course, Jessie asked.

Minutes later Sir Donald appeared, straightening the knot on the now familiar SACA tie. He was wearing exactly the same clothes as the day before – after, I suspect, Lady Bradman dutifully washed the shirt out overnight. He said 'G'morning' to all of us and sat down on the piano stool. 'It seems I've been rolled,' he said and smiled. 'It seems I'm briefly playing the piano, and then I'm walking in the garden with Jessie. Is that right?' All I could do was nod.

Maybe we just got lucky. Maybe he had mellowed. There's no question that he was deeply worried about Jessie's health, and he wasn't exactly as fit as the proverbial mallee bull himself. Yet he was warm and friendly and generous about everything we asked.

For our final pictures Jessie and Don strolled together like a pair of young lovers in their front garden, amongst Jessie's prize-winning roses. Amongst other things I told her that Don had called her 'the most wonderful person I've ever met'. She smiled demurely and said, 'Well, I think he's wonderful.'

'Oh, is that the best you can say?' he laughed, prompting Jessie to smile and suggest, 'I think that's probably enough.' That was our cue to switch off the camera, for the last time.

We adjourned for tea and Anzac biscuits while Sir Donald sat on the verandah signing bats and photos and books – endlessly, it seemed – for our Channel 9 crew. He wrote personal inscriptions to everyone. No problems.

Despite Kerry's dire warnings beforehand Sir Donald never asked for a preview of our interview before it went to air. I rang him to arrange a screening, but he told me not to bother.

Of course, the interview only added to The Don's post-office problems. He rang me later to say that he had been absolutely deluged, buried in mail from across the cricket world, receiving about four thousand pieces of correspondence in just a few days. Cards, letters, photographs and lots of memorabilia arrived. Much of it came from India, wrapped in brown paper, tied with string and simply marked 'Don Bradman, Australia'. Fans sought his wisdom on everything from marriage to money.

I think that Sir Donald Bradman is the only person I've ever met who was beyond question – beyond any doubt – the greatest in his field.

*   *   *

Sadly, Lady Bradman passed away from her cancer two years later. Without her companionship, and increasingly upset by commercial changes at the Bradman Museum that he hadn't approved, Don grew lonely and feeble. He survived just a few more summers, ending his glorious innings at ninety-two. The cricket world came to his memorial service in the big cathedral up on the hill overlooking his favourite Adelaide Oval, and Channel 9 broadcast it at the Bradman family's request.

A smaller private affair happened later, away from the cameras, at the Bradman Museum in Bowral. I felt honoured when John Bradman invited me. (John had proudly reverted to his father's name a few years earlier.) The simple ceremony was the final page of the final chapter of the great Australian love story. It took place out behind the iconic oval just a boundary throw from the old Bradman family home, the brick bungalow that Don had left in order to conquer the cricket galaxy when he was still in his teens.

I'm sure that Don Bradman and his beloved Jessie would have savoured this tender occasion. In a sense they were coming back home to Bowral, where their love first blossomed, when he was twelve and she eleven. 'I fell in love with Jessie the moment I set eyes on her,' he had said to me, with a rare romantic honesty for an Aussie bush boy. It took a decade after they met before Don was game enough to ask Jessie to marry him. For the next sixty-five years only cricket kept them apart. Now this little piece of home turf would be their sweet resting place.

'It's been a long and loving journey,' John said softly to the small crowd of family and friends, almost with a sigh of relief. In that sigh was a private sadness – amidst all the decades of glory and public adulation – that only he and his parents could ever understand.

John was joined by his partner, Megan, and children, Nicholas, Tom and Greta. In a red outfit, the brightness of which was matched by his shiny eyes and spirit, three-year-old Nicholas Bradman scattered a handful of the ashes of his famous grandparents across the memorial garden, amongst the Sir Donald Bradman rosebushes and the Lady Jessie pansies. Then, taking a small silver dish that Jessie had created herself years ago in a jewellery class, the family excused themselves for a quiet, private moment. Arm-in-arm, they walked out towards the centre of the oval in the darkness and cast the last of the precious Bradman ashes.

Chapter 29
The King

'In this business most tantrums are caused by fear.'
– Graham Kennedy

I had only just started on *ACA* in early 1994 when I was offered the final interview that Graham Kennedy would ever give. I accepted the offer, aware of how much I had enjoyed interviewing Don Bradman and Fred Hollows.

This would be very different. It turned out the only reason Graham agreed to the interview at all was because Channel 9 gave him an expensive four-wheel drive as payment. All I got was the pain.

The idea was that we would do a 60th birthday special and would troll through the highlights of Graham's quite extraordinary life. There would be no tricky questions – nothing about his abortive engagement to Lana Cantrell, nothing about his sexual preferences. It was a chance for him to tell us some anecdotes about radio and the glory days of *In Melbourne Tonight*, a chance to have a bit of fun.

Instead, he liberally sprinkled his answers with the f-word, and occasionally dropped in the c-word. Each time he'd look at the floor manager, have a chuckle and say, 'Let's see them try and cut around that, TC.'

Peter Wynne, who produced the hour-long special, managed to miraculously edit out the offensive language. He even made the interview look reasonably warm and friendly. Let me tell you, it wasn't. Graham was cantankerous and bitchy.

When we'd finally finished in the studio, I had no interest in sitting down to lunch with Graham. But David Leckie, the Channel 9 boss, rang and asked me to join them.

Kennedy came in, after a recuperative cigarette, and to my utter astonishment proceeded to thank me for my patience. He apologised for having been a complete arsehole and we had a relaxed meal – full of very funny anecdotes about his early days, none of which Graham had mentioned in our studio chat. He kept telling Leckie how good the interview was, how professional I was and how he wouldn't have done it with anybody else. I figured he was talking about another time, another place.

As he was about to leave – full of a couple of bottles of vintage Barossa red – I remember we had two unexpected visitors join us. Peter Meakin, the News boss, and Paul Lyneham, the ABC star, had just been to lunch to celebrate Paul being signed to the Nine network. That was quite a coup.

Kennedy proceeded to tell Meakin and Lyneham what a fun interview we'd just had. Then we all waved as Kennedy climbed aboard the Channel 9 chopper for the return trip to his farm outside Bowral.

I don't know why, but in later years The King would remember the interview as 'an ambush'. According to Melissa Fyfe in *The Age*:

[Kennedy's] last television appearance was a Ray Martin interview that he cites as the reason for never going back on television. He has told friends that Martin deviated from the agreed questions and asked about his personal life. Martin has disputed this.

I don't just 'dispute' it. It's simply not true.

The fact is, Graham hadn't been inside a studio for over three years before our interview, so he wasn't staying away from his television career on account of me.

David Lyle, the highly accomplished Nine executive who talked him into this interview, had been his producer at *Graham Kennedy's News Show*. Immediately after my interview Lyle came into the studio, shook his head and apologised for having asked me to do it. He'd set up the ground rules for the interview and knew that I hadn't deviated or ambushed Graham.

In a letter I received the next day, which I still have, Lyle called Graham's performance the most unprofessional and unpleasant he'd ever seen – and he'd witnessed some epic Kennedy temper tantrums over the years. Clearly Graham simply didn't want to be there.

Graham was eccentric and full of contradictions. Exceptionally talented performers often are. On the one hand he was well-mannered, very proper and didn't swear in mixed company. Yet he was irreverent, subversive and his comedy was crude and bawdy. (His interview with me certainly was.) I also suspect in his final years, given his illness and the booze, Graham wasn't what you might call 'a rational, reliable witness'.

This wasn't my first interview with Graham. He had made one appearance on *Midday* – I seem to recall it was to promote his return to television on his *News Show*. It wasn't an easy chat, even allowing for the fact that – on that occasion – all the questions had been vetted by Graham beforehand, by fax.

I had also been summoned by Sam Chisholm on occasion to his infamous third-floor 'bar' to 'keep Graham company'. It was too early for Sam's daily happy hour, but I guess because I had finished that day's *Midday Show* he thought I was available. And Graham 'approved' of me, Sam said.

They were amusing interludes. Graham was a great entertainer, even in Sam's bar. He was warm and witty. But he also had a stinging, piquant wit – with a sharp mind and a rapier tongue. It could make you wince and feel somewhat relieved that you weren't the target of his attack.

As it turned out, Graham was also behind a bizarre game of charades with my dressing room, which I had no idea about until much later. I cracked up when I finally heard about it.

It's important to understand that for fifty years 'dressing rooms' had been one of the lynchpins of the Channel 9 culture. Nowhere was it more entrenched than at GTV in Melbourne. Sam Chisholm liked to call television 'Australia's Hollywood', and nowhere was a star's status more on display than in the size and location of his dressing room.

Second only to the dressing room was the parking spot closest to the GTV studio doors. Depending on one's ranking at the time that could belong to Graham, Bert Newton, Don Lane, Daryl Somers or, these days, Eddie McGuire. By seeing the name imprinted on a block of wood at the head of that parking spot, everyone at Channel 9 knew exactly who the network's reigning star was.

But dressing rooms were what legends were made of. In Melbourne they included a few couches, a kitchenette with bar fridge, a writing desk, a big TV, a stereo player, a bathroom with a shower, a mammoth make-up chair and lots and lots of mirrors. Oh, and a separate *dressing room*.

The biggest one – in the central courtyard of GTV – had been Graham's original, with Bert's in the annex alongside. For some reason Graham later asked for a swimming pool in front of his, which was duly sunk and tiled. Not that anyone ever went for a dip, unless he or she was very drunk.

When Don Lane had his *Tonight Show*, Graham's dressing room was given a makeover by one of Melbourne's most expensive interior decorators before Don moved in. Bert stayed next door.

In fact Bert was shunted around quite a bit when Daryl Somers got the top car park, finally being assigned a cosy triple-roomed suite next door to the make-up room.

When Bert was let go from Nine by Sam Chisholm, Daryl made his power play and extended Gra Gra's old dressing room. Rumour has it amongst the GTV cognoscenti that Daryl actually passed up a zero or two in his new contract in return for 'the biggest dressing room in Channel 9 history'. Daryl was only ever there one day a week. The rest of the time it remained locked and off limits, even to the prime minister when he was about to be interviewed.

For some reason TCN in Sydney didn't have the same rich dressing-room tradition or culture, despite having had Bobby Limb, Barry Crocker and Brian Henderson as major network stars. It was only Mike Walsh who bothered, and his was *a cheap motel* in comparison with the five-star luxury at GTV!

Mind you, doing ninety minutes of live TV every day, Walshy deserved a bit of pampering. He actually put it to good use. The only trouble was that while Mike's dressing room was behind the studio, it was a long way from the *Midday Show* cottage, where he and his team prepared the show. Apparently a distressed Mike Walsh complained to Sam Chisholm, over a midnight-to-dawn drink one night, that every morning as he walked across to his dressing room he had to run the gauntlet of busloads of his female audience. So, Mike had come up with a solution. Why not excavate a tunnel under the roadway, from the *Midday Show* cottage to Mike's dressing-room entrance? Why not? That way he could avoid the fans before he was suitably buffed-up.

After Sam checked out the idea with the engineers, however, and found it was going to cost Kerry Packer a few hundred thousand dollars, the idea was dumped. I doubt Graham Kennedy would have let Chisholm off so lightly!

When The King came back to television, years after *Blankety Blanks,* he hosted *Eleven A.M.,* which was a quizzical look at the morning news on Channel 7. Colleagues who worked with him there tell riotous stories about Graham rejecting all the available dressing rooms and demanding a Winnebago caravan. That was duly imported and put on site in the studio props bay.

A few years later, when Kennedy returned to Nine to do his night-time news show, I got a call from Sam Chisholm. I was still doing *Midday* at that stage and had acquired Mike Walsh's old dressing room. Sam asked if it was okay for Graham to use it at night. I said I couldn't care less because it was empty anyway.

But that's when the dressing-room charades began.

Apparently every afternoon when I left all my pictures and photos came down and a batch of Graham's replaced them. On the same wall nails! There were shots of Kennedy and his then-favoured manager, Harry Miller, on horseback, Graham with Sammy Davis Jr, Graham with his dog, et cetera. As well as the pictures, each day a cast-iron St Kilda Football Club badge would be screwed into the door of his clothes cupboard. Early the next morning, in a clandestine swap, they'd all be changed over again!

Quite frankly I didn't care, but it was all so secretive.

Later still, as part of Graham's new contract to do *Coast to Coast*, he insisted on his own separate dressing room. A luxury one was duly built, down the other end of the corridor with its own dedicated exit, so that when the show was over he could walk straight down the stairs and into his waiting limo. As well as the huge fridge for the Cristal champagne, Graham insisted on a dishwasher. A dishwasher!

In the years that followed, when I shared that dressing room with Mike Munro, Jana, Liz Hayes and Tracy Grimshaw (not all at the same time, of course), we used to shake our heads and wonder what the dishwasher was for. Why would you need a dishwasher? It's still there, like some royal memento of grander times in television land, when dressing rooms really were the mark of the man!

Chapter 30
Frontline and Other Funny Business

Frontline went to air in early 1994, a few months after I started hosting *A Current Affair*.

The timing was a pain in the bum. I must admit, that first night when it was broadcast, I put on my flak jacket and crash helmet. But when it finished, I poked my head up from the bunker again feeling almost relieved. It could have been much worse.

Mind you, it would get much worse.

The early episodes gently targeted Mike Willesee and Stan Grant, as they'd been hosting the 6.30 nightly shows when the production company Working Dog first came up with the *Frontline* concept. It was in subsequent seasons, when I was in the host's chair, that they sharpened their machetes. In the mid-1990s, current-affairs shows were the tall poppies, winning the ratings and the Logies. And we know what always happens to tall poppies in Australia.

Admittedly, given what really goes on in the news and current-affairs business, *Frontline* did have a rich and colourful pool of characters and controversies to draw on. The world of journalism, by its very nature, has always attracted larrikins, crusaders and show ponies. Add to that the egos of television types and it's a satirist's playground. For years there'd been hidden cameras, chequebook journalism, foot-in-the-door reporters, bullying studio interviews and an obsession with ratings. None of that was new. In fact ABC precursors to *A Current Affair* and *Today Tonight* such as *This Day Tonight* and *Four Corners* had been guilty of many of the same sins that the ABC's *Frontline* now accused us of – without the chequebook, of course. But those two flagship ABC programs had had an extra charge levelled at them: that they were run by a biased cabal of lefties. I'm sure there were days when John Howard and his cohorts would have paid the Working Dog team good money to produce a similar *Frontline* show targeting *Four Corners* or Kerry O'Brien.

Frontline came along at an especially ripe time. The size of some of the cheques had become ridiculous: by now ordinary battlers with half a story to tell were putting their hands out for money, and often receiving it. There was also the competition factor. There was a fearsome rivalry between channels 9 and 7, but also between *60 Minutes* and every other show on the Packer network. Not since the afternoon-newspaper wars in Sydney in the fifties and sixties between *The Mirror* and *The Sun* had there been such bitter and intense competition as there was on TV at 6.30 on weeknights. That rivalry made journalists push the envelope.

I remember one good example: the first IVF mother-to-be in Australia had been paid by Channel 9 for her exclusive story. No one in Australia had seen her face. But a rival crew from Channel 7 drove up and parked outside her suburban home, waiting to get pictures. It spooked the Channel 9 producer, so he helped lift the heavily pregnant woman over the high back fence, where a waiting car whisked them off to a 'safe house': a resort motel hundreds of kilometres away. It was a ready-made subplot for the satirist's pen.

I recall one stake-out that took place over several nights, with the camera crew sleeping in the truck . . . outside the wrong house. It was even the wrong suburb. I remember one TV crew deliberately parking a car on an outer Sydney freeway for a story about gangs who were pinching wheels from broken-down cars. After waiting all afternoon without any action, the camera crew ducked away for a quick coffee. When they returned, all four wheels *and* the car were gone. Sometimes a reporter and his crew, with the camera rolling, did a walk-in at the wrong factory, confronting staff who didn't have a clue about the fraud they were being accused of. The illegal factory was actually next door. I recall doing a story on 'the worst emergency ward in Australia', where medicos were about to revolt because of overcrowding and staff shortages. We spent three nights camped at the hospital, and the only patients were one minor-car-accident victim, a woman who gave birth and a couple of drunks who'd fallen over. We dumped the story.

Then there was a much more serious yarn, an exposé of a killer psychiatrist, for which we'd mounted a six-week investigation. A new researcher went to the photo library and chose a picture for the report – but it was of a federal MP who happened to share the same name. This horrendous mistake was discovered, but only at the last minute. The story ended up winning us a Logie for Best Current Affairs report, but it could easily have lost us the whole program.

There was clearly no shortage of real-life material for *Frontline*. But the strange thing is, they turned some of *ACA*'s better and more worthwhile stories – exposés of nursing-home scandals, the shameful neglect of Aboriginals and the life-saving separation of conjoined twins from Bougainville – into ludicrous, far-fetched satire. But then you always can, with a clever jerk of the truth.

During the last *Frontline* series, in 1997, we were convinced that Working Dog must have had a mole within *ACA*. They had details about upcoming stories they couldn't have known without an insider. It annoyed us to think that someone on the payroll was leaking secrets to undermine our show. But, at the same time, over a beer we'd laugh our heads off at the nefarious tricks producers, reporters and crews really did get up to. Sometimes it reached ridiculous levels, with crazy car chases, decoys, the leaking of bogus information, bidding wars, lie-detector tests and the delaying of interviewees so they'd be too late to talk to the opposition show. 'Kidnapping' talent, like the IVF mother, was a common tactic. The tricks of the trade were endless and highly imaginative.

But there's a huge difference between this madcap competitive behaviour and journalists telling lies.

Frontline was such an entertaining and clever show that viewers could easily believe Working Dog got it right when they portrayed current-affairs shows deliberately deceiving the public. Well, they didn't get it right. I know there are times when individuals on current-affairs teams (or newspapers) misrepresent things, and occasionally they get the facts wrong. There remains a basic integrity in the TV news game. But, of course, that didn't quite fit the *Frontline* script.

All kinds of skulduggery went on in the editing room on the satirical TV show. I remember one episode when the tape editor deleted a word: 'have not' became 'have', I believe. But, you know, in four decades of sitting in TV editing suites I've never witnessed that kind of behaviour. As in newspapers, a misrepresentation is more often the result of a cock-up than a conspiracy. The culprit is usually the pressure of time, or just laziness in failing to check and double-check facts.

As fate would have it, in 2001, long after the show was off air, *Frontline* was part of Jenna's curriculum in her final year of high school. It must have been weird-crazy for her. After all, Jenna had grown up hearing me talk night after night at the dinner table about the trials and tribulations of *ACA*, including the occasional stray ethical dilemma. Now, years later, she was watching *Frontline* as the primary source in an advanced English unit called 'Telling the Truth'. I found the show as funny as all hell. But it didn't tell the truth. Jenna would come home from school and say she'd had to remind her teacher that *Frontline* was a spoof, that it wasn't a real program and that the airhead host, Mike Moore, was really a balding comedy writer/actor named Rob Sitch, wearing a bad rug. It was a satire. The trouble is, people often forgot and thought it was real. My daughter had the clear impression that the intent – or mal-intent as she put it – of this English unit was 'to expose how commercial current-affairs shows lie to us'.

I must admit that as Jenna's father, concerned more about her HSC marks than about debunking the ideology of the Board of Studies, I suggested she shouldn't buck the system. 'Give 'em what they want to hear' was my fearless advice. Jenna ended up getting an exceptional mark in English. We were having a chat after the exams, and I asked her what tack she'd taken on *Frontline*. She looked at me aghast, narrowed her eyes and asked rhetorically, 'What do you think, Dad?' Well, I think she probably gave it to them with both barrels.

Frontline often portrayed commercial TV current-affairs

shows as outrageously biased. In fact I don't know of any TV network or program that takes a position on political or social issues in the way newspapers regularly do, especially at election time. *A Current Affair*, *Today Tonight* and *60 Minutes* never do. When I was hosting *ACA* and I interviewed a politician, let's say Keating or Howard, afterwards I'd check the phone logbook in which viewers' calls were recorded. I'd know if I'd done a balanced interview because the complaints would also be balanced: a whole bunch of viewers whingeing about me being a blue-ribbon Liberal, while the other half insisted I was clearly a Labor Party stooge. They all watched the same interview; it's just that people see what they want to see. And often believe the worst.

I do think that for a time the undeniably successful *Frontline* seriously damaged the credibility of current-affairs programs, especially on commercial TV. There developed a kind of anti-current-affairs culture amongst young, idealistic Australians. At Nine I even argued that we should plan a counterattack, sending the most senior journalists into university media classes and other public forums to show the positive role of the media. But commercial TV management is as short-sighted as government. They only care about tomorrow's ratings, not the image of journalism in a decade's time, when they may have moved on.

Long after the ABC satire had gone to DVD, the crew and I would roll up for an interview with a housewife or a businessman – just a simple everyday story – and be greeted with, 'Now, you're not going to distort this, are you? We've seen the way you blokes do this on *Frontline*!'

We'd always laugh and make a joke of it, but it got a bit tedious.

*　　*　　*

Mind you, there were occasions when I just had to put my hand up and plead guilty as charged, of everything from being over-zealous to being boring and worthy. Sometimes at *ACA* we found ourselves accused of sensationalising stories, exploiting people, beating up issues, bullying and taking cheap shots. Occasion-ally they were justified complaints, especially towards the end of the 1990s. Within *ACA* we always had heated discussions when we received such brickbats about our ethics. There was a constant debate between the cowboys and the purists. I have to admit there were occasions I was in both camps, because in jour-nalism issues are not always black and white, and there's a fine line between being provocative, cheeky, crusading – and just plain wrong. In the pressured environment of a nightly current-affairs show decisions must sometimes be made on the spur of the moment. Notwithstanding the experience and excellence of those making the decisions, mistakes do happen. There were times when *ACA* simply stuffed up.

The saga of the Paxton family, in suburban Melbourne, is a case in point. *A Current Affair*'s treatment of them was over-the-top, and bad editorial judgements were made. I was in the middle of those decisions. There were reasons for the way we told their story, but no excuses.

The details of the long-running melodrama have become a bit murky over the years, but it was my clear understanding at the time that the Paxton story, which aired in 1997, was meant to be about the problems of living on the dole long term. Mike Munro insists it was never a hatchet job. On the contrary.

Taking Munro on a walk through the house, Shane Paxton, the eldest son, shouted at his brother, Mark, 'Get out of bed. It's twelve past twelve.' The electric guitars from their late-night jam session were spread around the lounge; a couple of huge dogs were waiting to be fed. Mum didn't work, and nor did their sister, Bindi. The story depicted a pretty dysfunctional family who were leading a life of indolence.

Now, I know there are often complex reasons people can't lift themselves out of a rut. It's often not simply a matter of getting a job. Nevertheless, Australia was outraged by the Paxton family's lifestyle and attitudes. When I came off air and went downstairs to the *ACA* office that night, the switchboard was ablaze. There were five staff answering the phones, but they couldn't keep up with the angry calls. The reaction in the Melbourne office was even more fiery.

A few nights later came the second story. After an offer from a resort owner who phoned in, *ACA* flew the three Paxton kids to South Molle, on the Great Barrier Reef. On this 'island paradise' the brothers knocked back job offers because they would have to cut their long hair short. Bindi turned down her job offer because she objected to the colour of the housemaids' uniform.

This time Australia simply went off! I've never seen a phone reaction like it. I've never seen *ACA* ratings like it, either. The story quickly took on a life of its own, becoming what one editorial dubbed 'a kind of shameful public stoning'. The media and audience frenzy was started and sustained by us at *ACA*, and whipped along by newspapers and talk radio. In Melbourne the *Herald Sun* conducted a poll, which found that 95 per cent of respondents were in favour of having the Paxtons' dole cut. John Laws, the nation's talk-radio king at the time, called Shane and Bindi Paxton 'putrid'. The Victorian Premier, Jeff Kennett, jumped on board, noting the 'public outrage' at the Paxtons' laziness. Even John Howard, who'd just been elected prime minister, fronted up on *ACA* and denounced the Paxtons as 'bludgers'.

The Paxtons insisted they'd been 'stitched up' by the producer, John McEvoy, which he denied. *ACA*'s official position was that everything was ethical and the Paxtons appeared on the show willingly and loved the limelight – until it all turned sour. But I'm now reliably informed that somebody at *ACA* fudged a few key details of the story. It seems, for example, that the South Molle resort owner only offered the Paxtons jobs to get some positive publicity. He'd actually gone into receivership six days earlier. He wasn't in a position to give anyone a long-term job, even if the Paxtons had been interested in working there.

On balance the Paxton saga wasn't *ACA*'s finest hour. The family had no way of dealing with the media circus as everything spun out of control. Few families would have. The fact is, the unbelievable ratings proved irresistible to Nine. Every time good journalistic judgement cried 'Enough!', the TV audiences wanted more. The Nine News boss, Peter Meakin, was quoted in one newspaper article cheekily saying, 'Quite frankly I wish I had more stories like that.' Meakin probably didn't help. In the long term I believe the Paxton story damaged *ACA*'s reputation. We certainly could have handled it better.

Surprise, surprise, *Media Watch*'s Stuart Littlemore and *The Australian*'s Phillip Adams were almost orgasmic in their attacks. It irked me that we'd given them an excuse to go off.

The Paxton story also brings me to my sordid little encounter with a serial pest named John Safran, which became – at least to *Media Watch* – a celebrated confrontation. Again, its effects would hang around like a rancid smell for years.

I had just returned from Indonesia, where we'd been filming stories for *ACA*, one on threatened orangutans and another on corrupt army generals. I'd worked eleven days straight. It was 9.30 in the morning when the buzzer on our gate at home blasted and a voice said over the intercom, 'A package for Ray Martin, from *A Current Affair*.'

Dianne answered, 'Oh, thanks, I'll come and get it. Please come in.' She pressed the buzzer to open the gate, stepped through the front door . . . and then hurtled back inside.

Coming up the driveway was an odd-looking trio: a bloke in a bizarre grinning Mike Munro mask; a heavily pregnant woman wielding a tiny digital camera; and another man, who turned out to be Shane Paxton, although Dianne didn't recognise him straightaway. I was unshaven and dressed in shorts and a T-shirt. Not exactly a good look for TV. The bloke in the mask proceeded to ring the doorbell nonstop for about a minute, like a madman. Then he banged on the glass, shouting, 'C'mon, Ray. We know you're in there. We just want to ask why you're still at home at nine-thirty, when the rest of Australia is at work.'

Having no joy, the noisy trio set up a desk and a chair across the road from our house, directly in front of the local primary school, where seven-year-old Luke was a pupil. They caused such a commotion that kids began hanging out of the classroom windows. Dianne walked quietly down the side of the house, trying to unravel the mystery of who these people were and what the hell was going on. That's when she recognised Shane Paxton. She heard the guy with the Mike Munro mask talking about the ABC, as they proceeded to film up and down our street, including the front of our house.

This was the period when I was covering Melbourne mafia drug dealings for *ACA* and had recently received a death threat, which New South Wales police had suggested I should probably take seriously. A woman had overheard a couple of blokes in a Lygon Street coffee shop threatening to take action against me.

She reported it to the Victoria Police, who apparently knew the blokes concerned and prompted the New South Wales cops to warn me. It was the second such threat I'd received in the space of six months, so for three nights Channel 9 posted an armed guard at our house. Understandably Dianne had been quite upset; it had reminded her of some of the unwelcome spin-offs that come from being married to a high-profile journalist. So I wasn't very happy about this idiot filming my house, my street and Luke's school.

I rang a couple of people I knew at the ABC. They told me it was almost certainly a character named John Safran, who was doing a comedy pilot for Aunty. They apologised for his behaviour and promised to get him to leave.

The next morning Dianne and I were at the shops when I received a phone call from Luke's primary-school principal telling us that 'the TV crew' were back outside our house. Only this time, she said, they had opened our letterbox and were rifling through our paper-recycling bin. Dianne was angry, so I did my best to calm her down on the short drive home. I was pretty relaxed when we arrived, even when they jammed the camera in Dianne's face. I still had myself under control when Safran tried to interview her.

'What are you doing going through our letterbox?' she asked, at the same time pulling off his silly Mike Munro mask. Safran reacted, shouting, 'Hey, look. You can't do that, Mrs Martin.'

That was the moment I lost my cool, my composure, my sang-froid. That's when I grabbed Safran by the throat, suggesting he should mind his manners.

In a high-pitched voice he chirped, 'We're doing a comedy show and wondered if we could ask you a couple of quick questions, please?'

I said okay. (I was now feeling a bit guilty about my overtly violent reaction.)

When he asked why I was at home so late in the morning, I explained my Indonesia assignment. He muttered something about knowing exactly what I was doing up there with that repressive totalitarian regime, or some such nonsense. He then asked if I wanted to know how he knew what I'd been doing. 'Yeah, tell me,' I replied, just a bit curious.

'Well, we have surgically implanted a mini camera in your forehead. So we know everything you've done for the past fortnight.' What?

I suggested that as a comedy this was about as funny as a toothache. The 'interview' was now over. I went inside and again rang my ABC friends.

Shortly after, I received an abject apology from Brian Johns, the corporation's managing director. He also promised that because the ABC was paying for the pilot of the comedy show, the video shot by Safran would 'never see the light of day'. A woman in the ABC's corporate-affairs office also sent a bunch of flowers to Dianne. The pilot show was dumped, presumably because it didn't make anyone laugh. But within a few weeks the photos of my confrontation with Safran were on the internet, and within a few months the video had appeared on *Media Watch*. In fact it graduated way beyond that, becoming part of *Media Watch*'s opening montage for the next couple of years. So much for the unbridled power of the ABC's brass.

*   *   *

Aside from the Paxtons there were one or two other *ACA* stories that hurt our reputation badly, though I'd argue that from a journalist's standpoint they were justified. They weren't yarns that made you feel especially good, but they were legitimate.

Like the episode on Benny Mendoza.

It was no secret at *ACA* that I strongly objected to reporters chasing people down streets and charging into offices with cameras rolling. I happen to think it's bad manners, and pretty ordinary journalism, anyway. Most times it just looks like bullying. But the *ACA* story with the most maligned and tragic outcome of all – the story on allegedly shonky TV repairman Benny Mendoza – in fact hadn't relied on that kind of journalism. Reporter Jane Hansen didn't use any of those antics with Mr Mendoza, who hanged himself, apparently because of the family shame after the story aired. All that matters is that he took his own life. His death was a shocking tragedy. No news story is worth a death.

Stuart Littlemore, of *Media Watch*, condemned the *ACA* story as 'media misconduct', 'bullying righteousness' and a 'sordid little entrapment'. It was none of those things. Jane Hansen is an experienced, compassionate journalist whose repertoire has never included set-ups, lies, deception or vilification, as was so cruelly alleged by her critics. She certainly did nothing to deserve Littlemore's abuse, such as calling her 'an unspeakable bastard'.

For decades newspapers and current-affairs programs have run stories exposing dodgy mechanics and tradesmen, fraudulent accountants, pill-popping truck drivers and paedophile priests. High-profile politicians who misuse their official credit cards to pay for prostitutes get a working over by the reputable broadsheets. There is always the potential that any of these people may harm themselves after being subjected to media scrutiny. Littlemore himself in his *This Day Tonight* and *Four Corners* days turned his camera and rapier-like tongue upon people who may well have reacted like Benny Mendoza.

Examples abound of legitimate stories resulting in emotional pain for those put under the media blowtorch. A psychiatrist treating Federal Court judge Marcus Einfeld for severe depression testified in court about the dangers of the media and the courts pursuing him further – but the news coverage didn't let up, and Einfeld was subsequently sent to gaol for three years. In recent times in politics we've had near-tragic examples such as Paula Wriedt, in Tasmania, John Brogden, in New South Wales, and Nick Sherry, in the federal sphere. They have all attempted suicide, unable to handle public scrutiny. The stockbroker Rene Rivkin took his own life after a public shaming for insider trading.

So at what point does a journalist pull back from a story? Who is fair game, and who is out of bounds? Are politicians okay? Is a corporate boss? What about a desperate farmer who diverts public water or sprays his crop with a banned pesticide? These are basic questions for any introductory seminar in a first-year journalism course. What's the answer? I believe you do the story, carefully and ethically. Compassionately, too, when it's called for.

I know that Jane Hansen was absolutely gutted when Mr Mendoza took his life. She met with his family, apologised and cried with them. Then, two years later, Jane underwent a course of counselling because she was plagued by nightmares, waking up hyperventilating and perspiring. Jane revealed in a book she wrote that eight years after Mr Mendoza's death, and after losing two premature babies, she rang the Mendoza family's pastor, the Reverend Denis Shelton, wondering whether this was God's revenge for what she had done. Reverend Shelton did his best to reassure her it wasn't.

In hindsight the *ACA* story could never justify Benny Mendoza's death. But that's the benefit of hindsight.

*   *   *

There was a bizarre spin-off from this sad story. Without bothering about the facts, a few talk-radio jocks condemned *ACA* for its role. Mike Gibson, in Sydney, was amongst them. One afternoon his editorial rant apparently included a litany of what he called 'grubby stories' done by *ACA* with me at the helm. Gibson, for some reason, made it a highly personal attack on my ethical standards. He focused on the fate of Mr Mendoza but also accused me of, amongst other things, once having made Lindy and Michael Chamberlain's eldest boy, Aidan, break into tears by asking him about the disappearance of his baby sister, Azaria. Michael had in the past publicly defended me, pointing out that he and Lindy requested that I ask Aidan about what he saw on that tragic August night back in 1980. They were standing beside the boy as I gently spoke to him.

Partway into the show, Dianne got a call from a friend who told her what Gibson had said; she quickly tuned in and caught the last of his verbal barrage. Mad as hell, she called him up, telling him on the radio what a mean-spirited goose he was. Dianne also suggested that he had ulterior motives for his attack. She knew he was angry about an exposé *ACA* did on a friend of his, a Gold Coast motel proprietor who'd been accused of spying on naked women guests.

I didn't hear what she said on the radio, but friends tell me she opened both barrels, which I would never have predicted. Not in a million years. Remember, Dianne is a woman who has studiously avoided publicity for decades, and she has a steely determination never to be provoked by the media. Never to play their game. She normally couldn't be bothered. But on this particular day Gibbo fired her up.

I have no idea what midlife crisis Gibson had been going through. But my former Nine colleague had turned from being a sports writer whom I regarded as one of the best I'd ever read and a good radio performer into a bitter, twisted drone who was angry at the world. Dianne gave him a free character analysis. Onya, Di.

Of course, the smart-arses at *Media Watch* regurgitated Dianne's radio confrontation with Gibson the next Monday night, with their usual smarmy exegesis. It was what I'd come to expect from Stuart Littlemore and his sidekick, producer David Salter, although I was a little unimpressed that they'd used Dianne's emotional outpouring as a way of having another bash at me. It was a pretty cheap shot, but why should I be surprised?

The *Media Watch* attacks had begun as regular gratuitous jibes while I was at *Midday*, but when I moved to *ACA* they became unrelenting. It got to the point where I almost felt disappointed if I didn't get a guernsey from Stuart. The truth is, *Media Watch* rarely bothered to check its own facts and never gave its victims a right of reply, the very same crimes it accused other journalists of committing. There was nothing you could do except cop it on the chin.

But then, one Monday night in the late nineties, Mr Littlemore QC accused me, in his rather arrogant and supercilious way, of having 'played the race card again' on *ACA*. This was in relation to a story the program had done about Asian students at the University of Wollongong. It was a good, solid story, which, as host, I had introduced amongst maybe four other stories that night. I was stunned that anybody would accuse me of playing the so-called race card after forty years of doing the exact opposite.

The next morning I rang David Leckie, the Nine boss at the time, and suggested Littlemore could get away with calling me stupid or ugly, but never racist. Not that Leckie needed reminding, but I pointed out that for many years I'd been chairman of the Fred Hollows Foundation, which worked directly with indigenous Australians and had restored sight to a million cataract-blind people in the Third World. I'd also been a member of the Council for Aboriginal Reconciliation for a decade. Apart from my own family's DNA, I had a public track record that proved he was wrong. I figured I was on pretty solid ground for defamation action. David Leckie, to his credit, didn't hesitate. 'Yeah, go get the bastard,' he said. So I did.

As we know, the justice system moves at glacial speed. Especially with defamation proceedings. But after about seven years of legal torpor, Littlemore and the ABC were keen to settle, for a hefty payout. It gave me a lot of satisfaction to pass the cheque directly to the Fred Hollows Foundation, to help continue its great work eradicating cataract blindness in Asia and Africa.

There was such a thing as karma.

Chapter 31
Revolts and Royals

Now, I'd hate to give the impression that I wasn't having fun. *A Current Affair* churns out over twelve hundred stories a year. That's an awful lot of television. Decisions have to be made on the run and under the gun, and that's when mistakes are sometimes made – but that's also when you get an adrenaline buzz. I still thrived on the daily pursuit of the big interviews and challenging stories. So, in spite of the stings from *Frontline* and *Media Watch*, I loved going to work.

Some of the biggest laughs and best times I ever had were on the road with *ACA* – from Ambon in Indonesia to Tenterfield and Marble Bar back in Australia. We seemed to take the show everywhere in those days, heading off to Ho Chi Minh City for the 20th anniversary of the end of the Vietnam War, to Townsville for the 50th celebrations of the War in the Pacific.

I remember we began one new season from Washington, where Bill Clinton was trying to save his presidency after the

Monica Lewinsky scandal, while another time we were in the jungles of Kalimantan, trying to save the threatened orangutans.

As I mentioned before, politics had become a ratings 'danger zone', but we went there anyway. Almost every day. At least we did in the first three or four years that I hosted the show. In fact I even had a dedicated producer, a political bloodhound named Warwick Adderley – who was ex-ABC radio like me – whose job it was to find *the* main interview of the day. The target was usually in Canberra, but often in big business, sport or even some news-breaking university. These interviews regularly got us headlines in the next day's papers.

In the midst of dozens of memorable stories towards the end of my first stint at *ACA* there were two standouts. Both are amongst my all-time favourites, yet both convinced me to leave *ACA*. They also reinforced one rule I have learnt over the years: in television an unforgettable story needs a great crew to tell it. On these two occasions I had the best: producer Steve Bibb, cameraman Mark Munro and sound recordist Jason McCawley. I'd trust them with my life.

The Sandline Affair, up in Port Moresby, was a huge story in 1997. It had all the makings of a first-class political scandal. Maybe even a political disaster that might result in Australian armed intervention. It was a cracker of a yarn, one of those stories that makes journalism so exhilarating. It just fell into our laps, as only happens when the gods are with you. To me it was one of *ACA*'s finest moments.

Steve Bibb had been tipped off that something was about to blow in Papua New Guinea, so we raced up to Moresby. The island of Bougainville was the hot topic at the time, as a bloody rebellion had shut down their incredibly rich copper mine. Thousands of local people had been killed in this long-festering conflict, while Australian diplomatic efforts to broker a peace had failed. The PNG prime minister, Sir Julius Chan, was convinced that his own army couldn't end the Bougainville stalemate. So he signed a top-secret agreement with Sandline International, a dodgy paramilitary mob who'd mostly worked in African trouble spots. Run by a colourful ex-lieutenant colonel in the Scots Guards named Tim Spicer, Sandline was contracted to bring in foreign mercenaries and sort out the rebels.

At the height of the PNG story there was an army mutiny, a dangerous stand-off between soldiers and police, mass demonstrations, a parliamentary siege and the sacking of the elected government by Brigadier-General Jerry Singirok. In the end it was a tin-pot revolt, but for ten days it loomed as a major crisis for Canberra.

Frontline ended up doing an episode based on commercial current-affairs coverage of the Sandline Affair. It would have been much funnier if they had known what really went on behind the scenes.

Kerry Packer owned the dominant Port Moresby commercial TV channel, which meant the locals had seen me on *The Midday Show* and everybody now watched *A Current Affair*. Each story we satellited back to Sydney was telecast in PNG half an hour later, and we quickly discovered that all sides in this fractured capital wanted to talk to *ACA*, in an attempt to use us to their political advantage. Army mutineers, army loyalists, expat Aussie businessmen, Chan's political rivals and even Lieutenant Colonel Tim Spicer's office were in touch with us. We had access to everyone.

First we interviewed Prime Minister Julius Chan, a clever, self-made, rich man. He expressed genuine surprise that Canberra, which pumped in over half a billion dollars a year in aid to PNG, hadn't bothered to call. 'I haven't heard a word from my friend Mr John Howard,' he said, loudly projecting his voice towards the ceiling and smiling. I suggested that it seemed Chan desperately wanted someone to hear about his concern.

'Oh, Canberra hears every word that's spoken in PNG – even in my office,' Sir Julius replied. When I asked if he was implying that Australian defence intelligence used bugs to eavesdrop in PNG, he just shrugged and said, 'Whatever.'

Later that afternoon Chan's Australian-born press secretary, Mark Lilleyman, called me at our hotel. 'Hey, guess what? Within two hours of Sir Julius's interview with you today, John Howard rang. Now isn't that a strange, strange coincidence?' It was indeed.

The next morning we learnt of a big union rally outside the Murray military barracks. Rioting had begun in the local business area behind it, with a row of shops being looted by a *rascal* gang. Police had cordoned off the area and were blocking traffic from going anywhere near the barracks. That is, until they saw our cameras and discovered we were from *A Current Affair*.

'Ahh, yewz can go down, Ray,' the sergeant said, 'but just be careful.'

At the rally I tried to inconspicuously stand off to one side. But the union leaders saw us turn up, handed me the megaphone and invited me to address the assembled brothers. It was seriously bizarre. I didn't even know why they were striking. And the closest thing I had to union credentials was that I *worked* on a TV program they all liked. I could see Steve Bibb chortling to himself as I spluttered out some inane 'power to the workers' platitudes. When we arrived at the street where the looting was taking place, the young thugs actually stopped heaving rocks through shop windows. At least for a moment. They ran over to have a chat, asking us to take their picture. All their questions were about what it was like to be 'on the teev'.

It seemed everybody was happy to talk to us. Like the next morning when Steve and I were having breakfast, and a business card suddenly dropped on the table, alongside my cereal bowl. I looked up to see a bearded man, who turned out to be an expat lawyer from Australia. He told us that he had a copy of the top-secret Sandline contract, which was the key to the whole mystery of the foreign mercenaries. I almost choked on my Special K. This was the way reporters got scoops in movies like *All the President's Men*, not in real-life journalism. Anyway, he wanted us to expose what he called Prime Minister Chan's illegal activities; the PM had signed the multimillion-dollar deal without even showing it to his Cabinet. The lawyer wouldn't let us take the contract from our hotel room, but he let us copy down the details. Bibb and I scribbled feverishly.

So that night on *ACA* we exclusively revealed that the Sandline contract provided for forty foreign mercenaries equipped with Russian-built helicopter gunships, troop carriers, automatic grenade launchers and assault rifles. It was fully two days later that the rest of the media were shown the secret contract.

Over the next week or so everybody talked to us. We met the elusive brigadier-general, the officer behind the military coup, and Major Walter Enuma, the man in charge of Operation Rausim Kwik. This was pidgin for 'Get rid of them quickly', with 'them' meaning the foreign mercenaries. I figured you couldn't dream up a funnier name.

When Lieutenant Colonel Tim Spicer was arraigned, the Papuan magistrate even offered me a seat inside his tiny courthouse to watch proceedings. (He was a viewer of *A Current Affair*, he told me.) That's when I met Roger, a plain-clothes police sergeant who would become a critical player in our story. Roger whispered to me that he had driven the Land Rover carrying Spicer from the British High Commission to the court. He gave me his card and told me to ring him later for an update. Again, I couldn't believe my luck. Sergeant Roger, who was now my instant best mate, laughed and said that all he wanted in return was 'an autograph for my teenage daughter, 'cos she loves *A Current Affair*'. No probs, Rog. It was the least I could do.

Over the next few days I travelled everywhere with Roger in his unmarked maroon Subaru, while the rest of the *ACA* team shadowed us in a red four-wheel drive we'd borrowed from Mr Packer's Port Moresby TV station. We weaved our way through every roadblock around Parliament House, right up to the Cabinet room. Sir Julius greeted us warmly and introduced us to the PNG Speaker. Some hours later, from a glass walkway above the parliamentary chamber, I saw that the rest of the Aussie press corps had finally arrived but were locked out of the building. I knew they'd be a trifle vexed, but I wasn't about to swap places. In the news business it's the quick and the dead.

That night our new 'best mate', Brigadier-General Singirok, decided on a total army blockade of Parliament House, which meant that all the PNG politicians who'd turned up for an emergency session remained locked inside for the night.

Now, as it happened I had the mobile number of the ex-prime minister, Sir Michael Somare, whom I'd interviewed earlier that day. I'd known Somare for more than thirty years, and I guessed that even though he was on the Opposition benches right now, having twice been PNG's prime minister, Sir Michael would be in the thick of things in the turbulent days ahead. I wanted to stay in close formation with him. So I rang Somare, who asked if we could fetch him a fresh pair of underpants and a clean shirt, along with a carton of cigarettes. All life's basic essentials when there's a siege happening.

Imagine what *Frontline* could have done if they'd known all these little gems.

But it was *The Age*'s veteran correspondents, all hot and sweaty hanging around Moresby, who were almost apoplectic about our exclusive access to the army coup leaders and politicians. We found ourselves starring in their stories, including a snide little piece about my cigarette delivery through the seemingly impenetrable roadblocks of Moresby. There was another gratuitous story about me wearing my sunnies inside the parliament chamber, 'lounging around insouciantly' like a character from *Hawaii Five-O*. If only. They happened to be prescription glasses, and because I'm short-sighted I couldn't see what was happening 20 metres away without them. Inside or out. I simply didn't have any other specs with me that sunny day.

The *Sunday Age* was even more pissed off. They devoted the best part of a page to highlighting 'ACA's sexy red four-wheel drive' and our 'rock-star-like access' to all the key players. They accused us of delaying the army's press conference (which was untrue), getting 'a cheering wave from Julius Chan' (which was true) and indulging in 'a kind of cargo-cult service', bringing chocolates and bread to the soldiers locked away in the barracks (hey, whatever it was called, it certainly helped us clear a few army roadblocks).

I felt like reminding Andrew Rule, the Gold Walkley Award-winning journo who wrote the diatribe, that there was an even better story: about an army revolt and PNG's democracy in strife. But I didn't bother. We were having too much fun.

Sir Julius Chan fled the parliament that night, somehow passing through the mobs of protestors. Nobody knew how he'd done it or where he was, until lunchtime the next day, when a police inspector walked up to Bibb and me. He turned out to be yet another happy Channel 9 viewer. 'G'day, Ray Martin,' he said, sotto voce. 'I've just delivered the prime minister. Do you want to know where we've been?'

This time I did my best to really look insouciant, as *The Age* boys liked to put it. As I ushered the inspector towards the parliament car park, he told me that he had hidden Chan, disguised in a police uniform, on the floor of his squad car the previous night and taken him to a private residence – as it turned out, just behind our hotel in suburban Moresby. If only we'd known. Still, this was valuable background for our *ACA* story that night.

The inspector also informed us that the PM would tender his resignation to parliament in about forty minutes' time. Which he did, again playing up to our *ACA* cameras at the press conference afterwards. (Sir Julius would later offer to fly us out to his home on New Ireland and take us fishing.)

Amazingly, despite all the civil unrest and the military coup, nobody was killed or even seriously injured in the PNG crisis. Lieutenant Colonel Tim Spicer, incidentally, would end up in charge of the second-largest military force in Iraq: twenty thousand mercenaries and security guards, paid for by a 300-million-dollar contract with the Americans. The abortive PNG operation didn't set back Lieutenant Colonel Tim's career, did it? And, reflecting the mercurial nature of politics PNG style, ex-prime minister Chan was cleared of any wrongdoing over the multimillion-dollar payout to Sandline and is still in parliament. As expected, Sir Michael Somare became prime minister again. And, with the help of Australian peacekeepers, copper is again being hauled out of Bougainville.

You only dream about getting this kind of story. We had an amazing couple of weeks. I can't pretend the PNG yarns blitzed the TV ratings back home, but they certainly gave us some badly needed credibility. Yet, after the first couple of nights, our PNG story was shunted towards the end of *ACA*, gazumped by stories about used-car scams or dodgy builders. The newspapers, on the other hand, were still running the PNG drama on their front pages. The clear message to me was that on *ACA* a supermarket war in the southern suburbs was always going to get priority over a civil war in the South Pacific, no matter how great the journalistic scoops. It was up in PNG in early 1997 that I first started to think it was probably time to move on from *ACA*, because the blokes in charge had a different agenda from mine. It must have been similar to the way Mike Willesee felt back in 1993, when he spoke to me in Monte Carlo about leaving the show.

*　　*　　*

I would have much the same feeling in London later that year when the same four-man team covered the funeral of Princess Diana.

It was a sad, sad time. It cast my mind back to the early 1980s, when I had reported on the start of Diana's liaison with the House of Windsor. It promised to be a fairytale life for the twenty-year-old and her Prince Charming. How poignant those memories now seemed to me. Back then I was in London for *60 Minutes* for a story we'd cheekily called 'Charlie's Angels'. It was meant to be a sordid tale cataloguing the playboy prince's many female conquests. But after interviewing the Aussie-born royal watcher Nigel Dempster, we had to change tack. He insisted there was now only one woman in Charlie's life: Lady Diana Spencer.

Dempster argued that the Queen desperately wanted Charles

to marry and settle down and that Lady Spencer had all the essential qualifications: 'She's young, a virgin and has great boobs.' (There's nothing subtle about the Fleet Street boys.) If true, this was an even better story, and Dempster's sources were usually spot on.

We managed to find Diana's address and even her phone number. We knew that she drove a British-racing-green Ford Escort hatchback, which we found parked just down the road from her Kensington flat. So my producer, Andrew Haughton, rang her phone. He explained to the young woman who answered that we were outside the flat with our TV camera, and that she shouldn't be alarmed. She thanked him and promised to pass the information on to 'Miss Spencer'. To this day Haughton is convinced he was speaking to Diana herself.

Anyway, about an hour later she walked down the street to her car. She smiled demurely and said hello to us. She was an English rose and strikingly beautiful. I told her that we were from Australia. 'Orstralia!' she said. 'Christ, what a long way to come.' We all remember the moment well, because as she swung her long legs into the tiny hatchback, she flashed a pair of bright-red knickers. We had nowhere else to look, I promise.

It was actually Charles who had bought her the Ford Escort – as a sweet engagement present – though nobody knew it at the time. He was apparently prompted by a few patriotic Fleet Street hacks who had whinged about the fact Ms Spencer was scooting around London in a French-built Renault. These narks had insisted that she should 'buy British' if she was ever going to get a parking place at Buckingham Palace. What's more, her boy prince had gone to the trouble of putting a distinctive frog insignia on the car's bonnet, perhaps a whimsical nod to the 'kiss a frog, marry a prince' fairytale. (The car, with eighty thousand miles on the clock, was sold in 2009 to a Californian car museum for 650,000 dollars. Dealers say that if it wasn't for Diana's connection, the car would have been worth about a thousand dollars.)

Haughton and I agreed that the best strategy was to be gentle and not push for an interview on this first meeting. We figured we'd come back the next day, now that she knew who we were. It seemed like a good idea at the time.

What we didn't realise was that the next day she was off to Australia to tell her mother that she and Charles were getting married. When one of her flatmates told us Diana had left London, we had no option but to change tack again and go after Prince Charles.

The Buckingham Palace media secretary, who happened to be an Aussie, told us that HRH was skiing in the Swiss Alps, so off we headed. In Klosters we discreetly filmed Charles as he walked through the village with his bodyguard, heading to the mountain ski lifts. Fearing we were about to lose him for the day, we jumped into the same cable car as he did, as the doors slammed shut. It was just him, his bodyguard and us. There's no way you could ever get that close today. After all, we could have been carrying weapons or a suitcase full of explosives.

Our cameraman filmed the Prince's ride for about a minute but then had to turn the camera off. As he explained later, the ice-cold Medusa stare was threatening to turn him into stone. Still, he'd captured a memorable picture of Prince Charles with an iconic Marlboro Man poster over his shoulder. Somehow the bronzed machismo of the American action man with the pecs rippling through his checked shirt was a perfect contrast to the balding, pasty English prince.

At the top, as he strapped on his skis, Charles finally turned and asked, 'And where, pray tell, are you from?' When I told him, he threw his head back and laughed, knowing full well that Diana was now secretly en route to Sydney. 'Orstralia? Bloody hell. Well, have a nice time.'

It would be fifteen years before I next spoke to Charles, in an hour-long interview for *ACA*. After his disastrous marriage break-up the heir to the British throne seemed less confident, less in control. I suspect Diana wasn't the only one who was scorched and traumatised by the media blowtorch.

We recorded that *ACA* interview at the governor's mansion in Brisbane one sunny afternoon. I was driven up there by a Queensland cabbie in shorts and long socks, who said, 'Oh. Charlie's got a bugger of a job, hasn't he?' When I told the Prince that, he laughed out loud and said, 'I do have a bugger of a job. He's right, you know.'

The news of Diana's terrible Paris car crash had come through early one Sunday morning in Australia, the last day of August 1997. As it happened, at 4 pm I was booked on a Qantas flight to Los Angeles and then on to Vancouver. I was heading off to do another assignment with the amazing Bronte Cullis. We'd been filming stories with Bronte for years, including her desperate, life-saving journey to a private clinic in Canada. Her irrepressible mum, Jan Cullis, who lived in Melbourne, was already on her way to Sydney with an *ACA* crew. Bronte, whose mind and emotions were extremely brittle, was expecting us, along with her mother, in British Columbia the next day.

But overnight the news world had suddenly gone on red alert because of Diana's tragedy. It was going to be a hard ask to get our four-man crew, with the usual twenty bags of camera gear, to London. This was the dilemma: we had Qantas tickets for a story in Canada that I now had to drop, but no tickets for a London story that I now had to pick up, and every flight to London had waiting lists just to get on their waiting lists.

'Who *must* go?' asked the unflappable Qantas booking clerk.

With a special one-hour edition of *ACA* already scheduled, I had to be in our London studio within twenty-six hours, but Bibb, Munro and Jason also needed to be there, so we could start filming reports. The Qantas lady just smiled and shook her head. Then she asked us to take a twenty-minute coffee break while she tried to somehow score one impossible ticket for me.

We ran into a bunch of journalist friends from newspapers and TV who were just as frantic for a flight. The best anyone had managed to scrounge was a flight via Tokyo later that night. My chances of hosting the *ACA* special were nil it seemed. But when we returned twenty minutes later, Miss Qantas Extraordinaire announced that she had not only found me a seat but one for producer Steve Bibb, too. Within another half-hour, she miraculously had seats for all four of us. I remember the lady's name was Ms Romanov, just like the Russian royal family. She deserved a Fabergé egg. (We sent her a big bunch of flowers instead.) I have no idea how she did it, other than stretching the jumbo jet. I wasn't going to ask.

We had forty minutes to get aboard. As we hurtled towards the gate, I ran smack bang into Bronte's mother, Jan. It was an awful moment. Nobody had been able to contact her about the change of plans, so I told her. Distressed beyond description, Jan couldn't understand why we were abandoning her terribly sick daughter in Canada to go to London to report on a dead woman instead.

All I could do was give Jan a cuddle and plead with her to understand that right now Diana's death left us no choice. We left Jan Cullis in tears – but fortunately, with help from Nine's LA trouper Robert Penfold, Bronte's story also went ahead brilliantly.

It took some deep breathing – plus a couple of deep Scotches – to calm me down on the first leg of the journey, our flight from Sydney to Bangkok. Then, at Bangkok airport a fuel truck broke down and our flight was delayed for an hour. As we approached Heathrow, the Qantas captain gave us our ETA. If I was going to host the hour-long Diana special, I would have less than an hour to get out of the airport, make my way through the morning peak-hour traffic to the studio, and get dressed and made-up. It seemed like Mission Impossible.

Waiting for me at Heathrow was a Qantas ground agent, who got me on a motorbike that took me across the airport. Then I took a helicopter trip to Battersea Power Station and had a fast drive in a hire car to the TV studio. I still had only the jacket and jeans I'd worn from Sydney, but I did manage to borrow a fresh shirt and tie. I had no chance to prepare but just winged it with three live interviews. It was an absolute miracle to be on air – live from London – against all those odds. We'd beaten everybody else. But during the show, the station received four angry phone calls from viewers who'd glimpsed my jeans. They rang to complain that it showed total disrespect for poor Diana. Sometimes you just can't win.

*   *   *

For the best part of a week we worked around the clock, without really noticing it. London, that marvellous old lady, was overwhelmed by sadness. Normally a taciturn, mind-your-own-business, private race of people, the English now just wanted to talk. Diana's death led to an outpouring of grief, almost a sort of public therapy. When they saw our TV camera, they stopped to tell us how they felt. Some even cried. I've spent a lot of time in the British capital over the past thirty-five years. Nothing could compare with this. Losing Diana had kicked the stuffing out of seven million Londoners. Even the pubs lost their raucous laughter.

At least during the London Blitz, when the Nazi bombs rained down, the English could hate the Germans. This time it was hard for them to settle on someone to hate. Back then they could see the fires and the city's destruction. This time there was nothing to see. In 1940 the old British bulldog spirit had a cause: Londoners were not going to let Hitler demoralise or destroy them. But this time there wasn't really anyone to defy. Fleet Street couldn't decide who to blame: the paparazzi, the drunken driver, the fact Diana had not been wearing a seatbelt, Camilla and Charles, the Queen for her recent rejection of Diana. The sorrow and, in some cases, the hysterical reaction to Diana's death in the Pont de l'Alma tunnel had also spread across Britain. We went into surrounding counties and found villages just as sullen and traumatised as London.

For a couple of nights I hosted *ACA* from an elevated platform at the end of The Mall, with Buckingham Palace as the backdrop. As I walked past Kensington Gardens each day, I saw the piles of floral tributes higher than my head. Everywhere you looked, there were mounds of flowers, festooned with cards, personal messages and flickering candles.

I also hosted the ITV/Channel 9 coverage of Diana's funeral, on a balcony directly across from Westminster Abbey. We were close enough to hear Elton John sing his mournful version of 'Candle in the Wind', which he'd just adapted for Diana's memorial service. I remember thinking that our lives really are circumscribed by time and place. I recalled the time of my brief street encounter with the lovely, innocent Lady Spencer all those years ago, and the place I'd first heard Elton sing this signature song. He was in the basement of our hotel in Beijing, and I was doing a story for *60 Minutes* on the Rocket Man as he toured China with his beloved Watford footy team. We'd lugged a piano down the stairs and then talked him into playing half a dozen songs, including the original version of 'Candle in the Wind'. As they listened to the words, the rowdy footballers fell silent and became almost melancholy. That occasion was not long after Elton attended Diana's wedding to Charles, in St Paul's Cathedral. Now I could hear his voice again, singing her requiem in the abbey. I looked around at the gathering of hard-bitten TV crews from across the world. Like the footballers in Beijing, nobody spoke.

*   *   *

Even though Princess Diana's death was easily the biggest news event of 1997, just as with the Sandline Affair, Bibb and I found that after two days we were having almighty blow-ups with Sydney about whether Australians were still interested in the story. Quite frankly I found *A Current Affair*'s judgement of the Aussie attention span mind-boggling. The story was still rating well, and the newspapers had no doubts, as they kept filling their pages with it. Out of total frustration, during one late-night phone call I told them I was quitting the show. I had never had a tantrum like that in my working life. It was crazy, and the next morning I had calmed down and was back out there filming on the streets of London.

But reporting the Sandline Affair and the aftermath of Diana's death served to remind me of why I'd become a journalist in the first place. And those stories came at a time when *ACA* had begun down a path that I didn't want to follow. As the show's host I had the privilege of reporting all the major stories, but as host I also had to present stories on miracle bras, backache cures and diets night after night. I didn't think such stories should dominate the program, given *ACA*'s rich journalistic past. I believed the reporters, producers, camera crews, editors and researchers deserved better. The *ACA* audience certainly deserved better.

On top of all that we were now being consistently beaten by *Today Tonight* in the ratings. It didn't make sense. Why didn't we switch back to the sort of *ACA* stories that had worked for so long?

I figured that if the Channel 9 bosses didn't want to change the program, then they should change the host. Nothing else was working. And I feared it was getting pretty damn obvious to *ACA*'s viewers that I didn't want to be there.

So I decided to walk.

Chapter 32
'Gentlemen, Include Me Out!'

I took Mike Munro for an early-morning coffee. It was late 1998. I wanted him to be the first to know I was quitting *ACA*. Mike had filled in as host when I was off reporting, so the job was clearly his. He was deliriously happy, thinking as I had before him that he could push the show back on track.

I had no intention of ever going back. I'd done the five years at *ACA* I had promised David Leckie. As the great movie mogul Sam Goldwyn said, 'Gentlemen, include me out!'

Leckie leant on me to stay, saying *ACA* was a network priority, so if I walked away I'd have to take a salary haircut. No probs, David, get out the clippers.

Kerry Packer could never understand why the *ACA* gig had become a revolving door, with Willesee coming and going, then Jana and now me. It's hard to explain, but let's just say that although the nightly news and *ACA* are both similar in that they're half-hour programs, hosting one is like lawn bowls while the other is a bloody kick-boxing contest!

Over the years lots of people – especially newspaper TV writers – have asked why I didn't try to change the direction of *ACA* if I didn't agree with it. It's a fair question. But it's not that simple.

The shift into what I call consumer heaven at *ACA* had been gradual. (Today it might as well be called *A Consumer Affair* as it's a totally different program.) I protested, lobbied and disagreed with the move away from what I call 'the Willesee formula'. That original mix of breaking news, real investigation, big interviews, feature stories, colourful characters, bush tales, the political issues of the day *and* consumer yarns.

David Hurley, the boss of the show, disagreed with me. He was a great newsman whom I'd first met when he worked as New South Wales Premier Neville Wran's media man in the early eighties. He had almost as many years in the business as me and remains a mate of mine. His *ACA* sidekicks were all experienced, good journalists, but they went along with Hurley. Peter Meakin, the highly acclaimed TV news guru who was at Nine during those years, also agreed with him.

Hurley is amusing, intelligent and a scholar of TV ratings. In fact, he dissects and analyses these mystical numbers as devoutly as a rabbi scrutinises the Babylonian Talmud. The trouble is, TV ratings are about as cryptic as those ancient, sacred scriptures. What still confounds me is that Hurley loves hard news and he luxuriates in politics – especially political intrigue. Yet he argues that going 'the consumer routes' at 6.30 pm has actually helped save the brand. I argue that it's helped kill it off. Still, I have to admit that if you look at the daily audience rating, both *Today Tonight* and *A Current Affair* consistently rate amongst the top-ten shows. What's more, three and a half million Australians watch these two shows every night, so that's a pretty persuasive figure.

Nevertheless, I would argue that Jana Wendt and I proved that you can get an even bigger audience if you give the viewers a fair-dinkum current-affairs show. You have to believe that Australians really do care about more than cabbage diets or the latest breast implant. I think the growing ratings success of *The 7.30 Report*, the ABC news and the Thursday-night *Q&A* show hosted by Tony Jones is tangible proof that there is an audience for relevant stories and issues of the day in Australia. They're certainly not watching *ACA* or *TT* for that, unless they're comparing the price of soapsuds at Woolies and Coles.

I used to argue long and loud that commercial-network programmers underrate the taste and intelligence of the average Aussie. (One senior executive producer used to disparagingly refer to the Channel 9 audience as 'the string bags'.) They still underrate them.

Kerry Packer once rang and told me to 'Please back off' when I was loudly complaining about too many consumer and fad diets on *ACA*. I didn't back off – I just lost the argument and eventually quit.

Dianne tells me that almost as soon as I'd left *ACA*, she could feel the tension inside me unravel and the pressure ease off. The past five years had been easily the most frenetic, full-on, batten-down-the-hatches time of my working life. I'd also been up to my neck in charity commitments, the Fred Hollows Foundation and Aboriginal reconciliation. Obviously none of that was going to ease off. But Jenna and Luke remained my most important priority and the joy of my life. I'd somehow always found free time for them, and now I figured I'd have more of it – for school sports, concerts and their unbridled passion for acting. I used to jokingly say that I was producing two out-of-work actors.

When I quit *ACA* that first time in 1998, Jenna was into her teenage years but was a lovely writer with more style and confidence than I had when I was twice her age; she was a natural student with a real lust for life, always laughing, all bubbly and fresh, 'like a mountain stream', I used to say. I'm afraid that anything I say about Jenna will make it seem like I'm besotted and that she is the perfect daughter. Well, I am and she is. The same applies to my boy, Luke. It seemed that Luke was always going to be tall, well spoken and a natural mimic, with a *Simpsons* sense of humour. He was eight, and crazy about astronomy, battlefields and *Monty Python*. He was endlessly interesting, and I loved whiling away time with him. Still do.

Dianne and I had now been together for over thirty years. She is my rock. Despite the glare of the public spotlight we have remained a tight family unit, cocooned in our private lives. Anyone who knows us would confirm that television never intruded. Dianne made damn sure of that. Still, if a bit of angst and pent-up frustration had now gone from my work life, that was probably a good thing for those I loved the most. Even I could see that.

My producer, Steve Bibb, and my clever personal assistant, Michelle James, left *ACA* with me. I figured they were so talented that if I stayed in their slipstream then together we could have a crack at anything. And we kinda did.

We set up a Special Projects unit down the road, in what used to be my old *Midday* production cottage, so in five action-packed years I'd come full circle. In TV speak, when someone says they're 'doing Special Projects' it usually means they're in limbo, nobody upstairs knows what to do with them, and they're about to go out the door backwards. On the contrary. We ended up doing a bit of everything: some Olympic Games previews, some documentaries, some show-business specials. Altogether

Bibb and I did ten one-hour one-off specials in the space of a year. They were all pretty cheap to produce and rated well. On reflection that's probably why the carpet strollers left us alone.

I also got the chance to have a go at something I'd never done before. I wrote the scripts and hosted a twenty-six-episode program called *Our Century*, working with an astonishingly talented documentary maker, Will Davies. Based on rare film from archives, newsreels and private collections, *Our Century* depicted Aussies at work and play in the years since Federation, when the movie camera came along to record their antics. So, there I was, after the addictive adrenaline rush of daily current affairs, back wandering through the dust and cobwebs of Australian history. It was exactly the sea change that I needed. It seemed to pump oxygen back into my lungs.

For a time I hosted a lively Saturday-night interview and variety show called *Up Close and Personal*, and another series called *Simply the Best*, which it wasn't. Mercifully that had a short season, marking the end of the millennium. Or something. There were always state and federal elections and the loveliest night of the year, the Melbourne *Carols*.

I also went on the road again with *60 Minutes*. I got to spend the best part of three months, on and off, working on a really special yarn for them. In the show's thirty-year history it was probably the longest anyone had spent on a single story before. It was about a young Brisbane mum named Mary Nolan. When we first met, she was pregnant with conjoined twin girls, who were attached at the back of the skull. The specialists I interviewed told us the odds of that happening were about five million to one. Mary and her laconic larrikin of a husband, Shaun, invited us to go with them on their emotional roller-coaster ride. We were there constantly for the last seven weeks of her pregnancy, the girls' birth and their heart-rending separation.

The Nolans were good people – in the truest sense of the word. They figured this was what God must have wanted, and as parents they were obligated to 'give the little darlin's every chance at life'. That's how Mary saw it, anyway. 'It's just the luck of the draw' was the way Shaun put it to me, with a resigned shrug of the shoulders. His attitude was: you cop life on the chin and just get on with it. Meanwhile, he had begun to carry rosary beads in his pocket and always seemed to be singing John Williamson's 'True Blue', almost under his breath. It had become his mantra.

The baby girls – Alyssa Grace and Bethany Rose – were delivered prematurely, by caesarean section. They shared myriad blood vessels to their brains and only one kidney instead of four, so the procedure to separate them would be about as tricky as it gets. Brilliant neurosurgeon Dr Scott Campbell, who was a dead ringer for Tom Cruise, delayed the intervention for as long as he could. Now, though the girls were only five weeks old, he had no choice but to operate: it was a matter of life and death.

As Shaun and Mary slumped with us in the cold linoleum corridor adjacent to the operating theatre, they knew there was a real chance that neither baby girl would survive the night. Shaun prayed a lot, and I noticed that he'd switched mantras to 'I Still Call Australia Home', which he hummed all the time.

Trauma, I'd long ago realised, plays itself out in many different tunes.

After twelve long weeks we were no longer just a TV film crew covering a story. We'd spent many eldritch hours with Mary and Shaun, filling in the empty time, driving Mary back and forth to the hospital and sharing with them the full compass of emotions. We'd almost become part of the Nolan family. We'd taken the twins' three older brothers, who loved cricket so much they just about played it in their sleep, to a Sheffield Shield game at the Gabba, and we'd barbecued with the Nolans' neighbours and countless friends.

Two surgical teams had been working a marathon sixteen hours when, after one o'clock on a frigid Sunday morning, Dr Campbell took Mary and Shaun aside with the sad news that Bethany had lost her battle. They'd saved her twice, but cardiac arrest and a brain bleed had finally beaten the surgeons and taken their precious baby girl. The news of Alyssa was hopeful. She occupied all our prayers through that long night.

It's a strange feeling to be a journalist at a wretched moment like this. It's quite different to, let's say, a police or ambulance officer at the scene of a tragedy. I'd been there when the girls were born. I'd held them in my arms and spent hours listening to Mary and Shaun talk about the hopes they had for them, despite the impossible odds. I wondered whether Dianne and I would have done what they did and gone ahead with the pregnancy. Once they'd made their decision, I desperately wanted them to win. At least there was a chance now that one of the tiny premature girls would make it. That was still in the lap of the gods.

As I sat silently in the hospital corridor with my arms around Mary, I wondered what priests say at such times of loss and tribulation. Or poets. After all, Shakespeare had a line for every dolour, every human pain. Later, I would go searching and find that the great Elizabethan wordsmith had answered my question: he scoffed at those who 'patch grief with proverbs'. No words are adequate, so a silent arm around the shoulder is about the only solace you can offer, I suspect.

Some hours later I raced out to Brisbane airport to pick up my producer, Peter Wilkinson, who'd been called back to Sydney the previous day. As I walked out of the hospital, I was surprised to see the early-morning fog blanketing Brisbane. On the northern ring-road I must have nodded off for a moment and ended up driving my hire car up onto a grassy verge. I found myself about 40 metres off the road, facing the wrong way. I had forgotten that I hadn't had any sleep for the past thirty-six hours. Thankfully, as it was Sunday morning the highway was empty. Somebody was looking after me, again.

And somebody has certainly taken good care of Alyssa Nolan. She's now at her local primary school, in Brisbane's northern suburbs. According to her father she's the boss of her three carrot-topped big brothers, indeed of the whole family.

I don't know if there was a family connection between the Nolans' awesome neurosurgeon, Dr Scott Campbell, and Alec Campbell, the last Gallipoli soldier left on earth, but just a few days after one Campbell had separated the Nolan girls, I was sailing with another Campbell in Hobart harbour. One minute I was crying over the loss of five-week-old Bethany, the next celebrating the life of one of Australia's living treasures, a 102-year-old Anzac who had also faced terrible odds but had somehow survived. That's been the potpourri of my life.

Alec Campbell, from Launceston in Tassie, had lied about his age at sixteen and joined up to go to war. They made him a water boy, running up the pock-marked gullies of Gallipoli, until he was hospitalised and sent home with Bell's palsy and a bout of uncontrollable fever. He got his chippy's ticket, worked on building Canberra's old parliament house, fathered nine children, got an economics degree as a mature-age student and sailed the Sydney–Hobart yacht race six times. 'And I got seasick every darn year,' he told me, with a cackle.

A million men fought on the Gallipoli peninsula in 1915,

and now Alec found himself the last man standing. 'I just can't believe it. Are you fair dinkum?' he kept saying to me, shaking his head. 'You mean to say that all the other boys have gone? I just can't believe it.'

To make a great television moment, Bibb came up with the idea of gathering all Mr Campbell's scattered family together for a birthday photograph in Hobart. So we did. If my memory serves me right, there were seventy-nine direct Campbell offspring smiling at the camera that day, including two great-great-grandchildren in swaddling clothes perched on Alec's lap as he sat in his wheelchair, grinning proudly.

A couple of things about this unique family snap were poignant to me. If a single Turkish bullet had found Alec, seventy-nine Aussie Campbells would not have been there that day. And if Alec hadn't suddenly achieved the status of being the last man alive who'd served at Gallipoli, no one would have bothered to listen to his remarkable life story.

You're left to wonder what baby Bethany might have done if she'd had a second chance, if she'd had a long and fruitful life such as Alec's. As Shaun Nolan said to us sagely, 'it's just the luck of the draw'.

I had taken Luke to Tassie with me to give him the privilege of meeting Alec Campbell. I thought he should soak up the moment with this reluctant anti-war hero.

Luke had once met General Peter Cosgrove at a cricket Test and plagued him with questions. Cosgrove had been uncommonly generous, as he always is, telling Luke not to be half-hearted about life, because it is there for the taking. He'd left an indelible mark on my son. Great men have that capacity. At 102, Alec seemed to be almost too old and frail to tell us much about his life for our TV special. Yet when Luke sat in a corner talking to him, the old soldier found his tongue and his memory once again. He and Luke had a lovely chat. On the flight home I asked him what they'd talked about. Luke said, 'Oh, just things. About war 'n' bullets 'n' stuff. And Mr Campbell told me, "You've gotta always have a go!"' I hope the advice dished out by Campbell and Cosgrove is tucked away in Luke's memory bank, to be drawn on in later life. Luke could do worse than act on their prescription.

When Alec Campbell died of pneumonia the next winter, someone wrote poetically that Gallipoli, that proud signpost on Australia's journey, was now 'just a country of the mind'.

By 2002 there was only a handful of Great War diggers still alive. It was hard to believe, but out of the many hundreds of Aussies who had been awarded military honours, there was now only one decorated soldier left: Corporal Frank McDonald, of Ulverstone, Tasmania, who was 105. Frank was awarded the Military Medal and was subsequently recommended for a Bar after conspicuous bravery outside Passchendaele, under General Monash. Frank had been a farm boy when he joined up, in 1916.

In my experience heroes – not just in war but civilian heroes, too – are usually a different breed. A hilariously funny bloke, Frank told me his real reason for going off to war had been because his next-door neighbours in northern Tasmania were German Australians.

'Me and me brother used to breed racing pigeons,' Frank laughed. 'One day they all died after being fed poison bait. We knew it was the family next door, but we couldn't prove it. So we decided to join up and kill some krauts, to even the score.'

His grand-niece, who was looking after him, was appalled.

'You can't say that, Uncle Frank!' she screamed.

'Well, it's the truth,' he replied.

When you're 105 and the only bloke still alive with a Military Medal, you can say what you bleeding well like.

It seemed Frank remembered everything about his eighteen terrible months along the Somme. He told me in great detail, almost minute by minute, about the battle action that won him his bravery citation. 'I just knew I wasn't gonna die that day,' he said, sounding like he meant it, too.

His long-term memory was amazing, going back almost ninety years. But then, later on, as we sat in the sun and shared a Scotch together like old cobbers, he looked at me and asked, 'What did you say your name was again? And where did you say you were from?' So I told him, for about the fourth time.

Not long after I met Frank McDonald, I went off to Gallipoli to do a story for *60 Minutes*. I'd driven reverentially through the battlefields of the American Civil War but I'd never paid homage at the places where Aussie battalions had perished. From everything I'd read, and especially Les Carlyon's magnificent tome *Gallipoli*, I knew this battlefield must be special. I found it to be the most ethereal, most sacred place I'd ever been. To see the blood-red stones in the clear water of Anzac Cove, where those innocent, wide-eyed boys leapt ashore, is guaranteed to bring tears to an Aussie's eyes. And a Turk's, too, I suspect.

I took a lot of photographs and had some time to spend just walking on my own, up Shrapnel Gully and around the other legendary battle sites. For an hour or so one day I sat quietly in amongst the thick trees and shrubs that have grown over what must have been a pitted lunar landscape in 1915. I can't say that I saw any ghosts in slouch hats or heard the muffled sounds of mortars, yet the hair on the back of my neck stood up as I sat silently there. At one point I was startled out of my reverie when a bird fluttered up from the bushes beside me. I didn't have to fossick far for shrapnel, bullet shells and even bone fragments, which our historian-guide was adamant were those of Australians. I handed everything to the museum curator.

Every day for the several days we filmed at Gallipoli, we caught a car ferry across from a nearby regional port and back. On most of these crossings there would be students from the local university who, keen to practise their English skills, asked us endless questions. (You'd wonder why, given our Aussie accents.) One evening after a sombre day spent out on Lone Pine, I got the question I'd been dreading.

'Please sir,' a young engineering student asked me, 'can you explain to me why your grandfather sailed across the world to kill my grandfather? What had he ever done to you Australians?'

It was a fair cop. All I could do was apologise to the young man and tell him I wished I had an answer. I couldn't tell him about the bravado of youth, the fiscal apron strings tying Australia to Westminster, or the folly of Empire. I bought him a coffee and thanked Atatürk for his munificence and forgiveness.

A few years later, again for *60 Minutes*, I was in Fromelles, in the far north of France. It was the site, in July 1916, of an even more disastrous battle than at Gallipoli. As a French war historian would put it to me, 'For the Aussie diggers Gallipoli was a picnic. Here it was the slaughterhouse.'

At Fromelles I would find the locals had a very different response to Australia's involvement in the war than I'd found in Turkey. In one battle we were the invaders. In the other, we'd come to help defend. In both we were there to kill.

The French citizens of Fromelles and other villages along the Somme simply could not believe that young Aussies in 1916 had crossed the world to die for them. Yves Fohlen, an infectiously enthusiastic French battlefield tour guide who helped us with our *60 Minutes* story, had tears in his eyes when he said, 'For me it is a mystery, but it is so wonderful. It is the most beautiful Australian mystery. Yes?'

The Battle of Fromelles turned out to be the most tragic night in Australian history, with 5533 of our soldiers killed or wounded in the space of a few hours.

In the twilight of summer I walked the vast killing fields, which were now pastures filled with wheat and barley. Up on the horizon were the remains of the giant concrete German blockhouses, now overrun with vines and graffiti. And scattered on the edge of the narrow ribbons of road were graveyards and monuments to the dead, most of them Australian. Surrounded by all this mellow, rustic beauty, at first I found it hard to see the summer fields as the slaughterhouse the French historian had referred to. But when I stood silent for a while it didn't take much imagination to see the apparitions of diggers running boldly into the German machine guns, and hear their pitiful cries of 'Don't forget me, cobber.' That is the poignant inscription on the base of the glorious monument to the diggers who fell at Fromelles.

And that's what our *60 Minutes* story was really all about: not so much the battlefield horrors but the cobbers it now seemed we'd forgotten. Lambis Englezos, an irrepressible Greek-born art teacher from Melbourne, had spent over a decade painstakingly sifting through microfilm and record books, and had come to the conclusion that as many as 250 soldiers had been dumped in giant pits just below the village, in a place known on military maps as Pheasant Wood. He knew that half of them had to be missing Aussie diggers. The rest of the bodies were likely to be British, and there were possibly even some Germans. Englezos was one cobber who would not forget the Australian soldiers. He demanded they be given the military respect they deserved.

On *60 Minutes* Englezos made a compelling case and showed ample evidence, such as aerial maps, photographs and German Red Cross documents. However, in Canberra, the Veterans Affairs Department, the Army and even the Australian War Memorial had long dismissed him. At best they'd been patronising to him.

So, in recounting Australia's darkest night, our intention was to tell the story of one man's magnificent obsession. Our wish was to spur a proper investigation, even an archaeological search, at Pheasant Wood for the biggest mass-burial site of the war.

And indeed, following our *60 Minutes* story, the Federal government launched an investigation into Englezos's claims. Everything he told us stood up to scrutiny, so for the last couple of years the Commonwealth War Graves Commission has been working to exhume all the soldiers' remains. Understandably, as the burials took place ninety years ago, it is a delicate and highly sensitive archaeological dig. The soldiers who were dumped in these burial pits in 1916 will now be buried nearby, with full military honours.

As a journalist it's not often you get the chance to help correct the history books.

Chapter 33
'This is Payback Time, Raymond'

For want of a better name, we called it *The Ray Martin Show*. That's what people used to call *Midday*, but this was the first program I'd ever had named after me, even after thirty-six years of working on radio and TV shows, many of which I'd hosted. While Channel 9 had made its fortune on the cult of personality – with every live show named after Kennedy, Newton, Sigley, et cetera – I hadn't bothered with it myself before. We'd tossed around a number of titles, but management argued that the name sold itself. So *The Ray Martin Show* it was.

It was to be a night-time live variety show, the sort of program I'd been talking about doing ever since *Midday*. Peter Wynne and I had played around with the concept for years, and *Up Close and Personal*, the Saturday-night show we'd done out of Nine's Melbourne studios a couple of years earlier, had been like a warm-up version. *Up Close and Personal* ran for about ten weeks, on a shoestring, and easily won its spot and made the network a bucket of money. That's probably why management finally agreed to *The Ray Martin Show*. But I can't pretend that they were busting out of their Armani shirts with excitement at the prospect. David Leckie and the Nine program directors promised me only a short season, just thirteen weeks, but to be honest I don't think they believed *The Ray Martin Show* would even last that long. I got the impression that they'd only agreed because I'd been agitating them about it for a while and they wanted to shut me up. So we kicked off in 2001 on a hiding to nothing.

Apart from Mike Walsh's abortive attempt when I took over *Midday*, there hadn't been live variety on TV at night since *The Don Lane Show* in 1983. *Hey Hey It's Saturday* had been cancelled in 1999, while Rove's late-night show lasted only a few months and was dumped from the 2000 schedule, which again would prove to be a programming debacle. Clearly Nine management's thinking was that Australian TV had moved on from variety to reality and lifestyle. Meanwhile, I'd been contacted by some of the biggest Australian show-business entrepreneurs, including Paul Dainty and Kevin Jacobsen, who said they'd tour major international acts if there was a prime-time TV show to promote them on. Film studios, record companies and book publishers made the same promise.

We planned to make the show a bit like *Parkinson*, rather than follow the standard *Tonight Show* formula of stand-up comics and regular so-called experts. With a budget of about a hundred thousand dollars a show, we simply wouldn't have the money for a live band as we'd had at *Midday*.

Steve Bibb was again my ace producer, and we had a small but perfectly formed team of five people, some of whom had worked with me on *Midday*. The show went out on Monday nights at 9.30. We were up against Paul McDermott's satirical *Good News*

Week and then the cult hit *The Secret Life of Us.* They were both on the Ten Network and consistently pulled in an audience of almost a million. That made for some crowded late-night Monday viewing. It's not surprising: audiences will actually turn on if you give them something to watch.

Despite our short season we still managed to interview quite a galaxy of stars, including Billy Connolly, Elton John, Michael Douglas, Ben Elton, Rod Stewart, Eric Bana, Robert Redford, Bryan Brown and Jack Thompson. Two soon-to-be-great sporting stars, Harry Kewell and Lleyton Hewitt, made their first-ever TV talk-show appearance on our program. In fact nobody we went after knocked us back.

We convinced another emerging new star, Heath Ledger, to overcome his reticence and suspicions about talking to the media. It was a real coup to get him. Heath rarely gave television interviews in those days, certainly not on live TV. I got a number for Heath's older sister, Kate, who was managing him at the time from Perth, where she lived. She said she loved the show and went in to bat for us, talking him into flying up from Melbourne with a couple of mates.

Heath was painfully shy, almost agonisingly so, fiddling with his hair, squirming around in the chair and stumbling over his words at times. But he was a delightful young bloke. Also a delightfully normal bloke, for an actor who was already being singled out for screen immortality.

After he died, I went back and viewed the tape recording. Looking at Heath Ledger again, after his accidental and tragic loss, he looked so young, so handsome and so dynamic. Of course this was long before the paparazzi started hunting him and eating away at his soul. Still just a kid from Perth, Heath seemed most relaxed when he spoke about what he missed when he was in Hollywood. 'Oh, ya know, I miss the Australian sense of humour, along with Mum and Dad and the family. There is a cultural difference. No question. It's mainly in the laughter, in the smile,' he said with sincerity.

So, who was Heath's inspiration? 'Oh, probably my sister, Kate. I watched and always admired her in amateur theatre.' Heath said to me after the show that he'd really enjoyed himself – but confessed he'd only done it because his big sister, Kate, had asked him.

The person Heath reminded me most of as an interviewee was Mel Gibson. They both loathed the publicity circuit. I think Mel would sooner have his fingernails ripped out than have to promote his latest movie before a live audience – even before his marriage break-up. Gibson said that he felt comfortable talking to me, but he never looked like he was.

For my interview with Gibson, Bibb edited together a dazzling montage of scenes from his best movies. It was a spectacular collection: love scenes, and action and comic moments. As the studio audience laughed and sighed, you knew he had them in the palm of his hands.

I looked across at Mel. The only thing in his palms at that moment was his face. Buried. He was grimacing and frowning, as if he was watching somebody being tortured. But he was the one being tortured – just by looking at himself on screen. He confessed that he just couldn't stand it. I wondered how he handled the making of *Braveheart*, when he was both star and director and had to constantly watch himself on film rushes every day.

About the only time I felt that Mel really relaxed during that show was when he volunteered to make his special hangover cure. Suddenly he was on stage again, performing like a character, not Mel Gibson. He blended celery sticks and carrots with milk, I think, and topped it off with a raw egg. Whatever it was, it tasted shocking. But he was hilarious.

When Mel was later arrested for drunk and disorderly behaviour in LA, I made sure nobody could find the tape of him mixing his legendary hangover remedy. I felt I had to protect him from that extra kick in the head.

The first guest we ever had on *The Ray Martin Show* was the notoriously volatile Russell Crowe. He brought his Oscar along in a brown-paper bag, like a wino's prized bottle, and stashed it under his studio chair. He brought along his band, 30 Odd Foot of Grunts, too. They had been due to fly out that night to LA for a twenty-two-city American tour. But when he found out that was the night I was starting my new show, he rearranged their itinerary. How good is that? They arrived in a couple of pick-up trucks. There's nothing fancy about Rusty. But he's a class act in almost everything he does, from winning an Academy Award to buying a losing football team and turning it around.

Someone had the nutty idea that since this was our opening show and he had just won an Oscar for his performance in *Gladiator*, maybe Russell should walk out first instead of me. In fact why not get Russell to introduce me? That'd certainly be different. Crazy, but different.

So when Russell and his band had finished their studio rehearsals, we asked him. Rusty loved the idea, saying that meant he could walk on 'without having to listen to one of Raymond's terminally boring introductions'. I think he was joking.

The fact is, I'd been introducing Mr Crowe for about fifteen years, mostly on *The Midday Show.* He'd always come on when he had a movie to flog, since his first, *The Crossing*, I think it was, in 1990. Then it was *Proof* and *Romper Stomper*, right through to *L.A.*

Confidential and *The Insider*. Over the years there had been some truly great movies to talk about. He even came on once wearing riding boots and a full-length Driza-Bone coat to promote a low-budget film called *The Silver Brumby*. He looked like a Snowy Mountains version of Curly from *Oklahoma!* Well, sort of.

I always found Crowe to be lively TV talent, irascible, witty and with lots of yarns to tell. Russell has often said that as an actor he's really just 'a gypsy storyteller'. He's a lot more than that, but you get the picture.

It's no secret that he has a short-fused temper at times. Especially around phones. Mind you, I suspect he's mellowing with age, although he'd hate me saying that. The suggestion of him mellowing would be blasphemy to Russell.

Even as a young bloke he had enough ego to light up a small town. His confidence bordered on arrogance, certainly when it came to the craft of acting. But quite frankly that never worried me, because you could say the same thing about Don Bradman or Fred Hollows in their respective fields. They didn't suffer fools, either. After all, mock humility can be a pain in the bum, especially when you're trying to get a good TV interview. Sarah Murdoch is very beautiful. Barry Jones is scary bright. Let's not stick beige wallpaper over them and pretend they're really just like the rest of us. They're not. And neither is Rusty.

I don't think anybody would ever suggest that Russell Crowe was at the back of the humble queue. But there were times he'd surprise people by just being normal. Just being himself. I've seen him get a cup of coffee for the make-up women at Nine. No big deal in that, I know. He didn't think it was special, either. But the women did. They'd had a conga line of stars through the door who regarded studio staff as their personal slaves.

The truth is, I like Russell a lot, and I think he's an exceptional human being – but he's a professional actor, so I had always treated our interviews as business. Fun, but business all the same. So that's why he shocked me that first night of *The Ray Martin Show*.

We were standing behind the set, about to begin. The make-up women did their final 'too late to make a scrap of difference anyway' touch-up. The floor manager shouted, 'Two minutes!' The audience was buzzing. It was time to tense up.

Russell reached out and shook my hand. At the same time he looked me in the eye, and in that deep, rich double-bass of a voice, said, 'There were times over the years in this studio when you said good things about me. You supported me when others had their doubts. Well, this is payback time, Raymond!'

And he gave me a huge bear hug. Then the opening music started, and out he went to take the piss out of me.

I'd have been very disappointed if he hadn't.

*   *   *

The Ray Martin Show averaged an audience of 1.25 million each night over the course of the series. Our audience peaked at well over 1.4 million for our interview with Tom Cruise not long after his separation from Nicole. She'd been the guest on our second show, which rated almost as highly.

The bizarre thing is, I couldn't talk Channel 9 into doing it again, despite the excellent ratings and the fact it had made a heap of money for the network. The Nine program directors, who'd become enormously powerful television deities, argued that there probably weren't enough big stars left to interview to justify another season. Andrew Denton, of course, proved them wrong over the next five years by winning ratings, Walkley awards and even a Logie for his splendid interview series *Enough*

Rope, in the same timeslot on the ABC. I'd always found that David Leckie, despite his bluster and bravado, would at least listen. Indeed, he usually backed us. The trouble was, at the start of 2002 Leckie had much greater worries than what to do with my Monday-night show: Packer was about to flick him from the top job at Channel 9. Leckie's departure would prove to be another big nail in the Channel 9 coffin.

I was really disappointed that *The Ray Martin Show* didn't get another run. Who knows, we might still be doing it, like Parkinson, whose show ran forever.

I should add a final word here. The galaxy of film and sports superstars I talked to during the course of my career is not a reflection of my day-to-day lifestyle and one of Dianne's favourite stories illustrates this. A few years ago we were on holiday in London. I was waiting for Dianne downstairs in the hotel lounge, when a voice behind me, hearing me order some coffee, asked if I was Australian. We started a conversation. We must have chatted for half an hour. He had one of those trans-Atlantic accents, was about forty and was an actor. He introduced himself as 'John'.

When Dianne eventually appeared, I introduced her to John, just before the hotel bell boy appeared and told him his limo was ready. So we shook hands and he left.

I told Dianne he was an actor and seemed a nice fellow.

'You have no idea who John is, do you?' she said.

'No, I have no idea. Should I?'

'That's John Malkovich. You're hopeless,' she said, a trifle unkindly I thought. 'He got two Oscar nominations last year and he's currently starring in the two hottest films in the world – he's been on the cover of almost every magazine and newspaper. You've even interviewed him on satellite!'

Chapter 34
Back to the Future

By 2002 my world was changing, it seemed. My friend Steve Bibb departed Channel 9 to become an independent TV entrepreneur, my magnificent PA, Michelle James, married and travelled north (to be replaced by the equally wonderful Kym Weatherley who still works closely with me), while the rest of *The Ray Martin Show* team moved on to become movers and shakers in the realm of lifestyle TV.

Jenna was unstoppable in her final year of high school; Luke had begun his first year. He was about the youngest in his class, but threatening to be the tallest. We'd just built a holiday house on the Sunshine Coast, and that became our regular retreat for family golf. Every day of our holidays we'd all hit off just after six o'clock onto dewy virginal greens. I remember saying to Jenna that heaven couldn't possibly be better than this, playing golf with the three people I loved most. Mind you, she'd usually start making colourful allusions to Hades when my putting went off, as it inevitably did.

I returned to reporting almost full time for *60 Minutes*, where I'd started at the network twenty-five years earlier. In some ways, as the song says about love, it was 'lovelier the second time around'. When we'd kicked off back in 1978 – with just George, Ian and me – as much as I enjoyed it, every story was a test. We always seemed to be on trial. We all knew how much was invested in the program and how many people depended on its success. We were breaking totally new ground, and on commercial TV you knew that if it didn't rate it wouldn't last.

In the earliest days, when we were overseas in some exotic place, I'd always go to bed anxious about the next day. What parts of the story did we still have to shoot? How would we make the talent sparkle? What had we forgotten? Did we have enough pictures? Could we trust the weather forecast?

But by the time of my *60 Minutes* encore, I'd done a couple of hundred reports, under all sorts of war and weather conditions. I knew by now we'd get the story. I'd discovered the truthfulness of what old fellas had been telling me for years: that there's no substitute for experience. And it was great to get back on the road again and enjoy the intoxicating variety of stories and locations with which *60 Minutes* provides a reporter.

Towards the end of 2002, with the worst drought in modern times threatening, I had the idea of taking a camera crew through a vast stretch of the parched outback, from Queensland to the Mallee, in western Victoria. Out along the old Cobb & Co coach routes. I didn't realise it when I set out, but that journey would almost certainly seal the fate of my career for the next three years. Maybe even for the rest of my days at Channel 9.

Executive producer John Westacott didn't see it as a *60 Minutes* story, but David Hurley, who was still in charge of Mike Munro's *ACA*, was keen to run a series on my journey through the dry backblocks. In the studio Munro would trace our travels on a large map of eastern Australia.

I embarked on this big-sky adventure with all the enthusiasm of a cadet reporter. If I had a choice of going anywhere in the world, I think my preference would be to go bush in Australia. For me there's nothing richer for the soul than wandering out along the Darling River.

We took along a mini production unit big enough to do a documentary. (Channel 9 still allowed that kind of extravagance, although the era was coming to an end.) The producer, Danny Milosevic, my brilliant PNG and London cameraman Mark Munro, a sound recordist Mat Brown and I travelled in a pair of four-wheel drives, while a technician and his offsider were in a satellite news-gathering truck, or SNG. The techs would set up base and establish a signal to send the pictures and words back to Sydney for editing. Meanwhile, we'd be driving ahead starting the next story. It was a highly productive, highly satisfying way to work. I could have worked like this forever. We shot, scripted and got to air a five-minute *ACA* yarn every two days, while at the same time travelling about a thousand kilometres.

I remember speaking to Dianne on the satellite phone one night from beside the Menindee Lakes in New South Wales. My mobile hadn't been working for about three days, so I quickly brought her up to speed on where we'd been and what we'd done. When I stopped for breath, she quipped, 'You hate this, don't you!' I had to confess I love it with a passion.

The range of stories we covered was as motley as the country we crossed. The only cocky shearing west of Walgett, New South Wales, had survived by burying his feed grain like the ancient Egyptians had. A bemused farmer who had been hand-feeding his stock because of flooding the last time we spoke to him was now doing the same thing because of drought. And an innovative bloke near Broken Hill had adopted the cockeyed idea of feeding over-sized onions to his sheep, because of their high moisture content. It kept them alive – despite giving them really bad breath!

We filmed dust storms so thick you couldn't see the road-side posts, and we embarked on the scariest night-time drive I can remember. For a 100 kilometre stretch, in the pitch black outside Brewarrina, in New South Wales, the narrow bitumen road was teeming with hungry wildlife. Countless roos, walla-bies, pigs, foxes and emus had gathered to feed off the grassy verge. There were hundreds and hundreds of them, all starving to death, panicking as we approached and dashing across the road or stopping, frozen in the headlights. It was like a real-life video game as we drove through, trying not to hit any. A few of them lost the game, I'm afraid.

One other memorable night we lit a midnight fire in a dry riverbed outside of Dirranbandi, just across the Queensland border, out the back of hell. We were with my favourite bushie, Ben Dark, the *Getaway* daredevil who used to run cattle on a property nearby. We drank some beers and yarned, so isolated that the man in the moon seemed our closest neighbour. Forget the five-star accommodation – we had five *million* stars twinkling at us.

I had an absolute carnival doing these stories, away from the confines of a studio. But the fun the crew and I had must have been transparent, because it was this trip that convinced Nine management to get me back into the *ACA* chair again.

This is where things started to get murky, in one of those all-too-familiar television tangles. Let me just set the scene of how my sweet world of TV had started to turn sour at Nine.

In late 2002 old man Packer sacked the loud, rambunctious but very capable David Leckie after more than a decade as boss of Nine. After the changeover to the daily-ratings system, which Leckie had driven, Channel 9 had come off a bad second best to Channel 7. That wasn't a position Kerry Packer was accustomed to, and after a bit of shadow-boxing the heavyweight contest ended the only way it could: with Leckie knocked out of the ring. He was gone from Channel 9, where he'd come to love the TV business.

John Alexander, an old Fairfax newspaperman who'd recently pulled off a profit bonanza for Packer's glossy magazine empire, took over. Someone who knew Alexander said to me at the time that 'compared to Leckie he was more antithesis than antidote'. I think what he meant was that, in his quiet, cerebral way, John Alexander was the direct opposite to David, but not the medicine that Channel 9 needed. He knew little about television.

We all quickly discovered that Alexander was clearly a man on a mission to shake up TV, as he had magazines. He was doomed to fail. Television is a different animal. Still, he'd long been a close confidant of both Packers, and that had given him riches and power beyond his early working-class dreams.

In early November 2002 I was summoned to John Alexander's office for a meeting, which also included Ian Johnson and David Gyngell. Johnson was the veteran manager of the station's Melbourne office and a Packer stalwart. I was pleased to see him at the meeting because Ian is one of those trustworthy executives who actually give management a good name. Gyngell, who is James Packer's best mate, was clearly being groomed to take over Channel 9, if Alexander would ever stop interfering.

I found John Alexander to be cold and aloof. He was the sort of bloke who would be nodding as you talked while clearly thinking something else. He asked me what I wanted to do at Nine. I told him that I was really enjoying being back at *60 Minutes*, but I'd also like to do a second series of the Monday-night *Ray Martin Show*. He said yes to that idea, assuring me that he would put $1.8 million aside in the network's budget to pay for the production costs, 'eighteen shows, at one hundred thousand dollars each'. (Although he was nodding, I never heard another word about that particular show.) But, Alexander insisted, the immediate network priority was *A Current Affair*, and he wanted me back in the host's seat at the start of 2003.

To each of my objections or queries he had a ready answer. He wanted *ACA* to return to being an up-market commercial current-affairs show, breaking news again, conducting investigations and producing the top political yarns and interviews, with colourful characters and the best pictures. He was going to ride shotgun to make sure of it, he insisted. Again, he did the opposite. When I asked what guarantee he could give me that we wouldn't head back down the old rutted road of consumer stories and diets, Alexander said that those stories should only be part of the night-time mix and shouldn't dominate. I totally agreed with that. When I said I'd learnt from bitter experience that TV management can't always be trusted, he announced he would sign Paul Barry, from the ABC, and Ellen Fanning, one of my favourite people, as senior reporters. He also wanted to bring Mark Llewellyn, who was second-in-command at *60 Minutes*, across as the executive producer. Alexander argued that showed how committed he was to changing the direction of the show. It would be his priority.

But there was still one outstanding question: what about Mike Munro? I said I wouldn't be party to dumping him. Alexander was adamant that whether I took the gig or not, he was moving Munro on from *ACA*. That decision had already been made. Alexander said he had other network plans for Mike and would talk to him within a day or so. 'Don't worry about Mike,' he reassured me. 'We'll look after him. But let me tell him first.'

I understand it was weeks before Mike was told.

After leaving the executive suite that afternoon, I went around to see the old Nine warhorse Peter Meakin. Quite frankly I was surprised that Meakin, the boss of Nine's News and Current Affairs programs, hadn't been at the meeting. I had no idea until that moment how much he loathed John Alexander. Channel 9 was becoming a management mess. Later it would become clear that Alexander had decided to bypass his News and Current Affairs chief in his negotiations with Barry and Fanning, and had deliberately kept him in the dark about his intention to sack one or two other key players at the network. Meakin would soon leave Nine in disgust and join Channel 7, turning his considerable talents against his old network.

Anyway, Meakin said he approved of me taking over as host and that the *ACA* team also favoured it, and Mike Munro was reconciled to going. 'Munro will be fine,' Meakin said. 'He's not happy down there anyway.' When I finally spoke to Mike some weeks later, he felt he'd been shafted by John Alexander and others, but he admitted he hadn't liked the sort of program *ACA* had become in recent times. Ironically, it was now his turn to wish me luck back in the hot seat.

After a private lunch with Kerry Packer, plus another couple of meetings and phone calls from KP, we relaunched the show. The funny thing was, John Alexander went AWOL after that. I never heard from him again, despite all the promises.

In the early years, especially when Willesee and Jana Wendt hosted, *ACA* had the pick of the stories. Now lifestyle and reality shows had gobbled up much of the show's fodder. Material that would once have appeared on *ACA* had been pillaged, mostly by other Nine Network shows such as the various backyard blitzes, *Border Security*, *Getaway*, *RPA* and a dozen such shows. *A Current Affair* was in danger of becoming increasingly sensationalist and superficial like the glossy magazines. It had always been tabloid, but now it was becoming tacky. The good stories were getting lost amongst the consumer stories, the council rorts and the weeping women at 6.30 pm. At least that's what I thought.

I figured if viewers were as bored as I was with the avalanche of lightweight stories, then we might be able to turn back the clock and become relevant again. Mark Llewellyn, the new *ACA* boss, whom I was very happy to work with, agreed on the need for a change. It worked like a charm for a while, too. Within a couple of months we'd clawed our way back in front of Channel 7 in the all-important ratings war. We'd done it with a bunch of strong, well-researched stories from Barry, Fanning and a top team, including Jane Hansen, who sent some excellent reports from the Iraq battlefront. There was once again an appealing mix of news, investigation and colour – as well as the occasional consumer rip-off potboilers. I remember thinking that this *ACA* unit was capable of taking on *60 Minutes* or *Four Corners*. Not that they wanted to.

But. One minute it was full steam ahead; the next we hit an iceberg. It was suddenly panic stations, and madness reigned.

Peter Meakin quit the network, calling Alexander 'a prize c***', and went to seek his revenge by joining Leckie at Channel 7. David Gyngell, who was now sitting in the CEO's office, was suffering from the same sort of interference from Alexander and within a year or so would spit the dummy and leave, too. It was management anarchy. Meanwhile, in Meakin's place as head of News, Gyngell appointed an Aussie ex-journo from Sky, in London, whom nobody knew or cared about. That appointment turned out to be a total disaster. So Gyngell took over running News himself, without any experience and taking the advice, it seemed, of whoever had walked into his office last. Just as we were back on track and winning the ratings towards the end of 2003, Gyngell inexplicably shifted Mark Llewellyn and *ACA*'s second-in-command, Darren Wick, to other programs. I knew nothing about these changes until they'd happened.

John Westacott, who had twice earnt the wrath of Kerry Packer for announcing to the world that he was deserting to Channel 7, was suddenly all powerful: he was made overlord of *ACA* as well as *60 Minutes* and was appointed to the board of the New Zealand branch of the Packer empire. For the life of me I couldn't figure out how that had happened. It meant he had a foot in too many camps to really focus on anything, especially *ACA*. Of his three jobs, Westacott clearly preferred tinkering with *60 Minutes* each week. *A Current Affair* was about to go off the boil.

Chapter 35
The Last Hurrah

The Boxing Day 2004 tsunami that wiped out parts of South-East Asia was the worst natural disaster in years. *National Nine News* and *ACA* sent crews crawling all over the devastation, recognising it as the biggest news story since the Bali bombings in 2002. I had no way of knowing it at the time, but events in Banda Aceh during the month following the disaster would determine my immediate future and that of a few other key people at the program.

Astonishingly, the *ACA* chiefs – John Westacott and his second-in-command, John McEvoy – went missing in action. Control of our nightly coverage and the program's substantial budget was left to a fill-in executive producer named Ben Hawke. Hawke, who now runs *The 7.30 Report*, was magnificent in their absence, staying on top of everything and everybody, in difficult, sometimes dangerous, conditions.

I was coming off a frustrating time. It had been a tough, thankless year at *ACA*, with the added pressure of a federal election.

We'd trailed badly behind *Today Tonight*, and there was no sign that anyone in charge had a strategy for changing the status quo.

I'd been in Melbourne doing *Carols*, had flown back to Sydney on Christmas morning and was driving up to Coolum for a month's holiday with Dianne, Jenna and Luke. We were off to play some golf. That's when the news broke about the cruel tsunami. As we travelled our favourite inland New England route, we listened to the ABC, which was now painting a horrifying picture of the waves and their trail of death and destruction. It was unimaginable.

I pulled over at Warwick, in Queensland, and rang David Gyngell, who was in the Sydney newsroom at the time with the redoubtable Max Uechtritz, who was now running News at Nine after an awesome career at the ABC. I believe Uechtritz's appointment was the only really astute, innovative decision made by Nine management in this whole chaotic period of four or five years. (Sam Chisholm would inexplicably get rid of Uechtritz the moment he returned to take over from Gyngell, in 2005. The madness continued unabated.)

I told Gyngell I wanted to cover the tsunami story. While I was happy to go anywhere, I was hoping I'd end up in Aceh, the most northerly Indonesian province, which seemed to have been the epicentre of the disaster. In the meantime Gyngell told me to at least get in one round of golf while they worked out a network strategy. Our family holidays were always strictly work free, and Dianne and the kids were miserable that this year our time together was about to be gazumped. That included a big New Year's Eve party at a friend's house, which we'd all been looking forward to. But as the first TV pictures came in of the tsunami's ferocious impact, they knew I had to go. There was no question about it.

In fact, early on 31 December, Gyngell called to say I was off to Aceh that night. I was itching to leave, but as I had breakfast with my family it was disturbing to think that the next morning I'd be in the middle of the Indonesian apocalypse, where tens of thousands of families had been obliterated. Just wiped off the face of the earth.

I welcomed in 2005 at 35,000 feet, somewhere north of Darwin. In the space of a few hours I had left the golf course, jumped the first plane to Sydney, got a couple of injections and a bagful of tablets and creams for every disease known, packed my kitbag, trusty camera and passport, and headed for Qantas.

As my producer for this new year at *ACA*, I had chosen Hugh Nailon, a rangy, frustrated amateur footy player from our Melbourne bureau. It turned out to be one of the smartest things I ever did. 'Huge', as we call him – because he's a big unit – has exceptional people skills, which are only matched by his production talents and impeccable judgement. No cameraman I have ever worked with is better than Tim Hawkins, whom I ended up with in Aceh. He simply will not let you down. Rounding out our quartet was a hard-working, unflappable sound recordist named Paul Jolly. Just the bloke you'd want on the toughest assignment.

On the tedious airport-hopping trip to the demolished provincial capital of Banda Aceh, at the far northern end of the island of Sumatra, I kept imagining what we were about to see. (The reality would turn out to be even worse.) Knowing the next few weeks would be traumatic, with too many dead bodies and too much devastation, we made a pact to closely monitor one another's emotional and physical shape. At least for the four of us it seemed to work. We came out of the whole experience pretty much unscathed, while I know some others who needed counselling and a bit of help with their emotions when it was all over. It was a wretched time, but an experience I feel really privileged to have had.

I got a sense of the scope of the human tragedy even while flying to Banda Aceh. Sitting beside me in the plane was a man going home to try to find his family. He told me he'd been working for two years on the oil rigs down in Sulawesi, and when he had rung his parents' farm outside Banda Aceh, ominously there had been no answer. Clearly anxious to talk, he said that his sisters and brothers all lived there with their families. They had eight small children between them.

There was no one at the airport to meet my new friend, which added to his uneasy feeling. We had arranged to be picked up by a small van with a driver, and I offered to take him out to his parents' house first. Although it was dark we could see that very little had been left standing. We could see silhouettes of broken palm trees, buildings reduced to rubble and roofless houses. We stopped at the gate to his farm, full of trepidation. As we shone the car lights on the remnants of his family home, he sank to his knees in the mud, crying uncontrollably. I could do nothing but join him. It seemed his world had been wiped away. At the local police station they confirmed his worst fears about his family.

I told the man's story that night on Nine's news. We would hear the same kind of heart-breaking saga again and again. Daylight revealed to us a vast, ruined cemetery. In fact there were more dead bodies in Banda Aceh than you'd find on a battlefield. There were too many babies and children. It would take some days before the authorities were able to place them all into the tiny, unmistakable body bags. The town looked the way I always imagined Hiroshima did after the A-bomb.

We ended up living in a half-built house that had a roof but no windows. That was our home, studio and editing room for over a month. There was a chorus of about fifteen snoring Channel 9 blokes each night, and we all used one open Indonesian bathroom. We threw water from a bucket over our heads to shower and brushed our teeth with bottled water. The toilet was a porcelain hole in the ground. We slept on thin grass mats on the concrete floor and ate rice laced with vegetables and . . . stuff.

The landlord hired a family to cook and do laundry for us. The father, who had been a high-school sportsmaster, and his wife, a primary-school teacher, along with their three gorgeous children and a grandmother, had lost their home in the tsunami. They bedded down in a tiny room that was barely a cupboard. Yet they always smiled. They kept us all sane with their dignity and good spirits. Their influence was quite remarkable. I never heard a cross word from any of our boys, despite the atrocious conditions and long hours everyone was putting in. I guess it was because we knew that we'd eventually return to the comforts of Australia. The Acehnese family faced life with nothing. We spent our spare time trying to win the attention of the kids, who spoke no English. We had varying success, from hopeless to cuddles. When we left, we managed to scrabble together enough rupiahs to see the family through for a couple of years. Hopefully, the mother and father were back working at their rebuilt schools long before the funds ran out.

Years later my mind's eye is a kaleidoscope of searing images of this extraordinary place and its resolute people. I can still see crowded vans overflowing with smiling, waving people, and market vendors wanting to shake hands and have their photos taken with us. Every person we spoke to – every one – told a horrific tale of lost loved ones. Yet they invited us in and always could find something to laugh and smile about.

One merchant, shovelling mud from his shop floor, turned out to be a commerce graduate from Wollongong University. He asked us to share the bowl of rice he'd been heating on his open stove; he spoke of how kind people in Australia had been to him and how he'd always watched *A Current Affair* and *60 Minutes*. He was so gracious and welcoming we figured that apart from his shop being flooded he must have been lucky. That was until he explained about his wife, his daughter and both parents. They'd all drowned. Maybe he was still in shock.

The Acehnese are a warrior race. Strict Muslims, they are proud and independent people. I don't know what it is in their cultural or religious make-up that gives them such resilience and yet such generosity of spirit. I admire it, but I can't begin to explain it.

Along the perimeter of a park in the centre of town we filmed countless hundreds of green and black body bags all lined up like a macabre picket fence around a cricket ground. A bright-yellow petrol tanker had been pitched onto the roof of a building as one of the gigantic waves thundered ashore. The tanker still hung there, twisted like a mangled spring.

In the nearby cemetery there were at least ten bloated bodies stuck in black mud amongst the marble gravestones. Dead bodies in a cemetery suddenly seemed ghoulish and strangely out of place.

There was a brown-skinned man, naked, lying on the footpath near our satellite station, in the only part of town left intact. He had a blanket loosely covering his legs. We figured he was dead – until he sat up, cringing in fear as we approached. Our interpreter handed him a water bottle to drink from and wrapped the tatty blanket around his shoulders. The man explained that he'd walked a jungle road from a town about 200 kilometres away, after his wife and daughters had been drowned. He cried that one minute he was huddled with them and the next they were swept away; 'stolen' was the Indonesian word he kept repeating. He was clearly demented because of his experiences. We got him some new clothes and some food. An Australian doctor at the psychiatric hospital arranged to collect him and care for him.

The next day we saw him back on the footpath, naked once again.

I noticed limp Indonesian flags everywhere I looked, red-and-white banners dotting the debris and rubble. I thought how patriotic it was in this time of national tragedy. A policeman explained, however, that every flag meant there were more dead bodies under the fallen concrete. As I scanned the immediate vicinity, there must have been at least five hundred flags.

In my opinion the Australian defence forces were the heroes of Aceh, always respectful of the locals, highly efficient and bloody effective in whatever they did. The water-treatment unit sent from Darwin, for example, went sleepless for thirty-six hours to get the gear up and running. Somehow they still found the energy to smile, speak kindly and even have a sly joke with the queues of locals. Their supply of fresh, clean water almost certainly saved the city from widespread disease. The Army Reserve doctors, surgeons and nurses were miracle workers, too. I don't think I've ever felt more proud to be an Aussie than when I watched these men and women in khaki do their stuff. I reckon they all deserve a medal.

We took a ride in one of the Navy's Seahawk choppers, which was the best way to see the devastation wreaked by the tsunami, and went out to the HMAS *Kanimbla*, anchored offshore.

The *Kanimbla*, the Navy's reliable workhorse, had turned up with four hundred men, helicopters, graders and heavy trucks. Without any fuss they rolled up their sleeves and got stuck into clearing the roads, blocked drains and sewers. The chopper had earlier ferried John Howard around Banda Aceh. It was the same chopper that so tragically crashed a few months later, killing nine Australians. The pilots had been our pilots, too. Lest we forget.

Just before we headed home from Banda Aceh, we filmed our farewell story near some of the worst destruction of all, down by the mouth of the river that sweeps through the town. A fisherman came down the road, wheeling a broken bicycle. I smiled at him and waved, so he stopped and came across to us. Through our interpreter he told us that he'd lost his wife of forty-eight years, taken by the raging waters. Looking at us with pitifully sad eyes, he said he didn't know how he could go on living. He said she used to take care of him and he loved her with all his heart. And now she was gone. And he was alone. He started to cry, tears pouring down his nuggety seaman's skin. I reached forward to calm him and he just wept on my chest. I gave him money to buy some food at the local markets. I had to force him to take the rupiahs. I honestly didn't know what else to do. I had nothing to say that could ease his pain.

The mud and slush that blanketed this neighbourhood was so full of chemicals and poisons that when we'd first arrived in Aceh it had rotted the soles of my Blundstone boots, which I had thought were indestructible. Yet now I saw that banana palms had grown through the same toxic waste and within the month of our being there were now head high. The awesome power of Mother Nature. Even amidst the grief and devastation, already there were signs of new life, of hope.

* * *

There was an uncomfortable, rather weird moment when I came back after the month spent sleeping on a concrete floor in Banda Aceh. I was standing at the *ACA* front desk talking to our two receptionists when John Westacott bounced through the front door. 'Welcome back,' he said, shaking my hand. 'How was it? All right? It all looked good.'

Westacott didn't wait for an answer, and I didn't get a chance to ask this dedicated yachtie how the summer breezes were. Perhaps if I'd had to choose between being stuck in *ACA*'s Sydney studio watching the reports come in from Sri Lanka, Thailand and Banda Aceh, or remaining on holidays, I might have preferred to stay on the golf course at Coolum. Or go sailing. But then again, that's why some journos go into management and others stay out on the road.

The ratings for *ACA* during our tsunami coverage easily won us January, another clear indication that audiences will watch if you give them stories that matter to them. The show's ratings collapsed again the moment we reverted to the normal consumer beat. Most nights in the east-coast capitals we'd actually win or be neck and neck, but Adelaide and Perth were still killing our national figures. There was no plan for a frontal attack in those cities. Morale was low and budget cutbacks were starting to hurt. A good, strong story always lifted the *ACA* team's spirits, but a growing number of on-camera stunts, more like *ACA* promos than serious reporting, were creeping into the show. It was getting harder for reporters to do investigative stories or even the quirky colour tales that had been such a feature of *ACA* in the past.

One of the secrets of success at Channel 9, especially at *ACA*, since the early days of Sam Chisholm was that you always knew you were working for and with the best in the business. Now

432

many at Nine had lost that faith. Ellen Fanning left *ACA* to have a baby, a happy event for Ellen's family but a sad loss for our team. Senior reporter Paul Barry had a Mexican stand-off with John McEvoy – the second-in-command – so Barry and his highly paid producer virtually downed tools. Suddenly two of the reasons that I'd agreed to come back to host *A Current Affair* had gone. When two journo mates rang me in tears of laughter about *ACA*'s in-depth study of the best toaster in Australia, I knew it was time to go.

That decision was only cemented by a series of drastic changes. In early 2005, with *ACA* still lagging in the ratings and clearly not a happy unit, David Gyngell suddenly removed the two men running the show, Westacott and McEvoy. Even as the host of the show I didn't know that they were about to be chopped. That became the Nine management modus operandi. I didn't get so much as a hint from anybody. The first I heard of it was when Gyngell rang me at home half an hour before he told the two of them. Gyngell sounded highly stressed and said he had no choice but to replace them with David Hurley. Clearly agitated, he said he knew that Hurley and I disagreed about consumer stories, but we'd 'just have to work it out'. Hurls and I certainly gave it another go.

But there was a bigger shock to come: David Gyngell suddenly quit the network, complaining about too much interference from the Park Street headquarters, presumably meaning John Alexander.

The whole sorry saga just got weirder and weirder. Some weeks after Westacott's removal I was astonished to learn that in late 2004 he had secretly built an expensive new *ACA* studio set. Apparently he had planned it for Peter Overton and Ellen Fanning, whom he intended to install as the new co-hosts of *ACA*.

Again, I knew nothing of this subterfuge. Not even a whisper. Having worked closely – and I thought pretty amicably – with him for at least fifteen years, I was astonished that Westacott hadn't bothered to tell me. I would quite happily have vacated the *ACA* chair if anyone had asked. I'd been staying on not because I was enjoying it but because I'd signed up for a three-year stint and the *ACA* team had pleaded with me to stay on.

When I later confronted Westacott about the plan to have Overton and Fanning co-host, he seemed embarrassed and evasive. He told me it was David Gyngell who had floated the idea. And indeed I can't imagine Westacott getting the budget for a new set without the CEO having first approved it. It was all too Machiavellian for me. It seems my work in Aceh had changed Gyngell's mind, and so the plan to replace me had never eventuated. There's a great word for this kind of behaviour – 'dissimulation', which means 'the act of disguising one's intentions or thoughts'. Let's just say somebody upstairs had been doing a lot of dissimulating.

I spent the next six months or so negotiating my way around *ACA*'s line-up of good, solid stories and half-baked consumer yarns. I'll give you an example of how absurd it got. Steve Barrett, who happens to be one of the very best crime reporters in Australia, was asked to do a 'walk-in' on a small Greek delicatessen in Sydney. The owner, George, was allegedly overweighing ham and cheese. With the cameras rolling and Barrett accusing him of this heinous crime, the baffled owner cried, 'Hang on, please, mate. Ray Martin and his wife, Dianne, shop here all the time. Ask them if I'm doing the wrong thing.'

Of course he wasn't. For years I'd seen George give people free food samples, undercharge pensioners, let others pay 'tomorrow', and show the same generosity that small shopkeepers do just to stay in business. Now a national TV show was accusing him of being a cheat, without any proper research.

Barrett was mortified. Back at the office he told me he had been against doing the story from the outset but had been instructed to do it. And he reminded me of the case of poor Benny Mendoza. He didn't have to. I drove straight down to see George and apologised to him. He was okay, if a little shaken up.

Needless to say, we never ran the delicatessen interview, but still, it was just about the last straw for me. We had the Howard government abandoning refugees in the Indian Ocean and locking up kids in detention centres; hospitals were going broke; Aboriginals were still dying too young; pensioners couldn't get their rotting teeth fixed – and here we were bullying some little delicatessen owner over a slice of ham.

I quit *ACA* the moment my second term was up, after three fascinating, frustrating and sometimes torturous years.

Chapter 36
The Years of Living Dangerously

It's hard to know when Channel 9 stopped being Channel 9.

There was a period in the 1990s when it was Australia's national broadcaster. Forget the ABC, Australians turned to Nine if they wanted sport, entertainment or news. Sam Chisholm and David Leckie built Kerry Packer one of the world's great TV networks. That's now gone. You don't have to work in TV to know that – just turn on your digital plasma screen.

I think it was David Leckie's decision to axe *Midday* in 1998 that started the rot. It was like turfing your favourite old aunt on the scrapheap. No flowers, no cup of tea, no chance to remember the good times together. It was a slap in the face for loyal *Midday* viewers – especially women, shift workers, the elderly and the lonely, who welcomed the show into their homes every lunchtime.

Leckie had taken over the Channel 9 reins from Sam Chisholm after Packer unceremoniously flicked Sam in 1990. (There were obviously no hard feelings because Sam came back to try to save the Nine ship fifteen years later.) Leckie was, like Chisholm, an ex-salesman, though a generation younger. Twice as big physically, he was also louder and swore even more than his predecessor, especially after a drink. I doubt that anybody who knew him talked about his couth. For a long time Leckie suffered from a real inferiority complex, underrating himself compared with Sam. Nobody else did because we thought he was an exceptional CEO. Leckie was just very different. He was extremely capable, and brave to stand up to the bullying of Kerry Packer. It finally cost him his job.

Given his strong feel for television, it remains a mystery to me why Leckie decided to dump *The Midday Show* – and Geoff Harvey with it. I admit to a bias on both counts, but I think Leckie must have had a brain snap. For me it was one of Australian TV's great mistakes and the beginning of Nine's fall from grace.

It was sad for Harvey to finally close the lid on his grand piano at Channel 9, after one of the longest and most successful stints anyone had had at the network. Everybody at Nine knew Harvey because of his musical talent and his merriment. More than anybody he made people laugh. Yet, unbelievably, when Leckie sacked Geoff he actually said to him, 'You're not f***ing funny.' (And worse.)

Oh yes he is, David. He's hilariously funny, and you know it. Everybody knows it. I can't tell you how deeply hurt Geoff was about the way he was dismissed. To his credit Leckie subsequently paid for a huge party down at the local Bridgeview Hotel, but the incident left an awful taste in everybody's mouth. That wasn't the way Channel 9 worked.

We all know that commercial TV is a hard-nosed business. It's about profits, not public service. But a few people, like Geoff Harvey, were an essential part of the most dominant TV brand – brand Channel 9! For almost four decades – television's golden age – he was one of Nine's happy, familiar faces. To Australian audiences he was an old family friend at a time when they really loved their television shows. When television really mattered to them. It doesn't anymore.

I constantly saw how universally recognised and liked Harvey was – at the football, in shopping centres, in pubs. It was overwhelming. In return I have to say Geoff was the original, rusted-on Channel 9 loyalist. The very few occasions I ever heard him get angry was when people – especially if they worked at Nine – started bitching about the network. Like mine, Harvey's years working there had been blessed.

Anyway, a few weeks after he was sacked, Geoff wrote Kerry Packer a letter. Harvey had had a closer relationship with KP than just about anybody, regularly playing music at various private functions in the Packer mansion. In his brief note, which was generous given the circumstances of his dismissal, he told the Big Fella that he'd loved his thirty-seven years at the network and he wondered whether in his incredibly busy schedule Kerry might find time for a cup of tea so Geoff could thank him personally. He never even got a reply.

We all know TV moguls are busy men, but that was a bit ordinary.

I hate to say it, but in the end business moguls don't really care about the foot soldiers. It seems that everyone's disposable, even the best and the most loyal.

If the rumours were right, *Midday*'s profits had fallen to half what they used to be. Regardless, five million bucks was not to be sneezed at. I can't help thinking that Channel 9 would love to have that profit these days. Besides, I'm convinced the benefits of an iconic show like *Midday* – because of its brand name, the platform it gave the network to promote other shows and the viewer goodwill it engendered – went way beyond simple bottom-line profits.

I'm afraid today's accountants and venture capitalists like CVC, Nine's current owners, can't even begin to understand the ephemeral side of TV. They're not there for a long time, just a rich time – which isn't going to happen, either. Alan Bond, at Nine, and Frank Lowy, at the Ten Network, would both scratch their heads and admit to me that television was a contrary, totally different business from all the others they'd known intimately like banking, real estate and shopping centres.

'In TV,' Bondy once said to me, 'one plus one doesn't always add up to two.'

Sam Chisholm didn't try to understand. He was smart. He just let creative people get on with their job. And sacked them if they weren't good enough.

Dumping *Midday* began what I call 'the years of living dangerously', the decade in which Channel 9 purged many of its key people and programs. In quick succession we witnessed the disappearance of shows that were identifiably Channel 9 such as *Hey Hey It's Saturday*, *Wide World of Sports*, *Burke's Backyard*, *Nightline*, *Business Sunday* and, finally, Kerry Packer's baby, *Sunday*.

Some of Nine's best on-air talent also disappeared – stars such as Don Burke, Jim Waley, Jeff McMullen, Brian Henderson, Brian Naylor, Richard Carleton, Mike Munro and, of course, Jana Wendt.

It was almost as if Channel 9's bosses had whacked on their Zegna overalls and shiny Blundstones and decided to demolish the TV tower. They would argue that they were carrying out essential life-saving repairs, but to me it was fear and loathing.

At a time when Australians were growing older, the TV execs seemed to be on their own personal search for eternal youth, chasing the volatile younger demographic. That's a highly dangerous pursuit.

The year after *Midday* it was *Hey Hey It's Saturday*'s and Daryl Somers's turn to be chucked in the dustbin. Again Channel 9 showed no respect for *Hey Hey's* and Daryl's extraordinary credentials. Or the fortune they had made the network. In 2009 somebody at Channel 9 decided to drag out the defibrillator and give Daryl, Ossie and the gang a belt from the old Packer whacker. The new TV promos were suddenly calling it 'Australia's favourite TV show' and 'good old-fashioned entertainment'. Funny about that. Yet I remember one drunken night in the Sydney boardroom years ago when an ad came on for *Hey Hey* featuring Daryl Somers. A senior executive pushed his way to the TV and switched it off. 'I can't stand that ****!' he shouted. Every on-air personality in the room must have thought to themselves, 'If that's what they think of Daryl, the network's number-one star, what do they say about me when I'm not in the bar?' That's certainly what I thought.

As a general rule I came to believe that the further you stepped away from the management floor, the more you could trust the word of whomever you happened to be talking to. Studio crews, the chopper pilot and the blokes in the gatehouse would never dud you.

In recent years there's been a cavalcade of calamities on Nine: *Monster House*, *The Singing Bee*, *Power of 10*, *homeMADE*, *Australia's Perfect Couple* and *Dance Your Ass Off*. That's just in recent times. I know that, as Sam Chisholm loved to say, finding a hit TV show is very difficult. But so many of the shows we see today on Channel 9 are simply embarrassing. Maybe that's because executives no longer face Kerry Packer's wrath – or his chequebook.

Maybe the programmers have lost the plot. Women decide the fate of many TV shows, yet there are few women executives at Channel 9. Do these blokes really think they know what women want? Well, check the scoreboard – Channel 9's only new home-grown runaway successes over the past eight years have been *Underbelly* and *The Block*.

At a charity event in Melbourne for Cathy Freeman recently some Macquarie Bank executives asked me, 'What's happened to Channel 9?' I pointed out that in the space of five years – 2002 to 2007 – there were *seven* network CEOs and *five* network News chiefs in succession, and the network lost the heads of sport, entertainment, drama, sales and programming. They were either sacked or walked. A few of them headed straight off to the enemy's camp. The Macquarie execs shook their heads in amazement.

The fact that Channel 9 is still in the TV game is a tribute to the survival skills of its management team. Or perhaps luck. Remember, in quick time Leckie was sacked, Alexander simply interfered, Gyngell quit, Chisholm was undermined, and then there was Eddie.

Eddie McGuire's appointment as CEO was a James Packer experiment that failed miserably. There was the infamous 'boning' incident with the lovely Jessica Rowe. There was the morning Eddie summoned everyone to the canteen and announced that a hundred News and Current Affairs staff would have to go, which would make Channel 9's news presence 'stronger'. (How does that work?) Shortly after, the new boss of News and Current Affairs, Mark Llewellyn, was dumped. He sued the network and won a reported million-dollar-plus settlement, all carried out in a blaze of damaging publicity. Finally, in August 2006, Eddie publicly promised that Jana Wendt was 'very much part of going forward at Channel 9'. The game-show king assured us, 'She's someone we hold in the highest regard.' A week later Jana was shafted.

There were some unbelievably loopy decisions being made.

Then, in 2005, in the middle of this tumultuous period, the grandmaster, Kerry Packer, sadly died. Less than two years later the private·equity firm CVC Asia Pacific paid James Packer five billion dollars to buy the family's TV and magazine empire. As I've said, CVC knows nothing about television and couldn't care less. Their approach is simple: a quick six- or seven-year hit and they're out of there.

Saddled with seemingly insurmountable debts, the bank creditors have given Channel 9 a moment to catch its breath. But the corporate lungs will soon have to start pumping again. It's going to be tough to pay the bills.

* * *

It was in late 2005, in the middle of all the corporate chaos, that I left *A Current Affair* for the last time. I was so unhappy in the final few months that I was becoming a pain in the bum to myself, let alone my workmates. It must have been obvious to viewers by then that I loathed the endless consumer stories we were doing. *ACA* and *TT* were jumbled together, like the letters in alphabet soup. I used to hear talkback-radio callers say things like 'Well, I saw it on TV last night. I forget whether it was *A Current Affair* or *Today Tonight*'. How could they possibly differentiate?

I was in the *ACA* chair years earlier, in 1997, when Jana Wendt delivered her searing Andrew Olle Media Lecture about the evils of commercial-TV current affairs. Settling a few old scores, I suspect, she condemned the networks for their 'mass-produced vulgarity'. To her credit Jana did acknowledge that over the years she had made many dollars from the commercial-television beast, which she now denounced as being filled with 'venality and hypocrisy'.

I certainly didn't agree with her at the time. *ACA* was already under a heavy barrage of criticism – from Phillip Adams, *Media Watch* and *Frontline* – without copping friendly fire from Jana, a former host. After all, I was fronting a show that at the time was still doing a swag of good stories with a team of journalists, producers, editors and camera crews who were – and still are – an awfully long way from exhibiting venality, vulgarity or hypocrisy. Jana's message was simplistic and I'm sure wasn't directed at them. I think Jana was just being prescient in her 'tough love' speech.

In my own Olle lecture, in 2008, I picked up from where Jana had left off, suggesting that as the media moguls die out, true journalism is dying out, too. Accountants and program managers, who can't stand news and current-affairs shows, now rule TV. Although one in five Australians watches *ACA* and *TT* nightly, those shows have no relevance to the big issues or events of our lives (unless the price of a toaster is a major concern for you). It's not current affairs and that's a pity.

Chisholm asked me to say nothing yet about leaving *ACA*. The next day, on holidays at Coolum, I spied a *Courier-Mail* billboard outside the newsagents, which screamed 'Nine Axes Ray'. I was livid at this distortion of the truth. After brooding over it for a fortnight, I rang Chisholm and told him I wanted to leave the network. He flew me down to Sydney, took me to lunch and gave me the title 'Nine Network's Senior Correspondent' and a

443

pay increase. During the same lunch Chisholm sacked *Sunday*'s executive producer, John Lyons; he was promptly reinstated by John Alexander a few hours later. Shortly after that Chisholm left. They were turbid times, as the network unravelled before our eyes.

I went back to reporting for *60 Minutes* in 2006, with a spring in my step. I was also asked to do a major network special called *Who Killed Harold Holt?* I must confess the special wasn't my idea, but the bonus was that I got to work with a sparkling new talent, a young producer/reporter called Jo Townsend. The program cost well over a hundred thousand dollars and took the best part of three months' work, here and overseas. It was meant to go to air in the last week of the 2007 ratings period, just prior to the fortieth anniversary of the prime minister's mysterious disappearance at Victoria's Cheviot Beach. Yet, without even bothering to watch it, the program director, Michael Healy, decided it wouldn't go to air until *after* ratings had finished. The goalposts had shifted. I went off my skull. It was a complete contradiction of what I had been promised, not to mention an absurd waste of Nine's money and the time of everyone who'd worked on the show. Thankfully, David Gyngell, who was now back in the chair as CEO, agreed that our opus deserved to be shown during the ratings period. Gyngell also made sure it got some publicity, and *Who Killed Harold Holt?* was a triumph, peaking at over 1.2 million viewers, which wasn't bad for a story about a long-ago prime minister.

Garry Linnell, the Channel 9 News boss who'd commissioned *Holt*, left Nine totally frustrated and eventually became the editor of the Sydney *Daily Telegraph*. He was yet another highly skilled casualty of the corporate anarchy.

The whole episode added to my growing disenchantment with Nine.

I had also been asked to do some stories for Jana, who was hosting *Sunday*, where oddly enough I'd never worked. But in what became Channel 9's longer version of the Night of the Long Knives, Jana was forced out, Ellen Fanning and finance wizard Ross Greenwood replaced her, and *Sunday*'s budget was slashed in half. Then, a few weeks later, Greenwood was sacked by Ian Law, the same interim CEO who had appointed him. Having seen off Jana, John Lyons duly resigned as *Sunday*'s executive producer to return to the refuge of newspapers. I was then asked to join Fanning as co-host.

By the time I began to co-host *Sunday*, I'd already done stories for the program on a range of topics, like the ongoing traumas of Vietnam veterans, the tribulations of being an Australian Muslim and the injustice of David Hicks's five-year incarceration at Guantanamo. At least you could still do such worthwhile yarns on *Sunday*, even on a rag 'n' bone budget. Despite benign neglect by management it remained a high-quality enclave, a rare backwater in commercial TV. I couldn't help thinking how satisfying it must have been in Jim Waley's salad days, when they had enough staff, a travel budget and Kerry Packer's blessing.

But in February 2008 what had once been the most highly respected show on commercial TV was finally given a lethal injection. David Gyngell decided to shift the show from the 9 am timeslot it had held for almost three decades to 7.30 am. Neither Ellen Fanning nor I, the hosts of the show, were told. We read about it in the paper.

When I spoke to him about it, John Westacott, who was now the third boss of News and Current Affairs in the space of a couple of years, looked me in the eye and insisted that the decision wasn't yet final, but it clearly was. He had never been a fan of the program. Gyngell argued convincingly that the new owners,

CVC, had given him no choice. The move was 'a cost-saving measure', he said, and I accepted that. Still, I asked him how in business you could ever put a bottom-line figure on excellence and quality. He suggested the new network owners didn't care.

In the end *Sunday* simply bled to death in its new timeslot. But ironically *Sunday*'s gun reporter Ross Coulthart and producer Nick Farrow won three 2008 Walkleys, including the most prestigious in journalism, the Gold Walkley, which had never been won by Channel 9 before. They actually collected their awards after *Sunday* had been dumped from the network and they had moved on to work at Channel 7. John Westacott couldn't find the money to fly them to Melbourne for the grand occasion so Channel 7 picked up their travel costs. It was a sad, sad reflection of how Nine has abrogated its commitment to serious news.

Still, I loved my too brief time at *Sunday*, working again with Ellen Fanning.

*   *   *

There's no question that David Gyngell's decision to move *Sunday* forced my hand to finally leave Channel 9, though I understood he had to pay the bills – and please his new network bosses. Gyngell offered me a new two-year contract, at my existing salary. That was very generous considering the drastic cutbacks that were being made across the network. But that contract required me to host the new early-morning *Sunday* show, which I knew would fail in that timeslot.

Gyngell was aware that I'd also recently knocked back an offer to co-host *The Today Show* with the delightful and talented Jennifer Byrne. I had no interest in returning to a lifestyle that meant getting up at 4 am every day. I'd already done that as a cadet journalist, more than forty years before. A late-afternoon news show had also been dangled in front of me, which I had no interest in, either. I knew there simply wasn't the money or resources at Channel 9 anymore to do it properly. That show has since been tried, and it failed.

Finally, Gyngell proposed that I do fifteen stories a year for *60 Minutes* – a program that I still loved – on a fee-per-story basis. That was a badly disguised way of putting me back on the road full time again, at a much reduced rate. Thanks, but no thanks.

I'd been getting restless anyway over the previous year or so and all the signs were obvious that Aussie TV had moved into a different era and that the old days would never return. Besides, I'd made up my mind to write a book. Or maybe several books. I also wanted to go bush and take some serious photographs, and maybe come up with a few new TV programs.

So after talks with David Gyngell, on 8 February 2008 I quit – having enjoyed three exhilarating decades in the Nine stable.

Despite some nonsense written in the newspapers, the truth is Gyngell and I had no arguments when I resigned. There was no rancour, not even a raised voice. The fact that he asked me to write the network press release about my departure is proof of that. In it I thanked the Packers – Kerry and James – for my job on *60 Minutes* and everything that came after that. I still thank them, as I reflect on some of the experiences I've recounted in these pages.

I sent Gyngell the press release mid-afternoon on a Thursday. He asked me not to say anything publicly until the next morning, as he wanted Peter Harvey to write the story for Friday night's news bulletins. Apart from being a mate, Harvey is a beautiful writer, so I was delighted.

But by 5.30 pm on Thursday the news had broken on Macquarie radio. A 2GB producer, whom I'd worked with on *Midday*, rang to say they were about to run a report claiming that after a noisy quarrel with Gyngell I had stormed out of the Sydney Channel 9 headquarters. According to this (highly unreliable) report I'd almost had a smash as I tore out of the Channel 9 car park.

Hello?

I told her the truth: no arguments, no storming out. I hadn't even been at Channel 9 that day, but instead had gone for a long, lazy bowl of spaghetti with Luke at our local trattoria. The report was total fiction. She asked if I would go on air and say just that. So I did.

Still, at my peril, I ignored the squad of newspaper reporters out the front of my house. There must have been five journos sitting in their cars in the pouring rain. Luke, now eighteen, was at home playing video games with a couple of schoolmates. They couldn't believe the reporters' stake-out and the incessant ringing of the doorbell. I asked Luke to go down and tell them I wouldn't be saying anything until Nine's official press release came out the next morning. It was getting late anyway, so the reporters all left. But then, under pressure from the Nine publicity department, Gyngell released the official statement later that night. He didn't have much choice.

The initial confusion and the mixed messages probably explain why so much rubbish – so many fabricated stories – came out over the next few days. The TV writers, whom I hadn't spoken to at all, opened up both barrels. I understood.

I had a strange, empty feeling that night as Dianne and I ate dinner and opened a bottle of wine. Jenna was in London at drama school. We missed her wisdom and warmth, although she rang several times during the night. Luke was a great comfort, but a bit perplexed, like Dianne and I. This wasn't how I'd ever imagined leaving Channel 9. But then, I'd never really thought of leaving until recent months. I just figured I would be there for 'the term of my natural life'. That's what James Packer had said to me several times, although surprisingly I never heard from him after I left. Still haven't. That disappoints me, because we'd become quite close. But I guess with the global economic meltdown James has had bigger things to worry about than me pulling up stumps at his dad's old TV network.

Over the years there had always been rumours about me signing with Seven or Ten. Jenna and Luke would get upset and ask, 'You're not going to leave Nine, are you?' I'd always reassure them that I had no such intention and that Nine was my television home. After all, I knew everybody there, even Frank the cleaner, who would regale me with his latest real-estate ventures. Despite all the tectonic shifts up on the third floor, life down on the studio floor was calm and stable – until the sackings started making people nervous. That's when I found myself a bit like a shop steward trying to reassure loyal long-term workers – like Nobby, the devoted studio sound engineer, and Katrina, the Croatian make-up artist, and Fay, the smiling Lebanese lady in the canteen – that everything was going to be fine and they shouldn't worry about what they read. Now suddenly, I was gone, too.

To his credit David Gyngell told me not to feel any pressure to clean out my office. It contained a library of books and mountains of story files, and the walls were festooned with photos from so many TV shows over the years. My phone didn't stop ringing for days. I got calls from all across the network. Old producer mates now working at *The Footy Show*, clerks in finance whom I only ever saw at the Christmas party and mates like Murph, the original floor manager from GTV in Melbourne – everyone called. I was quite overwhelmed.

Gyngell said he wanted to throw a big farewell bash for me in my old *Midday* studio – 'something befitting thirty great years'. I told him I didn't want it, because I'm really uncomfortable at farewells. Maybe it's a hangover from my childhood, when we always seemed to be moving on, saying goodbye. I settled instead for a couple of noisy dinners with good mates from *A Current Affair* and *60 Minutes*, for which Gyngell, it should be said, picked up the hefty bills.

He made it clear, publicly and privately, that he was anxious to maintain my strong connection with Channel 9. I was pleased about that. He said he wanted me to keep reporting for *60 Minutes*, which I happily continue to do.

My only sadness was in losing my favourite *Carols by Candlelight* gig. I would have celebrated my twenty-first year in 2008, which is pretty remarkable for such a mammoth seat-of-the-pants telecast.

Carols was when we usually got together with our Victorian rellos – Dianne's younger brother, Ian, and his family. Nothing underlined the reality that I'd moved on from Nine more than the fact we weren't in Melbourne on the loveliest night of the year. Dianne cooked a fabulous duck dinner for just the four of us. We laughed as we shared our *Carols* memories, argued about our favourite singers – was it Hugh Jackman, John Farnham, Rhonda Burchmore or Marina Prior? – and unforgettable moments, like when cousin Amy's candle set her hair on fire. One thing we all agreed on was that there was life after *Carols*.

* * *

I was shocked to get a call from Sydney's Catholic archdiocese just a few weeks after quitting Nine. Divine intervention, I call it. Cardinal George Pell was inviting me to host the worldwide telecast of Pope Benedict XVI's visit to Sydney for World Youth Day, with a potential audience of a billion people. I explained to George that since the innocence of my baptism I had lapsed into a less-than-perfect Catholic life, and I'd married a Presbyterian. In a Presbyterian church, to boot. (I felt like I was back in the confessional, about to cop twenty Hail Marys.) But His Eminence assured me that he'd dealt with much greater sins and that my taking part in the telecast would prove how ecumenical and forgiving the Vatican really is. I couldn't counter that pitch.

World Youth *Day* ended up occupying *two months* of my life, and was totally different to any other major event I've ever done. It was a bit like covering a moon mission, when you've got to keep talking for hours, although nothing much is happening. I was pleased with the reaction we got. Especially from Catholics who felt that we'd managed to avoid the dirge and dogma and had shown respect for their faith. I was never going to do it any other way.

But my greatest satisfaction came from using my new-found connections with Cardinal Pell to help Lauren Huxley and Sophie Delezio get papal blessings.

I'd earlier done a *60 Minutes* story with Lauren, who at eighteen had been brutally bashed and set on fire by a monster she'd never met before. The Huxley family had simply refused to give up on gravely injured Lauren, turning to prayer when all else had failed. And she pulled through. It was Lauren's and her dad Pat's dream to meet the Pope, and I am glad that I could help make that a reality.

The family of Sophie Delezio, who was severely burnt and injured at a young age in two serious car accidents, had been informed that a meeting with His Holiness was impossible. Her father, Ron, and mother, Carolyn, had already proved that anything's possible. After all, they'd helped Sophie pull through a long-running medical nightmare. In the end it was just a matter of putting the Delezios in the right spot on stage at Pope Benedict's final function, which I hosted. As the Pope passed, he couldn't miss Sophie, looking innocent but clearly damaged from her terrible accidents. So he stopped to bless the eight-year-old beauty, and then the whole Delezio family. Now, if anyone in the world deserved a blessing from God it was the Delezios, given that they'd been to hell and back.

To get me out of the garret, where for months I'd been writing this book, I did a few stories in 2009 for *60 Minutes*; hosted a funny interview sketch called 'Small Talk' in an episode of *The Chaser*, on the ABC; and introduced two episodes of *Australian Story* that focused on a truly inspirational farmer named Peter Andrews, on whom I'd long ago reported.

But, perhaps most significantly, I did a story for *The 7.30 Report* about Palm Island, the former gulag where the biggest Aboriginal community in Australia lives in woeful disadvantage. It was the first time I had done a television report for the ABC since I resigned from my New York correspondent's job to join *60 Minutes* thirty years previously. For a moment I was back at the ABC, where I'd started in journalism in 1965.

I'd come full circle.

Epilogue
The Full Circle

From where I sit now, I have to say my three decades at Channel 9 were utterly fantastic, as were my earlier ABC years. I've been a lucky bloke.

When I took the leap of faith from the ABC to Channel 9 in 1978, if anyone had suggested that I would end up handsomely paid to wander the world, talk to paupers and princes, and work with the colourful colleagues that I have, I would have laughed at them. In so many ways my working life has been a playful exemption from the real world, certainly from the mundane.

Every Christmas holidays for about twenty years we had a tradition of going up to South West Rocks, on the New South Wales Mid North Coast. I'd stand in the tepid waters of Trial Bay with my favourite brother-in-law (FBIL), Brian (I have to call him that or else he turns nasty), and we would reflect on what sort of a year we'd had. Our kids frolicked in the gentle waves in front of us or chucked a tennis ball at our heads. My FBIL was a shiftworker at the Kurnell Oil Refinery, in Sydney.

He'd always insist that he'd spent the year at work while I'd been off having a good time at Kerry Packer's expense. He was right. Brian couldn't retire quickly enough. I still can't stop chasing stories.

But having soared with eagles, as they say, it's a bit hard scrabbling around in the pigeon droppings that much of commercial TV has become today. I think it's accepted that we've seen the passing of the golden age of television (and of journalism, I suspect). I may sound like some old fart banging on about how things aren't as good as they used to be in my day, but the fact is they're not! That's despite the wonder and amazement of the internet and the digital revolution. I can picture Kerry Packer screaming his nicotine-clogged lungs out in dismay.

But the true storyline of my life had begun before my days in radio and TV, when I slept in those slow-moving trains and drank railway coffee with condensed milk – always under the powerful influence and unconditional love of my mother.

Mum spent the last few years of her colourful life in a nursing home close to our house. Physically she'd become a little brittle, but she still had plenty of spirit, especially when she saw her kids or grandchildren. I'd pick her up and take her for a drive, or we'd just sit down near the harbour in the sun. If I happened to sneeze or cough, Mum would always put her hand on my arm and tell me I was working too hard and that I needed to take better care of myself. Old habits die hard.

She'd smile as we reminisced about the early days at Yarrangobilly and Jannali, and even my old man's dereliction. I think she'd long gone past the bitterness and pain. She'd just chortle about some of the absurdities of our lives, knowing that in the end she'd won the game.

Mum's nursing home was a pleasant enough place, with

seventeen women and just three old codgers living in up-market motel-style accommodation. They each had their own bed-sitting room, private bathroom and balcony, all leading off a long corridor. To make sure they didn't get confused, they each had a little photo in a frame outside their door, to identify their room. Mum had a picture of her and me. The trouble was, one demented old bloke who was obviously a rusted-on Channel 9 viewer saw my familiar face and thought it was his room.

When Mum was watching TV in the communal lounge room, he'd regularly strip off his clothes, dump them on her bed and jump into her shower. Mum would go absolutely apoplectic at the thought of a naked man in her bedroom. Given her bittersweet experience of marriage, Mum had little time for men, except for me and my brothers-in-law. No matter how many times we explained the mix-up, she was hell-bent on torching the whole place to overcome the toxic shock. But she was too stubborn to take down my photograph.

She would often come to our house and bathe in the attention she'd get from Jenna and Luke. Luke had actually stopped going to the nursing home when he was about five, because all the old ladies would pinch his cheeks and cuddle him and make him wait until they fetched lollies from their room. They were mostly just lonely, and he was a cherubic little boy.

One Sunday morning in September 1997, I'd taken Luke to the preview of a new kids' film. My niece rang me in the car to say that Mum had taken a bad turn overnight. When I got to the nursing home, she'd passed away. She was coming up to her 86th birthday. I sat holding Mum's hand for about an hour, thinking how lovely she looked. She'd have laughed to hear me say that all the wrinkles on her face, which so bothered her in later life, had disappeared.

Dianne's father, Bruce, had died almost a year earlier, living up to the adage that good blokes die young. He was only in his early seventies and had never quite recovered from the triple bypass he'd had many years before. Although I didn't meet Bruce until I was about nineteen, he became, in a sense, the father I never had. A simply wonderful bloke, he was a vital cog in our lives. The truth is since we returned from America, Dianne and I spent more time with her family than mine, although I still remain close to my sisters. That was just the way things panned out.

Before Jenna and Luke were born, we spent an inordinate amount of time with Dianne's sister Susan and Brian's three boys, Jeff, Chris and Brad. We were like their alternative parents, going to their soccer and cricket games, birthdays, any excuse for a barbecue and especially holidays. For at least a fortnight before Christmas we'd rent the same flats at South West Rocks, halfway between Sydney and Brisbane. This was a fishing, swimming, golfing, game-playing binge that has brought us great memories, a thousand photos and a million lies about who caught the biggest fish, won at golf or failed to shout at the town's only pub, The Seabreeze Hotel.

Without places like South West Rocks the stories of my life would be as flat as a badly poured beer. Barbecues lit by warm sunsets on the best beaches in the world, catching sweet whiting off the rocks at the river mouth, feeding cocky bream to hungry pelicans, bumping over the sandbar, heading out in a tiny fishing boat to drag tiger sharks out of the nets, mercilessly cheating at Trivial Pursuit, sticking cigarettes in Brian's nostrils as he slept in front of the TV and then taking photos to prove it – the list of small but treasured moments is endless. As it is for so many families.

Susan and Brian's boys have grown up to be a policeman, a

builder and an IT specialist, and all have wives and children of their own. They remain an integral part of our lives. We recently all made a long-overdue pilgrimage back to South West Rocks. I doubt it'll be the last now that the new generation has indulged in the simple but delicious pleasures of the place. With their boys grown up, Susan and the FBIL have gone on holidays with the four of us over the last ten years to Canada, America, Europe and New Zealand and joined us on driving safaris around Australia. They fill our lives with love and laughter.

I make mention of this perfectly normal family life in order to put my encounters with princes, presidents and popes into proper context. These family moments remain the real stories of my life, the real colour in the tapestry.

Late last year Jenna organised a party for Dianne and me on our fortieth wedding anniversary, with the complicity of her brother, Luke. Now, I'm easy to fool, but they managed to pull it off at home – bringing in hired tables, chairs, live music and about thirty of our friends – without Dianne even getting a whiff that something was amiss. It seems our kids are getting smarter.

Jenna got her BA Hons in theatre in London and came home at last. It was only three years but seemed like a lifetime. She's worked in theatre and TV, but like everybody else in this capricious game Jenna awaits her big break. From across the oceans Barack Obama sparked a genuine fascination in Luke for international relations and politics. He's now about to go into his final year at Sydney Uni, and he's still only nineteen but almost six foot five. He also dabbles in theatre and musical comedy, with a passion that matches Jenna's. Where they'll both end up is anyone's guess. No matter what, they bring me happiness beyond reason.

As for Dianne, she remains *the* story of my life.

Acknowledgements

Samuel Goldwyn, the Hollywood legend, once famously declared that 'no man should write his autobiography until long after he is dead'. Well, my bright yet indefatigable agent, Deb Callaghan, convinced me I probably shouldn't wait.

My sincere thanks to everybody at Random House. Publishing Director Nikki Christer made me an offer I'm very glad I didn't refuse. Along with her equally talented colleagues Sophie Ambrose and Catherine Hill, they somehow got me across the (dead)line. Just. And my long-distance editor, Vanessa Mickan, did a marvellous job of untangling my stories and syntax.

I want to thank Karen Reid, who's the publicity queen at Random House, in advance of our barnstorming promotional tour – just in case she's not talking to me at the finish.

My thanks to Channel 9 for the use of the *Midday* archive photographs and to the extraordinary illustrator Bill Leak for the use of his two cartoons. Thanks also to the immensely talented *Daily Telegraph* cartoonist, Warren Brown, for the use of his *Midday* cartoon.

I owe so many details of my early stories, and my early life, to my remarkable sisters Lorraine, Kay and Joyce. They insist we had it easy in comparison with *Angela's Ashes*. Of course we did. And of course I write this book in celebration of my mother's memory. My wonderful niece, Kathy O'Donnell, helped locate the early family photographs and I thank her.

Two young, sexy chicks from my *Midday* era – Leslie Moy and Nicole Anthony – were tireless in fossicking for many of the dog-eared photos of that star-studded time. *Midday* wouldn't have happened without them and their exuberant producer mates who made *Midday* such a joy – especially colourful stalwarts such as Pat Lovell, Bill Wallace, Hilary Innes, Rory Callaghan, Richard Stomps and the late Chris Fyfe. And all those other *Midday* marvels whom I've now offended by not naming. You know I love you, along with the hardworking studio crews and the *Midday* musicians, who never once let us down. I couldn't have done it without my *Midday/ACA* floor manager, Jenny Ward, either.

In twenty-five years I've only ever had three personal assistants. Lisa Danson, Michelle James and Kym Weatherley are all brilliant and have saved my life.

From my earliest years in journalism Dan Speight, Russell Warner, Charlie Buttrose and Stuart Revill were instrumental in my development. In my New York days Carole Pierce was a trusted friend and safety net, Jeff McMullen was a midnight companion in many Village music bars, and the 'Pundit', Peter Barnett, kept me informed and amused.

The legendary *Four Corners* executive producer Peter Reid, who happens to be Karen Reid's dad, gave me the TV break I needed and believed in me.

At *Sixty Minutes* Gerald Stone and Peter Meakin led an unmatchable bunch of producers, editors and sound recordists. Of the latter I must mention Micky Breen and Terry 'Skeeter' Kelly, who were a joy to travel the world with.

Over the years cameramen have made the difference in making good stories memorable. Along with those I've already mentioned go the talents of men like Mick Morris, Paul Boocock, Brendan Ward and Drew Benjamin. They don't come any better.

Similarly, film and tape editors have routinely saved me from embarrassment, and tried to make me look good. I especially enjoyed the creative hours with Laura Battistel, Gia Thompson and Renee Hudson at *ACA*, while Thomas Pokorny, Mike Chirgwin and Gary Albery at *60 Minutes* constantly amazed me.

Two invincibles who made my life easier are Geoff Cameron, the unit manager from *60 Minutes*, who somehow makes sense of taxi dockets from Kabul and buries bar bills from Riyadh (which is dry), and Robyn Nailon, the human dynamo from *ACA* who helped me locate any satellite link in the universe or missing tape.

From the list of journo mates who have taught me so much I would like to make special mention of Paul Lockyer, Cliff Neville, Alan Hogan and John Muldrew, who have always given me wise counsel.

And finally old friends like Katrina and Geoff Harvey, Anne and Peter Wynne, Glenys and Gary Clark, Vicky and Mike Perjanik – and all of their families – who have been so much a part of our lives for so long.

Which only leaves me to give the last word of thanks to *my* family: Dianne, Jenna and Luke; along with all my sisters' children, the Dean mob; the Stevos from Wentworth; and Ian, Karen and the gang from the Mornington Peninsula. And Nancy and Bruce, Dianne's wonderful parents. Thank you all.

Index

A Current Affair, 206, 234, 260,
  315–96, 416–18, 420–35, 442, 443
  Ray hosting, 323–96
  Ray leaving, 392–6, 435, 442
  return to, 420–35
ABC, 65–163
  resigning from, 163
Aboriginal people
  Aboriginal Employment Strategy,
    305–6
  apology to, 304
  Australian Indigenous Education
    Foundation, 306
  Council for Aboriginal
    Reconciliation, 303–5, 375
  Fred Hollows and, 299–303
  neglect of, 299–306, 362, 435
  Palm Island story, 452
  Ray's heritage, 8, 9
  referendum 1967, 84
Aceh, tsunami, 424–31
Adams, Gerry, 180
Adams, Phillip, 329, 367, 443

Adderley, Warwick, 377
Adelaide, 46–8
Afghanistan, 180
Ainsworth, Roy, 250–2
Air Cadets, 51
Alexander, John, 246, 419–22, 433,
  441, 444
Ali, Muhammad, 117–121
Allen, Dave, 253
Allen, Woody, 116
AM, 75, 79–80
  East Timor story, 155–8
  Perth correspondent, 81–4
America's Cup, 139–44, 153, 216
Amos, Lou, 49, 55
Anderson, Angry, 235, 239, 243, 326
Andrew Olle Media Lecture, 442, 443
Andrews, Peter, 452
Angleton, James Jesus, 145, 149–53
anti-war demonstrations, 103, 115,
  117, 130
Apollo 13, 100
Apollo 14, 100

Appin coalmine tragedy, 194
Argentina, 223–4
Armstrong, Neil, 99
Ashbolt, Allan, 67, 75
Aussie bush stories, 214–21
Austin, Ward 'Pally', 79
Australian Indigenous Education
    Foundation, 306
Australian Story, 452
Australian Women's Weekly, 3, 165,
    310, 322

baby rescue in Spain, 184–7
Bacall, Lauren, 117, 125, 286
Bacon, Wendy, 205–6
Bailey, Dr Harry, 203, 204, 206
Baird, Bruce, 314
Bana, Eric, 409
Banda Aceh, 426–32
Barber, Tony, 279
Barnes, Pam, 280
Barnett, Peter 'the Pundit', 114, 129
Barrett, Steve, 434, 435
Barry, Paul, 144, 420, 421, 422, 433
Bassey, Shirley, 253
Battistel, Laura, 328
Beatty, Warren, 125, 126
beautiful women, 285–97
Beazley, Kim, 242
Beirut, 187–90
Belafonte, Harry, 114
Benaud, Richie, 54, 55, 273
Bennett, Tony, 231, 255
Benussi, Nadia, 259
Bertrand, John, 14
Bettridge, Bill, 8
Bettridge, Mary, 7, 8, 15–16
Bibb, Steve, 377, 379, 380, 383, 388,
    391, 396, 397, 401, 408, 410, 415
Bich, Baron Marcel, 142
Biggs, Ronald, 145–9
Bingara, 7

birth, 13
birth of Jenna, 228
birth of Luke, 273–3
Bisset, Jacqueline, 287
Bjelke-Petersen, Flo, 242
Bjelke-Petersen, Joh, 219, 242, 300
Black Panthers, 107–9
Black Ronnie, 237, 238
Blencowe, Tanya, 267
Blowfly (maths teacher), 49
Blundell, James, 253
Bogan Gate, 1, 2, 3, 14, 15, 44
Bogart, Humphrey, 286, 292
Bombay, 86–8
Bond, Alan, 143–4, 153, 160, 202, 320,
    439
Boon, David, 54
Borches, Wendy, 153
Bourne, Shane, 235
boxing, 37–9, 117–21
    Ali vs Frazier 1971, 117–20
Boxing Day tsunami, 424–31
Boyce, Christopher, 199–202
Bradman, Don, 54, 87, 218, 338–52,
    412
Bradman, Greta, 351
Bradman, Jessie, 338–51
Bradman, John, 339, 343, 350, 351
Bradman, Megan, 351
Bradman, Nicholas, 351
Bradman, Shirley, 343
Bradman, Tom, 351
Brennan, Father Frank, 306
Breslin, Jimmy, 102
Brill, David, 151, 152, 153, 223
Brogden, John, 372
Brown, Bryan, 409
Brown, Mat, 417
Brown, Noeline, 127
Bryant, Martin, 331, 334
Burchmore, Rhonda, 450
Burke, Don, 235, 439

Burns, Creighton, 157
Burns, Gary, 234, 240
Bush, George Snr, 136
Bush, George W., 123, 124, 136, 199
Buttrose, Charles, 97, 113, 114
Buttrose, Ita, 97
Buttrose, Margo, 97
Byrne, Debra, 276
Byrne, Jennifer, 446

Caine, Michael, 233
Campbell, Alec, 400–2
Campbell, Glen, 235
Campbell, Dr Scott, 398, 400
Canadian Ladies Marching Band, 235
Canberra, 84, 90, 92
Cangai seige, 317
Cantrell, Lana, 352
capital punishment, 197–9
Carleton, Richard, 68, 75, 86, 321, 439
Carlton, Mike, 68
Carlyon, Les, 403
Carmichael, Alan, 67, 75
Carmody, Rob, 337
Carols by Candlelight, 252, 260, 275–8, 397, 425, 450
Carr, Bob, 76
Carrey, Jim, 260
Carson, Johnny, 253
Carter, Jimmy, 136, 155
Casey, Ron, 238
Castro, Fidel, 107, 109–12
Castro, Ramón, 111, 112
Castro, Raul, 111
Chamberlain, Aidan, 373
Chamberlain, Azaria, 310–13, 373
Chamberlain, Ingrid, 312
Chamberlain, Lindy, 298, 310–13, 373
Chamberlain, Michael, 310–13, 373
Chan, Sir Julius, 378–83

Channel 7
  rivalry with Channel 9, 314–25, 360, 419
  60 Minutes job offer, 159
Channel 9, 163–7, 418–23, 433, 436–50
  current affairs, 314–25, 360
  decline of, 436–42, 454
  Keating and, 244–6
  Ray as face of, 259–60
  Ray leaving, 447–50
  rivalry with Channel 7, 314–25, 419
  Special Projects unit, 396
Chapman, John, 227
The Chaser, 452
Chelmsford Private Hospital, 203–4, 206
childhood, 13–45
children, 224–5, 228–30, 269–78, 322, 327–8, 395–6, 457
Chipp, Don, 232
Chisholm, Sam, 168, 193–5, 207, 226–9, 233, 239, 242, 319, 320, 355–7, 425, 432, 436, 437, 439, 440, 441, 443, 444
CIA, 149, 154, 155, 200
Clapton, Eric, 115
Clinton, Bill, 136, 376
Coates, John, 314
Cocker, Joe, 114
Cole, Frank, 312, 313
Collins, Joan, 286
Cometti, Dennis, 77
Commonwealth Games host, 163, 260, 279
Connolly, Billy, 236, 409
Constantinidis, Al, 244
Cosgrove, General Peter, 401, 402
Cosser, Steve, 319
Costello, Peter, 245, 335
Coulthart, Ross, 446

Council for Aboriginal
  Reconciliation, 303–5, 375
Courtenay, Bryce, 305
Crawford, Michael, 235, 265–8
cricket pitch 'vandalism', 54–5
criminals, 196–207
Crocker, Barry, 253, 323, 356
Crowe, Russell, 274, 411–13
Cruise, Tom, 264, 274, 290, 292–4,
  413
Cruz, Penelope, 290
Crystal, Billy, 114
Cuba, 109–12
Cullis, Bronte, 298, 308–10, 311, 387
Cullis, Graham, 309, 310
Cullis, Jan, 309, 310, 387, 388–9
current affairs rivalry, 314–25, 360
Curruthers, Jimmy, 38–9
Curtin, John, 13
Curtis, Tony, 260
CVC, 442, 446

Dainty, Paul, 408
Dallas, Texas, 133–6
Dame Edna Everage, 295–7
dangerous assignments, 179–95
Danson, Lisa, 281
Dark, Ben, 418
Davies, Brian, 152
Davies, Will, 397
Davis, Sammy Jr, 130, 357
De Castro, Raimunda, 147
De Niro, Robert, 131
Dean, Brian, 453–4, 456–7
Dean, Brad, 456
Dean, Chris, 456
Dean, Jeff, 456
Dean, Susan, 61, 170, 272, 456–7
death threat, 368
Deep Sleep Therapy, 203–4
defamation action, 375
Delezio, Carolyn, 452

Delezio, Ron, 452
Delezio, Sophie, 451–2
Dempster, Nigel, 384, 385
Denton, Andrew, 413
Denver, John, 114, 261–4
Derek, Bo, 229, 288
Derek, John, 288
Dingo, Ernie, 235
Donoghue, Phil, 175, 176
Douglas, Michael, 260, 409
Downing, Malcolm, 76
Duckmanton, Sir Talbot, 78, 156, 157,
  163, 167
Duncan, Ken, 14
Durham, Judith, 278
Dylan, Bob, 114

East Timor, 154–8
Edgley, Michael, 232
Einfeld, Marcus, 372
El Salvador, 222–3
Elton, Ben, 260, 409
Emmanuel, Tommy, 253
Englezos, Lambis, 405, 406
Enuma, Major Walter, 380
espionage, 149–58, 200–2
Estens, Dick, 306
Evangelista, Linda, 288–9
executive producers, 328–9

Fahey, John, 314
The Falcon and the Snowman, 200,
  201
family history, 7–13
Fanning, Ellen, 76, 420, 421, 422, 433,
  434, 445, 446
Farnham, John, 277, 450
Farrow, Mia, 141
Farrow, Nick, 446
fatherhood, 224–5, 228–30, 269–78
Ferguson, Sarah, 295, 296
Finch, Peter, 142

Fleetwood Mac, 181

Flynn, Julie, 76

Fohlen, Yves, 404–5

Fonda, Jane, 131, 233, 286

food, 208–13

Ford, Gerald, 123, 136, 137

Forrest, Lisa, 235

Fort Leavenworth, 200, 201

fortieth wedding anniversary, 457

Four Corners, 67, 76, 285, 360, 371, 422
   US stories, 104, 109, 125, 131, 132,
      144, 152, 153

Frager, Peter, 193

Fraser, Malcolm, 154, 248–9

Frazier, Smokin' Joe, 117–20

Fred Hollows Foundation, 300, 302,
   305, 375, 395

Freeman, Cathy, 117, 441

Friend, Rachel, 235

Fromelles, 404–6

Frontline, 317, 359–64, 376, 378, 443

Fyfe, Melissa, 353

Galbally, Frank, 239–40

Gallipoli, 400–4

Geller, Uri, 14

Genet, Jean, 107–9

Gibson, Jack, 272, 273

Gibson, Mel, 410–11

Gibson, Mike, 373–4

Gillespie, Des, 56

Gillespie, Lorraine, 2, 12, 18–20, 23, 26,
   27, 31–3, 43, 48, 56, 64, 91, 122, 323

Glatzle, Mary, 106

Gocup, 24

Gold Logies, 165, 279, 297

Goldberg, Whoopi, 236

Gooding, Cuba Jr, 294

Goodrem, Delta, 287

Gorton, John, 80, 84

Grace, George, 2, 6, 11–45, 57

Grant, Stan, 316, 329, 359

Greenwood, Ross, 445

Grenada, 222

Grimshaw, Tracy, 358

gun laws, 335–6

Gunnedah, 8, 9, 12, 13, 15–16, 57

Gymea Squash Club, 60

Gyngell, David, 419, 422, 423, 425,
   426, 433, 434, 441, 444–50

Hadley, Ray, 79

Hall, Richard, 153

Hamill, Pete, 102

Hansen, Jane, 371, 372, 422

Hanson, Pauline, 218

Hardy, Frank, 306

Hardy, Sir James, 143

Hargrave Park, 4, 33–41

Harris, Rolf, 195

Harvey, Geoff, 91, 228, 235, 237, 238,
   247–58, 273, 276–8, 282, 283, 323,
   437–8

Harvey, Neil, 77

Harvey, Peter, 447, 448

Haughton, Andrew, 178, 187, 193, 222,
   385, 386

Hawke, Ben, 424

Hawke, Bob, 232, 242–4, 256, 303,
   339–40

Hawke, Hazel, 338

Hawkins, Tim, 426

Hayes, Liz, 358

Healy, Michael, 444

Helpmann, Sir Robert, 97

Hemingway, Ernest, 73–4, 121

Henderson, Brian, 253, 356, 439

Hepburn, Audrey, 291–2

Hepburn, Katharine, 115, 117, 125

Hewitt, Lleyton, 409

Hewson, John, 318

Hey Hey It's Saturday, 166, 233, 408,
   439, 440

Hicks, David, 445

Hinch, Derryn, 323
Hinze, Russ, 219
Hodgson, Virginia, 234
Hoffman, Dustin, 93, 94, 115, 125
Hogan, Alan, 75–6, 125
Hogan, Paul, 165, 264, 279
Hollows, Fred, 84, 218, 298–307, 352, 412
Hollows, Gabi, 300, 303, 306
Holly, Buddy, 53, 54
Holt, Harold, 72, 444
Honey, John, 52–3, 55
Hookes, David, 338
Hoover, J. Edgar, 149, 152
Horowitz, Rafi, 191, 193
houseboat, 30
Howard, Jeanette, 242
Howard, John, 212, 242, 244, 273, 303–5, 330, 335, 360, 364, 366, 379, 431
Huckstepp, Sallie-Anne, 205–7
Humphries, Barry, 296, 297
    Dame Edna, 295–7
Hurley, David, 394, 416, 433
Huxley, Lauren, 451

Iglesias, Julio, 256
India, 86–90
Indonesians in East Timor, 154–8
Innes, Hilary, 289
Iran, 180–4
Irwin, Steve, 280, 307, 308
Irwin, Terri, 280, 298, 307–8, 330
Isom, Dr Wayne, 245

Jackman, Hugh, 277, 450
Jacobsen, Kevin, 408
Jagger, Mick, 220
James, Clive, 41, 260
James, Michelle, 396, 415
Jannali Primary, 41
Jenner, Sir Edward, 228

JFK assassination, 133, 135
Joel, Billy, 260
Jolly, Paul, 426
John, Elton, 390, 391, 409
Johns, Brian, 370
Johnson, Ian, 419
Johnson, Lyndon, 114, 123
Jones, Alan, 79, 80
Jones, Barry, 412
Jones, Caroline, 84
Jones, Tom, 233, 253, 256
Joyce, Tony, 76

Kamilaroi people, 8, 9
Kayleen and Guido, 184–7
Keating, Paul, 229, 242–6, 330, 364
Keepit Dam, 9
Keepit Station, 9
Keller, Amanda, 235
Kellogg's factory rip-off, 63
Kelly, Grace, 141, 315
Kennedy, Bobby, 99, 125
Kennedy, Graham, 253, 259, 279, 352–8, 407
Kennedy, Nigel, 236
Kennedy, Stephanie, 235
Kennerley, Kerri-Anne, 253
Kennett, Jeff, 366
Kewell, Harry, 409
Khomeini, Ayatollah, 180–4
Kidman, Janelle, 294
Kidman, Nicole, 254, 286, 292–5, 413
Killeen, Gretel, 235
King George VI, 342
King, Martin Luther Jr, 99, 131, 201
King, Marty, 328
Kissinger, Henry, 153
Kozlowski, Linda, 264
Kruszelnicki, Dr Karl, 243

Lamey, Annie, 18, 270, 323
Lamey, Bertha, 8, 9

Lamey, Frederick, 7, 8
Lamey, Jack, 29–30
Lamey, Jane, 9
Lamey, Jim, 16
Lamey, Mary Jane *see* Martin, Mary Jane
Lamey, May, 29
Lamey, William, 8, 9
Lane, Don, 253, 259, 279, 297, 323, 355, 356, 408
Lanfranchi, Warren, 204, 205, 207
Lara, Brian, 347
Launceston, 49–56
Lavelle, Pat, 242
Law, Ian, 445
Laws, John, 79, 80, 366
Lawson, Henry, 1, 6, 7, 11, 82, 219
Lawton, Fred, 141
Lebanon, 187–93
Leckie, David, 245, 260, 318, 322, 353, 375, 393, 408, 414, 418–19, 422, 436, 437, 441
Ledger, Heath, 409–10
Ledger, Kate, 409, 410
Lee, Daulton, 201
Lee, Nick, 173, 193, 209–11, 225
Lee, Suzie, 225
Leigh, Vivien, 142
Lemmon, Jack, 233
Lennon, John, 115–16
Leslie, Ian, 164–8, 310, 416
Leslie, Jan, 165, 166
Lilleyman, Mark, 379
Limb, Bobby, 127, 203, 253, 323, 356
Lingiari, Vincent, 301
Linnell, Garry, 444
Lionel, 215, 216
Little Pattie, 127
Littlemore, Stuart, 86, 367, 371, 374, 375
Llewellyn, Mark, 420, 422, 423, 441
Lockyer, Paul, 322

Logies, 165, 195, 204, 231, 279–81, 297, 321, 361
Lopez, Jennifer, 289–90
Loren, Sophia, 290–1
Louis, Joe, 118
Lowy, Frank, 439
Lucas, George, 264
Luck, Peter, 167
Luigi, Sergeant, 105, 106
Lyle, David, 354
Lyneham, Paul, 244, 245, 353
Lyons, John, 444, 445

McAvaney, Bruce, 315
MacCallum, Mungo Snr, 73
McCawley, Jason, 377, 388
McClellan, Anthony, 194, 200, 202, 203
McDermott, Paul, 408
McDonald, Frank, 402–3
McEvoy, John, 367, 424, 433
McGilvray, Alan, 77
McGovern, George, 124–8, 131–3, 137
McGuire, Eddie, 279, 355, 441–2
McKay, Heather, 60
MacLaine, Shirley, 124–8
McLean, Don, 54
McMahon, Billy, 80
McMullen, Jeff, 68, 114, 439
Macpherson, Elle, 287, 302
Madison Square Garden, 117–20
Madonna, 260, 289, 290
Maharishi, 83
Mailer, Norman, 115
Malkovich, John, 414
Mamma Maria's, Beirut, 189
Mandela, Nelson, 342
Mangos, John, 273
Manhattan Transfer, 114
Mansfield, Bob, 340, 344
Marchetti, Victor, 154, 200
Markson, Max, 207

Marley, Bob, 109
Martin, Clare, 76
Martin, Dianne, 56, 59–62, 81–2,
    90–2, 95, 115, 116, 121, 138, 155,
    161, 164–5, 169–70, 224–5, 228, 249,
    259–60, 271–2, 322, 323, 327, 338,
    368, 369, 373–4, 395, 396, 414, 417,
    425, 449, 457
    marriage to Ray, 84, 90–2
Martin, George, 233
Martin, Jenna, 115, 164, 228–30,
    268–75, 309, 322, 328, 334, 363,
    395–6, 415, 425, 448, 449, 455, 457
Martin, Joyce see Snape, Joyce
Martin, Kay see Truscott, Kay
Martin, Lorraine see Gillespie,
    Lorraine
Martin, Luke, 4, 164, 272–5, 322, 327,
    328, 334, 369, 395–6, 401–2, 415,
    425, 448, 449, 455, 457
Martin, Mary Jane, 2, 6, 9–13, 16–45,
    53, 56–9, 84, 91, 122, 161, 270, 274,
    323, 454–5
Masters, Chris, 76
Mathis, Johnny, 255
May, Norman 'Nugget', 77
Meakin, Peter, 162, 318, 353, 394, 421,
    422
Meat Loaf, 236
Media Watch, 329, 367, 370, 371, 374,
    376, 443
Meekatharra, 83–4
Melbourne Olympics, 47
Melville, Paul, 234
Mendoza, Benny, 371–3, 435
Menzies, Robert, 14
Midday, 226–323, 331, 338, 354, 436–40
    hosting, 127, 226–323
    leaving, 321–3
Midler, Bette, 114
Midnight Cowboy, 93–4
Mikac, Alannah, 330, 332, 333, 334

Mikac, Danny, 331
Mikac, Madeline, 330, 333
Mikac, Milka, 331
Mikac, Nanette, 330, 331, 332
Mikac, Walter, 330–6
Miller, Harry M., 310, 357
Milosevic, Danny, 417
Mitchell, Neil, 79, 80
moon landings, 99–101
Mooney, Neil, 322, 325
Moran, Bugs, 201
Moy, Lesley, 254
Muggable Mary, 106
Muldrew, John, 322, 330, 335
Munckton, Peter, 156
Munro, Mark, 377, 388, 417
Munro, Mike, 334, 335, 358, 365, 416,
    417, 420–1, 439
Murdoch, Rupert, 318
Murdoch, Sarah, 287–8, 412
Murph, the floor manager, 450
Murphy, Lionel, 151, 152–3
Murphy, Pat, 104
Murphy, Paul, 75
Muskie, Ed, 128

Nailon, Hugh, 426
Namco Industries job, 64–5
Naylor, Brian, 276, 439
Negus, George, 164–9, 237, 310, 416
Neill, Sam, 294
Neville, Richard, 243
New York, 93–162, 169
    arrival in, 93–7
    leaving, 161
    politics, 123–37
New York Yacht Club, 140, 141, 142
Newman, Paul, 131, 176–7
Newport, Rhode Island, 139–44
Newton, Bert, 253, 259, 279, 283, 355,
    356, 407
Newton-John, Olivia, 277, 286, 287

Nichols, Mike, 125
Nixon, Richard, 99, 103, 117, 127–33, 136–7, 150, 153
Nolan, Alyssa, 398–400
Nolan, Bethany, 398–401
Nolan, Mary, 397–9
Nolan, Shaun, 397–401
Normie and Wayne, 214–17
Northern Tasmanian Cricket Association, 54–5

Oakes, Laurie, 245
Obama, Barack, 457
O'Brien, Kerry, 360
O'Donnell, Simon, 254
O'Keefe, Johnny, 203
Oliver, Bert, 77, 140
Olivier, Sir Laurence, 142
Olle, Andrew, 86
Onassis, Jacqueline Kennedy, 115, 141
O'Neill, Norm, 77
Ono, Yoko, 115
Operation Snatchback, 185–7
O'Reilly, Bill, 13
Orient Express, 171–6
Oswald, Lee Harvey, 133
Our Century, 397
Out of the West, 82
Overton, Peter, 433, 434

Packer, Sir Frank, 142, 143, 160
Packer, James, 144, 340, 419, 441, 442, 447, 449
Packer, Kerry, 144, 160–2, 164, 166–9, 171, 219, 220, 232, 244–5, 289, 319, 320, 335–6, 340, 343, 344, 349, 378, 393, 395, 414, 418, 419, 421, 423, 436, 437, 438, 441, 442, 445, 447, 454
Paisley, Ian, 180
Palm Island story, 452
Palme, Olof, 127

Papua New Guinea, 377–84
Parkinson, Michael, 230, 253, 338, 408, 414
Patten, Chris, 245
Paxton, Bindi, 366
Paxton, Mark, 365
Paxton, Shane, 365, 366, 368
Peacock, Andrew, 127–8
Pell, Cardinal George, 451
Penfold, Robert, 389
Perth, 81–4
pest control job, 62–3
Peterson, Governor, 124
Pierce, Carole, 113
Pilbeam, Rex, 219–21
Pockley, Dr Peter, 100, 101
Poland, 174–5
police corruption, 205–6
Ponting, Ricky, 54
Pope Benedict XVI, 451, 452
Port Arthur massacre, 330–6
Port Moresby siege, 377–84
Prime TV, 283
Prince Andrew, 295
Prince Charles, 229, 384–7
Princess Diana, 294, 384–92
Prior, Marina, 277, 450
prisons and prisoners, 196–202

Queen Elizabeth II, 41, 384, 390

Raffaele, Paul, 76
Rafferty, Chips, 71
railways, 1–6
Raja, Mr, 88–90
Rampling, Charlotte, 287
Raper, Johnny, 273
Rasa, 183, 184
Ray, James Earl, 201
The Ray Martin Show, 407–14, 420
Reagan, Ronald, 136, 222, 223
Real Life, 316, 325

Reasoner, Harry, 159
Redford, Robert, 141, 409
Reg, the chopper pilot, 216, 217
Renouf, Alan, 157, 158
Revill, Stuart, 113
Richard, Cliff, 256–7
Richmond District Hospital, 4, 14
Rio de Janeiro, 146–8
Rivkin, Rene, 372
Robards, Jason, 286
Roger, Sergeant, 380–1
Rogerson, Roger, 204–7
Romania, 175
Romanov, Ms, 388
Rosewall, Ken, 273
Rowe, Jessica, 441
Rowe, Normie, 238
Royal Easter Show interview, 69–70
Rudd, Kevin, 80, 304, 306
Ruddock, Philip, 304
Rule, Andrew, 382

Safer, Morley, 159
Safran, John, 367–70
St Martin, 162
Salter, David, 374
Salvation Army People's Palace, 32
Samaranch, Juan Antonio, 314
San Quentin Prison, California, 196
Sandline Affair, 377–84, 391, 392
Saudi Arabia, 208–9
Schiffer, Claudia, 288–9
schooling
    Air Cadets, 51
    correspondence course, 19
    Launceston High, 49–56
    Jannali Primary, 41
    school radio station and magazine,
        52, 66
    Sydney University, 58–9
Scone, 17
Scott, Evelyn, 304

The Seekers, 278
The 7.30 Report, 326, 395, 424, 452
Seymour, Les, 125, 128
Shapiro family, 190–1
Sharon, Ralph, 255
sheepdog trials, 85–6
Shelton, Rev Denis, 372
Shepard, Alan, 100
Sherry, Nick, 372
Simon & Garfunkel, 97, 125
Simon, Carly, 115
Simon, Paul, 115
Simply the Best, 397
Sinatra, Frank, 110, 115, 119, 141, 253,
    286
Singirok, Brigadier-General Jerry,
    378, 381
Sitch, Rob, 363
60 Minutes, 57, 65, 76, 95, 159–226,
    285, 299, 304, 310, 364, 397, 416,
    422, 423, 444, 447, 452
    Keating piggery story, 244–6
    Ray leaving, 226–8
    return to, 416, 444
Skase, Christopher, 202
Smith, Neddy, 206
Smith, Red, 140
Smythe, Mr and Mrs, 25–6
Snape, Joyce, 2, 13, 18, 19, 24, 32, 33,
    45, 46, 53, 59, 323
Somare, Michael, 69, 70, 381, 383
Somers, Daryl, 253, 259, 279, 355, 356,
    440
South Sydney Rabbitohs, 28–9, 91,
    170, 274
South West Rocks holidays, 456
Spain, baby rescue, 184–7
Speight, Dan, 74–5, 79, 94, 161
Spenkelink, John, 197, 198
Spicer, Lieut Colonel Tim, 378, 380,
    383
Spock, Dr Benjamin, 103

sport, love of, 37, 54, 59
Springsteen, Bruce, 114, 125
Spry, Colonel, 152
squash, 60
Stallone, Sylvester, 256
Stannard, Bruce, 153
Stephen, Brian, 61, 122, 170
Stephen, Bruce, 61, 121, 161, 170, 346, 456
Stephen, Dianne see Martin, Dianne
Stephen, Ian, 450
Stephen, Nancy, 61, 81, 91, 121, 272
Stephen, Susan see Dean, Susan
Stephenson, Pamela, 236–7
Stewart, Rod, 115, 409
Stone, Gerald, 86, 160–2, 164, 166–8, 177, 207, 226–8, 310, 316, 317
Stone, Irene, 227
Streisand, Barbra, 115, 119, 125
Suharto, President, 154
Sullivan, Robert, 197–9
Sunday, 76, 322, 439, 444, 445–6
Sydney, move to, 28
Sydney University, 58–9

Tabberer, Maggie, 296
Taiwan
  baby racket, 195
  eating birds in, 210–11
Talese, Gay, 102
talk-radio, 79–80
Tasmania, 48–53
Taylor, James, 115, 125
Tehran, 180–4
television
  introduction to, 53
  trying to break into, 82, 86
Tendulkar, Sachin, 347
tennis in India, 88–90
This Day Tonight, 75, 76, 86, 315, 360, 371
Thomas, Ted, 159, 160

Thompson, Hunter S., 102
Thompson, Jack, 127, 409
Thorne, Len, 185, 186
The Today Show, 446
Today Tonight, 230, 325, 360, 364, 392, 394, 395, 425, 442, 443
Tottenham, 1, 3, 14
Towns, Ched, 250
Townsend, Jo, 444
Truscott, Kay, 2, 8, 13, 18–20, 23, 24, 26, 31–3, 43, 45, 323
tsunami coverage, 424–32
Tumut, 23–4
Tunney, Gene, 97
Turnbull, Malcolm, 245
Twain, Mark, 5

Uechtritz, Max, 425
Uganda, 90
United States see also New York
  espionage, 149–58
  gun culture, 133–6
  1972 elections, 124–33, 136–7
  politics, 123–37
Up Close and Personal, 397, 407
Urban, Keith, 253, 254–5
Uris, Leon, 191
Ustinov, Peter, 233

Vidal, Gore, 102
Vietnam War, 72, 103, 124, 126, 131, 132, 166
  anti-war demonstrations, 103, 115, 117, 130
Village People, 114

Wagstaff, Stuart, 232
Waitara (property), 14–15
Waley, Jim, 439, 445
Walkleys, 446
Wallace, Mike, 159
Wallace, Rowena, 232

Walsh, Mike, 79, 226, 227, 230, 253, 279, 323, 356–7, 408
Walsh, Sean, 307
Walters, Barbara, 307
war zones, 180, 187–93
Warlow, Anthony, 253–4, 277
Warne, Shane, 347
Warner, Russell, 75, 79, 86, 87, 88
Watanabe, Noriko, 294
Watergate, 129, 131, 132
Waugh, Steve, 347
Wayne, John, 129
Weatherley, Kym, 415
Webb, Graham, 179
wedding, 90–1
Wendt, Jana, 178, 220, 238, 260, 310, 316, 319, 320, 322, 324, 329, 337, 358, 393, 395, 421, 439, 442–3, 445
Westacott, John, 244, 319, 416, 423, 424, 432, 433, 434, 445, 446
Whiteley, Brett, 220, 303
Whitlam, Gough, 126, 127, 150–4, 201, 202, 242, 243, 310, 314
Whitlam, Margaret, 242, 314

Wick, Darren, 423
Wilkinson, Peter, 245, 399
Willesee, Mike, 75, 86, 160, 206, 230, 260, 279, 315–21, 324, 329, 337, 359, 384, 393, 421
Williams, R.M., 217–19
Williams, Robin, 295
Williamson, John, 277
Withers, Tony, 79
Wonder, Stevie, 261
Woodward, Joanne, 176, 177
Wooley, Charles, 76
Wordley, Dick, 185–7
World War I, 400–6
World War II, 13
World Youth Day telecast, 451
Wriedt, Paula, 372
Wright, Stevie, 203
Wynne, Peter, 260–2, 265, 266, 276, 341, 342, 343, 353

Yarrangobilly, 18–22
Yunupingu, Galarrwuy, 211–13